Dismissed

A Study of Unfair Dismissal and the Industrial Tribunal System

Linda Dickens
Michael Jones
Brian Weekes
Moira Hart

The research and analysis on which this
book is based was carried out by Linda Dickens,
Michael Jones, Moira Hart and Brian Weekes
during their employment with the ESRC
Industrial Relations Research Unit.
Linda Dickens co-ordinated the research
and wrote this book.

BASIL BLACKWELL

© Economic and Social Research Council

First published 1985
Basil Blackwell Limited
108 Cowley Road, Oxford OX4 1JF, England

British Library Cataloguing in Publication Data

Dickens, Linda
Dismissed : a study of unfair dismissal and
the tribunal system. —(Warwick studies in
industrial relations)
1. Employees, Dismissal of—Great Britain
2. Labor courts—Great Britain
I. Title   II. Series
344.104'18915   KD3110

ISBN 0-631-13925-7

Typeset by Styleset Limited, Warminister, Wiltshire

Printed in Great Britain by Billing and Sons Ltd, Worcester

Contents

Contents

List of Figures

List of Tables

Editors' Foreword

The University of Warwick is the major centre in the United Kingdom for the study of industrial relations. Its first undergraduates were admitted in 1965. The teaching of industrial relations began a year later in the School of Industrial and Business Studies, and it now has one of the country's largest graduate programmes in this subject. Warwick became a national centre for research into industrial relations in 1970 when the Social Science Research Council (now the Economic and Social Research Council), a publicly-funded body, located its Industrial Relations Research Unit at the University. In the Summer of 1984 it was decided that the Unit should be reconstituted as a Designated Research Centre of the School of Industrial and Business Studies.

The series of Warwick Studies in Industrial Relations was launched in 1972 as the main ~~~~~~~~~~~~~lication of the results of the Unit's projects. It i~~~~~~~~~~~~isseminate the research carried out by staff teaching ind~~~~~~~~~s in the University, and the work of graduate students. The ~~~~~tles in the series were published by Heinemann Educational Book~~~ London, and subsequent titles have been published by Basil Blackwell of Oxford.

This book examines an important area of individual employment rights, protection from unfair dismissal, and the use, nature, operation and effects of the institution responsible for its enforcement. The industrial tribunals were described in the 1960s as a valuable experiment in our industrial relations system. Twenty years on they handle some 40,000 cases a year and it is generally assumed the experiment has succeeded. Using the results of extensive research, this book examines whether that assumption is justified.

The importance of assessing how the industrial tribunal system has operated is underlined by the tendency of governments to add to its jurisdictions, edging into areas of industrial relations where previously the law abstained. This book assesses the extent to which the industrial tribunal system provides the accessible, informal, expert adjudication mechanism which was intended and it explores whether the intentions and expectations behind the introduction of statutory protection from unfair dismissal have been fulfilled. It thus deals with both the direct and indirect outcomes of the unfair dismissal legislation as operated by the tribunals. Finally, having identified various problems with the industrial tribunal system, the book explores whether an alternative based on arbitration might provide a better means of dismissal dispute resolution.

George Bain
William Brown
Hugh Clegg

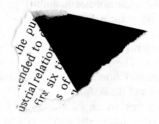

Acknowledgments

The work on unfair dismissal and the industrial tribunal system developed as part of a wider research project concerned with third parties in dispute settlement funded by a grant from the Leverhulme Trust. The research on which this book is based depended upon co-operation from various agencies involved in the industrial tribunal system: the Central Offices of Industrial Tribunals in London and Glasgow, various Regional Offices of Industrial Tribunals, the Department of Employment, and the Advisory, Conciliation and Arbitration Service. A number of people involved in these organisations were most generous in helping set up the research, in co-operating with it and in commenting on its findings. Grateful thanks are due also to the many hundreds of workers and employers who agreed to talk about their experiences of unfair dismissal claims, and to others — trade union officers, employer association officials, law centre and citizens advice bureaux staff, tribunal lay members and chairpersons — whose co-operation helped make the research possible.

In the early stages of the project, Alan Anderson carried out some research interviews and Cliff Allum, Jill Greenwood and Jill Hardman helped in obtaining the sample of unfair dismissal cases which formed the basis for the large interview survey which provided much of the core data. The survey and data processing were carried out by Social and Community Planning Research under the efficient direction of Julia Field. The Industrial Relations Research Unit provided a valued base from which to conduct the research and being part of a research community helped ameliorate some of the problems caused when the project team dispersed at the early drafting stage.

Large-scale research makes considerable demands not only on the researchers but also on those who provide essential administrative and secretarial back-up. The project team was extremely fortunate to have Annemarie Flanders as secretary throughout the research and early drafting stages of the project. I am grateful also to Vivien Collett and

Norma Griffiths for typing successive drafts of the manuscript skilfully, despite the obstacle posed by my handwriting, and to Judith Auty who performed the copy-editing. I would like to thank also those people, in addition to my research team colleagues, who commented on the manuscript, in particular Bob Hepple, Michael Terry, David Deaton and Roy Lewis. Of course they bear no responsibility for the final product.

Linda Dickens
May 1984

1

Introduction and Background

This book is about challenging employers' dismissal decisions through law. It critically examines the legal right to challenge the fairness of a dismissal, now part of the Employment Protection (Consolidation) Act 1978 (EP(C)A), and the mechanism for that challenge, the industrial tribunal system. Our focus, therefore, is on a certain kind of job loss and one type of challenge to it.

In the early 1980s unemployment is high and mass redundancies commonplace. Individuals are not just losing their jobs; jobs as such are disappearing. This is now true of all sectors but manufacturing has experienced a notable decline (Massey and Meegan, 1982:4). Economic recession highlights clearly the extremely limited nature of any job security workers can attain. Yet the law has sought to provide workers with protection from being unfairly deprived of their jobs in certain circumstances.

In Britain a distinction is drawn between dismissal for economic reasons of the firm, redundancy, and dismissal for reasons relating to the individual, although the distinction may blur in practice. Workers meeting certain requirements (for example, concerning age and service) who are made redundant are entitled to receive a severance payment.[1] Those dismissed for reasons other than redundancy may be compensated under statute for loss of employment only if their dismissal is found to have been unfair. Crudely, the distinction between the two kinds of job loss is between, on the one hand, the decision that a particular job or jobs should no longer exist and, on the other, the decision that a particular individual should no longer continue to be employed. The law of unfair dismissal provides workers with the right to challenge the latter kind of decision but there is no legal right to challenge a decision that redundancies are required, although notification and consultation may be necessary.[2] The unfair dismissal legislation,

1. EP(C)A 1978 s.81.
2. Employment Protection Act 1975 ss.99, 100.

however, may be used to challenge the selection of workers to be made redundant or the way in which the redundancy was carried out.[3]

Where there is no legal protection, and even where there is means of challenging employers' decisions other than through law may be available. In March 1983, for example, a worker at the Ford Motor Company's plant at Halewood on Merseyside was dismissed for allegedly maliciously damaging an unfinished car by bending a bracket. Assembly workers on the night shift responded by going on strike. Other workers joined in, getting union support for their demand for the reinstatement of their colleague whom, they said, had been unfairly dismissed. A few days later the *Financial Times* (*FT*) (11 March 1983) reported that some 4,500 workers were on strike and a further 3,700 were laid off as a result. The dispute finally was settled following the report of an arbitration panel. By that time 126,000 working days and £90 million worth of production had been 'lost' (Department of Employment (DE), 1983d: 543; *FT*, 8 April 1984).

On every weekday that the collective, industrial challenge was being made to the Ford management's decision, some sixty tribunals sat at locations throughout Great Britain to settle peacefully legal claims made by other workers who alleged that they too had been dismissed unfairly. In this book we examine who it is that chooses to use the legal route to challenge employers' dismissal decisions; what happens to their claims and why. We discuss the nature, operation and outcomes of the institution, the industrial tribunal, which has been given the role of impartial adjudicator in such legal disputes and of conciliation provided by the Advisory Conciliation and Arbitration Service (ACAS), which attempts to dispose of disputes without need of a tribunal hearing. We look too at the wider impact of the unfair dismissal provisions as operated by the industrial tribunals to assess the extent to which the intentions behind the legislation are being met. The Ford dispute, mentioned above, was settled by arbitration, not by judicial determination in the industrial tribunal system. At the end of the book, having identified various shortcomings of the industrial tribunal system, we examine how arbitration differs from the industrial tribunal system and explore whether it might provide a better mechanism for dismissal dispute resolution.

The importance of assessing how the industrial tribunal system has operated in the area of unfair dismissal is underlined by the tendency of governments to add to its jurisdiction, gradually moving, as we describe below, into areas of industrial relations where previously the law abstained. Indeed, the industrial tribunal system is being

3. EP(C)A 1978 s.59.

advocated, sometimes implicitly, sometimes openly, as a model whereby more controversial areas of industrial relations might come to be regulated by law. Such developments appear to assume that what the then Minister of Labour referred to in 1965 as 'a valuable experiment' has succeeded.[4] This book examines whether that assumption is justified. We are concerned with law, institutions and processes: with the nature, operationalisation and effect of the legal right not to be unfairly dismissed and the nature, functioning and outcomes of particular forms of third-party intervention in disputes, the industrial tribunal and ACAS individual conciliation.

In this chapter we sketch the background to the system and the law, outline the nature of the industrial tribunal system and the unfair dismissal provisions and provide details of the research on which the analysis in the book is based.

A Background Sketch

Industrial tribunals (ITs) had been set up some six years before the unfair dismissal provisions were introduced as part of the Industrial Relations Act 1971. Originally their task was to adjudicate in disputes arising out of the imposition of levies on employers by Industrial Training Boards set up under the Industrial Training Act 1964. A legally qualified chairperson was assisted by two lay members, one drawn from each side of industry. The selection of members for administrative tribunals from interest groups whose members may be involved in the cases coming before the tribunals was a frequently used device 'for reconciling the conflicting interests which may be represented in the decision-making process to see that fair play is done' (Elcock, 1969: 36). Additionally, such people are able to supply an expertise in the form of knowledge about the area in which the interest groups are involved.

Initially, therefore, the industrial tribunals appeared as just another form of administrative tribunal. Such bodies generally hear appeals against decisions of government, its agencies, or some other public body concerning rights or obligations under a statutory scheme (Wraith and Hutchesson, 1973). Other jurisdictions of this 'administrative tribunal' kind followed under the Selective Employment Payments Act 1966 and the Docks and Harbours Act of the same year (Whitesides and Hawker, 1975: 4). But under the Redundancy Payments Act 1965, the industrial tribunals had received jurisdiction of a slightly different kind: that involving disputes between employers and employees. It

4. 711 HC Deb, 26 April 1965, 46.

was not unknown for administrative tribunals to hear disputes between citizen and citizen but it was the exception, the main concern being conflicts between 'the individual' and 'authority'.

The Redundancy Payments Act provided no right to challenge managerial decisions that redundancies were necessary. Rather it provided for severance pay under certain conditions (for details of the legislation see Grunfeld, 1980). The industrial tribunals were empowered to hear disputes over entitlement to, and amounts of, redundancy pay. As the payments are met in part from a state-administered fund the government had some direct interest in such cases but gradually the industrial tribunals came to be seen less as administrative tribunals in the traditional sense and more as potential labour courts.

The idea of the industrial tribunals as embryonic specialist labour courts, to which all types of employer/employee dispute might be referred, was floated by the Ministry of Labour in the 1960s in its evidence to the Royal Commission on Trade Unions and Employers' Associations (the Donovan Commission). Clark and Wedderburn (1983: 176) note that, with hindsight, one can detect the importance of the civil service thinking in the development of the present-day industrial tribunals. At the time the Ministry of Labour was suggesting the tribunals might deal with all employer/employee disputes 'no political party, no employers' organisation, no trade union made a central demand for new labour courts'. The Donovan Commission proposed (1968: para.573) that the jurisdiction of the labour tribunals (as it suggested the revamped industrial tribunals be called) 'should be defined so as to comprise all disputes arising between employers and employees from their contracts of employment or from any statutory claims they may have against each other in their capacity as employer and employee'. Although they continue under the name industrial tribunals, these bodies have had their jurisdiction widened to cover a number, but not all, of the areas envisaged by the majority of the Donovan Commission and, indeed, some areas which the Commission had felt should be excluded from judicial determination. The Commission (1968: para. 576) did

> not propose that they should be given the job of resolving industrial disputes or differences arising between employers or employers' associations and trade unions or groups of workers, since these are matters which must be settled by procedures of, or agreed through, collective bargaining. Nor do we envisage that any matters arising between trade unions and their members or applicants for membership should be within the jurisdiction of the labour tribunals.

The Commission, as far as disputes with employers were concerned, attempted to make a distinction between individual and collective conflicts, wishing only the former to come within the ambit of the tribunals. The distinction in practice is difficult to draw. For example, the right not to be unfairly dismissed, which the Commission recommended be adjudicated by the tribunals, was intended to affect collective relations. Some of the individual rights enacted during the 1970s which were added to the industrial tribunals' jurisdiction, such as time off for trade union duties,[5] are similarly likely to involve tribunals in collective matters while s.59 of the EP(C)A requires tribunals to ensure a collectively agreed redundancy procedure, if one exists, is followed. It is possible, however, to distinguish those legal rights which are to be exercised by individual employees against their employers (as is the case with unfair dismissal) from those to be exercised by trade unions against employers or by individuals against trade unions.

Most of the enlarged jurisdiction[6] of the industrial tribunals concerns rights given to individuals (employees or potential employees) to be exercised against employers, for example the right not to be discriminated against because of sex, married status or race.[7] But the tribunals do hear claims made by trade unions against employers concerning consultation regarding redundancies, where the sanction is an award to individual employees,[8] and, since the Employment Act 1980, disputes between individuals and trade unions alleged to have expelled or excluded them from membership.[9] As Table 1.1 shows, the unfair dismissal jurisdiction remains the source of most of the caseload handled by the industrial tribunal system, accounting for about 75 per cent of applications registered in 1983.

The Donovan Commission recommended that adjudication in unfair dismissal cases be entrusted to the industrial tribunals despite some reservations expressed in certain quarters. For instance, a committee of the Ministry of Labour's National Joint Advisory Council (NJAC), composed of representatives of employers and unions, when reporting in 1967, had said that it did not think one should assume that the industrial tribunals were the right bodies to handle unfair dismissal questions. In particular, the NJAC Committee questioned the need for a legal chairperson and suggested that representatives of employers and workers might take the chair in turn (Ministry of Labour, 1967: 42).

5. EP(C)A 1978 s.27(7).
6. A complete list of jurisdictions is given in Hepple and O'Higgins, 1981: 362–4.
7. Sex Discrimination Act 1975 (SD Act) s.63; Race Relations Act 1976 (RR Act) s.54.
8. Employment Protection Act 1975 s.101(1).
9. s.4.

TABLE 1.1

CLAIMS REGISTERED BY JURISDICTION 1983

	England and Wales	Scotland
	%	%
Unfair dismissal	72.9	78.0
Redundancy payments	9.3	10.8
Unfair dismissal/redundancy pay	5.5	5.6
Employment protection	4.8 ⎱	4.1
Contracts of employment	0.9 ⎰	
Equal pay	3.5	0.1
Sex discrimination	0.9	0.3
Health and safety	0.4	0.3
Industrial training levy	0.3	0.3
Race relations	1.5 ⎱	0.1
Miscellaneous	0.09 ⎰	
	N = 35,890	N = 4,069

SOURCES: Central Office of Industrial Tribunals (COIT) Fact Sheet, February 1984; Scottish Central Office of Industrial Tribunals (SCOIT) Fact Sheet, April, 1984.

There appears, however, to have been little detailed debate about the institution which was to enforce the new rights that legislation was conferring on employees (Wedderburn, 1965: 9; Wedderburn and Davies, 1969: 245). It would appear that, the NJAC's comments notwithstanding, the choice was seen as being *within* judicial institutions rather than, say, as between a judicial body and an arbitral one.

This no doubt reflects the proposed form of the new rights as individual legal rights giving rise to a dispute between an individual employee and his or her employer. Although, as we discuss in Chapters 8 and 9, private procedures or arrangements for appealing against decisions to dismiss might culminate in arbitration, legislators generally have seen arbitration as appropriate only where positive rights are conferred on trade unions, for instance the right to information from the employer which is necessary for collective bargaining purposes (Davies, 1979: 36). Where rights have been conferred on individuals, despite the clear collective implications of certain individual rights, judicial determination has been seen as most appropriate.

Given the perception of the choice as between court and court-substitute for enforcing the unfair dismissal provisions, the industrial tribunals were seized on as an already established form of the latter. These tripartite bodies could be seen to offer advantages over the ordinary courts because of the way the courts had traditionally approached employment questions, the attitude of trade unions towards the courts and the operational advantages which the tribunals displayed. Judges tend to read statutes in the light of common law but the unfair dismissal legislation in some respects was to represent a radical departure from the common law on contract of employment: it was, for example, to introduce a remedy – reinstatement – which common law had never been willing to develop (Dickens et al., 1981: 170; Farmer, 1974: 55). Tribunals were seen as bodies which would be able to pay attention to the social policy intentions underlying legislation, in the way the courts had failed to do (Bell, 1969: 17). The attitude of the unions towards the courts placed a questionmark over the appropriateness of giving them the new jurisdiction. Although the judiciary may be suited to deal with enforcement of individual rights, they have dealt less happily with collective interests and at the time the possibility of statutory protection against unfair dismissal was being considered in the 1960s, the trade union movement saw itself as being attacked by the courts in decisions such as *Stratford v Lindley*[10] and *Rookes v Barnard*.[11] Judicial creativity in this latter case so undermined the protection which unions considered they had under the Trade Disputes Act 1906 that a new Act had to be passed in 1965 (Wedderburn, 1971: 361). In 1969 came another blow to the unions in *Torquay Hotel Co. v Cousins*.[12]

As we discuss in Chapter 8, if the 'voluntary tradition' in British industrial relations did not necessarily mean keeping the law out, it did embrace the desire to keep out the courts. Further, disputes at the workplace were seen to require speedy resolution and, as the new rights were to be pursued by individual employees, a channel of enforcement was needed which was also less formal and expensive than the ordinary courts. The development of a positive legal framework of individual employment rights therefore necessitated a new mechanism which could overcome these difficulties.

The Donovan Commission (1968: para. 572) called for a dispute

10. *Stratford Ltd v Lindley* [1965] AC 269; [1964] 3 All ER 102, HL.
11. *Rookes v Barnard* [1964] AC 1129; [1964] 1 All ER 367, HL.
12. *Torquay Hotel Co. Ltd v Cousins* [1969] 1 All ER 522, CA.

settlement procedure 'which is easily accessible, informal, speedy and inexpensive, and which gives [employers and employees] the best possible opportunity of arriving at amicable settlement of their differences'. This last point refers to the Commission's suggestion that tribunal hearings be preceded by informal, round table conciliation meetings between the parties and the tribunal, or one or two of its members, in order to settle the case on a consensual basis.

This particular form of tribunal-based conciliation, similar to that practised in the German labour court, was not adopted. Instead the task was given to the Department of Employment which already had experienced conciliators. There were soon a number of people designated to handle pre-tribunal conciliation, a function handed over to ACAS along with other third-party functions in the mid-1970s. Conciliation is a traditional form of third-party intervention in British industrial relations. Its essence is that the conciliator acts to help the parties reach their own resolution of the dispute. It is generally seen as preferable to other forms of third-party intervention because of its voluntary and consensual nature; it is the disputing parties who have to reach agreement and any agreement or settlement is clearly their own responsibility. As will be discussed in Chapter 6, a pre-tribunal conciliation stage was considered desirable both because settlements reached in this way are seen as qualitatively superior to imposed outcomes and also because it was expected that a large proportion of claims could be disposed of without the need for a formal hearing.

The pre-tribunal conciliation stage was a novel feature of the industrial tribunal system introduced with the unfair dismissal jurisdiction. This emphasis on the opportunity to reach a voluntary settlement without the need for tribunal adjudication was very much in line with the way in which the Donovan Commission saw its recommendation of statutory protection against unfair dismissal: as a way of encouraging the development and reform of voluntary procedures for handling dismissal disputes. The tribunal was meant to be a longstop rather than the major mechanism for settling dismissal disputes. The law was to be a catalyst to voluntary reform which would make actual recourse to law unnecessary. As we discuss in Chapter 8, the statutory protection was seen by the Commission as a prop to, not a substitute for, voluntary action as well as providing 'safety net' protection for those outside collective bargaining and for nascent union organisation.

The legal position at that time of the Donovan Commission, as the Report noted (1968: para. 141), was that 'an employer is legally entitled to dismiss an employee whenever he wishes and for whatever reason, provided only that he gives due notice. At common law he does not even have to reveal his reason, much less to justify it'. This was so despite the British government's acceptance of International Labour Office (ILO) Recommendation 119 which provided that 'termination of employment should not take place unless there is a valid reason for such termination connected with the capacity or conduct of the worker or based on the operational requirements of the undertaking, establishment or service'. It listed certain reasons as invalid – for example, trade union membership, race, colour and sex – and laid down that there should be some right of appeal against dismissal decisions. The adoption of the ILO recommendation in 1963 was one stimulus to considering statutory dismissal protection. For instance it led to the NJAC being asked to examine the question. There had been little pressure from the trade unions for any change. In 1961 the Trades Union Congress (TUC) had questioned its affiliated unions on their attitude towards legislation against unfair dismissal. The majority of respondents, 44 out of 57 unions with a membership of 4,600,000, said they preferred the matter to be dealt with by collective bargaining; 11 unions, with 225,000 members, favoured legislation (*The Times*, 15 March 1965).

The introduction of the Redundancy Payments Act 1965, although not providing the right to challenge employers' economic decisions, had introduced the notion of compensation for 'no fault' job loss, a principle which logic indicated should also apply to arbitrary and unfair dismissals for non-economic, personal, reasons. The redundancy payments legislation had been introduced to facilitate labour mobility and reduce resistance to changes seen as necessary to improve Britain's economic growth, productivity performance and competitiveness (National Economic Development Council (NEDC), 1963; Fryer, 1973: 5). The unfair dismissal provisions were concerned more with job protection than had been redundancy payments legislation since they provided for the possibility of job retention. But they too had an economic rationale since it was recognised that 'the efficient operation of the production process required an effective means of assuring peaceful enforcement of industrial rights' (McPherson and Meyers, 1966: 1).

In the 'full' employment, tight labour market conditions of the 1960s, many workers were in a position to insist, often through industrial action, on what they saw as their industrial rights, including the right not to be disciplined or dismissed unfairly or arbitrarily. The introduction of statutory protection and the provision of a dispute settlement mechanism was seen as a way of reducing the need for, and likelihood of, industrial action over dismissals. In proposing legislation in this area, the Conservative Party (1968: 42) was concerned that 'about two-fifths of all stoppages and about one-fifth of days lost through strikes stem from disputes about "the employment or discharge of workers and other working arrangements, rules and discipline" ' and when the Donovan Commission proposed that statutory machinery be set up, whereby a speedy and impartial decision might be obtained about a contested dismissal, it hoped the number of stoppages arising out of dismissal other than redundancy, then some 200 a year, would be reduced (1968: para. 528).

The Donovan Commission reported in 1968. The then Labour government introduced its proposals for industrial relations legislation, *In Place of Strife*, in 1969. The proposals included the protection against unfair dismissal recommended by the majority of the Commission but contained other provisions which went 'beyond Donovan' and which the unions found objectionable. After the ensuing 'battle of Downing Street' (Jenkins, 1970) the *In Place of Strife* proposals were dropped. The Labour government's Industrial Relations Bill 1970 contained unfair dismissal protection but it was the Conservative government elected in June 1970 which finally introduced it, as part of its own industrial relations legislation. The Industrial Relations Act 1971, which enacted the unfair dismissal protection, was designed to introduce a new framework of law into British industrial relations, a framework which the trade union movement found unacceptable (Weekes et al., 1975; Thompson and Engleman, 1975). In both instances the protection against unfair dismissal, and some other measures such as a procedure whereby unions could seek bargaining rights from employers, were perceived by the unions as sugar on an otherwise bitter pill.

In countering allegations that their legislation was 'anti-union', Conservative speakers pointed to the unfair dismissal protection as evidence of an even-handed, balanced approach. Unions were to be expected to act in a fair and reasonable manner but so too were employers.[13] Although the major planks of the Industrial Relations Act 1971 had been formulated in *Fair Deal at Work* (1968) and echoed proposals in an even earlier document, *A Giant's Strength* (1958), some provisions, such as those concerned with unfair dismissal, could be pointed to as proof that the government had taken account of the findings of the Donovan Commission and not ignored them, as the TUC claimed.[14]

The right to receive compensation for unfair dismissal was seen generally, in the words of the leaderwriter of the *Financial Times* (6 October 1970), as a proposal 'every unionist is bound to welcome'. But the right was not dependent on union membership. The 'floor' of

13. For example, Robert Carr speaking at the Conservative Party Conference in 1970, *The Times*, 8 October 1970.
14. For example, Sir Geoffrey Howe's address to the Industrial Law Society, November 1970.

employment protection rights for employees in their relationship with employers can be seen as favourable to trade unions (e.g. Anderman, 1979: 243). It is a floor upon which unions can build (Wedderburn, 1980: 83) and provides the building blocks for collective rights (Wedderburn, 1976: 169). And yet, because the legal rights provide a protection for employees not dependent on trade union membership, they can be seen also as in keeping with other aspects of the Industrial Relations Act aimed at weakening trade union authority (Barnes and Reid, 1980: 143). Such an argument, however, fits uneasily with the fact that when the Industrial Relations Act was repealed, the unions requested that the unfair dismissal provisions be salvaged and strengthened. This was done by the Trade Union and Labour Relations Acts 1974–6 and the Employment Protection Act 1975. The development of the legislation since its introduction is considered in the next section of this chapter, after an outline of the industrial tribunal system.

Outline of the System and the Law

This section provides a brief description of what is meant by the 'industrial tribunal system', outlining the various stages through which an application for unfair dismissal can progress, the institutions involved and the various regulations governing the tribunals' operation.[15] It also explains the nature of the statutory provisions, in particular who can claim unfair dismissal and reasons which can justify dismissal.[16] This section is not intended to provide detailed guidance on how to bring or defend a tribunal case[17] nor do we seek to present detailed description or analysis of the statutory provisions.[18] Rather the aim is to provide a fairly broad-brush exposition for those with little or no familiarity with the unfair dismissal provisions or the statutory machinery for enforcing them.

The Stages of the Industrial Tribunal System

Figure 1.1 shows the stages of the industrial tribunal system. An application for unfair dismissal is made in writing — normally on application form IT1, available from job centres or unemployment benefit offices —

15. Industrial Tribunals (Rules of Procedure) Regulations 1980 (SI 1980 No. 884). Similar regulations are in force in Scotland (SI 1980 No. 885). See Appendix III.
16. The statutory provisions are embodied in Part V of the EP(C)A 1978 as amended. See Appendix II.
17. Books providing such guidance include Angel, 1980 and McIlroy, 1983.
18. For this see, for example, Hepple and O'Higgins, 1981.

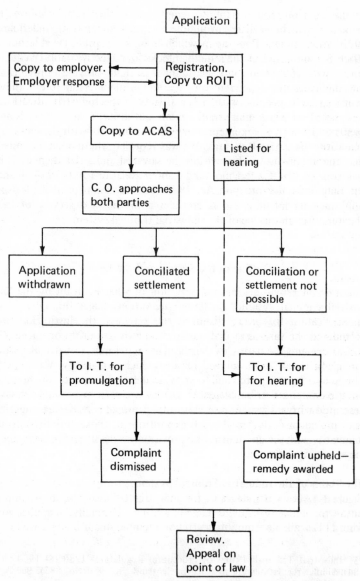

FIGURE 1.1   THE INDUSTRIAL TRIBUNAL SYSTEM FOR
DISMISSAL CASES

NOTE: The figure does not include the possible pre-hearing assessment, preliminary hearing and interim relief hearing stages.

to the Central Office of Industrial Tribunals (COIT) in London, for those in England and Wales, or in Glasgow, for those in Scotland.[19] The information necessary for the application to be accepted by the tribunal office is the name and address of the applicant, the name and address of the person against whom the claim is being made (the respondent) and the particulars of the claim. In fact the IT1 goes beyond these basic requirements asking additional questions considered helpful in processing the claim and useful for statistical purposes. The form has been modified over the years, partly to suit new statutory provisions. In addition to the basic information it asks about length of employment and hours of work (which help determine whether the applicant is qualified to bring a claim), age of applicant, details of any chosen representative, information on gross and take-home pay and other employment benefits; the position held by the applicant and the place of work. As well as asking for full particulars of the grounds of the application the IT1 form provides the opportunity for applicants to say what in their opinion was the reason for dismissal and to state which remedy (reinstatement, re-employment or compensation) is being sought.

An originating application may be lodged any time from the date of notice of dismissal until three months after the effective date of termination, though any applications mistakenly sent to a Regional Office of Industrial Tribunals (ROIT), rather than a Central Office, normally will be accepted if they arrive within the time limit. There is provision for applications which arrive outside the time limit to be accepted where a tribunal is satisfied that it was not reasonably practicable for the complaint to be presented in time and that the complaint was presented within a further period that the tribunal considers reasonable. The application time limit was originally four weeks from dismissal; following the increase to the present level in 1974 tribunals became more reluctant to allow out of time claims.

It is when the application has been received by COIT that the first filter comes into operation. Before the application is registered it is checked to see whether the applicant's length of service, employment status etc. are those required by the statute for claiming unfair dismissal. Where the applicant appears unqualified to bring a claim a letter will be sent advising this and unless the applicant replies in writing that he or she wishes the claim to proceed it will not be registered. In 1983 almost 1,800 would-be applicants were filtered out at this stage; about 40,000 were registered. The Secretary of the Tribunals's vetting power

---

19. There is also a Central Office in Belfast, covering Northern Ireland, but this book is concerned only with the system in Great Britain.

relates only to jurisdictional matters and not to the merits of a case and an application has to be registered if the applicant insists, but, as we shall see, there are a number of other filters later in the system which can remove claims thought to be meritless or outside the tribunal's jurisdiction. Where there is doubt over whether or not a tribunal does have jurisidiction, a preliminary hearing may be held to determine this question.

Once the application has been registered centrally and given a case number it is forwarded to a Regional Office of Industrial Tribunals, the appropriate region being chosen according to the place from which the employee was dismissed. Regional offices have been established in Ashford (Kent), Birmingham, Bristol, Bury St. Edmunds, Cardiff, Exeter, Leeds, London (Central, North and South), Liverpool, Manchester, Newcastle-upon-Tyne, Nottingham, Sheffield, and Southampton. There are no regional offices as such in Scotland but tribunal offices exist in Edinburgh, Dundee, Aberdeen, and Inverness. The ROIT copies the application form to the employer stated as respondent and to ACAS. In Scotland the applicants also receive a copy of their applications, in England and Wales only an acknowledgment is sent.

The respondent employer is required to 'enter an appearance'. This is done by returning a completed form to the tribunal office stating whether the applicant was dismissed and, if so, for what reason and whether the applicant's claim is to be resisted. If so, the employer is required to state on what grounds. The form, IT3, also requests details of the respondent's name and address, details of any chosen representative and information regarding the applicant's length of service and remuneration. This form has to be returned within fourteen days. Failure to enter an appearance (that is return the form or provide the required information in writing) bars the employer from taking part in any subsequent proceedings or the tribunal hearing, unless called by someone else as a witness. In practice, however, applications for extensions to the fourteen-day time limit are invariably granted, and any late notice of appearance is automatically treated as if it contained a request for an extension.

In 1978 the IT1 and IT3 forms were amended to require 'full particulars' of the claim and reasons for resisting the claim so that the parties, and the tribunal, might have a better picture of the allegations being made. Since 1980 the employer can ask that further particulars of the applicant's claim be provided before returning the notice of appearance, instead of only after, as under the previous regulation. The tribunal may, on its own initiative, request that more information of some ground or fact relied upon be provided by either party. If the particulars are not provided as ordered all or part of the notice of appearance may be struck out or the application may be dismissed. Before taking this step, however, the tribunal has to notify the party in default, providing an opportunity to show reason why this should not be done. This ability of the tribunal to initiate, introduced in 1980, supplements the right of either party to apply to the tribunal for an order requesting the other side to supply 'further and better particulars' of the case. Witness orders, orders for the production of documents and inspection of documents may also be made on request of the parties. A tribunal chairperson decides whether such orders should be made. Until 1980 the penalty for failing to comply with such an order was, on summary conviction, a fine not exceeding £100. This has now been supplemented by the power of the tribunals to strike out the notice of appearance or dismiss the application.

If the information coming into the tribunal office on the application form and employer's notice of appearance, or other document, appears to indicate that either party's case is unlikely to succeed, the ROIT can notify the parties that it intends to hold a pre-hearing assessment (PHA). This special filter procedure was introduced in the 1980 Regulations to weed out unmeritorious cases by threatening an award of costs (see below, p. 104). As well as the tribunal taking the initiative either party can ask that a PHA be held. The tribunal considers the contents of the application form and notice of appearance and any written representations. The parties or their representatives may make oral representations, but no witnesses are called. If the tribunal considers that the application is unlikely to succeed or if the contentions of a party have no reasonable prospect of success it can indicate that costs may be awarded against the party with the apparently hopeless case should that party lose at the main tribunal hearing. Costs may be awarded where it is thought a party brought or conducted proceedings 'frivolously, vexatiously or otherwise unreasonably'. If the application continues to a tribunal hearing, a differently constituted tribunal hears the case. The tribunal will have on file a sealed envelope containing the PHA opinion which is opened if necessary after the decision. In fact, as we shall discuss later (p. 105), most PHA costs warnings are made against applicants and secure the withdrawal of the claim.

Although the tribunal regulations provide various filter mechanisms in the processing of claims, the major filter in the system which stops cases proceeding to a hearing is the ACAS conciliation stage. As we shall see (Chapter 6) in 1982 only 35 per cent of applications went beyond this stage. The industrial tribunals and ACAS are separate institutions. Having sent ACAS a copy of the application form and, in due course, the employer's response, the ROIT goes ahead with listing the case for hearing. In the meantime a conciliation officer from the appropriate ACAS region will contact each of the parties, or their representatives, if any, to see if the case can be settled without the need for a tribunal hearing. If the case is settled, or if the applicant decides to withdraw the claim, this is notified to the tribunal normally on an appropriate form signed by the party or parties involved and the tribunal will record this. Once an agreement has been reached with the assistance of a conciliation officer from ACAS a tribunal is prevented from hearing the case. Where conciliation fails to bring about settlement or the applicant's withdrawal of the claim the case will proceed to tribunal hearing. Anything communicated to a conciliation officer during conciliation is not admissible before an industrial tribunal without the consent of the person who communicated it.

The parties have to be given at least fourteen days' notification of the date, time and place of the hearing; in practice some three weeks' notice is usually given. Hearings may be postponed on request of either party. Where the postponement is to facilitate a conciliated settlement it will normally be granted. Tribunals in England and Wales may also be willing to exercise their discretion to grant a postponement where holidays, other commitments, or inadequate time for case preparation are given as reasons for the request. In Scotland, however, a slightly different system operates (which is being adopted by some other regions) whereby the parties are asked to indicate any dates which are not suitable within a specified two- or three-week period. Once this has been notified the tribunal office chooses a mutually convenient date. Because the date is selected in view of the parties' preferences, postponements are requested, and granted, less often.

The tribunal is chaired by a solicitor or barrister of at least seven years' standing and there are two lay members appointed for their industrial or commercial experience. Hearings are generally held in public. Parties may present their own cases or be represented as they choose. Legal aid is not available for representation at a tribunal hearing, but pre-tribunal advice and assistance from a solicitor up to a certain value is obtainable under the means-tested Legal Advice Scheme. The parties are entitled to give evidence, to call witnesses, to question witnesses and to address the tribunal. The party bearing the burden of proof begins. This means that where the employer denies dismissal the applicant has to start and where dismissal is admitted the employer goes first. If a party fails to attend the hearing or send a representative the tribunal may dispose of the application in the absence of that party or adjourn the hearing to another date. Since 1978 the tribunals have had the power to dismiss the application if the *applicant* fails to appear or be represented. A party who is absent from the hearing may ask for a review of the decision if good cause for absence is shown and if, were the case re-heard, there is a reasonable prospect of success.

Having heard the case, the industrial tribunal may dismiss the application or may uphold the complaint and award one of three remedies: reinstatement in the same job, re-engagement with the same or an associated employer, or compensation. The decision of the tribunal, which can be a majority decision, usually is given orally at the hearing and written reasons sent to the parties later. Once the decision is entered formally in the register it is binding on the parties. Before then any obvious mistakes can be corrected or the oral decision varied but after it has been registered it cannot be altered other than by the correction of clerical errors or accidental slips under the chairperson's authority, and by review or by appeal.

Application for a review may be made by a party within fourteen days from the date on which the decision was sent to the parties. A tribunal can review a decision if it was wrongly made as a result of an error on the part of tribunal staff; if a party did not receive notification of the hearing or the decision was made in the absence of a party or person entitled to be heard; if new evidence has become available since the making of the decision, the existence of which could not reasonably have been known or foreseen, or if the interests of justice require such a review. The President of the Tribunals, the regional chairperson or the person who chaired the original tribunal may refuse an application for review if it appears to have no reasonable prospect of success. If a review is granted the full tribunal hears it and may revoke or vary its original decision or order a rehearing.

An appeal against the decision can be made on a question of law to the Employment Appeal Tribunal (EAT) where a High Court Judge sits with lay members. Appeal beyond that is with leave, to the Court of Appeal (Court of Session in Scotland) and then the House of Lords. Notice of appeal to the EAT has to be given within forty-two days of the date on which the written decision was sent to the parties. On appeal the decision of the tribunal may be reversed or altered or the case sent back for rehearing.

Before turning to the legal provisions, the special interim relief procedure needs to be mentioned.[20] This applies to claims where unfair dismissal is alleged on grounds of trade union membership or activities or, since 1982, for non-membership of a trade union. In these particular cases an application may be made for interim relief within seven days of the dismissal. Where membership or activities dismissals

---

20. EP(C)A 1978 s.77.

are alleged the claim must be accompanied by a certificate from an
authorised trade union official stating that there are reasonable grounds
for supposing the dismissal was related to membership or activities. The
application triggers off an expedited procedure whereby a hearing takes
place as soon as practicable after the receipt of the application, with
seven days' notice being given to the parties of the date, time and place.
If, at this hearing, the industrial tribunal decides that it is likely that an
unfair dismissal complaint on the grounds alleged will succeed then it
can order the reinstatement or re-engagement of the employee or, if
the employer is not willing to accept this, order that the contract of
employment continue in existence until the full hearing of the case.

The Unfair Dismissal Provisions

a) *Scope of protection.* The law on unfair dismissal, first introduced
in the Industrial Relations Act 1971, is now contained in the Employment Protection (Consolidation) Act 1978, as amended by the Employment Acts 1980 and 1982. Section 54 of the EP(C)A provides 'every
employee shall have the right not to be unfairly dismissed by his employer'. Although it is a general legal protection, the scope of the
protection is not unlimited. Certain occupations are explicitly excluded,
among them the police, sharefishers and registered dock workers.
Some workers are excluded because they work for their spouses or
because their work is ordinarily performed outside Great Britain. Other
workers employed on a contract for a fixed term of one year or more,
will be deemed to have excluded themselves if they agreed to waive
their rights to claim unfair dismissal. Those covered by an approved
dismissal procedure will be excluded also. At present there is only
one such procedure, that in the Electrical Contracting Industry (see
p. 238).

Other employees are covered by the protection if they meet certain
qualification requirements, as shown in Figure 1.2. The provisions cover
'employees' and so exclude, among others, independent contractors and
the self-employed. Distinguishing between employee and non-employee
has posed problems for the courts (Clark and Wedderburn, 1983:151–5;
Leighton, 1984: 62; Hepple and O'Higgins, 1981: 65–8). In deciding
whether an unfair dismissal applicant is an 'employee' the tribunals
consider all aspects of the relationship rather than rely on single indica-
tors such as whether the person is registered as 'self-employed' for
personal taxation. For example, it is widely believed by employers and
the Inland Revenue that homeworkers are self-employed but the EAT
has held that there are circumstances where homeworkers would be
employees under the legislation, as for example in *Nethermere (St Neots)*

FIGURE 1.2   ELIGIBILITY TO CLAIM UNFAIR
DISMISSAL

An employee	Excludes self-employed
Who is dismissed	i. employer terminates contract ii. employer does not renew fixed-term contract iii. employer's conduct leads to worker's resignation (constructive dismissal)
Has 1 year's continuous service or 2 years' if fewer than 20 workers employed	Does not apply if dismissal is on grounds of sex or race discrimination or membership or activities of trade union or non-membership of trade union
Worked 'full-time'	Contractually obliged to work at least 16 hours a week or 8 hours a week after 5 years' continuous employment
Not past retirement age	60 for women 65 for men or normal retirement age for job (does not apply if dismissal is on grounds of sex or race discrimination or membership or activities of trade union or non-membership of trade union)
If not otherwise excluded	Certain occupations; waived rights; exempt procedure; industrial action dismissal etc.
Application made to IT during notice or within 3 months of dismissal	

SOURCE: Derived from EP(C)A 1978 Parts V and IX.

v Gardiner and Taverna ([1983] IRLR 103), a decision upheld by the Court of Appeal. Many homeworkers and those classed as casual or temporary workers however, who are often subject to irregular work patterns and vulnerable to short-time working, would be unable to satisfy both this 'employee' requirement and the further requirement of continuous employment for sixteen hours a week (Ewing, 1982a: 109). Until the Employment Protection Act 1975 only those employees working twenty-one hours a week were eligible to claim unfair dismissal. The present requirement is sixteen hours a week and employees working between eight and sixteen hours qualify for protection if they have five years' continuous service.

The provisions concerns 'dismissal'. Generally this is the termination of the employment contract by the employer, with or without notice. Under s.55 of the EP(C)A non-renewal of a contract for a fixed term (that is for a specifically stated period, even if it may be determined by notice within that period) is included within the definition of dismissal. So is 'constructive dismissal', the termination of the contract by the *employee* in circumstances where this is justified by the employer's conduct in breaching a fundamental term of the contract of employment. The inclusion of constructive dismissal in 1974 was designed to prevent employers circumventing the unfair dismissal provisions by harassing unwanted workers and so forcing them to resign. It also enables workers to claim dismissal where they resign because the employer changes the employment or behaves in an outrageous manner. Termination of the contract by agreement or frustration does not come within the statutory definition of dismissal.

The service qualification has been changed several times since the introduction of the legislation. It started off at two years, a period chosen for administrative convenience to allow time to gauge the demand under the new provisions without immediately swamping the industrial tribunals (Weekes et al., 1975: 26). It was reduced during the 1970s to one year and then to six months but was increased again in 1979 to one year. In 1980 a special provision was introduced for workers in small firms. Where no more than twenty workers are employed (and no more have been employed in the past two years) workers have to have two years' service in order to claim unfair dismissal, unless dismissal is alleged to be on grounds of union membership activities or non-membership or sex or race. The statute provides, in Schedule 13, how to determine the length of continuous service, ensuring that continuity is preserved despite certain changes of employer (for example, through transfer of ownership or death of employer), certain periods of absence from work (for example, sickness or confinement absence) and certain fluctuations in the hours of work per week. The Transfer of Undertakings (Protection of Employment) Regulations 1981 introduce the principle of automatic transfer of contracts of employment in the case of certain transfers of commercial ventures (see Hepple, 1982: 29).

Tribunals cannot consider the fairness of the dismissal of an employee who is dismissed while taking part in industrial action or while locked out by the employer, unless the employer has dismissed selectively among those taking part in such action (see below, p. 247). The industrial action dismissal bar on tribunal jurisdiction has always existed in the unfair dismissal provisions but the Employment Act 1982 made substantial amendments to widen the opportunity for employers to discriminate between workers.

b) *Reasons for dismissal.* The statute provides that some reasons for dismissal are *automatically unfair*, some are *automatically fair* and other reasons *may be fair*. Figure 1.3 summarises the position regarding

FIGURE 1.3 FAIR/UNFAIR DISMISSAL

Reason for Dismissal	Legal Position
Race Sex Married status[a]	Unlawful discrimination under Race Relations Act 1976 and Sex Discrimination Act 1975
Pregnancy Trade union membership Trade union activities Non-membership of a union Redundancy selection in breach of custom or agreed procedure	Automatically unfair under EP(C)A
Non-membership of a union where UMA applies	Automatically fair unless exemption applies
Capability Conduct Redundancy Contravention of an enactment Some other substantial reason	Potentially fair, depends on reasonableness

SOURCE: Derived from EP(C)A 1978 ss.57—60
SD Act 1975 s.6
RR Act 1976 s.4.

NOTE:

a. In the employment field the SD Act 1975 covers discrimination against a married person of either sex.

reasons for dismissal. Automatically unfair reasons are those concerned with trade union membership or activities or non-membership of a trade union which, until 1982, were referred to as 'inadmissible reasons'. This covers being, or proposing to become, a trade union member or taking part, or proposing to take part, in trade union activities at an appropriate time (that is outside working hours or in working hours with the consent of the employer). It also covers not being a member of any or a particular union or refusing, or proposing to refuse, to become a member. Automatically unfair reasons also cover unfair redundancy selection. Where the principal reason for dismissal is redundancy but it is shown that the redundancy situation applied equally to other workers in similar positions to the applicant who were not dismissed, then s.59 of the EP(C)A provides dismissal is unfair if the selection of the applicant was because of trade union membership, activities, or non-membership or was an unjustified contravention of a customary arrangement or agreed procedure. Dismissal because of pregnancy or reasons connected with the pregnancy or denial of the worker's right to return to work after confinement is also automatically unfair. Because of the provisions of the Rehabilitation of Offenders Act 1974 s.4 it is also likely to be automatically unfair to dismiss a worker because of a spent conviction (Hepple and O'Higgins, 1981: 287). Convictions become 'spent' after a specified time, depending on the severity of the crime. The Race Relations Act 1976 and the Sex Discrimination Act 1975 make it unlawful to discriminate by dismissing someone on grounds of colour, race, nationality, ethnic or national origins, sex or because he or she is married.

Although the dismissal of someone for not being a member of a trade union is generally automatically unfair, it will be automatically *fair* where there is a closed shop, that is a union membership agreement (UMA), requiring membership. Automatically fair dismissal applies to those covered by the UMA who refuse to join a specified union and who cannot claim one of the exemptions provided by the Act. Where an exemption does apply, however, dismissal will be automatically unfair. The list of exemptions from compulsory union membership was considerably extended by the Employment Acts 1980 and 1982 and so closed shop dismissals are more likely to be automatically unfair than was previously the case. Exemptions now cover those employees who genuinely object to union membership, or membership of a particular union, on grounds of conscience or other deeply held personal conviction; those non-members employed before the UMA came into effect who have not joined since; those with professional obligations embodied in a written code which would be incompatible with the taking of industrial action and those whose non-membership arises from unreasonable exclusion or expulsion from the union. In addition it is automatically unfair to dismiss for non-membership unless the UMA has been properly approved. 'Proper approval' depends on the outcome of a periodic ballot requiring high levels of support in favour of the UMA. The balloting provisions came into effect in November 1984.

The reasons which *may* be fair are set out in s.57 of the EP(C)A 1978. A potentially fair reason is one which

(a) related to the capability or qualifications of the employee for performing work of the kind which he was employed to do, or
(b) related to the conduct of the employee, or
(c) was that the employee was redundant, or
(d) was that the employee could not continue to work in the position which he held without contravention (either on his part or on that of his employer) of a duty or restriction imposed by or under an enactment

or is 'some other substantial reason of a kind such as to justify the dismissal of an employee holding the position which that employee held'. Capability is assessed 'by reference to skill, aptitude, health or any other physical or mental quality' and qualifications means 'any degree, diploma or other academic, technical or professional qualification relevant to the position which the employee held'. The employer has to show a reason for the dismissal and that it falls within one of the categories just outlined. Having done that then s.57 of the statute goes on to provide that

the determination of the question whether the dismissal was fair or unfair, having regard to the reason shown by the employer, shall depend on whether in the circumstances (including the size and administrative resources of the employer's undertaking) the employer acted reasonably or unreasonably in treating it as a sufficient reason for dismissing the employee; and that question shall be determined in accordance with equity and the substantial merits of the case.

Before the Employment Act 1980 amended this section, the tribunals were not required explicitly to consider the employer's size or resources in determining reasonableness and the burden of proof was on the employer rather than neutral as now. As we shall discuss in Chapter 4, in practice the question of reasonableness, rather than the reason for dismissal, generally is the key issue in determining whether a dismissal was fair or unfair.

c) *Remedies.* Where a dismissal is found unfair, the tribunal may award re-instatement (return to the old job on the same terms and conditions and privileges, with back pay, as if applicant had not been dismissed), re-engagement (return to the same, or associated employer, on terms decided by the tribunal) or compensation. These are discussed in detail in Chapter 5. Since 1976 the tribunals are required by statute to explain the re-employment remedies and ask whether a re-employment order is wanted by the applicant. The tribunal also has to take into account whether it is practicable for an employer to comply with a re-employment order and, where the applicant is found to have caused or contributed to some extent to the dismissal, whether it is just to order re-employment. If an order for re-employment is not made, compensation is awarded, calculated as provided by the statute, subject to a maximum which is revised periodically. When an order for reinstatement or re-engagement is not complied with by the employer the tribunal has to award compensation plus an additional award or an enhanced special award where dismissal was for trade union membership, activities or non-membership. There is no specific enforcement or contempt of court sanction.

The tribunals in England and Wales cannot enforce their own decisions. Any sum payable as a result of tribunal decision is recoverable by execution issued from a county court after the making of an order of execution by that court. In Scotland any sum payable may be recovered by sheriff officers provided with a copy of the registered decision of the tribunal or extract prepared by the Secretary to the Tribunals. How the industrial tribunal system and the legal provisions which have been outlined here actually operate and with what effect was a major focus of the research.

The Research

Multi-method data collection was used, fuller details of which are contained in Appendix I. The major data source for the study was interviews conducted with about one thousand unfair dismissal applicants and the respective employers. The cases were selected from three regions covered by the England and Wales Central Office of Industrial Tribunals and from Scotland. The research did not cover Northern Ireland where there is a similar system. The sample proved representative of unfair dismissal applications generally; it included cases which were heard by industrial tribunals and cases which were abandoned or ended by settlement. The interviews, based on four questionnaires, provided information on the nature of the parties; what happened to them; their expectations, experience, perceptions and assessments of the industrial tribunal system. Interviewing a large representative sample of employers and dismissed employees provided data from which generally applicable conclusions could be drawn in a way that in-depth case studies of particular applications could not, but necessarily meant the richness of some individual experience or particularity of individual case histories was submerged.

As with most, if not all, research methodologies, what we did was moulded by operational and access constraints and chance happenings. An original intention had been to follow a number of dismissal cases as they progressed through the industrial tribunal system, building up a series of case histories. Access to any non-public process involving an official agency, however, was not granted. We were unable to sit in on ACAS conciliation, and the Department of Employment and Central Office of Industrial Tribunals would not grant access to case files or to the tribunal decision-making stage of the hearing. An alternative approach of reconstructing what happened in particular cases, by piecing together information obtained after the event from all participants, also was ruled out as we could not discuss particular cases with conciliation officers nor could we question tribunal members about how or why particular decisions were reached. At the time the research was being set up the industrial tribunal system was becoming subject to criticism from various quarters. Sensitivity to this, and necessary respect for confidentiality of certain information, helps explain some of our access problems.

As it was becoming clear that the original access requests would not be met, money became available to finance a large-scale interview survey and so the viable methodology emerged as one focusing on the aggregate and general rather than the particular. ACAS, the Department of Employment and the Central Offices of Industrial Tribunals felt able to co-operate in our revised approach and we are very grateful to them for their assistance. Contact was maintained on a continuing basis throughout the research with staff at ACAS Head Office responsible for individual conciliation and with the Presidents of the Industrial Tribunals.

We attended residential training for individual conciliation officers and a feed-back information gathering technique was developed to help examine their work. Meetings were held in various ACAS regions with individual conciliation staff at which we discussed their work with them using as a focus the information and comments we had gathered from our interviews with applicants, respondent employers and representatives. We conducted semi-structured interviews with local full-time officers of seven major trade unions; local officials of two major employers' associations who advised and represented members at industrial tribunals, and with a number of Citizens Advice Bureaux (CAB) and Law Centre staff in various parts of the country.

Information on the characteristics, training, role perception and views of tribunal members came predominently from postal surveys of chairpersons and lay members undertaken with the co-operation of the two Central Offices of Industrial Tribunals. Access gatekeepers are always in a position to influence the scope and nature of research and in this instance control affected both the design of the chairpersons' questionnaire (questions thought by COIT to impinge on judicial integrity were dropped) and the kind of initial co-operation-seeking approach which we were able to make to tribunal members. Our original request for a list of names and addresses of tribunal members was not granted. Instead we selected people from lists of names by region which were provided, and questionnaires were sent to them via the regional tribunal offices with an accompanying letter from the then President of Industrial Tribunals.

To obtain an 'outside' perspective on, and evaluation of, certain aspects of the industrial tribunal system discussed by users and operators, we carried out an observation exercise in four tribunal regions using an observation schedule. The experience of Frost and Howard was useful to us in this respect (1977: 18). A number of other, ad hoc, visits to tribunals were made during the research to provide continuing contact. The published decisions of tribunals and the appellate courts were monitored to enable us to analyse the interpretation and application of the unfair dismissal law. Our reading of published reports was supplemented by an examination of all unfair dismissal decisions registered in the Central Office of Industrial Tribunals for a selected period. This enabled us to look beyond cases establishing important principles to examine general tribunal practice, for example, in regard to compensation calculations (discussed in Chapter 5).

The formal research methods described above were augmented by informal discussions with industrial relations practitioners, operators of the system and those who had experienced it; by examination of academic and other literature and of official, pressure group and other publications and statements relevant to the area of research.

The research was concerned with the British system of handling unfair dismissal but included some examination of the way this issue is handled in other countries.[21] Our aim was not to provide a comparative

21. In this we were helped by academics, practitioners and organisations in several countries. Among them were Eugene J. Barry, Paul Yager and Sam Kagel in the USA, the American Arbitration Association and the Federal Mediation and Arbitration Service, members of the Sozialwissenschaftliche Forschungsgruppe of the Max-Planck-Institut, Hamburg, and of the Freie Universtät, Berlin. Our investigations in Sweden were aided by Alan Neal.

examination. Rather, a limited international focus was designed to help us perceive the British system more clearly, bringing into sharper focus various assumptions and characteristics of the British system which otherwise might have gone unexamined or unquestioned. The book, therefore, while not presenting descriptions of other countries' methods of handling dismissal disputes is, we hope, informed by them.

Structure of the Book

Chapter 2 examines the potential and actual use made of the right to challenge the fairness of a dismissal through the industrial tribunal system, discussing the characteristics of applicants, the employers who dismissed them and the help and representation which the parties obtain.

Rather than then adopt the sequence of the industrial tribunal system for our examination and analysis, we turn immediately to its central aspect, the industrial tribunal. Although the ACAS conciliation stage occurs prior to the hearing, our argument is that ACAS conciliation is affected considerably by the context in which it takes place and is understood better once that context has been examined. After discussing, in Chapter 3, the composition of the industrial tribunal; the role of its members; its decision-making and the nature of hearings, Chapter 4 examines the reasons why unfair dismissal cases are won and lost. In Chapter 5 we describe and explain the kind of remedies obtained by applicants found to have been dismissed unfairly.

ACAS conciliation is the subject of Chapter 6 where we examine why some applicants do not proceed to hearing, the organisation and nature of conciliation and its outcomes. We evaluate ACAS conciliation in that chapter and then move on, in Chapter 7, to an evaluation of the industrial tribunal system as a whole. We assess whether it does offer a cheap, accessible and expert means of resolving unfair dismissal disputes in a way that is also free from technicality. That is one measure of the efficiency of the industrial tribunal system but also we raise the question of its efficiency when judged by the needs of different parties and in terms of what is demanded by the type of dispute being dealt with.

While Chapter 5 deals with the direct impact of the unfair dismissal provisions in terms of the outcomes of applications to tribunals, Chapter 8 looks at the wider impact which the existence and operation of the provisions has had. The framework for this examination is the effects expected or hoped for by those advocating and introducing the right not to be unfairly dismissed. Finally, in Chapter 9, we examine one alternative mechanism for dismissal dispute resolution, arbitration. We suggest that had the unfair dismissal provisions been entrusted to an arbitral rather than judicial system things might have worked out rather differently.

The unfair dismissal legislation gives employees the opportunity to challenge the fairness of their dismissal via the industrial tribunal system. It confers a right on employees which inevitably involves a cost to the employer; a restriction on employer freedom. The granting of the right not to be unfairly dismissed in the starting point of the investigation in this book. The interests of employers are not neglected but a central perspective underlying the work is an assessment of the extent to which the position of the individual dismissed worker has been improved by the existence of the statutory protection.

2

Parties and Representatives

The right to challenge the fairness of a dismissal is a general right but, as we have seen, not a universal one. Some workers will not be able to bring claims before a tribunal. Others, as we saw in the Ford example, will choose not to. This chapter explores the potential and actual use of the tribunal system by dismissed workers. In 1981, 37,000 unfair dismissal applications were registered, an increase over the previous year's total of 33,000 and a reversal in the slight downward trend which had been taking place since 1976. The effect of more stringent qualifications for applicants in reducing the level of applications appeared to have been balanced by an increased willingness of workers to challenge dismissal as increasing unemployment reduced the likelihood of finding new employment. In 1982, however, the number of unfair dismissal applications registered dropped again, to 35,000.

We look at the characteristics of applicants and then examine the type of employers who get involved as respondents in tribunal proceedings. We also examine the kind of help sought by the parties in tribunal cases. This will be influenced partly by the characteristics of the parties and partly by the system itself and their perception of it. For instance the absence of legal aid for representation at tribunals and the official emphasis on the flexibility of hearings and the ability of parties to present their own cases may serve to lessen the incidence of legal representation, although other factors, not least the definition of unfair dismissal as a legal problem to be determined by a quasi-court, may make this kind of representation appear most suitable. We discuss the representation chosen and the determinants of this choice.

Applicants

Potentially an unfair dismissal application can be made by anyone who has been dismissed (or is under notice of dismissal) as defined by the

statute. As noted in the preceding chapter, not all job loss is challengeable on grounds of fairness through the industrial tribunal system. The
statute encompasses forced resignation and the termination of fixed-
term contracts within the definition of dismissal, along with straightforward termination by the employer, but affords protection only to
'employees'. This excludes various sections of the working population.
Nearly two million people in the UK are self-employed and it has been
estimated, probably conservatively, that there are some two hundred
thousand to four hundred thousand homeworkers who, in the main,
fall outside the protection (Ewing, 1982a: 94).

Among those who are employees, the chance of becoming a member
of the potential pool of unfair dismissal applicants is not evenly distributed, as some are more likely to face dismissal then others. White-
collar workers generally enjoy greater security than manual workers;
dismissal is more common in the private than the public sector and is
practised proportionately more by small employers than large ones. A
survey of manufacturing industry establishments with fifty or more
employees undertaken in 1977–8 found the risk of dismissal to be
fifty times greater in establishments employing fewer than a hundred
workers than those with a thousand or more (Brown, 1981: 116). The
Policy Studies Institute (PSI) also found that 'workplaces employing
50–199 people had dismissed one in every 58 of their employees in
the previous 12 months. Plants employing 1,000–5,000 had dismissed
only one in every 200' (Daniel and Stilgoe, 1978: 62). A survey of
establishments in all industries in 1980 found a similar picture: 'the
absolute number of dismissals reported by larger establishments was
higher; but the rate of dismissal relative to the number of employees
was lower' (Daniel and Millward, 1983: 171). This survey found the
highest rate of dismissal in single establishment companies in the small-
est establishment size group, 25–99 workers.

The potential pool is also defined by the statutory requirements
concerning such matters as the age and service of applicants. Those who
have not served what, in effect, is a probationary period cannot generally
challenge the fairness of their dismissal. Changes in these statutory
requirements affect the definition of the pool and consequently the
characteristics of those who actually apply to the tribunals. For example, about a quarter of the applicants in our sample had between
26 weeks' and 52 weeks' service and would be ineligible to make a
claim under the present service qualification. People who do not conform to the requirements do sometimes try to apply. In past years some
10 per cent of applications received by COIT were not registered because
the would-be applicant withdrew after being notified by the tribunal
office that he or she did not seem to be qualified. In 1981, just under

2,000 applications were not registered due to the operation of this arrangement.

Differential risk of involuntary job loss both between and within industries and the legal parameters both help to delimit the range of potential applicants. Unfortunately, it is not possible to assess accurately the size of the pool and so calculate what proportion of those who could apply to a tribunal actually do so. What evidence is available, however, indicates that claiming unfair dismissal via the industrial tribunal system is an atypical, minority response. The survey of manufacturing establishments employing over 50 workers referred to earlier (Brown, 1981), found just under 2 per cent of the workforce had been dismissed for reasons other than redundancy in the previous two years but less than 10 per cent of them had sought to challenge their dismissal via the industrial tribunals. The 1980 survey of establishments of all sizes across industries found an average dismissal rate of 11 per 1,000 employed. Tribunal applications for that year however numbered some 33,000 which, given a total employed labour force of 25,300,000 (Institute of Employment Research (IER), 1983: 30), is only 1.3 per 1,000. This is an application rate of some 12 per cent. As noted, not all those dismissed will have been eligible to apply for unfair dismissal (for example because of inadequate service) but it appears likely that if we could accurately quantify those in the dismissed population able to bring a claim, the proportion of them actually applying would still be quite small. Applying to an industrial tribunal is not the usual response of a dismissed worker.

By the very fact that they do not apply to a tribunal we know little about the characteristics of the majority of dismissed workers or their reasons for not seeking to challenge their dismissals. Various explanations may be suggested, however, for the apparent acceptance of the fairness of their dismissals. Discussion of dismissed workers *choosing* whether or not to apply to a tribunal presupposes knowledge of the right to apply and some idea of how to go about it. Although it is perhaps unlikely that many dismissed workers are completely unaware that there is 'a law against unfair dismissal', a general awareness may be insufficient to bring about an application. For example, without some knowledge of the detailed provisions, someone who is forced to resign may not realise that this can amount to a dismissal and is challengeable before an industrial tribunal. Only 8 per cent of the applicants in the survey were claiming constructive dismissal (that is, forced resignation). Similarly, knowing that a law exists is of little value without also knowing both that an individual can initiate action and how to do so.

As Table 2.1 shows, applicants in the sample reported that they found out about industrial tribunals most commonly from job centres or

TABLE 2.1

APPLICANTS' SOURCES OF INFORMATION ABOUT INDUSTRIAL TRIBUNALS

Source	%
Trade union	12
Company	1
Solicitor/lawyer	3
Citizens Advice Bureaux	6
Department of Employment	26
Law Centre	—
Media	21
Friends/workmates	25
Other	6
Don't know/can't remember	2
	N = 1,063

SOURCE: IRRU survey of applicants.

unemployment benefit offices (here referred to generally, although not with total accuracy, as Department of Employment offices). This was particularly so among the 29 per cent of applicants who had not known about industrial tribunals prior to their dismissal. Thirty three per cent of these mentioned the DE offices compared with 23 per cent of those who did know prior to dismissal.

The prominence of the Department of Employment is not really surprising as people who have lost their jobs will begin looking for others and/or will attempt to draw unemployment benefit. In so doing they may discover their right to challenge their dismissal. Indeed in some cases it is only when benefit is refused that someone may discover he or she has been dismissed for 'misconduct' or is held to have left voluntarily and may wish to dispute it. Application in such cases may be less a challenge to the fairness of the dismissal per se than an attempt to secure unemployment pay.

The importance of the Department of Employment as a source of information about the existence of the tribunal system may be part of the explanation for the under-representation of women among tribunal applicants, compared with their proportion in the workforce as a whole. Men made up 71.5 per cent of the unfair dismissal applicants in our

sample, compared with 59 per cent of the workforce as a whole.[1] Since
dismissed women may be less likely to 'sign on' because of ineligibility
for unemployment benefit, or to use the DE as a job search agency,
they are less likely to be exposed to this source of information about
their right to apply to a tribunal. Female applicants mentioned the DE
as a source of information about industrial tribunals slightly less than
male applicants (24 per cent compared with 27 per cent) and were
more likely than men to have found out about industrial tribunals
from friends and workmates or Citizens Advice Bureaux. Their lesser
use of the DE here would appear important given that female applicants were less likely than men to know about industrial tribunals prior
to their dismissal (only 57 per cent of female applicants compared with
76 per cent of male applicants) and suggests that more women than
men may remain unaware of their rights. Awareness of rights may be
unevenly distributed in other ways also. One might expect unionised
workers to be more likely to know than non-unionists, for example.
It may also be the case that immigrant workers, particularly non-
English speakers, are less aware of their rights.

Other explanations for the under-representation of women may be
that they get dismissed less often than men or that fewer women
than men are eligible to apply for unfair dismissal. The first explanation
appears unlikely. A third of the female labour force is in public administration and professional and scientific services, industries which as we
shall see below, p. 42) are under-represented in tribunal claims. But
women constitute the majority of workers in sectors such as miscellaneous services where employees appear far more vulnerable to dismissal.
It does appear, however, that because of the nature of their employment women may be less likely than men to be eligible to claim unfair
dismissal, because of insufficient service or because they work part-
time. Part-time work is done predominently by women. The EEC
Labour Force Survey in 1979 found 15 per cent of employees in Britain
reported that they worked part-time and 80 per cent of the part-time
employees were women. The reduction in the hours required for statutory protection made by the 1975 Act (see above, p. 20) will have
brought more part-time women within the coverage of the provisions
since two-thirds of them work less than 22 hours a week (Robertson
and Briggs, 1979: 672).

Lack of knowledge about how to apply, and lack of eligibility, are
two likely explanations for non-application by dismissed workers.
Others can be sought in the dismissed worker's lack of any grievance,

1. Total workforce from *Employment Gazette* (December 1978), 1422. Figure as
at June 1977.

the grievance having been aired already, and in perceptions of the tribunal remedies as inappropriate or inadequate or available only at an unacceptable cost. To be motivated to apply to an industrial tribunal, a dismissed person firstly needs to feel aggrieved by the dismissal and, secondly, to see the industrial tribunal system as a way of satisfactorily resolving the grievance at an acceptable cost. Some dismissed workers no doubt accept that their dismissal was justified or do not view it as unfair and so do not feel aggrieved. The clearest example is perhaps the employee caught with a 'hand in the till', but it is wider than this. Although workers may not share management's view of what constitutes unsatisfactory behaviour or satisfactory performance, or the appropriateness of various sanctions, they may none the less acquiesce in, or acknowledge, management's claimed right to determine these matters. Further, the economic circumstances of working class experience, particularly in certain occupations or industries, probably fosters a kind of fatalism concerning job loss, with the result that dismissal is not viewed as exceptional or as something which can be questioned usefully.

Workers who have already challenged their dismissal or, more likely, the decision to dismiss, within the company or via some other procedure, may be more willing to accept it or see little point in trying another challenge via the industrial tribunal machinery. It may be indicative here that 57 per cent of the 1,063 applicants in the sample said that they had not discussed their dismissal or appealed against it within the company before applying to a tribunal. Most applicants, therefore, had not aired their grievance about their dismissal. Only 10 per cent of applicants reported using a formal procedure to try to discuss or challenge their dismissal within the company before applying to a tribunal. The remaining one-third had tried to raise the matter informally. Most (67 per cent) of those who had not attempted anything within the company said no opportunity to do so had existed (another 18 per cent said they did not know whether there was such as opportunity).

The probability of being able to challenge a dismissal decision, other than through the industrial tribunals, is highest where workers are unionised. Dismissal decisions can be contested through a grievance or disputes procedure, by negotiation possibly backed by collective action. The positive correlation between union organisation, size of firm, and the existence of discipline/dismissal procedures (Brown, 1981: 44; Daniel and Millward, 1983) means that where workers are organised dismissals are in any case less likely to be arbitrary and hence give less cause for grievance.

The nature of the grievance felt by the dismissed worker and the nature of the remedies offered by the industrial tribunal system will act to encourage or discourage application. The legislation and the industrial tribunal system define unfair dismissal as a legal problem. Workers may experience it rather as a social or psychological problem, causing trauma and stress or strain on family relationships. The grievance of the dismissed worker may be a feeling of betrayal after years of loyal service or a lessening of self-esteem or reputation. Unless the dismissed worker sees the system's remedies of money or re-employment as a way of resolving these problems application will not be seen as useful. Some workers will see the available remedies as solutions to their problems or as symbolic acknowledgement that they have been mistreated. Others perhaps will see the industrial tribunal hearing as a way of exposing publicly the employer's 'wrongdoings' or having a cathartic effect and so consider application. These potential applicants have to consider the likelihood of success and the costs of pursuing an application.

As we shall see in Chapter 4 the outcomes of industrial tribunal hearings are not encouraging to would-be applicants but it is perhaps unlikely that many dismissed workers will be aware of the low rate of applicant success or of the extreme rarity of re-employment. They are, however, likely to think about the costs involved in applying to a tribunal. As there are no application or hearing fees and the awarding of costs against the losing party is not automatic or even common, the costs are not primarily financial but have more to do with personal resources and consequences. Some workers who feel aggrieved over their dismissal may wish to distance themselves from it as quickly as possible. To challenge it via an industrial tribunal would only prolong the upset and unpleasantness occasioned by the event. Others may feel themselves unequal to the process with its attendant form-filling and appearance in front of, even an informal, court. The possibility of support and representation, dealt with later, is of course a factor here, but for some the worry and bother application would involve may act as a deterrent. Other factors, such as success in finding new employment or fear of adverse repercussions on job prospects if there were publicity as a result of applying, may also affect the number and nature of applicants.

The characteristics of industrial tribunal applicants are thus determined by differential likelihood of dismissal, the differential eligibility of dismissed workers according to the legal provisions and by a certain amount of self-selection. The typical tribunal applicant, as revealed by our survey, is a male, manual worker, not in membership of a union, who has been dismissed after relatively short service by a small employer in the private sector. The over-representation of men compared to their proportion in the working population has already been discussed. Table 2.2 shows the broad occupational breakdown of appli-

TABLE 2.2

APPLICANTS' OCCUPATIONAL CATEGORIES

	Applicants[a] %	Total Employment[b] %
Professional/managerial	12	15
Other non-manual	21	33
Total non-manual:	33	48
Skilled manual	38	24
Other manual	29	28
Total manual:	67	52
	N = 1,063	N = 24,624,000

SOURCES:
a. IRRU survey.
b. Lindley, R. (ed), *Britain's Medium Term Employment Prospects* (Warwick: Warwick Printing Co., 1978), 62. Family workers and HM forces are excluded.

NOTE: Slightly different definitions of the categories within the 'manual' classi- fication were used.

cants in the sample. Sixty-seven per cent were manual workers. This compares with 52 per cent in the workforce as a whole in 1976.

A lower proportion of applicants were members of trade unions than is true of the workforce as a whole. Only 32 per cent of applicants were union members at a time when some 52 per cent of the labour force was unionised (Bain and Price, 1980: 38). The disparity is more marked given the high proportion of skilled manual workers among tribunal applicants as this group has higher than average unionisation among the labour force as a whole. We noted earlier that the propensity to dismiss is greater in smaller firms and, as these are less likely to be unionised, it might be that the level of union membership among applicants is more representative of that among the dismissed population as a whole. In- deed, given that union members may be more aware of their right to challenge a dismissal through the industrial tribunals and more able to obtain help in so doing, the proportion of applicants who are union members may even be higher than among the dismissed population as a whole.

Table 2.3 shows the length of service applicants had in the job from which they were dismissed compared with a random sample of full-time employees. The proportion of short-service applicants, 60 per cent having under three years' service, is much higher than among the working population generally. However, a high proportion of dismissals occur during the first two years of service (Ministry of Labour, 1967)

TABLE 2.3

APPLICANTS' LENGTH OF SERVICE

	Applicants		Employees[a]
	%		%
6 months	4 } 27		12
Over 6 months up to 1 year	23		
1 year up to 3 years	35		24
3 years up to 5 years	15		13
5 years up to 10 years	14		20
10 years up to 15 years	5 } 9		31
15 years up to 20 years	1		
20 years and over	3		
	100		100
	N = 1,063		N = 129,916

SOURCE: IRRU survey; NES 1976, table 169, p. F41.

NOTE:

a. New Earnings Survey figures are for April 1976 (1977 figures not available). Refers to all full-time men and women.

and so in this respect the unfair dismissal applicants are probably more representative of the total *dismissed* population.

Respondent Employers

Those who are cited as respondents in unfair dismissal applications to tribunals are predominantly small employers. In 44 per cent of cases surveyed the establishment from which the applicant was dismissed was the company's only premises. Three-quarters of these single-establishment employers had fewer than 100 workers, 46 per cent of them fewer than 20. Table 2.4 shows the establishment and company size of the respondent employers in the sample. Almost half the unfair dismissal applications involved employers with total labour forces smaller than 100 and about a quarter involved employers with fewer than 20 workers. As noted earlier (p. 20), legislative change in 1980 means workers in these very small firms generally have to satisfy the longer, two-year service qualification before being able to challenge their dismissal before an industrial tribunal. This provision was not in existence at the time of the survey and may be expected to reduce the proportion of employers with fewer than 20 workers among respondent employers.

TABLE 2.4

SIZE OF RESPONDENT EMPLOYERS

Workforce	Establishment		Company	
	No.	%	*No.*	%
below 10	285	26	264	24
10–19	174	16		
20–99	327	30	276	25
100–499	185	17	193	18
500–999	40	4	75	7
1000+	41	4	238	22
Don't know	28	3	54	3
	N = 1,080		N = 1,080	

SOURCE: IRRU survey.

Small employers are found in particular industrial sectors. It is known, for example, that whereas only some 7 per cent of the labour force in manufacturing industry (orders III–XIX) is employed in establishments of fewer than 20, in the construction industry 24 per cent of the workforce is employed in such establishments (Census of Production 1977, table 6). The construction industry provided a substantial proportion of the unfair dismissal applications in our sample, as did miscellaneous services, distributive trades, and food, drink and tobacco. Given the regional dispersion of certain industries, however, the basis of our sample, drawn from four tribunal areas, may be a source of some distortion here. For this reason Table 2.5 which shows dismissal applications by industry uses the latest available national sample figures produced by the Department of Employment.[2] Construction (13.9 per cent of applications), distributive trades (16.6 per cent), and miscellaneous services (16 per cent) feature prominently. The table also shows the proportion of the labour force employed in each industry. This reveals that the three industries mentioned have a higher proportion of applications than their share of the working population would suggest. Construction, for example, employs 5.7 per cent of the labour force but produces 14 per cent of applications for unfair dismissal. By contrast, professional and scientific services employs 16 per cent of the labour force but produces less than 4 per cent of unfair dismissal applications.

Table 2.6 presents this picture in a slightly different way. The number applying to an industrial tribunal from each industrial classification during a one-year period is expressed as a proportion of the average workforce in the industry during that year. The industries are then ranked highest to lowest. It is, of course, possible that some industries with a below average proportion of applications dismiss the same proportion of their workforce in a year as those industries with above average application rate but that a smaller proportion of those dismissed actually apply. To test this would require better statistics than are available on the number of people dismissed from each industry during the course of a year and the proportion who then apply to a tribunal. Some of the reasons suggested above for non-application may apply more strongly to certain industries, but none the less it seems reasonable to suppose the rank order given in Table 2.6 is a rough approximation to the industries' relative dismissal rates. Using the DE/PSI/SSRC 1980 survey, industries were ranked by their dismissal rate (proportion of labour force dismissed other than for redundancy in previous year). The only industry with an above average dismissal rate which did not also have an above average application rate, on the basis of Table 2.6, was metal manufacture. Although the general picture was similar in terms of industries found near the top and bottom of the ranking the correspondence was by no means exact. The different time periods concerned and changing employment patterns obviously hinder comparison.

The contrast between the public and private sectors is clear: very few unfair dismissal applications originate from the public sector. Those industries with the highest application rate are those in the

2. Statistics on characteristics of the parties in unfair dismissal cases were not published for any year after 1976.

TABLE 2.5

DISMISSAL APPLICATIONS AND EMPLOYMENT BY INDUSTRY

Industry	Proportion of Labour Force[a] %	Unfair Dismissal Applications[b] No.	%
Agriculture, forestry and fishing	1.7	985	4.2
Mining and quarrying	1.6	137	0.6
Food, drink and tobacco	3.1	738	3.1
Coal and petroleum products	0.2	30	0.1
Chemicals and allied industries	1.9	460	2.0
Metal manufacture	2.1	459	2.0
Mechanical engineering	4.2	1,135	4.8
Instrument engineering	0.7	123	0.5
Electrical engineering	3.3	703	3.0
Shipbuilding and marine engineering	0.8	165	0.7
Vehicles	3.3	301	1.3
Metal goods not elsewhere specified	2.4	1,096	4.7

Textiles	2.2	533	2.3
Leather, leather goods and fur	0.2	71	0.3
Clothing and footwear	1.7	451	1.9
Bricks, pottery, glass, cement, etc.	1.2	265	1.1
Timber, furniture, etc.	1.2	422	1.8
Paper, printing and publishing	2.4	457	1.9
Other manufacturing industries	1.5	407	1.7
Construction	5.8	3,263	13.9
Gas, electricity and water	1.6	117	0.5
Transport and communication	6.6	1,521	6.5
Distributive trades	12.1	3,902	16.6
Insurance, banking, finance and business services	4.9	742	3.2
Professional and scientific services	16.1	848	3.6
Miscellaneous services	10.2	3,760	16.0
Public administration and defence	7.2	408	1.7
		N = 23,499	

SOURCES:
a. As at June 1976 (*Employment Gazette* (December 1977), 1404—5).
b. January—June 1976 (*Employment Gazette* (November 1977)).

TABLE 2.6

PROPORTION OF LABOUR FORCE CLAIMING UNFAIR DISMISSAL BY INDUSTRY

Industry	Proportion of Labour Force Applying (%)
Construction	0.23
Agriculture, forestry and fishing	0.23
Leather, leather goods and fur	0.19
Miscellaneous services	0.16
Timber, furniture, etc.	0.16
Metal goods not elsewhere specified	0.16
Distributive trades	0.14
Mechanical engineering	0.14
Other manufacturing industries	0.14
Transport and communication	0.13
Bricks, pottery, glass, cement, etc.	0.12
Textiles	0.12
Food, drink and tobacco	0.11
Chemicals	0.10
Clothing and footwear	0.10
	mean — — —
Paper, printing and publishing	0.09
Electrical engineering	0.09
Instrument engineering	0.09
Metal manufacture	0.09
Shipbuilding and marine engineering	0.07
Insurance, banking and finance	0.06
Coal and petroleum products	0.06
Vehicles	0.05
Gas, electricity and water	0.03
Mining and quarrying	0.03
Public administration and defence	0.02
Professional and scientific services	0.02

SOURCE: *Employment Gazette* (November 1977). Year of 1975 chosen as it is the last complete year for which the Department of Employment produced the information on applications by Standard Industrial Classification.

private sector characterised by small employment units and unionisation lower than the average of about 50 per cent. For example the industries at the top of the ranking for unfair dismissal applications in 1975 had relatively low union density: construction 32 per cent, agriculture and forestry 24 per cent, leather, leather goods and fur 27 per cent and miscellaneous services only 7 per cent (Price and Bain, 1983: 64).

The size and industrial distribution of respondent employers means that the proportion recognising trade unions is lower than among employers generally. The 1980 survey of establishments across all industries found that 67 per cent reported that a union was recognised (Daniel and Millward, 1983: 18). In the sample of respondent employers 51 per cent of establishments recognised trade unions, ranging from 32 per cent of those establishments with fewer than 10 employees to 95 per cent of those with 500 employees or more.

Size and union recognition have been found to associate positively with the existence of formal procedures (see Chapter 8), and it is not surprising that respondent employers as a group were slightly less likely to report the existence of written procedures for handling discipline/ dismissal disputes than employers as a whole. In our sample, 72 per cent of respondent employers reported that they had such a procedure at the time of the dismissal in question, whereas 83 per cent of all employers claim to have such procedures written down (Daniel and Millward, 1983: 163).

Examination of the characteristics of the parties shows that employers in the public sector, and in large and well organised companies in the private sector, do not generally find themselves having to defend industrial tribunal claims for unfair dismissal. Rather it is the small, often single-establishment employers who find their dismissal decisions most likely to be challenged at law. Those challenging their dismissals are generally non-union male manual workers who may have no other opportunity of airing their grievance or seeking redress. We noted earlier that the provisions of the law and the features of the industrial tribunal system help determine the nature of the parties who will use it. But these things are interrelated and the nature of the parties will itself affect the operation of the system. One area where this interrelationship can be seen is representation. As we shall now discuss, the characteristics of the parties is one determinant of the type and extent of representation used.

Representatives

Formally the parties have a free choice of representative:

> any person may appear before an industrial tribunal in person or be represented by counsel or by a solicitor or by a repre-

sentative of a trade union or an employers' association or by any other person whom he desires to represent him (EP(C)A Sched. 9 para. 6).

Similarly the parties have freedom of choice in whom, if anyone, they turn to for advice or representation prior to the hearing. However, the choice open to any particular applicant or respondent employer may be narrower than the formal position suggests. Table 2.7 shows how the parties surveyed were represented prior to the hearing and at the hearing. The table shows that in about one-fifth of cases the company's case was handled by an internal specialist, defined as an industrial relations or personnel manager or a legally qualified employee of the company. It is only the larger companies which have this representation option. Forty-one per cent of the 1,080 respondent employers reported that they had 'a personnel, industrial relations or welfare officer or department' but a majority 'yes' response was obtained only from companies employing over 500 workers. Only 13 per cent of respondent employers in the 20—99 size band reported the existence of an officer or department.

For these smaller employers representation from within the company of necessity is 'lay', non-specialist representation: the managing director, a line manager or supervisor, the company secretary or accountant. If specialist representation is required it has to be obtained from outside the company: for example, from an employers' association or a lawyer in private practice. Even here the small employer's choice may be constrained as membership of an employers' association which advises on industrial relations matters is more common among larger companies. In our survey 56 per cent of the 1,080 respondent employers said they were in membership of an employers' association (this appears to have been fairly widely interpreted and included Joint Industrial Councils and bodies which are perhaps more accurately seen as trade associations). Half the single-establishment employers and over half of multi-establishment employers with fewer than 20 workers said they were not members of an employers' association. Among the larger employers membership was more common: less than one-third of those with over 500 workers were not members of any employers' association. Those who were members of employers' associations appear to have made little use of them, however, in connection with the unfair dismissal claim. Only 14 per cent of members actually sought advice from their associations on being notified of the unfair dismissal application against them and only 5 per cent used their association for representation. This is of course partly due to larger companies, who are more likely to be members, having the option of using their own specialist staff but also

TABLE 2.7

REPRESENTATION

(a) AT CONCILIATION[a]

Applicants	%	Respondent Employers	%
Self	57	Internal company:	
Legal	21	lay	41 }63
Trade union:		specialist	22 }
full-time official	15 }17	External legal	31
shop steward/lay	2 }	Employers' association	4
Other	5	Other	2
	100		100
N = 1,063		N = 1,080	

(b) AT HEARING

Applicants	%	Respondent Employers	%
Self	45	Internal company:	
Legal:		lay/unidentified	
solicitor	21 }23	status	33 }52
barrister	2 }	specialist	19 }
Trade union:		External legal:	
full-time official	20 }22	solicitor	37 }41
shop steward/lay	2 }	barrister	4 }
CAB/Law Centre/		Employers' association	5
Representative Unit	2	Other outsider	2
Other	7	Don't know	1
	99		101
N = 596		N = 443	

SOURCE: IRRU surveys.

NOTE:
a. Representation at conciliation does not mean necessarily that only the representative had contact with the conciliation officer.

indicates that not all associations will offer a representation service, although they may provide advice.

The Engineering Employers' Federation (EEF) does provide representation for its member firms and although the EEF accounted for only 15 per cent of the employers' association membership among respondents, it provided 58 per cent of the, albeit limited, employers' association respresentation at the conciliation stage and 55 per cent of that at the hearing. Employers' associations may also be selective as to which cases they will support and member firms may be expected to fulfil certain conditions before the representation service is provided: following an approved procedure, perhaps consulting the association prior to dismissal.

Only 7 per cent of employers' association members were represented by their associations. Among applicants, 50 per cent of trade union members were represented by full-time or lay officials of their unions at conciliation and 52 per cent at hearing, but overall this type of representation accounted for only about one-fifth of applicants because, as we have seen, the majority of applicants were not members of a union. Further, some union members did not have union representation. Those union members who were not represented by their union may not have sought such representation or may have had it refused. Of those union members who said they sought advice on how to apply for unfair dismissal 44 per cent did so from their trade unions. Where a union member works in a weakly organised, or even unorganised establishment, there is no steward to contact as a first stage in getting union assistance and so recourse may be made elsewhere. In other cases, the applicant may see the union as an inappropriate source of advice and assistance; for example if a union representative was involved in or agreed to the dismissal or if the union had already sought, unsuccessfully, to challenge the dismissal decision via an internal procedure. In this latter instance the union might in any case be unwilling to support its member's application to a tribunal for fear of undermining the status of an agreed procedure.

Of the sixty-seven union members who went to a hearing without representation by their unions, eighteen (27 per cent) said this was because they had been refused such representation. Our interviews with full-time officials from seven unions revealed differing policy and practice on handling unfair dismissal claims both between and within unions. One area where differences were found was in the degree of specialisation. In some regions or districts there is formal or informal specialisation with a particular officer handling all, or most, of the tribunal work. We found this was sometimes the case in the General and Municipal Workers' Union (as it then was) where the person concerned might be

the Legal Officer (which does not necessarily denote any legal qualification) who was also responsible for such matters as industrial injury
claims and national insurance tribunals. Formal specialisation was
found less often in the Transport and General Workers' Union (TGWU)
where officers generally handled those cases coming from their area
although some districts had decided that it would be advantageous if
one officer took all cases and so developed familiarity with the area —
both with the law and procedure and with the personalities of those
chairing the local tribunals.

Theoretically officers in all the unions could call on the services of
the legal department at their union head offices but this did not appear
to be common except in those unions where some central control was
exercised. This was the case in the Union of Shop, Distributive and
Allied Workers (USDAW) where applications for assistance from
members had to be sent to the legal department which would decide
whether to handle the case itself or leave it to the local officer. There
was also variation in the stage at which the union officer liked to be
involved. Some preferred members to contact the union before sending
off the application form and in some areas members had been circulated
to this effect. The agricultural workers' union (now part of the TGWU)
operated a system whereby the application was actually completed
by head office on the basis of information provided by the divisional
organiser. Other officers were content not to get involved until a later
stage, providing representation at a tribunal hearing if the case reached
this stage.

Earlier involvement obviously allows more opportunity for the
union to be selective in which cases to pursue. Generally union officers
seemed to feel that they should offer some assistance to all properly
paid-up members who requested it but factors were identified which led
to some selectivity, particularly in terms of cases to be taken to a
hearing. One was simply lack of resources or competing demands for
the time and energies of full-time officers. Occasionally a branch
secretary or other lay officer, particularly a shop steward, might be involved in representing a member but, as Table 2.7 shows, this is rarely
the case either at the stage prior to the tribunal or at the hearing. Some
officers were prepared to offer all members some initial assistance in
applying and at the conciliation stage but would then attempt to dis-
suade those with weak cases from continuing to the hearing.

Officers rarely reported that they would refuse outright to provide
assistance although they would try hard to get applicants to realise their
cases were unlikely to succeed where they believed this to be the case.
An argument for not taking every case which was often mentioned was
that if the union officer gained a reputation at the local Regional

Tribunal office for taking 'no-hope' cases this could prejudice the chances of a member with a good case. Some officers also appeared to want to maintain as good a success rate as possible in the cases they did take to tribunals. There were circumstances however where officers felt it would be worthwhile to take a case which appeared unlikely to win. Generally these were where the case had collective implications. This might be because of the issue – a trade union activities dismissal for example – or because the union thought some spin-off advantage might accrue. For example, being seen to be prepared to tackle the employer's dismissal decision in situations where it was attempting to organise might encourage membership.

The extent of experience of, and expertise in, bringing unfair dismissal claims varied among the officials interviewed. It depended partly on whether there was specialisation within the union and whether the union had provided any training but also on the nature of the industries or geographical area for which the official was responsible. In some sectors it was extremely rare to receive a request from a member that an application be made to an industrial tribunal (see also Evans et al., 1984: s.4).

Membership of a trade union gives an applicant, at least potentially, a wider choice of representation. Self-representation was far less common among trade union members (36 per cent at conciliation and 27 per cent at hearing) than non-members (66 per cent of whom represented themselves at conciliation and 56 per cent at hearing) as was representation by lawyers. Twenty-six per cent of non-members had legal representation at conciliation and 27 per cent at hearing compared with 11 per cent and 15 per cent of union members at each stage. Some legal representation of union members may indirectly be union-assisted representation in that the union employs a solicitor to take the case to hearing. Our interviews did not reveal this to be common practice although it did appear to be an option sometimes used by union officers in Scotland.

As Table 2.7 shows, most commonly, at conciliation and hearing, applicants in our survey represented themselves. This remains the case although as we discuss later (below p. 78) legal representation is increasing. Self-representation for applicants is almost always lay representation. Few will have specialist qualifications of the kind some employers can call upon. For the non-union applicant, therefore, skills have to be obtained by engaging a lawyer, which one-fifth of applicants did, or possibly by using the services of voluntary and other agencies such as Citizens Advice Bureaux, Law Centres, or Tribunal Assistance Units. Some of the 'other' representation – usually friends or relatives

– may be specialist, but this is unlikely. Use of the voluntary agencies was small, covering only 2 per cent of applicants at hearing.

The availability of this kind of provision has increased slightly since the time of the survey. In 1976, for example, there were fifteen full members of the Law Centres Federation, in 1980 there were thirty-one full members, half of them based in London (Zander, 1980: 11). The greater availability of 'poor man's lawyer' facilities in the capital, where there is also a Free Representation Unit, staffed by Bar students, barristers and law students, is reflected in the regional breakdown of our sample. Of those applicants with representation in the London South region, 17 per cent at conciliation and 9 per cent at hearing were represented in this way, compared with only one per cent or less in the other three areas. Financing of Law Centres is often precarious, however, and some may have closed since 1980.

The seven hundred or so Citizens Advice Bureaux are geographically widespread, but the number of full-time staff and services available vary. As the National Association of Citizens Advice Bureaux (NACAB) stresses, it 'does not at present purport to provide nor participate in any semblance of a national network of assistance to tribunal appellants and applicants' (1978: i). Some Citizens Advice Bureaux, for instance Nottingham, employ salaried lawyers and others have established various tribunal assistance or representation schemes, but at the time of the research only those in Newcastle and Chapeltown (Leeds), appeared to undertake industrial tribunal cases regularly.

For the smaller employer and the non-union applicant, therefore, choice of representative is limited. Effectively, if they do not wish to represent themselves, the only option is to engage a lawyer. But, unlike the other forms of representation discussed, external legal representation has to be bought. This may mean that for some it ceases to be an option at all. The reasons for self-representation given by those 192 applicants who represented themselves at hearing reveal that for a high proportion (43 per cent) this was the only possible choice. Lack of representation was explained by comments such as 'I had no other way, I couldn't afford a solicitor's fee' and 'I had no alternative, there was nobody else to do it short of employing a solicitor which would have cost me a bomb'. Employers who handled their own cases were more likely than applicants to give positive, non-financial reasons for so doing. Only 14 per cent of the 137 employers who were represented at the hearing by someone from the establishment where the applicant had worked said this was because it was cheaper. The most common reason, given by 38 per cent, was that the person chosen to represent the company had been directly involved in the case or knew most about it. As

Table 2.7 showed, a higher proportion of respondent employers buy in legal representation than do applicants. Forty-one per cent of employers had this kind of representation at the hearing compared with 23 per cent of applicants. Although the average cost of legal representation at hearing incurred by respondents (just over £200 at 1976—7 prices) is not an insignificant amount for the small employer, the dismissed applicant is likely to face greater deterrent in the average cost of legal representation of £100 which applicants who used this form of representation at hearing incurred.[3] Only 14 per cent of applicants surveyed had obtained new employment before applying to the tribunal. Most applicants therefore will be unemployed at the time they have to decide on representation and, given that many will have been dismissed from relatively low-paid jobs (Dickens et al., 1979: 13), they are unlikely to have savings from which to finance legal representation.

Generally applicants who went to hearing retained the form of representation they had at conciliation. Of the 102 applicants who had solicitor representation at conciliation, however, 20 per cent changed to self-representation at the hearing. As it might be supposed that the particular skills of a legal representative would be seen as *more* useful at the hearing, the cost of such representation may be the explanation for this shift. Under the Legal Advice and Assistance Scheme, free or subsidised legal help can be obtained in preparing a case but, although it has been recommended by the Royal Commission on Legal Services (Benson, 1979: ch. 15), there is no provision for legal aid for representation at an industrial tribunal hearing. The different financial position of the employer is shown again in that, although there was some slight movement away from legal representation at conciliation into self-representation at hearing (5 per cent), there was greater movement in the other direction: 19 per cent of employers who had self-representation at conciliation switched to external legal representation for the hearing.

In about half the 308 tribunal hearings covered by the survey where information was obtained from both parties, there was a lawyer — usually a solicitor — present as a representative for one or both sides. In 16 per cent of all heard cases both sides had external legal representation, but the greater use of lawyers by respondent employers meant that in 28 per cent of heard cases (representing 55 per cent of those

---

3. Some indication of what current average costs might be is given by the fact that, between the period covered by the survey and January 1984, the Retail Price Index (All Items) virtually doubted (DE, 1984b: 558).

where a lawyer was present) the employer alone had this kind of representation. In later chapters we examine the importance of representation for the outcome of tribunal hearings (Chapter 4) and the implications of representation patterns for the efficiency of the tribunal system (Chapter 7).

Summary

This chapter has shown that challenging the fairness of a dismissal via the industrial tribunal system is not the usual response of a sacked worker. Who uses the tribunal is determined by differential likelihood of dismissal, the eligibility of dismissed workers to claim according to the legal provisions and some 'self-selection'. It was suggested that self-selection is affected by the dismissed workers' knowledge concerning the legal right; the nature of the felt grievance; and the perception of what is offered by the industrial tribunals and at what cost. Applicants are typically male, non-union manual workers dismissed after relatively short service. Respondent employers are generally small companies, often single-establishment employers. Those industries characterised by small employment units and below average unionisation produce most unfair dismissal claims.

The formal position of free choice between handling one's own unfair dismissal case or having legal or other representation was found to be constrained in practice by the nature of applicants and employers; the availability of specialist in-house, or free legal representation; the cost of external legal representation; the membership of a trade union or employers' association; and the policies and practices of those bodies on tribunal representation.

Before we can assess the importance or consequences of the nature of the parties and their form of representation we need to examine the operation of the tribunal system. We look first at its central aspect, the tribunal hearing.

3

The Industrial Tribunal: Members and Hearings

The formulation of protection against unfair dismissal as an individual legal right, calling for the interpretation and application of rules to a particular set of facts, pointed to judicial adjudication as the most suitable form of decision-making. Although judicial decision-making is not the monopoly of the courts the body chosen was a quasi-court, the industrial tribunal. With lay members experienced in industry or commerce sitting with a legal member, industrial tribunals were expected to show the sensitivity to industrial relations practice and problems and different employment circumstances which was considered necessary in adjudicating unfair dismissal disputes. There was little debate about the machinery to implement the new legislation but it seems to have been intended that the industrial tribunals would provide adjudication in a way that was less formal, less legalistic, than the ordinary courts while the provision for appeal would ensure that this was not achieved at the expense of consistency in decision-making.

Tribunals have been described as a specialist, modern form of court (Abel-Smith and Stevens, 1968: 228) and their distinctiveness lies in their composition and the way they conduct their business. These aspects are examined in this chapter. We look at those who sit on industrial tribunals, the functions they are expected to perform and the context within which they have to perform them. In particular we explore the industrial and legal knowledge and experience which the tribunals' membership encompasses; the factors which affect the mix of these elements in decision-making in unfair dismissal cases and the nature of the industrial tribunal hearing.

Composition of the Tribunal

The industrial tribunals consist of a legally qualified chairperson and two lay members who together represent both sides of industry. In October

1983 there were 64 full-time and 129 part-time chairpersons in England and Wales appointed by the Lord Chancellor and in February 1984, in addition to the President, 9 full-time and 16 part-time chairpersons in Scotland appointed by the Lord President of the Court of Session. They are barristers or solicitors of at least seven years' standing appointed for five years and eligible for reappointment.

The Ministry of Labour's National Joint Advisory Council, when reporting in 1967, had questioned the need for a legal chairperson and suggested that representatives of employers and workers might take the chair in turn (Ministry of Labour, 1967: 42). The TUC also considered the case for legal chairing was not conclusive because of the need to achieve informality of procedure and the adoption of a conciliatory approach. Although the French *conseils de prud'hommes* provided an example of a non-legal panel, the influence of the Franks Commitee recommendations and the general power and standing of the British legal profession made such a departure most unlikely. The Franks Committee, which had reported on administrative tribunals in the 1950s, had been critical of rent tribunals which did not have legally qualified chairpersons and were 'insufficiently judicial in their methods of handling cases' (1957: para. 161). Although the possibility of 'particularly suitable' non-lawyers chairing tribunals was not ruled out entirely, the Franks Committee (para. 55) felt that 'objectivity in the treatment of cases and the proper sifting of facts are most often secured by having a legally qualified chairman'.

The composition of the industrial tribunals had been decided when they were set up under the Industrial Training Act 1964 and to dispense with the legal chairperson in unfair dismissal cases would have been a significant change and against the trend towards legal chairing, encouraged by the Franks Committee Report. As it was there was no marked pressure for changing the composition of the tribunals when the unfair dismissal provisions were being discussed. Indeed there was not much debate at all about the nature of the body which was to play the crucial role in interpreting and adjudicating on the new legal right (Wedderburn, 1965: 9).

Initially barristers were preferred as tribunal chairpersons. Perhaps paradoxically, given the explicit move away from the courts which tribunals represented, this was because of their judicial and court experience. A survey of tribunal chairpersons in 1973 showed the distribution between barristers and solicitors to be 6:4 (Whitesides and Hawker, 1975: 26). It now seems that more solicitors have been appointed. In 1978 we surveyed a one in two sample of the full-time chairpersons and a one in three sample of the part-timers, obtaining response rates of 50 per cent and 43 per cent respectively (see Appendix I). This revealed that 31 per cent of chairpersons surveyed were, at the time of their appointment, practising barristers or held judicial office and 47 per cent were practising solicitors, the remainder holding other legal posts. We did not find support for the argument that 'admirals, brigadiers and former colonial judges' are familiar among those who chair tribunals (Hendy, 1983: 5), although this may have been the case originally (Rideout, 1968: 178). The small size of the achieved sample (38) means that the distribution we found may not accurately reflect the distribution among all chairpersons but, inasmuch as two-thirds of those responding to the survey had been appointed within the preceding three years, it might indicate that the growing case-load meant increasing reliance on solicitors rather than barristers or other judicial office holders, particularly for part-time appointments. Women are under-represented among barristers and solicitors of seven years' standing and few tribunals are chaired by women (Equal Opportunities Commission (EOC), 1978: 14, 19). In mid-1982 only three of the 77 full-time chairpersons were women.

Although industrial tribunals are specialist bodies, those who chair them are not required to have any experience or particular knowledge of commerce or industry nor indeed at the time of appointment of labour law. Two full-time chairpersons responding to our questionnaire noted under 'industrial experience' that they had experience as company directors while three part-timers said they had experience as solicitors or legal officers in local authorities or private companies. But the majority of respondents — 74 per cent of full-timers and just over half the part-timers — had what might be termed purely legal careers, generally in private legal practice. Those appointed to chair tribunals receive no formal training on appointment. New appointees are given introductory talks by the President or Regional Chairman and sit in on some hearings before chairing any themselves. Tribunal practice is to allocate experienced lay members to sit with new chairpersons for the first few hearings they chair. In some regions those who chair tribunals meet twice a year to discuss common concerns.

Opinion on the usefulness of training was divided among the respondents in the survey of chairpersons. Those who thought training on appointment would not be useful generally felt that what mattered was selecting the right people for the job and that, as one put it, 'any civil litigation lawyer should be able to do the job without training'. Some said it was difficult to see what training might consist of as what was required was a combination of particular personal qualities and experience which could be gained only by actually chairing tribunals. Others noted that informal help and advice were available from Regional Chairmen on a continuing basis. Half of the part-time chairpersons and of the full-timers, however, did think initial training would be useful but many qualified this response by saying it would depend on the past experience of the appointees, for example whether they had court experience or had acted as representatives at tribunals. The full-time chairpersons who thought training on appointment would be useful generally wanted an extension of the existing introductory programme, particularly more seminars and discussion with experienced chairpersons. Parttimers who thought initial training would be useful highlighted more particular requirements. The small size of the sample means each suggestion was made by only one or two respondents, but they included simulated or 'mock' hearings with the new appointee taking the chair; instruction on framing decisions, on the processing, promulgation and enforcement of awards; and greater contact with management and labour to obtain some understanding of industry and to help break down misunderstanding and suspicion.

The lack of training for those who chair industrial tribunals is in keeping with the general British practice of not training judicial appointees. There have been some developments — such as the 'sentencing conferences' for criminal court judges, which have an echo in the regular meetings of the President of Tribunals in England and Wales with the regional industrial tribunal chairpersons — but the qualities and experience which suit people to be appointed to judicial office are seen as equipping them to perform that office.

The need for chairperson training depends partly on whether the role they are expected to play is particularly different from any they would have encountered in their general court experience. Legal training and experience no doubt is one way of equipping people to evaluate evidence, sift facts, formulate and decide relevant questions, and apply general rules to a particular situation. Those not familiar with the particular legislation or relevant precedents can soon familiarise themselves with these things. However, the specific training suggestions made by chairpersons in our survey related not to the legal side of their job but more to the procedural side. It can be questioned whether legal training and experience necessarily equip people to be able to conduct tribunal hearings, the responsibility of the chairperson. Traditional court experience may indeed be as much a handicap as an advantage to chairpersons in view of the desired differentiation between tribunal and court proceedings, for instance the perceived need in the former for an informal, non-legalistic, more inquisitorial approach. Although tribunals can devise their own procedures, those trained in the legal profession are likely to see the procedures in which they are trained and with which they are familiar as the best or most appropriate. The need for training also depends upon the extent to which any 'deficiencies' in the chair (for example lack of knowledge about industrial practices or a tendency to use terminology unfamiliar to those not trained in law) are made good by the other, lay, members of the tribunal.

The tribunal regulations provide that at a hearing, in addition to a legal chairperson, one lay member is an employers' organisation nominee and the other an employee organisation nominee. In October 1983 there were 1,816 lay members in England and Wales and some 200 in Scotland. They sit as requested by the regional tribunals to which they are allocated. The Secretary of State for Employment seeks nominations from the major interest groups representing employers and workers. The main organisations are the Confederation of British Industry (CBI) and the Trades Union Congress (TUC). Nominations are sought also from other bodies such as the Local Authorities Board and its Scottish equivalent and some other employers' organisations, but on the worker side the TUC, with a membership of over ten million in its affiliated unions, claims to be, and until recently has been recognised as, *the* representative employee organisation. Because the TUC withdrew co-operation from bodies operating the Industrial Relations Act 1971 the two panels were abandoned and only one panel of lay members was in operation during that period and until October 1977. People on this panel nominated from other sources had to seek nomination from bodies such as the TUC or CBI in order to remain on the two new panels drawn up in 1977.

The decision that the TUC should be the sole nominating body on the employee side is consistent with the policy of successive governments which have rebuffed attempts of non-TUC organisations to claim consultation rights in government decision-making. In April 1981, however, the Secretary of State announced that nominations for industrial tribunal lay members would be sought also from non-TUC sources such as the Managerial, Professional and Staff Liaison Group, a grouping of various employee organisations, notably in the medical field. By April 1982 seven people had been appointed as lay members from this source of nomination. While this development may weaken any disruption which the TUC might effect by instructing its nominees not to participate in certain tribunal proceedings, as for example is the case concerning dismissals for non-membership of a closed shop union (Dickens, 1983a: 27), perhaps the major significance of this development lies more in the threat to the TUC monopoly as representative of the working population vis-à-vis government. In-creased recruitment from non-TUC sources may lead to a gradual change in the characteristics of a typical lay member since the source and method of nomination are major variables in determining this.

Although the TUC is still the major nominating body for the employee panel, it undertakes no vetting of those nominated for tribunals (although it does for EAT lay members), merely forwarding names sent by affiliated unions, regional and trade union councils. These bodies vary in their method of obtaining nominations with consequent effect on the type of lay members. Those unions whose national or regional committees handle the nominations generally forward the names of current or retiring full-time officials, whereas those unions which send the TUC circular requesting nominations to their branches are more likely to nominate lay officials or members working at the trade. There is, however, also variation within unions according to regional or local practice.

At the time of our postal survey there were 1,139 trade-union-nominated lay members. We approached a 15 per cent sample and received 102 completed questionnaires, a response rate of 60 per cent (see Appendix I). Thirty-seven per cent of union-nominated lay members in the sample were union full-time officials at the time of their appointment; 27 per cent were working in manual and 30 per cent in non-manual occupations. Those who were not full-time officials often were active within the union, some as lay officials, others as delegates. About one in five of the union-nominated tribunal lay members had retired from their occupations after appointment as lay members, joining the 5 per cent who were already retired at the time of appointment. The ability to offer the time necessary for this post, as well as the attraction of an additional source of income, obviously increases on retirement and such people may put themselves forward to the TUC for nomination. The DE is unlikely to appoint anyone who would not be able to sit an average of fifteen days a year but prefers to appoint lay members who are still active in employment since it feels the experience which they bring to the tribunal should not be of a previous era. Lay members are retired at the age of 70.

The Department does try to obtain a spread of lay members in terms of age, union, industry, and occupation and would like women to be represented in proportion to their share of the labour force.[1] However, this has not been achieved and there is an under-representation of women as there is of the younger age groups. In 1982 only 21 per cent of industrial tribunal lay members were women. This is the same proportion reported by the EOC in 1977 (EOC, 1978: 27). Among the respondents in our survey two-thirds of the union-nominated lay members were over 56 and only 6 per cent were aged below 45. A similar distribution is found in the employers' panel: 73 per cent of the 108 employer lay members responding to the survey were over 56 years old

---

1. In sex discrimination and equal pay cases the ROIT is encouraged to select at least one woman member (*Equality for Women*, Cmnd 5724, 1974, para. 83).

and 10 per cent below 45. A higher proportion (19 per cent) of employer than union lay members had already retired at the time of their appointment and a further 20 per cent had subsequently retired. Among those in work, personnel and industrial relations functions were well represented: 38 per cent of employer-nominated lay members were personnel and industrial relations officers or managers at the time of appointment; 6.5 per cent were directors with personnel or industrial relations responsibilities, but a higher proportion (20 per cent) were directors with other or non-executive responsibilities. Production or production related management was sparsely represented (4 per cent) and 6 per cent of lay members were self-employed.

Newly appointed lay members are given a short introduction consisting of lectures or seminars, for instance on the philosophy of tribunals, how they operate and aspects of the law with which they deal, and sit in as observers on a few hearings. Of the 207 lay members who provided information on this in the survey, 141 (68 per cent) said they had received initial 'training', 41 per cent of them had attended lectures and sat in on hearings, 30 per cent had just attended lectures and 18 per cent had just sat in as observers. Generally less than two days were devoted to lay member induction. Only 22 per cent said the training period was longer than this. About two-thirds of the lay members in the survey reported they had received some training since appointment. Generally this was a short (half-day) updating exercise, often following legislative change or the introduction of new jurisdiction. Post-appointment training is a matter for the regional tribunal offices and the replies indicated some variation between regions in this provision. The practice in recent years has been to have two half-day sessions annually. Lay members are provided with copies of the relevant statutes, procedural regulations and guidance booklets, and many reported that they received Incomes Data Services *Brief* on a regular basis. It is now the practice to send the *Brief* to all lay members.

The majority of trade-union-nominated lay members and between a third and a half of the employer-nominated lay members who had received training on and/or after appointment suggested ways in which it could be improved. The majority of those lay members who said they had received no training felt it would be useful and made suggestions as to content. Generally those who had received training wanted an extension of the existing programme: longer initial training; more sitting in on hearings; and discussion and more frequent and refresher training. Over a fifth of the improvements to training suggested by trade-union-nominated lay members concerned training in the legal aspects of tribunals: the provisions and interpretation of the relevant legislation and the nature and implications of appeal decisions and case law. The desire for such training was even greater among those trade union lay members who had received no training; 54 per cent of the suggestions from those members concerned legal aspects. Among employer-nominated members, a quarter of those who had received training wanted training on legal aspects, as did 28 per cent of those who had received no training. But, as with training for those who chair tribunals, the desirability and nature of lay member training can only be considered in the context of the role which lay members are expected to play.

Role of Lay Members

The role which lay members are to perform on the industrial tribunal is nowhere explicitly laid down but has to be deduced from the tribunal regulations.[2] Lay members are not referred to as advisers, assessors or representatives but as members of the tribunal, of equal status to the chairperson. Their source and method of appointment indicates that they are there because of their industrial experience and practical knowledge. The lay member as provider of knowledge and experience of industrial relations or 'shopfloor life' is a common description. One chairperson (Jukes, 1978: 5) has stated:

> Lay members, experienced in industrial relations, know what an employer should or should not put up with, equally they know what an employee can expect. They know the unwritten custom and practice which form such an important part of industrial relations. Thus they have a most valuable part to play in reaching a just decision.

This view of the lay members' function is one echoed in the replies of the vast majority of the chairpersons responding to our survey. Some quotations from answers to the open question 'how would you describe the role of a lay member?' illustrate this; first from some part-time chairpersons:

> He brings his knowledge of human nature and industrial practice and uses it to assess the facts within a legal framework

> an equal judge of fact: a judgement he/she reaches in the light of industrial experience

and from some full-time chairpersons:

> assess credibility, apply common sense and industrial experience

2. Industrial Tribunals (Rules of Procedure) Regulations 1980 (SI 1980 No. 884). See Appendix III. Similar Regulations exist for Scotland (SI 1980 No. 885).

to bring their proved experience and knowledge of industry and its practices including that of shopfloor relations to bear on the particular case and act as jurors in assessing the evidence.

Among lay members surveyed the contribution of practical knowledge and industrial experience was less of a widespread role description, although still the single most common one. Thirty-two per cent of trade-union-nominated members (31) and 48 per cent of employer-nominated members (52) who responded described their role as being to contribute their knowledge or experience of industry or commerce, while 5 per cent and 11 per cent respectively said they contributed common sense or a practical approach. For example:

> we supply a common sense, down to earth approach to problems of the workplace and often have actual experience of things being discussed — timeclocks, contracts etc.

and

> to help the chairman assess commercial or industrial matters with which he may not necessarily be familiar.

Although lay members are appointed to contribute industrial and commercial knowledge and experience, the contribution is a general rather than a specialised one. No attempt is made to match lay members to the type of case being heard. Thus a school teacher and director of a retail business may sit as lay members on a case involving the dismissal of a farm labourer, engineer or construction worker. Some lay members commented that they did not think their particular knowledge or experience was being fully or best used while some others mentioned their lack of knowledge of particular industries as a difficulty in fulfilling their role as lay members. The lack of correspondence between lay members and the nature of the case constrains the extent to which lay members can offer a particularly expert or unique contribution.

Perhaps for this reason 23 per cent of the trade-union-nominated lay members and 19 per cent of those nominated through employers' organisations described their role more generally, as being to ensure a fair hearing or natural justice. As one lay member described it, the role is 'to see a fair hearing: to make sure it is fair and is seen to be fair'. Ensuring that fairness was seen to exist because each tribunal had a lay member drawn from each side of industry was specifically mentioned as part of their role by 9 per cent of all lay members. It may be assumed, however, that part of the rationale underlying the two panel method of nomination and appointment of lay members is the notion of balance and fairness in decision-making. The contribution of lay members to justice not only being done but being *seen* to be done depends on the knowledge and perception of those attending tribunal hearings.

Among applicants in our sample, however, knowledge of how the tribunal was composed was lacking or partial. Twenty-nine per cent of the 417 who attended the hearing of their case said they did not know how the tribunal was made up. Two per cent in fact did not know how many people had been on the tribunal, while another 7 per cent thought there were four members, probably including the tribunal clerk in the count. Of those applicants who thought they did know who the tribunal members were, only 45 per cent knew that one lay member was nominated via the trade unions and 34 per cent that one lay member was nominated by the employers' organisations. The level of knowledge among respondent employers was higher than among applicants. Only 44 (10 per cent) of the 443 employers in heard cases said they did not know how the tribunal was composed. Of those who did describe who the tribunal members were, 82 per cent said one lay member was nominated by the trade unions; 70 per cent said one was nominated by employers' organisations. It should be noted that exact description was not required; replies such as 'one came from the workers' side' or 'one was an employer' were taken as indicating knowledge of composition.

Those employers and workers who are aware of the background of the lay members may feel that their cases will be better understood or that justice will be dispensed with due regard to practical considerations. But they would be mistaken if they went further than this to think that the union- or employer-nominated lay member was there to act as representative of their interests. The regulations are interpreted to forbid such a role. As equal members of the industrial tribunal, the lay members are to be impartial judges, not representatives of either side. It is not just the notion of *mandat imperatif* which is prohibited, for example, a pledge that the union's lay member will always support the worker's claim, as demanded of *conseil de prud'hommes* members by the Confédération Générale du Travail (CGT) in France (McPherson and Meyers, 1966: 19; Napier, 1979: 283), but the whole notion of a representative or interested role. The Lord Chancellor made this clear in 1968:

> One sometimes hears the members erroneously referred to as 'the employers' representative' or 'the employees' representative'. They are not. They represent no-one, except the interests of justice. Each is an entirely independent judicial officer who decides a case upon its merits, upon the evidence and law applicable (quoted in Cavenagh and Newton, 1971).

The first President of the EAT reiterated the point a decade later in stressing that lay members 'do not support one side or the other and are totally objective and impartial' (Phillips, 1978: 137).

It was noted earlier that no attempt is made to match lay member experience with type of case. To do so would cause administrative problems but these could be overcome, for example by having divisions by industrial sector as in some labour court systems. But the main reason for not attempting this, indeed for actually avoiding it by, say, not listing a lay member nominated through the shop-workers' union to sit on a case involving a shop-worker, is that the lay member might be thought to have an interest in the case which would endanger his or her role as impartial judge. Similar reasoning appears to lie behind the lack of encouragement from the Department of Employment for lay member training by the nominating organisations. Employer-nominated lay members generally did not think training provided by employers' organisations would be useful, generally seeing training as best provided within the industrial tribunal system. The position was different, however, among union-nominated lay members surveyed. Nineteen (19 per cent) of the 102 union-nominated lay members had received some training from their union or the TUC since their appointment as a lay member. Although this training was part of general provision and not specifically because they were lay members, most had found it useful to them in that capacity. Of the others 40 (52 per cent) thought training by their union or the TUC would be useful to them in fulfilling their role as lay members. For the most part the kind of training they wanted to see was similar to that sought from within the tribunal system and concerned the legislation and case law and the role of the lay member, but a quarter of these lay members indicated that the TUC could make more specialised provision. This included sessions on the TUC view of the law and procedure operated by tribunals and union aims and objectives in this field; sessions on union agreements, grievance and disciplinary procedures in various industries; and the opportunity for union-nominated lay members to exchange notes and discuss their experiences.

Arguably such training is not incompatible with an impartial approach to deciding dismissal cases but may enable lay members to make their contribution more effectively. However, lay member training by external agencies has been discouraged. Following the introduction of the Sex Discrimination Act 1975 the Equal Opportunities Commission raised the question of training for those chairing and sitting as lay members on tribunals to assist in their 'interpretation and application of complex and novel legislation'.

The Lord Chancellor's office replied that the Lord Chancellor 'must be careful not to do anything which could be construed as an attempt by the executive to guide or influence the decisions of the judiciary' (EOC, 1978: 28).[3]

No lay member saw it as part of his or her role to promote the interests of one side or to act in a representative capacity. Lay members accept the non-representative, impartial nature of their role on industrial tribunals. There are ways, however, in which lay members could be of assistance to the parties appearing before the industrial tribunal without having to adopt a representative stance. It has been suggested for example that the lay members provide a 'common touch' (Fulbrook et al., 1973: 9). Only a very small number of replies concerning the role of the lay member indicated any awareness of this possible role. These were made by 5 per cent of the lay members, particularly union-nominated members, who saw it as part of their function and in the interests of 'fair play' to help overcome various problems which might be faced by applicants. One of these rare descriptions of the lay member role was

> A lay member must have the ability to translate behaviour or sayings which sometimes shock the other members of the tribunal. This behaviour is often caused by the applicant's frustration or inability to express his own feelings or view.

The 'common touch' contribution has a number of different aspects but in particular, as indicated by the quotation, it may serve to bridge the social and educational gap which can exist between those who chair tribunals and those who bring cases before them. It may be thought that, as all kinds of workers face dismissal, less of a gap exists in industrial tribunals than has been documented in some welfare tribunals (Frost and Howard, 1977: 42). But, as seen earlier (p. 36) most unfair dismissal applicants are manual workers and it can be questioned how well equipped those in the legal profession are to understand and deal with the non-legal aspects of disputes which are concerned with, and arise out of, predominantly working class experience. While the importance of social distance is difficult to evaluate and should not be overstated, it may lessen the possibility of empathy and reduce the extent to which applicants in particular but also others, for example

3. When a sex discrimination or equal pay case is being heard, however, the ROIT tries to select at least one woman for the tribunal and, in race discrimination cases, at least one member with special experience of race relations. This may be the chairperson or a lay member. An applicant has no right to insist on a member with specialised knowledge (*Habib v Elkington Ltd* [1981] IRLR 344).

the employer's witnesses, are likely to feel at ease and able to make themselves understood at tribunal hearings.

During our tribunal observation exercise, instances were recorded of communication problems between the chair and applicants not only because of regional accents or technical or industry-specific terminology which the chair found difficult but because of different English usage or norms reflecting a social difference between the parties and the chair. For example, confusion arose as to the facts of one case because the applicant, and respondent, used the word 'dinner' to refer to the midday meal and the chairperson assumed it referred to the evening meal. In another case the chair's liking for naval terminology – 'was he paraded on the quarter-deck?'; 'do you work a dog watch?' – although possibly a well-intentioned attempt at informality, served only to baffle the works' supervisor to whom the questions were addressed. An example of conflicting norms is provided by another case where the question arose as to whether the applicant had actually been dismissed. In the event it was held that the applicant had failed to prove dismissal. Something which appeared to influence the chairperson at the hearing was that following the meeting at which the applicant – a farm labourer – alleged he had been dismissed he did not sit down with his wife to discuss the problem and assess the family finances and commitments. Although such discussion was seen by the chairperson to be the normal reaction of someone who thought he had been dismissed, studies of segregated role relationships and marital communication in working class families indicate that the norms being applied are middle class ones (see for example Komarovsky, 1967: 155–9).

These observations are anecdotal in the sense of being unquantifiable and not necessarily generalisable, but they provide examples of a problem that the lay members' 'common touch' may be expected to overcome. In the instances cited, however, this was not apparently the case. Providing a 'common touch' or social bridge requires active participation in the hearing, performing what Bell has termed an enabling role. Speaking of appellants at social security tribunals she says (1982: 145):

> They felt strongly that lay members should actively assist the chairman during the hearing; that they should play an *enabling* role towards the appellant by listening carefully, understanding the problem and asking relevant questions, thus drawing him out and enabling him to sort out his case and make his points.

Industrial tribunal lay members did not see their role in these terms. Only 9 per cent of the 204 lay members described part of their role as participating in hearings, asking questions, helping elicit facts and so on. While more than this may actively participate in practice, and in our observation exercise there were examples of lay members asking particularly pertinent questions which helped adduce necessary or important information, this is clearly not seen by lay members to be a major part of their job. The legal member takes the chair and controls the conduct of the hearing. This is one of a number of factors which are now examined which influence the relationship between the legal and lay members.

The Legal/Lay Member Relationship

On any particular tribunal the nature and personalities of the individuals concerned, of course, will help define the relationship between the three members, the part they play and the relative influence they exercise. There are, however, situational factors which also affect the relationship and which, we argue, tend to promote the legal member as first among equals, *primus inter pares*.

As noted, the legal member of the tribunal is the one who takes the chair and controls the conduct of the hearing. While the active participation by lay members in the hearings is not discouraged (only 2 per cent of employer-nominated and 5 per cent of union-nominated members said their involvement in hearings was discouraged by chairpersons), it is generally minimal when compared with that of the chair. Following an expression of disquiet by the TUC, a past President of Industrial Tribunals in England and Wales encouraged chairpersons to invite the lay members to ask questions at suitable points during the hearing. This occurred in all the hearings we observed except in a small proportion where lay members asked questions without waiting for the invitation from the chair.

We are not arguing that the part played by lay members is unimportant and, of course, orderly proceedings require that one person, rather than three, has overall responsibility for the conduct of the hearing. Monopoly of the chair by the legal member, however, has implications for the procedure and tenor of the hearing and bestows an authority on the legal member which partly gives rise to the different status of the legal and lay members. Those who chair tribunals receive more information on tribunal and appeal decisions than do lay members; they may be the only member to see papers and documents relating to the case prior to the day of the hearing; they generally take the only note of evidence and write the decision of the case. The legal and lay members are rewarded differently. The day rate for lay members in 1983 was £50 and for part-time chairpersons £109.

Importantly, the legal members also get more experience of sitting on tribunals than do lay members. The full-time chairpersons do of course sit most frequently, but part-timers are also called upon more often than are lay members. Seventeen of the 19 part-time chairpersons in our survey had sat on average once a week in the previous year; only 3 per cent of lay members reported this frequency. Only 17 per cent (34) of the 199 lay members who gave this information said they had sat more than 26 times over the preceding year. The difference cannot be explained wholly by availability as 30 per cent of the lay members said they were available to sit more than 51 times a year, as did 41 per cent of part-time chairpersons. Infrequent and widely spaced sittings can make it difficult to build up expertise as a tribunal member and to develop confidence in performing that role.

While the *primus inter pares* position of the legal member partly results from his or her occupancy of the chair, the influence of the chairperson in turn partly results from its incumbent being the legal member. This is because of the context in which the legal/lay member relationship operates: the tribunal members are part of a quasi-court operating within a structure providing for appeal to both a specialist tribunal and the ordinary courts. Inevitably such a context gives primacy to legal considerations.

The right of appeal and consequent handing down of precedents and the setting of guidelines to impose a consistency of approach on tribunals operating all over the country can constrain their flexibility and freedom as expert bodies. This obviously affects all the members of the tribunal but inasmuch as the constraints of the appellate system affect them differently, it is to be supposed that it is the lay members rather than the legal member whose particular contribution is more affected. After all it is the legal member who provides knowledge of, and guidance on, the law, including that laid down by the appeal courts. The lay members' main contribution is practical knowledge and experience. This contribution, however, is being made in a context where if the solution which the norms of industry, custom and practice or pragmatic 'common sense' might indicate is the one which will 'work' is not also that which the chairperson indicates is legally 'right', then it will not be adopted. The lay members are not part of an industrial arbitration body whose prime purpose is to settle the dispute in a practical acceptable way, rather they are part of a court concerned with the adjudication of legal entitlements set out in statute and interpreted in case law.

We did not directly question lay members about the constraints imposed by operating within a court structure but we did ask whether they experienced any difficulties in performing the role of lay member as they saw it. A substantial minority, 40 per cent of the 204 lay members, did encounter problems. The responses to an open-ended question on the nature of the difficulty encountered ranged very widely and made grouping difficult. They included problems in determining who was telling the truth, in assessing evidence, and their own lack of legal knowledge and ability to question properly. However, the single most common difficulty stated, given by 27 per cent, was that industrial or practical considerations took second place to legal ones in decision-making. The flavour of the replies can be gauged from the following statements:

> case law and legal decisions can sometimes upset what may be as plain as a pikestaff (union-nominated member)

> the chairman accepts the lay member role (to give him some idea of what conditions are like in modern industry) but is more interested in making sure the case has been dealt with correctly at law (employer-nominated member)

> legislation sometimes shackles common sense solutions (employer-nominated member)

> if a case depends on legal rulings the lay member has no choice — one must remember that 'the law' is not always 'justice' (union-nominated member)

> irrespective of the submissions of the parties, the 'legal reality' must take precedence (employer-nominated member).

These are, of course, responses from only a minority of lay members, but they do indicate that while lay members are there to contribute their industrial and commercial knowledge and expertise, they have to do so as members of a court-substitute body operating within a legal framework.

It would seem that the greatest scope for the lay members' contribution exists where the appeal courts allow the tribunals discretion. Where a matter is a question of fact the scope for intervention by the appellate courts will be reduced, since appeal is on point of law only. The EAT's early policy of taking a wide view of what constituted a question of law (Phillips, 1978: 139) has been restricted by the Court of Appeal which has held that a number of issues are to be regarded as questions of fact. These cover, among others, whether an employee has been constructively dismissed,[4] which was previously regarded as at

---

4. *Woods v W./M. Car Services (Peterborough) Ltd* [1982] IRLR 413.

least a mixed question of fact and law, and whether someone is an employee.[5] The lay member contribution is also facilitated where what for convenience we might term 'legal' and 'industrial' considerations point in the same direction or where what the statute requires is unclear, perhaps because a particular provision has not been addressed by the appeal courts. Instances of this last kind are of course likely to become increasingly infrequent in the absence of legislative amendment.

In such circumstances the lay members' experience and knowledge may be deferred to by the legal member but it has to be noted that the lay members' contribution is not necessarily seen as a unique one in the way the chair's legal contribution may be. This is because those who regularly chair tribunals become familiar with aspects of industrial or office life through hearing cases. This point was made by one senior chairperson (Smailes, 1971: 32) as follows:

> of course you have the two lay members, who will give the benefit of their industrial experience, but the idea that members of the judiciary are an isolated sect remote from the rest of the community I think is a fallacy. If somebody says to me as the chairman 'what do you know of industrial relations?' I say 'I don't know much because it's a very complicated subject but as regards conditions in industry I find I know about industry in general rather more than the average trade union officer' . . . I say 'I have been sitting full time for four years, a year or two before that part time, every day dealing with instances in somebody's working life and one goes into all kinds of occupations and the average trade union officer knows an awful lot about his own industry but he does not know a large amount about the others'.

This perception is in keeping with the fact that, although the judge and jury analogy is sometimes used both by chairpersons and lay members, in describing their respective roles, the 'industrial jury' notion in fact applies to the tribunal as a whole. The judge and jury analogy implies a division of labour between chairperson and lay members corresponding to law and fact. The chairperson in practice may rule on the law but he or she also takes part in deciding the facts and assessing the credibility of witnesses and so on. (See, for example, *Earl v Slater Wheeler* (*Airlyne*) *Ltd* [1972] IRLR 115.) We noted earlier (p. 53) the Franks Committee

---

5. *O'Kelly v Trust House Forte plc* [1983] IRLR 369.

view that the ability to sift facts was a skill more likely to be possessed by those with legal training and experience. Fact finding is an important aspect of the tribunals' work but, as we argue later, it is not aided by the adversarial nature of the hearings (see also Hepple, 1983a: 414).

We have argued that, although the three members of the tribunal are formally equal judges, various factors operate to make the legal member first among equals. Legal and lay members surveyed were not asked directly to assess their relationship but some pointers as to whether they share the *primus inter pares* perception can be gleaned from the descriptions given of the lay member's role.

In describing the role of the lay member a few chairpersons echoed the formal position, for example, 'he/she is a full member of the court on law and fact', but generally where the 'equal judicial' role was noted it was qualified, as in 'he exercises judicial functions in the same way as a chairman, and accepts the ruling of the chairman on a point of law', or 'an equal judge of *fact*' (emphasis added). The legal members did, however, use descriptions of equality far more frequently than did lay members. Only three union-nominated lay members and nine employer-nominated members, together making 6 per cent of the 204 respondents, directly or by implication (usually by a team analogy) described their role as one of equality with the other members. Even here, though, there was sometimes qualification, as in the reply from one lay member who wrote 'on an equal basis with the chairman but obviously very much in need of his guidance'. Slightly more lay members although still a small proportion (11 per cent) explicitly described their role as *subordinate* to that of the chairperson, often describing themselves as advisers or assistants. One employer-nominated lay member, when asked 'how would you describe the role of a lay member', wrote simply 'a chairman's assistant'; another 'supportive to the chairman but also able to advise in respect of practical industrial relations considerations'; while a third employer-nominated member apparently saw 'support' going beyond assistance, saying lay members 'must be painstaking, neutral, helpful, searching, quiet spoken, patient and above all loyal to the system and the chairman'. Among the 'subordinate role' replies from union-nominated lay members was the description of the lay member as 'an experienced and practical adviser to the chairman' and as one whose role is 'to assist the chairman in reaching *his* verdict' (emphasis added).

Decision-Making in the Tribunal

Another indication of the members' perceptions is provided by considering tribunal decision-making. As Table 3.1 shows, those who

TABLE 3.1

**PERCEPTIONS OF LAY MEMBER INFLUENCE IN
TRIBUNAL DECISION-MAKING**

	Chairpersons' *View*	*Lay Members'* *View*
	%	%
Very influential	87	58
Fairly influential	8	39
Not very influential	—	2
No influence	—	—
Other	5	—
	N = 37	N = 209

SOURCE: IRRU surveys.

chair tribunals regarded lay members as very influential in decision-
making: 87 per cent claimed they were 'very influential' and 8 per cent
'fairly influential'. Lay members generally shared the view that they
were influential in decision-making although they perceived themselves
as having slightly less influence than was attributed to them by the chairpersons: 58 per cent describing themselves as 'very influential' and 39 per
cent as 'fairly influential' with 2 per cent considering themselves 'not very
influential'.

It is extremely difficult to determine the effect which the *primus
inter pares* position of the chair has on tribunal decision-making. Certainly it would be wrong to infer from our discussion that those who
chair tribunals are able, or would seek, to impose their decisions on
lay members. None the less the status of the chair and the greater
experience and particular, legal knowledge which the chairperson brings
to the situation can be expected to have some effect on the process
of decision-making in the tribunal. Some indication of the process is
provided by a consideration of the unanimity of tribunal decisions.
Although majority decisions are possible, some 95 per cent of tribunal
decisions are unanimous (Hepple, 1983a: 411). Some of the factors
identified in the discussion of the legal member as *primus inter pares,*
for instance the acceptance that industrial relations considerations or
pragmatic 'common sense' should give way to the law where there
is a conflict between them, help explain the unanimity.

TABLE 3.2

WHY UNANIMOUS DECISIONS ARE REACHED

	Lay Members' View %	Chairpersons' View %
Facts are clear/case is clear-cut	16	19
Members act judicially/not as representatives	18	30
All reasonable people/common-sense	9	24
Decision has to conform to the law/chairperson says what law requires	13	14
Discussion brings about unanimity	27	–
Unanimity seen as desirable	3	5
Tendency/willingness to compromise/go along with majority view	5	19
Can't explain/difficult to say	4	–
Not usually unanimous	5	–
Other	3	–
(Multi-response possible.)	N = 186	N = 37

SOURCE: IRRU surveys.

Table 3.2 shows the explanations for unanimity given by legal and lay members in our survey. The general picture which an examination of the detailed replies to the open-ended question reveals is that where there is difference of view between the lay members on the one hand and the chairperson on the other, which reflects a conflict between 'common, industrial sense' and 'the law', then the lay members give way since the appeal system usually ensures that 'the law' wins in the end. As one employer-nominated lay member said, 'I have only sat on one case where the lay members outvoted the chairman. On appeal the lay members were proved wrong. Very deflating but interesting. The lay members in that case were morally right but legally wrong!' Conformity to the law as indicated by the chairperson was given as an explanation for unanimity by around 13 per cent of both chairpersons and lay members.

Where the union-nominated lay member and employer-nominated lay member disagree, the view of the chair can be decisive in determining what eventually becomes a unanimous decision. As one union-nominated member explained, there is 'mainly a clash of views between the worker representative and that of the employer, the chairman in a sense having the casting vote'. Once the chair has supported the views of one lay member the tendency is for the other to accept or acquiesce in the majority view unless some important point of principle (but not partisanship) is felt to be involved. The acceptance of an impartial, non-representative role appears important here. Eighteen per cent of lay members and 30 per cent of chairpersons gave the 'judicial' stance of members as an explanation for unanimity.

A part-time chairperson commented:

> If the votes of the chairman and members were taken without private discussion I believe there would be many more majority decisions. Quite often one member is disposed to accept the evidence of a witness whom the other two do not believe. After discussion there is unanimity, or perhaps more accurately, the would-be minority member is no longer unwilling to fall in with the majority opinion. No pressure is brought to bear.

As Table 3.2 shows, lay members attach a lot of importance to the post-hearing private discussion between the three members of the tribunal in securing unanimous decisions, 27 per cent citing this in explanation. Although 'no pressure is brought to bear', various factors operate towards bringing the 'odd member out' into line with the other two, among them the importance attached to the chairperson's view, the reluctance to go out on a limb or to appear partisan, and an awareness that unanimity is a desired goal. The following quotations are from some of the replies indicating these various factors.

> Usually it becomes clear that all three have reached the same conclusion, with varying degrees of reluctance. On occasion fairly long objective discussion is necessary while a member wrestles with his conscience. Chairmen are most scrupulous about avoiding putting pressure on a member but clearly do feel it their duty to reach unanimity if possible. On the whole I think the lay members share the view that unanimity is desirable (employer-nominated lay member).

> Reluctance inherent in sticking out for a point of view if two experienced colleagues differ from you (full-time chairperson).

> Although there are many cases where the three members do not entirely agree it is usually possible to reach a compromise through discussion. There have been instances where I have not agreed fully with a decision but never enough to require a majority decision (union-nominated lay member).

The replies also indicate that unanimity is seen to result because the case is clear-cut; the facts are clear: 19 per cent of chairpersons and 16 per cent of lay members gave this explanation. The 'facts of the case' which provide the basis for decision-making, however, are not all the data and information relating to the dismissal. 'What happened' as seen by the tribunal will be what emerges from information volunteered, allowed, or obtained by questioning at the hearing. It will depend on such things as what information the parties and the tribunal see as relevant; which statements are supported by documentation or by witnesses; whose testimony is preferred where evidence conflicts. In short, the 'facts of the case' which emerge will depend in part on the context in which they have to be obtained. This is the tribunal hearing, to which we now turn.

The Hearing

The intention behind tribunal hearings is clear. As noted by the one-time President of Industrial Tribunals, Sir Diarmaid Conroy (1971a: 4, 5):

> the tribunals are meant to provide simple informal justice in an atmosphere in which the ordinary man feels he is at home . . . an atmosphere which does not shut out the ordinary man so that he

is prepared to conduct his own case before them with a reasonable prospect of success.

Perceived trends towards legal technicality have been met by renewed emphasis on informality and flexibility, as in the 1980 Industrial Tribunals Regulations[6] which state that the tribunal

> shall so far as appears to it appropriate seek to avoid formality in its proceedings and it shall not be bound by any enactment or rule of law relating to the admissibility of evidence in proceedings before the courts of law.

Part of helping 'the ordinary man feel he is at home' has been the eschewing of various trappings associated with court hearings, such as imposing architecture and wigs and gowns. Other features, however, remain: evidence is given under oath, a seat apart is used by those giving evidence and in some tribunals we observed those attending were asked to stand when the members of the tribunal entered or left the room. The general picture of the tribunal's form which emerged from our observation of tribunals operating in four different regions was of the three tribunal members sitting behind a bench on a raised platform. The parties and their representatives sat facing the tribunal behind tables, and behind them sat any witnesses, members of the public and press. The 'witness box' (usually a small table) was to one side of the tribunal bench, to the other generally sat the clerk. The atmosphere or feel of the hearing varied to some extent from region to region and within regions. An important determinant of this was the chairperson and his or her conduct of the hearing which appeared to depend both on personal qualities and attitudes and the nature and quality of the parties' representatives. But whatever the personalities of those involved, there are various features of the tribunal system which pull against the intention that hearings be flexible, informal and non-legal, enabling people to present their own cases with a reasonable prospect of success.

A major constraint is the underlying accusatorial or adversarial model of hearings, part of the quasi-court nature of the industrial tribunal. The expectation of the accusatorial or adversarial model, as opposed to that of an inquiry, is that the parties, normally through representatives, will give evidence, call witnesses, cross-examine and make submissions to the tribunal. That is to say they take the initiative in the presentation of the case and the judge will remain passive

6. Industrial Tribunals (Rules of Procedure) Regulations 1980 (SI 1980 No. 884) reg. 8(1).

and quiet. The adoption of this court-like approach has implications in terms of the skills and knowledge needed by the ordinary person seeking to handle his or her own case. In a book designed to help people prepare and present industrial tribunal cases the subheadings of just one section on presenting a case, which deals with the 'art of cross-examination', give some indication of the skills of advocacy which may be required. Among the points dealt with are: highlighting the conflict of facts; exploring inconsistencies in the evidence; showing the tribunal where evidence or opinions have been based on invalid assumptions; refuting allegations; putting evidence into proper context; and correcting misleading or confusing testimony (Angel, 1980: 170–71).

A hearing based on the accusatorial model is one in which those who are used to legal proceedings are more likely to feel at home than lay people, whether bringing or defending cases or sitting as lay members. We noted earlier (p. 64) that lay members do not see it as part of their function to play an enabling role towards the parties. Because part of the tribunal ideology is that people should be able to present their own cases, however, attempts are made to help parties who are unfamiliar with such procedures and lacking or inexpert in the particular skills required. This generally consists of the chair taking a more active role in the hearing, asking more questions, and indicating to the parties how they should proceed. Where both parties are legally represented the tribunal can generally sit back and let them get on with presenting the case, concentrating on evaluating the evidence rather than obtaining it. Where this is not the case, however, the chair may have to come 'down into the arena' and participate more. Thirty-two of the thirty-six chairpersons in the survey reported that the part they played varied according to the nature of the parties and the type of representation. A more active role where there was a lack of representation was seen in part by the chairpersons as preventing an unrepresented party being disadvantaged, but was also necessary for the tribunal to obtain the facts for it to make a decision.

Greater involvement by the chair in obtaining the facts of the case is often characterised as a move towards a more inquisitorial style. The inquisitorial model, which forms the basis of court procedure in mainland Europe, however, differs fundamentally from the Anglo-American adversary system (see, for example, Danet and Bogoch, 1980: 37). Given the underlying adversarial model of the industrial tribunal hearing the more active involvement of the tribunal is better seen in terms of the chair playing the role usually assumed by a representative. That is to say, the tribunal, particularly the chair, takes over some of the questioning and cross-examination in an attempt to overcome the disadvantage (to both the party concerned and the tribunal) which is entailed by the lack of skilled representation within an accusatorial system.

The extent to which the chair does or can perform the role of representative substitute, however, is limited. Firstly there is the fear that the tribunal may appear biased when only one of the parties requires this help. Secondly, in so far as a more participative role by the chairperson attempts to compensate for the lack of representation, it does so only at the hearing stage and can do nothing to overcome the difficulties which may be experienced in preparing the case. Also, without the pre-hearing contact which representatives have with their clients, some important or fundamental point may never be raised because the unrepresented party may not recognise its importance and the chair, in ignorance of what is in the party's mind, fails to ask the relevant question which would elicit it.

The nature of the legislation which the industrial tribunals have to operate is another constraint on dispensing justice in a 'simple informal' atmosphere where the ordinary person feels at ease. The unfair dismissal provisions are complex and give ample scope for subtle legal reasoning, while the appellate structure has naturally resulted in the handing down of precedents and setting of guidelines for the tribunals to heed in making their decisions. The belief that somehow labour law might be lay law is mistaken (Munday, 1981: 149).

The creation of, and adherence to, guidelines and legal principles are to be expected in a system where higher courts are given appellate jurisdiction, particularly where a specialist appellate body is created which may feel it is particularly well qualified to interfere with tribunal decisions (see the EAT's decision in *Williams and others v Compair Maxam Ltd* [1982] IRLR 83); where lawyers play an important part (in chairing tribunals and representing people appearing before them); and where decisions are reported and available for citation. There has been developing, however, an awareness that legalism of this kind is contrary to the intended nature of industrial tribunals. There was early judicial criticism of the accumulation of case law on various aspects of the unfair dismissal provisions where tribunals were meant to exercise discretion (see, for example, Lord Denning in *Walls Meat Co. Ltd v Khan* [1978] IRLR 499). Then followed attempts to curb the EAT's creation of guidelines and legal principles (for example Lawton LJ in *Bailey v BP Oil Kent Refinery Ltd* [1980] IRLR 287 and *O'Kelly v Trust House Forte plc* [1983] IRLR 369). Most recently the newly appointed EAT President has noted that 'a pre-occupation with guideline authority' jeopardises the likelihood that parties conducting their own case 'would be able to face the Tribunal with the same ease and confidence as those professionally represented' (*Anandarajah v Lord Chancellor's Department* [1984] IRLR 131).

As the new EAT President implies, it is not surprising that in a system which appears legalistic legal representation will be seen as appropriate. The more court-like the tribunal system appears, the more appropriate, necessary or useful will legal representation appear, both at the hearing and in the stages leading to hearing. And the more legal representation occurs, the more court-like will the tribunal system appear. For example the use of interlocutory steps is generally associated with legal representation. Although details of the grounds for application and grounds for resisting an application which are given on the application and employer response forms are generally sparse, the provisions for either party to obtain further and better particulars of the other's case or to request discovery and inspection of documents, are used only infrequently. The use of these interlocutory steps is more common where legal representation is used. For example, 34 per cent of the 97 applicants in our sample who were represented by a solicitor at the hearing said further and better particulars were requested (a further third did not know), whereas of those represented by trade unions only half this proportion requested better particulars (25 per cent not knowing) and only 7 per cent of those representing themselves did so. The calling of witnesses is the responsibility of the parties, not the tribunal, and again this was more common where legal representation was used. Forty per cent of applicants represented by solicitors called witnesses compared with half that proportion of self-represented applicants. Employers generally were more likely than applicants to call witnesses. Seventy-two per cent of all employers did this, 85 per cent of those with external legal representation.

Despite the intention that the tribunal's procedure should be such that people could present their own cases without going to lawyers for help, the majority of all lay members and chairpersons surveyed thought that self-representation should not be encouraged. This view, held by just over half the chairpersons, was shared by 65 per cent of union-nominated and just under three-quarters of employer-nominated lay members. Generally the chairpersons surveyed saw few advantages in self-representation either from the parties' point of view or that of the tribunal itself. Where certain advantages were suggested — sometimes speedier, less formal, cheaper — they were generally felt to be outweighed by the disadvantages. These were that self-represented parties do not understand the procedure and cannot handle examination and cross-examination and they may fail to bring out relevant or important points; they lack objectivity in presentation and waste time on irrelevancies. Self-representation meant more work for the tribunal and was thought either to cause delays or postponements, because of inadequate preparation and failure to bring correct documents or necessary witnesses or, alternatively, to mean the tribunal has to reach its decision based on insufficient or unsatisfactory evidence.

Although some chairpersons thought that legal representation was only really *necessary* where difficult points of law were likely to be involved, there was general agreement that legal representation was preferable to having the parties — particularly applicants — representing themselves. The majority of chairpersons surveyed thought legal representation should be encouraged, although some drew a distinction between lawyers, favouring those who were familiar with tribunal work. About three-quarters of the lay members, however, thought legal representation should not be encouraged, favouring instead the encouragement of representation by union and employers' association officials. Seventy-one per cent of union lay members and 60 per cent of employer lay members thought this kind of representation should be encouraged, a view supported by about half the chairpersons. Some chairpersons criticised the standards of advocacy and lack of knowledge of tribunal procedure on the part of union and employers' association officials, particularly the former. The difference between the legal member of the tribunal and the two lay members as to which type of specialist representation should be encouraged obviously reflects their different backgrounds. It may also reflect a different assessment of the advantages and disadvantages of legal representation for the tribunal system as a whole. It is often thought that the greater use of legal representation would inevitably mean greater legal technicality at the expense of cheapness, speed and informality. As we discuss later (Chapter 7), such fears are not groundless. Legal representation may be seen as a consequence of increasing legalism in tribunals but it may also be a cause.

Whatever the exact causal relationship, the trend in both legalism and legal representation is upwards. Increasing legalism has been commented on by those involved in operating the system as well as by critics of it (for instances, see Munday, 1981: 146−7). The increase in legal representation can be quantified, if only roughly. Table 3.3 shows the proportion of applicants and respondent employers who had external (i.e. not in-company) legal representation at tribunal hearings in 1973, 1976−7 and 1982. While exact comparison between the years is difficult, it would appear that employers made greater use of legal representation than did applicants in each of the periods examined but that the greater increase in use over the years has been among applicants (see also Hawes and Smith, 1981: 21).

We have discussed factors which pull the tribunals from the achieve-

TABLE 3.3

USE OF EXTERNAL LEGAL REPRESENTATION AT INDUSTRIAL TRIBUNAL HEARINGS

	1973[a]	*1976*[b]	*1982*[c]
	%	%	%
Applicants	20	23	36
Respondent employers	37	41	49

SOURCES:
a. DE interview survey: unfair dismissal and redundancy payments.
b. IRRU interview survey: unfair dismissal.
c. COIT Fact Sheet February 1984: all jurisdictions, England and Wales.

ment of the ideal which was described at the beginning of this section — simple informal justice in an atmosphere where the ordinary person can conduct a case with reasonable prospect of success. But the ideal is there and those who operate the system are keenly aware of it. Thus, where possible within the constraints, attempts are made to achieve it. The greater involvement of the chairperson in hearings where one or both parties are unrepresented is an example of this. To deny the continuing validity of the model expressed in the ideal would have important consequences. It would be difficult, for instance, to continue to deny extension of legal aid to tribunal hearings if it were officially conceded that they were such that ordinary people could not bring their own cases without prejudicing their chances of success.

Our survey of the parties revealed that the model does appear to have a continuing validity although, as we shall discuss, applicants in particular do experience problems. Despite the features of the tribunal system which tend towards legalism, tribunal hearings at the time of our survey were experienced in the main as 'relaxed and informal'. Just over half of those applicants who attended their hearings found this as did 60 per cent of employers. This is shown in Table 3.4 which also shows, however, that the proportion who thought the hearing was not relaxed or informal was quite high, particularly among applicants. Agreement and disagreement was recorded with two other statements designed to explore the extent to which the tribunal hearings were experienced as free from legal technicality and their proceedings as comprehensible to the ordinary person. Only small proportions of

TABLE 3.4

THE PARTIES' VIEWS OF TRIBUNAL HEARINGS

Statement	Agree[a]		Neutral		Disagree	
	Applicants %	Employers %	Applicants %	Employers %	Applicants %	Employers %
The hearing was not relaxed or informal[b]	37	29	7	9	55	60
It was difficult to understand and follow what was going on	35	6	5	3	59	91
There was too much legal 'jargon'	45	14	10	6	44	79

SOURCE: IRRU surveys.

NOTES:
a. A five-point agree/disagree scale has been reduced to three.
b. This statement and the responses have been reversed for consistency in presentation. As put it was 'the hearing was relaxed and informal'.

respondent employers said they found it was difficult to understand and follow what was going on or thought that there was too much legal 'jargon' at the hearing. Over a third of applicants, however, reported comprehension difficulties and a substantial minority, 45 per cent, thought there was too much legal 'jargon'. Differences between those with representation and those representing themselves were not marked, although we found self-represented applicants were more likely than those with representation to report that it was difficult to understand and follow what was going on at the hearing of their case, 43 per cent of self-represented applicants agreeing with this statement compared with 35 per cent of all applicants.

The fairly favourable view of the atmosphere and tenor of the hearings which Table 3.4 shows does not mean, however, that the parties necessarily felt they succeeded in getting their case across to the tribunal – the essence of feeling able to conduct one's own case without disadvantage. Table 3.5 shows the opinions on this of self-represented applicants and self- (internal lay) represented employers. Only 17 per cent of the 148 employers who presented their own cases (with a lay person from the company) thought their case did not get across well, whereas the majority (53 per cent) of the 192 self-represented applicants thought they failed to get their cases across satisfactorily. The tribunals appear, therefore, to succeed where the ordinary person is an employer

TABLE 3.5

HOW WELL SELF-REPRESENTED PARTIES' CASES GOT ACROSS TO THE TRIBUNAL

	Applicants %		Employers %	
Very well	22		51	
Fairly well	25		28	
All well		47		79
Not very well	27		6	
Not at all well	26		11	
All not well		53		17
Can't say	–			4
	N = 192		N = 148	

SOURCE: IRRU surveys.

but do less well when the ordinary person trying to conduct a case is a sacked worker.

The reasons given by those self-represented applicants who felt their cases had not got across well are shown in Table 3.6. They are mainly concerned with difficulties encountered in case preparation and presentation. The lack of legal representation, particularly where the employer had this kind of representation, was felt to be important by 38 per cent of these applicants. The following quotations give an indication of the problems which applicants thought accounted for their cases not getting across well to the tribunal.

> I think we should have been represented by a solicitor — he would have got our facts more emphasised. Once we got talking we were like fish out of water — no experience. We did not represent ourselves properly at all.

> I felt something had been left out that should have been said. There were certain accounts I wasn't given a chance to answer because we weren't prepared for them.

> I think at least two members had preconceived ideas of both me and my case. They weren't really interested. When I heard the

TABLE 3.6

**REASONS FOR FAILURE TO GET CASE ACROSS
SELF-REPRESENTED APPLICANTS**

	%
Case not well prepared	13
I was not represented by a solicitor/other side had a solicitor	38
I could not express myself well/I made a bad impression	27
Decision made on irrelevant or incomplete facts	15
Employer denied my statement/told lies	12
Case was rushed/not given as much time as employer	16
Tribunal was hostile/biased against me	20
I lost/other reasons	15
	N = 101

(Multi-response possible.)

SOURCE: IRRU survey.

employer's side lying I interrupted and when I'm angry I shout a bit. This didn't help.

Because with us not having anything in black and white, not a concrete case, it's very easy for a learned man to bring out the points — most of our case was just word of mouth.

In the next chapter we explore the relationship between representation and outcomes. Here the point is that, although the ideal is a tribunal hearing where the ordinary person does not need skilled representation, the majority of those applicants who bring their own cases feel they fail to get their case across well to the tribunal.

Summary

This chapter has examined the composition of the industrial tribunal, the role of its members, its decision-making and the nature of tribunal hearings. Entrusting the determination of dismissal disputes to tribunals composed mainly of lay members rather than professional lawyers can be seen as part of a desire to 'distance labour law from the mainstream of English legal method' (Munday, 1981: 150). In a similar way the emphasis on informality and official encouragement to tribunals to eschew legalism is part of the distinguishing of tribunals from the ordinary courts and of promoting simple informal justice.

In practice we find the context within which the tribunals operate, the fact that they are quasi-courts, places constraints on the atttainment of this ideal. The differences between the tribunals and the ordinary courts are differences of degree not kind (Abel-Smith and Stevens, 1968: 224). This is seen to affect the roles, influence and relationship of the tribunal members and the nature of tribunal hearings.

All tribunal members accept the impartial, judicial role of the lay member but the notion of the lay member as equal judge, with the chairperson, of law and fact was articulated less often. The lay members' contribution of industrial and practical knowledge and experience is a general rather than specific one and, although at times important, has to be made in a context where the question to be decided is who is *legally* right? The legal member of the tribunal emerges as first among equals, a reflection of the court-like nature of the system which gives primacy to legal considerations, and of situational factors arising from the legal member being the chairperson. These considerations are seen to influence, and help explain the unanimity of, decision-making in unfair dismissal cases.

Lay members do not see their role as an enabling one vis-à-vis the parties and in practice generally do not play an active role in hearings.

Hearings are intended to be informal and flexible to enable unrepresented parties to bring their own cases without being disadvantaged but we identified various features of the tribunal system which have pulled against the attainment of this ideal. Notably, these were the underlying accusatorial model of hearings and a tendency towards legalism.

Although the informal model of tribunals was found to have a continuing validity, the majority of self-represented applicants thought they failed to get their case across at their hearing and the majority of both chairpersons and lay members thought self-representation should not be encouraged. The lack of legal representation in a quasi-court system may affect the outcomes of unfair dismissal cases. This is explored in the next chapter where we discuss the extent to which the lack of representation can explain the low level of applicant success.

4

Winning and Losing at the Industrial Tribunal

The majority of applicants who pursue their unfair dismissal claims to a hearing by an industrial tribunal have their complaints dismissed. As Table 4.1 shows, the applicants' rate of success until 1982 was declining. In 1976 about 38 per cent of applicants won their cases but in 1981 only 23 per cent were successful. In 1982 the success rate increased to 30.7 per cent.

This chapter examines why it is that the majority of applicants who go to a hearing have their unfair dismissal complaints dismissed. Two main explanations are forwarded. First, developing an argument of the preceding chapter, we seek to provide an understanding of the low applicant success rate by examining the relative disadvantage of applicants, compared with employers, in their ability to get their version of the facts of the case across to the tribunal. Second, and more importantly, we examine the concept of unfair dismissal which derives from the statute and the way in which it has been interpreted. These two factors are found to have more explanatory power than the argument that applicants bring meritless cases.

Relative Disadvantage

Applicants' relative disadvantage in getting their cases across at tribunal derives from their inferior resources compared with those of employers. This affects their ability to prepare and present their cases. The system demands that applicants initiate action. To do so they need to be aware of their rights and how to apply. They need to be able to comprehend and complete forms. The guidance leaflets, intended to help unadvised parties, themselves demand quite a high standard of comprehension and literacy. Although the formalities and procedures of the industrial tribunal are more simple and straightforward than those of other

TABLE 4.1

APPLICANTS' SUCCESS RATE AT TRIBUNAL HEARINGS

Year	No. of Complaints Heard by Tribunals	No. of Complaints Upheld	Percentage of Heard Complaints Upheld
1976	13,803	5,191	37.6
1977	12,842	3,954	30.8
1978	11,828	3,277	27.7
1979	11,705	3,187	27.2
1980	10,037	2,778	27.7
1981	13,436	3,134	23.3
1982	11,509	3,535	30.7

SOURCE: Table based on parliamentary written answer 15 December 1981 and *Employment Gazette* (1982), 520; (1983), 449.

courts, they still pose difficulties and disadvantages for unrepresented applicants. Employers are likely to have had more experience of dealing with officialdom, if not necessarily in appearing before courts, and may be better able to cope with the style and nature of communications from the tribunal office. The head of even a small firm may be expected to be better equipped than the typical dismissed manual worker in terms of articulateness and confidence which are at a premium in a system which relies on the production of evidence by oral testimony and question and answer. Even if the employer's personal resources in a particular instance are not superior to those of the applicant, the employer is generally better able to support his or her case with detailed information, documents and witnesses. We now examine some of these differences.

As noted earlier (p. 77), the provisions enabling one side to request further and better particulars of the other's case are little used. This does not mean, however, that each side is equally ignorant of the other's case. Employers did not request more details of the applicants' cases because, as the dismissing party, they generally did not require more information. Applicants on the other hand did not consider using the provisions mainly because they were ignorant of them. Only 17 per cent of the 429 applicants and 5 per cent of the 443 employers whose cases were heard said they or their representatives had requested further or better particulars. Generally, where information was requested it was given, although 12 of the 74 applicants requesting information required a tribunal order (granted in all but one case) as did 3 of the 24 employers (all granted). The vast majority (87 per cent) of those employers who did not request information said they did not think it would have helped them to have had more details of the applicant's case. About half of the employers not using this facility knew it existed, whereas only 13 per cent of applicants who did not request further and better particulars knew they could have done so. Unlike employers, half the applicants who did not seek more information of the other side's case thought it would have helped their case to have done this. It appears, therefore, that employers are more aware than applicants of the interlocutory steps but see no advantage in using them. Applicants, who in the main would welcome more information about the employer's case, generally are ignorant of the way to obtain it.

But even though with hindsight a number of applicants felt it would have been useful to have had more information about the employer's case in order that they might have been better prepared for the hearing, for various reasons there is no certainty that they would have used the provision even if they had known of it. Firstly, there is the difficulty or reluctance which may be involved in actually framing and sending a request to the ex-employer. Secondly, and relatedly, there is the problem of identifying, prior to the hearing, what information to ask for. To know what information might be useful, one needs to know how tribunals decide dismissal cases, what facts will be relevant. This will depend on the law. It is necessary to know what has to be proved or refuted and what facts have to be established to know what evidence is required and hence what information to seek. Unrepresented and un-advised applicants are therefore ill-equipped to formulate requests.

Employers, by virtue of their position, are in possession of more information, records and documents concerning the employment relationship and its termination and, in addition, are better able than applicants to call witnesses on their behalf. Applicants often have no one to support their version of events, and even if there is somebody appropriate, he or she is likely to be still in the respondent's employment and applicants will be reluctant to involve them. Almost three-quarters of employers in heard cases called witnesses compared with only a quarter of applicants. Of the 306 applicants who did not call witnesses, just over a quarter thought there was no one appropriate to call; a fifth wanted to call people but were reluctant to do so or were refused. Ex-workmates may be unwilling to give evidence against their employer. A tenth of these 306 applicants said they did not call witnesses because they did not know they could; twice as many said they had not thought or realised it might be useful to do so. Only a very small proportion, 3 per cent, of applicants not calling witnesses said this was because the employer would be calling those people whom they wanted to give evidence on their behalf. Those with specialist representation, particularly legal representation, made greater use of the interlocutory provisions and were more likely than those representing themselves to call witnesses in support of their case.

Employing a skilled representative, of course, is an important means whereby ignorance and personal inadequacies or lack of ability in case preparation and presentation can be overcome. Because of their greater needs and fewer resources, applicants attribute greater importance to representation than do employers. Sixty-three per cent of the 417 applicants in our survey who attended their hearings thought their type of representation had made a difference to the outcome of the case. Self-represented applicants generally felt their form of representation harmed their case while those represented by specialists saw this form of representation as beneficial. Just under two-thirds of each group thought their particular type of representation had made a difference to the outcome of their case: 82 per cent of the self-represented applicants who thought it had made a difference saw their form of representation as detrimental to their case while over two-thirds of those with specialist representation thought the difference was a positive one. Employers were less likely than applicants to see the way in which the applicant was represented as affecting the outcome of the case, but in those cases where they did think it made a difference their views were similar to those of the applicants, namely that where the applicant had self-representation it generally harmed the applicant's chances and specialist representation generally helped.

The outcome of the case may well influence the applicants' evaluation of the representation they had. Overall the majority of those who won, 52 per cent, thought their form of representation had helped. Only 6 per cent of these applicants thought their representation had harmed their case. Of the losing applicants, only 13 per cent thought their type of representation had helped and 50 per cent thought it had harmed their case. As Table 4.2 shows, the success rate for self-represented applicants in the survey, 31 per cent, was slightly below that of applicants represented at the hearing by trade union officials, 35 per cent, and those represented by solicitors or barristers, 41 per cent. Information provided in response to a parliamentary question (DE, 1984a: 127), showed the average rate of success at hearing between 1979 and 1982 for self-represented applicants was 25 per cent; for those represented by trade unions 28 per cent and 32 per cent for those with legal representation. The higher success rate of applicants who are represented by specialists at hearing probably partly reflects differences in the applicants themselves and their cases. It may also reflect some

TABLE 4.2

OUTCOME BY APPLICANTS' REPRESENTATION

Outcome	All	Representation at Hearing		
		Self	Trade Union	Solicitor/ Barrister
	%	%	%	%
Applicant won	34	31	35	41
Applicant lost	66	69	65	59
N =	429	192	96	97

SOURCE: IRRU survey.

selectivity on the part of specialists in the cases they take. But even allowing for this, specialist representation does make, and is seen to make, a difference to applicants, a finding in keeping with research on other types of tribunal (see Bell, 1982: 144; Frost and Howard, 1977: ch. 6; and Benson, 1979: 169).

Generally, when compared with applicants, respondent employers placed less importance on their representation as an explanatory variable in matters such as the outcome of the case and how well their case got across. Whereas almost two-thirds of applicants thought the way in which they were represented had made a difference to the outcome of their case, only 43 per cent of respondent employers thought this about their representation. Of these employers a majority in each representation category considered their form of representation had helped their case. With respondent employers the effect of representation is less clear as there are some marked differences within the specialist-represented group between those employers with internal specialist representation (personnel managers, legal officers, etc.) and those employing private practice lawyers. This latter group is often closer to those employers with company lay representation (accountant, line manager, director), as is the case with success rate at tribunal, shown in Table 4.3. About one-third of employers with lay representation and one-third of those with external legal representation were found to have unfairly dismissed the applicants in question whereas only one-fifth of those with company specialist representation had a finding of unfair dismissal against them. This reflects the nature and resources of the employers concerned.

As noted earlier (Chapter 2), the employers using 'company lay' and 'external legal' representation are predominantly small employers; larger employers using internal specialists. The likelihood of the employer winning an unfair dismissal case increases with size. Those establishments with fewer than twenty workers had a below average success rate and those with over a hundred employees had an above average success rate. The relative advantage of the larger company does not rest only in its ability to call upon internal specialist representation which combines intimate knowledge of the workplace with legal and procedural knowledge of tribunals. The same departments or personnel which provide representation will provide advice on how to discipline a workforce with the minimum risk of contravening the law. Such companies are more aware than smaller employers of the need and way to handle dismissals 'reasonably', for example to have and follow discipline and dismissal procedures and, in addition, they are more likely to have had previous experience of defending themselves at an industrial tribunal. Overall 48 per cent of the 1,080 respondent employers in the

TABLE 4.3

OUTCOME BY EMPLOYERS' REPRESENTATION

Outcome	All		Representation at Hearing[a]			
		Company Lay	External Legal	Company Specialist	Employers' Association
	%	%	%	%	%
Company won	70	66	68	79	70
Company lost	30	34	32	21	30
	N = 443	148	183	82	20

SOURCE: IRRU survey.

NOTE:

a. 'Other' representation not included.

survey said they had experienced at least one other unfair dismissal claim within the previous two years, but the proportion with this experience increased with size, varying from 28 per cent of single-establishment employers up to 80 per cent in companies employing 500–999 and to 86 per cent in companies of 1,000 workers or more.

Although applicants experience a greater need for representation than do employers and attribute more importance to it as a factor influencing the outcome of their cases, they are less likely than employers to have access to it. Chapter 2 examined the representation options open to the two parties, noting that the larger companies can generally call on a specialist form of 'self' representation while the smaller employer, like the majority of applicants, is effectively faced with a choice of lay self-representation or engaging a lawyer. Legal skills are expensive to buy and neither party will regard the cost of this kind of representation as insignificant. However, it is a cost more easily borne by the employer, who may also claim it as an allowable expense for tax purposes, than by an out-of-work applicant. It is not surprising, therefore, to find that employers make greater use of this kind of representation than do applicants.

The differential access to representation means that where representation at a tribunal hearing is unequal (one party having specialist representation and the other lay) it is the applicant who is usually disadvantaged. This can be seen in Table 4.4 which shows the representation used by each party in 308 hearings where applicants and respondents in our survey provided information about the same case. 'Other' representation is a mixture of specialist and lay representation, including Citizens Advice Bureau staff, friends and relatives, but has been classified as 'lay' which it predominantly is. The applicant was at the 'wrong end' of unequal representation in over a quarter of the hearings; in 13 per cent of hearings the applicants handled their own cases while employers had external legal representation (solicitors and barristers). Obviously Table 4.4 makes certain assumptions concerning the equality or otherwise of various kinds of representation. The data have been presented to produce the *highest* proportion of hearings in which representation could be said to be equal (62 per cent). If it is assumed that external legal representation is superior to, rather than as in the table equal to, trade union and employers' association representation (a viable assumption given the examination of the nature of hearings in the last chapter), then the proportion of hearings in which the applicant was disadvantaged increases from 27 per cent to 37 per cent.

It might be argued that some of the applicant's relative disadvantage in case preparation and presentation is offset by the the burden of proof being placed on the employer. Inasmuch as this is true, it is a compensatory factor which is being eroded. Until recently employers who admitted dismissal had to prove both that they had a fair reason for dismissal and that they acted reasonably in treating the reason as sufficient. The second part of the burden was lifted from the employer by changes to s.57(3) of EP(C)A 1978 made by the Employment Act 1980, in response to what the government described as a 'widespread feeling among employers that they are "guilty until proved innocent"' (DE, 1979b: 874). It is difficult to gauge exactly what effect this change in the burden of proof is having but, in cases where the evidence is evenly balanced, it has been suggested that a neutral burden of proof may favour the employer (Pitt, 1980: 234; Lewis and Simpson, 1981: 31).

The relative advantage of employers in case preparation and presentation means they are better placed than applicants to put forward their views at the hearing. This perception of relative strength is shared by both parties as shown in Table 4.5. Over half of all applicants who attended their hearings thought the employer was in the stronger position. This was also the view of 40 per cent of the respondent employers, lower than among applicants but still the largest category of response. Employers were less likely than applicants to think the applicant was the stronger party, 17 per cent of all employers thinking this compared with 27 per cent of applicants. The effect of representation on perceived strength in getting one's views across to the tribunal is also shown in the table. Sixty-three per cent of self-represented applicants said they thought the employer was in the stronger position compared with 42 per cent of specialist-represented applicants.

As might be expected, further analysis showed the outcome of the case appears to affect perceptions of who was in the stronger position to get his or her views across at the hearing. A higher proportion of losing applicants (66 per cent) than those who won thought the employer had been in the stronger position. But none the less 27 per cent of successful applicants thought the employer had been in the stronger position and among employers who lost 31 per cent still considered they had been in the superior position at the hearing.

Poor preparation and presentation of cases by applicants is seen to be a contributory factor in low applicant success. Applicants who blamed these factors for their failure to win, however, may have lost even if these problems had been overcome because of the nature of the legal tests which are applied in unfair dismissal cases.

TABLE 4.4

EQUALITY OF REPRESENTATION AT HEARINGS

Respondents' Representative	Applicants' Representative	% of Cases
Company lay	Self (no representative)	22.4
Company specialist	Trade union	5.2
External legal	Trade union	10.0
Employers' association	Trade union	1.0
Company specialist	Legal	2.6
External legal	Legal	15.6
Employers' association	Legal	1.3
Company lay	Other	2.9
Other	Self	1.3
	Total representation equal	62

Company specialist	Self	4.9
External legal	Self	13.0
Employers' association	Self	1.6
Company specialist	Other	2.3
Employers' association	Other	0.3
External legal	Other	4.9
Total applicant disadvantaged		**27**
Company lay	Trade union	7.5
Company lay	Legal	2.9
Other	Legal	0.3
Total employer disadvantaged		**11**

N = 308

SOURCE: IRRU surveys.

TABLE 4.5

RELATIVE POSITION AT HEARING BY REPRESENTATION

	Applicants			Employers		
	All	Self-Rep.	Specialist Rep.[a]	All	Lay Rep.	Specialist Rep.[b]
	%	%	%	%	%	%
Applicant stronger	27	22	32	17	22	16
Both the same	16	12	21	33	38	31
Respondent employer stronger	53	63	42	40	36	43
Unable to say	4	4	5	9	4	11
	N = 417[c]	N = 192	N = 187	N = 443[c]	N = 148	N = 285

SOURCE: IRRU surveys.
NOTES:
a. Trade union and external legal representation.
b. External legal, internal specialist and employers' association representation.
c. This figure includes those with 'other' representation.

The Legal Tests

The more important explanation for the low rate of applicant success at tribunals is the very notion of unfair dismissal itself. Even if the facts of the case which the tribunal obtains are those which the applicant would have wanted to have got across, the application of legal principles to those facts may result in the claim of unfair dismissal being dismissed.

As we described in Chapter 1, the employer has to show a reason for the dismissal. Some reasons are stipulated as automatically unfair, some as automatically fair (see p. 21). In other cases, s.57 of the EP(C)A requires the employer to show what was the reason, or principal reason, for the dismissal and that the reason related to the employee's capacity, or conduct, or redundancy, or contravention of an enactment, or that it was 'some other substantial reason' justifying dismissal of an employee holding the position which the dismissed employee held. Where these requirements are fulfilled, s.57(3) provides:

> the determination of the question whether the dismissal was fair or unfair, having regard to the reason shown by the employer, shall depend on whether in the circumstances (including the size and administrative resources of the employer's undertaking) the employer acted reasonably or unreasonably in treating it as a sufficient reason for dismissing the employee; and that question shall be determined in accordance with equity and the substantial merits of the case.

The concept of fairness encompasses both substantive and procedural aspects and on the face of it the tribunals are left a lot of discretion to operationalise the concept of unfair dismissal on a case by case basis, in determining, for example, what is 'reasonable'. In performing their function of clarifying the law, however, the appellate courts have handed down judge-made law embodying their own conceptions of fairness which the tribunals have to follow and the EAT until very recently showed an enthusiasm for laying down guidelines on how tribunals should handle a whole range of cases, setting down what it saw as the correct approach (Phillips, 1978: 139). As we discussed above (p. 76), the Court of Appeal in various decisions tried to curb the guideline practice, which the EAT reasserted in *Compair Maxam*, but, as we shall see, the Court of Appeal decisions themselves place important constraints on the tribunals' decision-making freedom.

This section does not attempt to provide a detailed analysis of the statute nor of case law on unfair dismissal, but briefly considers the statutory provisions and their interpretation in order to indicate that the law which tribunals apply to the cases they hear does not go very far in challenging managerial prerogative in the area of discipline and dismissal, a fact which helps account for the low applicant success rate.

If there is a dispute as to whether a dismissal has taken place, the applicant has to establish that it has. This has proved a heavy burden on the applicant particularly, but not only, in cases where constructive dismissal is alleged. The definition of dismissal rests upon the foundations of the contract of employment, a fact which opens the way for a whole hinterland of legalistic common law considerations to be brought into tribunal decision-making. The term dismissal is treated as synonymous with the common law idea of repudiation. In *Western Excavating (ECC) Ltd v Sharp* [1978] IRLR 27, the Court of Appeal held that the common law rules governing repudiatory breach of contract were the correct test for the tribunals to apply when hearing claims based upon constructive dismissal. The applicant has to show that the employer's conduct, which led to resignation, amounted to a fundamental breach of contract; that the employer acted in such a way that he or she demonstrated an intention no longer to be bound by one or more of the essential terms of the contract. Only then is the worker entitled to treat himself or herself as dismissed.

Where dismissal is not disputed or is held to have taken place the burden of proof is on the employer to show a reason for dismissal which falls within the categories specified in the statute. It is not difficult for employers to surmount their first hurdle. This is partly because the scope of the residual category, 'some other substantial reason', has become very wide and partly because of the nature of the 'reason' required by the tribunals. We shall examine each of these aspects in turn.

In their examination of how the courts have interpreted the statute's residual category of 'some other substantial reason', Bowers and Clarke argue that it has become an 'employers' charter' providing a wide 'ragbag of gateways to fair dismissal' (1981: 35, 43). For example, this category has been used to enable the fair dismissal of workers who refuse to accept changes in their contractual terms and conditions relating to such fundamental matters as job content, place of residence, wages and hours of work.[1] Where an employee refuses to do something which would involve a change in the contract tribunals have been reluctant to see this as misconduct but have allowed it under 'some other substantial reason'. Where the employer would not be unduly affected

---

1. Important cases on 'some other substantial reason' include *Hollister v National Farmers' Union* [1979] IRLR 238, CA; *Bowater Containers Ltd v McCormack* [1980] IRLR 50, EAT and *Gorman v London Computer Training Centre* [1978] IRLR 22, EAT.

by the worker's refusal to accept the changes in the contractual terms the dismissal may not be fair; some evidence of commercial need is required.[2] Originally, however, the contractual changes had to be *necessary* for the economic efficiency of the business but now case law rules they need only be beneficial.

The view that emerges is that it is substantively fair to dismiss when the dismissal is in the interests of the business as defined by the employer. This can be seen particularly in the area of reorganisation dismissals — where changes in work organisation result in the dismissal of workers in circumstances which fail to satisfy the detailed requirements of the redundancy definition. A review of the case law 'shows the EAT and Court of Appeal appearing to accept as valid employers' claims that to compete efficiently in a free market they must be allowed latitude to trim their workforce and make "efficient" their work methods without being hampered by laws protecting their workers' (Bowers and Clarke, 1981: 39).

In addition to allowing a range of reorganisation and non-contractual duty dismissals, the residual category has been held to include reasons relating to breakdown in relationships at work[3] and employees' personal characteristics, for example homosexuality,[4] as well as the ending of temporary contracts[5] and a miscellaneous collection of reasons including failure to disclose certain information to the employer at the time of appointment.[6]

As well as being a wide residual category, providing a virtual 'catch all' for employers who cannot fit their reason for dismissal into the specified categories of capacity, conduct, redundancy and contravention of an enactment, 'some other substantial reason' has been used also to expand the scope of the specified categories. For example an employer who dismissed a Tunisian national because he was informed by a section of the Department of Employment that it would be in contravention of an enactment to continue his employment had, in fact, been misinformed. It was held that the category 'contravention of an enactment' did not extend to a situation where the employer believed honestly but wrongly that the employment was illegal. However the EAT (albeit hesitantly) held that the employer's belief in this case did constitute some other substantial reason justifying dismissal.[7]

2. *Evans v Elementa Holdings Ltd* [1982] IRLR 143.
3. For example *Gorfin v Distressed Gentlefolks' Aid Association* [1973] IRLR 290.
4. *Saunders v Scottish National Camps Association* [1980] IRLR 174.
5. *Terry v East Sussex County Council* [1976] ICR 537.
6. For example, *O'Brien v Prudential Assurance Co.* [1979] IRLR 140.
7. *Bouchaala v Trust House Forte Hotels Ltd* [1980] IRLR 382.

Even without the elasticity provided by 'some other substantial reason', the specified categories of reasons for dismissal are wide because, on appeal, reason for dismissal has been interpreted to encompass not only the set of facts known to the employer which lead to the dismissal but also *beliefs* held by the employer which cause the dismissal.[8] Thus, showing a reason for dismissal is made easier for the employer because the statute has been interpreted to mean that employers do not have to prove to the tribunal's satisfaction that the dismissed worker *was* incompetent or guilty of misconduct or whatever, only that, at the time of the dismissal, the employer *reasonably believed* this to be the case. An early case in which this issue arose concerned a dismissal following an act of vandalism in the company's toilets for which the dismissed worker claimed he was not responsible. The industrial tribunal stated:

> we have considered the whole of the evidence in this case, and although there is a great deal of suspicion against the applicant we have reached the conclusion that we are not satisfied that he committed the offence, either on the balance of probabilities or beyond reasonable doubt.

When the employer appealed against the finding of unfair dismissal the EAT held that the industrial tribunal, in asking 'are we satisfied that the offence was committed' had asked itself the wrong question. It should, said the EAT, have asked 'are we satisfied that the employers had, at the time of the dismissal, reasonable grounds for believing that the offence put against the applicant was in fact committed?' (*Ferodo Ltd v Barnes* [1976] IRLR 302). That the employer's belief may be a fair reason for dismissal has been reiterated by the EAT on various occasions and has been supported by the Court of Appeal. In a case concerning the alleged incompetency of an airline pilot the then Master of the Rolls, Lord Denning, said:

> If a man is dismissed for stealing, as long as the employer honestly believes it on reasonable grounds, that is enough to justify dismissal. It is not necessary for the employer to prove that he was in fact stealing. Whenever a man is dismissed for incapacity or incompetence it is sufficient that the employer honestly believes on reasonable grounds that the man is incapable or incompetent. It is not necessary for the employer to prove that he is in fact incapable or incompetent (*Taylor v Alidair Ltd* [1978] IRLR 82, 85).

8. *Abernethy v Mott, Hay and Anderson* [1974] IRLR 213, CA.

The reason for dismissal, therefore, may be what the employer believes at the time of dismissal. The legal test requires not that he or she satisfies the tribunal that the belief was in fact correct but that the employer sincerely believed it to be so, and had reasonable grounds for so doing. In view of this interpretation of the statute the key question becomes what does an employer need to do to demonstrate to the tribunal that there were reasonable grounds for the belief which led to the dismissal. Guidelines were provided on this by the EAT in 1978 in a case concerning the dismissal of a shop assistant for alleged dishonesty:

> First of all there must be established by the employer the fact of that belief; that the employer did believe it. Secondly that the employer had in his mind reasonable grounds on which to sustain that belief. And thirdly . . . that the employer . . . had carried out as much investigation into the matter as was reasonable in all the circumstances of the case (*British Home Stores v Burchell* [1978] IRLR 379, 380).[9]

The nature of the statute and the way it has been interpreted mean that employers experience little difficulty in providing a portentially fair reason for dismissal; the substantive challenge has been severely constrained. But s.57 also requires tribunals to consider whether the employer acted reasonably. It is here that questions of procedural fairness arise. Initially at least, the courts appeared more willing to set procedural standards than to question the substance of the employer's decision. In judging procedural fairness they have the explicit guidance of the ACAS Code of Practice on Disciplinary Practice and Procedures in Employment (1977). A failure to observe the provisions of the Code does not of itself render a person liable to any legal proceedings but, under s.6 of the Employment Protection Act 1975, the Code is admissible in evidence in proceedings before an industrial tribunal and any provision which appears relevant shall be taken into account by the tribunal. The Code embodies notions of natural justice and advocates a 'corrective' rather than 'punitive' approach to discipline. The standards of reasonable procedure laid down in the Code include the giving of warnings, oral and then written, in the case of minor offences, stating the nature of the offence and allowing time for improvement; the right of the employee to state his or her case before dismissal; and the right of appeal to a higher level of management or appeals body. They also emphasise the need for the employer to undertake proper investigation. Although the provisions of the Code are not absolute requirements, it

---

9. This was approved by the Court of Appeal in *Weddell & Co. Ltd v Tepper* [1980] IRLR 96.

was held in the House of Lords that 'a failure to follow the procedure in the Code may lead to the conclusion that a dismissal was unfair which, if that procedure had been followed, would have been fair' (Dilhorne in *Devis & Sons Ltd v Atkins* [1977] IRLR 314).

The tribunals' emphasis on procedural fairness led to complaints from employers that they were losing cases on 'technicalities' but procedural fairness is clearly an important component in the notion of fairness contained in the statute and is an essential feature of managerial 'good practice' which is the hallmark of the 'reasonable employer'. The initial emphasis on the importance of employers adhering to the basic procedural standards of fairness, however, was considerably weakened by subsequent appeal decisions. In the early days of the legislation, for example, it was held that a dismissal for misconduct without giving the employee a chance to state a case would be unfair unless it was almost inconceivable that the hearing would have made any difference.[10] Now, however, the test is whether, on balance of probabilities, the employer would have taken the same course even if a hearing had been afforded. The leading case here is *British Labour Pump v Byrne* [1979] IRLR 94, an EAT decision unanimously approved by the Court of Appeal in *Wass v Binns* [1982] IRLR 283, but subject to academic criticism (see for example Schofield's discussion of subsequent EAT decisions, 1983: 171). In practice tribunals today rarely refer to the ACAS Code of Practice looking rather to decisions of the appellate courts for guidance on reasonableness in dismissing for reasons of, for example, ill-health[11] or redundancy.[12]

The weakening of procedural requirements by the courts, well documented by Elias (1981), has been taken up in the legislation itself. Since 1980, s.57(3) expressly directs the tribunals to take account of the size and administrative resources of the employer in determining reasonableness. The legislative change was anticipated by the EAT which was already instructing tribunals to take account of the special circumstances of small employers, whom the change was designed to help. For example, in *The Royal Naval School v Hughes* [1979] IRLR 383 the EAT considered that the Code of Practice was 'not necessarily apt' in the context of an independent school with a staff of forty.

The legal test of fairness directs the tribunals to focus attention on the conduct of the employer and not on whether the employee in fact suffered any injustice. Further tribunals are required to judge the

---

10. *Earl v Slater Wheeler (Airlyne) Ltd* [1972] IRLR 115.
11. e.g. *East Lindsey District Council v Daubney* [1977] IRLR 181; *International Sports Co. Ltd v Thomson* [1980] IRLR 340.
12. *Williams and others v Compair Maxam Ltd* [1982] IRLR 83.

reasonableness of employer conduct not by their *own* view of whether they would have dismissed in the same circumstances but by the standard of the 'reasonable employer'. In practice this need not have made too much difference since in deciding what a reasonable employer might do the tribunal members would draw on their own intuitive views. However the appellate courts have emphasised on a number of occasions that there may be a range of responses which reasonable employers might adopt – some dismissing where others would not – and only if the employer's decision falls outside this range should the tribunal find the dismissal unfair. It is sufficient that *a* reasonable employer would dismiss.[13] This 'range of reasonable responses' approach obviously limits the tribunal's power of intervention in the employer's dismissal decision and so further reduces the applicant's chance of succeeding.

Section 54 of the statute says that, with certain exceptions, 'every employee shall have the right not to be unfairly dismissed by his employer'. Some dismissed workers who feel they have been treated unfairly, therefore, seek redress. However, as Phillips J. has explained, and as our examination of the legal tests makes clear, 'the expression "unfair dismissal" is in no sense a common sense expression capable of being understood by the man in the street' (*Devis v Atkins* [1976] IRLR 19). The applicant's conception of what is unfair may not accord with the conception developed by the courts. It is in part this disjuncture between felt unfairness (which prompts the application) and the conception of unfairness operated by the tribunals (which leads to the application being dismissed) that lies behind the low rate of applicant success. We suggest that this, together with the problems faced by applicants in case preparation and presentation discussed earlier, provides a better explanation of the statistics on applicant success rate than the one more usually heard which is that dismissed workers pursue meritless claims.

Meritless Claims

The 'meritless claim' argument is that, because it costs nothing to apply and there is always a chance that the employer may be prepared to pay some money in order to avoid the time and expense of going to a tribunal hearing, people who have been dismissed have 'nothing to lose'

13. See for example *Union of Construction and Allied Trades and Technicians v Brain* [1981] IRLR 224, CA; *Rolls-Royce Ltd v Walpole* [1980] IRLR 343, EAT; *British Leyland UK Ltd v Swift* [1981] IRLR 91, CA; *Vickers Ltd v Smith* [1977] IRLR 11 and *Watling & Co. Ltd v Richardson* [1978] IRLR 255.

by putting in an application even where they know their case is without foundation. When these cases come to be determined by a tribunal they are thrown out.

This kind of argument prompted changes in 1980 which increased the scope for awarding costs against the losing party to discourage applications. Costs could be awarded previously against someone pursuing a case 'frivolously or vexatiously', that is, knowing it to be without substance or acting from an improper motive. The new regulations widened this to include 'or otherwise unreasonably'[14] and, as we saw in Chapter 1, provided for pre-hearing assessment (PHA) at which people with *prima facie* weak cases can be warned that the tribunal considers it unlikely that they would succeed and that they risk costs being awarded against them.[15] Since the beginning of the provision's operation to the end of December 1982, 5,299 pre-hearing assessments were called. Costs warnings were issued against 2,029 applicants, over 80 per cent of whom subsequently did not pursue their cases to full hearing. Of those who did carry on with their cases, 7 per cent in fact succeeded at hearing. A third of those warned applicants who lost their cases at full hearing had costs awarded against them (DE, 1982a: 520; DE, 1983a:449).

Our research evidence does not support the view that applicants who think they will lose none the less pursue their claims in the hope of achieving some 'nuisance settlement' (see also Dickens, 1978–9: 18). As we noted earlier (p. 31), making an application to a tribunal for unfair dismissal is a course taken by only a minority of those who lose their jobs. The 'ordinary man' referred to by the first President of Industrial Tribunals (p. 73) is not in a position to evaluate the strength of his case at law. In the event the chance of success may be slight, and the claim may be misconceived, but for the most part 'the ordinary man' pursues his case out of a genuine sense of having been treated unfairly. The reasons given by applicants in our survey for withdrawing cases before reaching a hearing (p. 143) indicate that even before the risk of costs was increased many applicants did not pursue cases once they realised or were advised that they lacked the necessary qualification or were unlikely to succeed.

Our findings also indicate that it takes a certain amount of resourcefulness and perhaps even courage on the part of applicants, particularly those without representation, to continue to the hearing stage. Applicants were asked 'how much did going through with this case make you nervous, worried or upset?'. Sixty-five per cent of those who went to a

14.   1980 Regulations, reg. 11.
15.   1980 Regulations, reg. 6.

hearing found it a worrying or upsetting experience; 39 per cent said 'very much' and a further 26 per cent 'quite a bit'.

In the strict sense a meritless claim is one without any foundation. The clearest case is a claim which falls outside the provisions of the legislation (because of inadequate service for example). Few claims are dismissed at tribunal hearing because they are 'out of scope'. Only 11 per cent of heard cases (3.9 per cent of all applications) in 1982 were dismissed for this reason (DE, 1983a: 449). In 1979, before the introduction of the PHA filter, 9 per cent of heard cases (3.2 per cent of all applications) were dismissed by tribunals as out of scope (DE, 1981a: 82). The majority of claims which are dismissed by the tribunal do not lack merit in that there are grounds which an applicant, not knowing the law, reasonably might feel justify a complaint. But, as discussed above, the law allows employers considerable scope before the actions which may give rise to such complaints will be held to constitute unfair dismissal.

Summary

Less than a third of the unfair dismissal cases heard by industrial tribunals result in a finding against the employer. This chapter has rejected the 'meritless case' argument as an adequate explanation for the low and declining rate of applicant success. The relative disadvantage of the applicant, vis-à-vis the employer, in case preparation and presentation, in getting the 'facts of the case' across to the tribunal, was examined. Use of interlocutory steps and calling of witnesses was associated with legal representation and their non-use by applicants often resulted from ignorance. Those applicants who represented themselves at the tribunal hearing had the lowest success rate. Despite their greater needs and fewer resources, applicants were less likely than employers to be able to employ skilled representation. In a large proportion of cases, representation was equal but in around a third of heard cases applicants were disadvantaged in that they were at the 'wrong end' of unequal representation, most commonly bringing their own case with the employer being represented by a lawyer.

Applicants attached a lot of importance to representation as an explanation of outcomes, seeing legal representation as advantageous. We suggest, however, that a more important explanation of low applicant success is the legal tests: the concept of unfair dismissal which derives from the statute and the way in which over the years it has been interpreted by the courts. The broad interpretation of the categories of reasons for dismissal given in the statute and the existence of a wide residual category of 'some other substantial reason' means employers have no difficulty in showing a reason which may justify dismissal, while procedural standards have been weakened over time both through case law and legislative change. The legal test of fairness which has been developed is concerned not with whether the employee suffered any injustice but focuses on the conduct of the employer and asks whether it falls within the range of 'reasonable employer' conduct. Consequently, management prerogative has proved 'a strong fortress' (Bowers and Clarke, 1981: 43).

The legal tests which we discussed have been developed by the judges in the course of clarifying the law as laid down in the statute. But the courts' apparent willingness to protect the interest of the individual employee in holding on to his or her job only in so far as it does not undermine the employer's interests, mirrors the ideological perspective of the statute. The concept of fairness in the statute is not a philosophical one but an ideological one, firmly located within a framework which takes for granted the inequality of the employer-employee relationship; which accepts that the employer has the right to dismiss where this is neccessary to protect or further his or her business interests.

Elias argues that the law obliges employers to adopt a pluralist perspective in that they 'should not remorselessly pursue their own interests. They must also take into account the interest of the worker whose dismissal is under consideration' (1981: 211). If this is the intention of the statute, then the unitary perspective of the courts lessens this obligation. As Phillips J. explained in *Cook v Thomas Linnell & Sons* ([1977] IRLR 132), 'it is important that the operation of the legislation in relation to unfair dismissal should not impede employers unreasonably in the efficient management of their business which must be in the interest of all'. By subsuming the interests of employees in general under the 'needs of the business' the interests of any individual employee in retaining his or her job can be overridden.

5

Tribunal Awards

An important feature of the unfair dismissal legislation is that it provides for the reinstatement of workers found by tribunals to have been dismissed unfairly. Reinstatement has been seen to represent 'the ultimate loss of employer control and the final symbol of worker ownership of a post of employment' (Meyers, 1964: 115). The provision for reinstatement was seen to distinguish the unfair dismissal provisions from those of the Redundancy Payments Act and to indicate a concern for employee job security (Martin and Fryer, 1973: 247; Wedderburn, 1971: 151).

Reinstatement, where the applicant returns to the same job as if there had been no dismissal, is the primary legal remedy for unfair dismissal. Alternatively the statute provides for re-engagement, a different form of re-employment, where return is to the same or an associated employer in a comparable or otherwise suitable job. The third remedy which an industrial tribunal may award to an unfairly dismissed worker, where re-employment is not wanted or not practicable, is compensation, calculated in accordance with the statutory provisions and subject to certain maxima.

In practice the tribunals rarely award the primary re-employment remedies. The most common remedy is an award of compensation, the average amount of which falls far short of the statutory maximum. This chapter explores and explains the pattern and nature of industrial tribunal awards. Why do so few successful applicants get their jobs back? Why are compensation levels so low? These two questions are addressed after an outline of the general picture of tribunal awards.

The Pattern of Awards

The emphasis in the statute on re-employment as the primary remedy has been evident since the introduction of the unfair dismissal provisions by the Industrial Relations Act 1971, although at this initial stage only re-engagement was mentioned. In 1974 the Trade Union and Labour Relations Act specified reinstatement separately from re-engagement, and in 1975 more weight was given to both these remedies when the Employment Protection Act empowered tribunals to order, and not merely to recommend, re-employment. This came into effect in 1976 with the sanction for non-compliance being the payment of compensation of between thirteen and twenty-six weeks' pay, or double this if the dismissal was on grounds of sex or race. Special enhanced compensation provisions apply where trade union membership, or non-membership, or trade union activity was the reason for dismissal.

In determining the remedy, tribunals are instructed to consider whether re-employment is 'practicable' but, generally speaking, the fact that the employer has taken on a permanent replacement should not be taken as rendering it impracticable. The applicant's wishes must be taken into account, and tribunals have an express duty to explain the specific remedies to unfairly dismissed employees and to ask whether either reinstatement or re-engagement is wanted. Underlying these changes was a concern that re-employment, regarded as a remedy superior to compensation, was not being awarded in unfair dismissal cases and a belief that this was due in large part to tribunals' lack of enthusiasm for it.

Although reinstatement is clearly the primary remedy for unfair dismissal provided by law, very few successful applicants are awarded it. The usual remedy for successful applicants is compensation. As Table 5.1 shows, compensation has accounted for at least two-thirds of the successful tribunal outcomes each year since 1972 with the exception of 1981 and 1982 when the proportion of 'other remedies' increased. This increase appears to reflect an increasing tendency of tribunals, having found dismissal unfair, to leave the remedy to be agreed by the parties. This is more likely to happen where both sides are legally represented and the increase probably reflects the increasing use of legal representation noted in Chapter 4. The legislative changes in 1976 did not halt the downward trend in the level of re-employment. The level of re-employment awarded by tribunals has always been low. In 1980 re-employment made up only 2.8 per cent of the remedies awarded by tribunals, the lowest proportion ever. In 1981 there was an increase in the frequency of this remedy and for the first time since 1976 it constituted almost 5 per cent of all the awards made by tribunals but this level was not sustained in 1982.

In discussing the level of re-employment awarded by tribunals, it should be noted that there are reasons to doubt the accuracy of the actual figures relating to re-employment which are produced by the Department of Employment, although the general picture is unaffected.

TABLE 5.1

REMEDIES AWARDED BY TRIBUNALS 1972–82

	1972	1973	1974	1975	1976	1977	1978	1979	1980	1981	1982
	%	%	%	%	%	%	%	%	%	%	%
Reinstatement/ re-engagement	4.4	6.2	4.3	5.1	5.5	4.3	3.2	3.1	2.8	4.8	3.8
Compensation	76.8	68.4	71.7	75.9	76.1	78.8	75.6	74.9	71.8	62.1	57.8
Other remedies[a]	18.8	25.4	24.0	19.0	18.4	16.9	21.2	22.0	25.4	33.1	38.3

SOURCE: *Employment Gazettes* 1974–83.

NOTE:

a. 'Other remedies' includes cases where a redundancy payment is ordered and where the dismissal is held unfair but the parties are left to agree on the remedy.

When Williams and Lewis (1981) tried to trace all the cases recorded by the Department as having resulted in tribunal re-employment rulings, they found about one-fifth were misrecorded and no re-employment award had been made, while a further 25 per cent had to be discarded because the DE figures are based on the first outcome of any complaint and this may be overturned later. Although this would seem to indicate that the official statistics overstate the level of re-employment awards other evidence indicates that the way the statistics are compiled and presented may in fact conceal some re-employment. The survey undertaken for the present work revealed a higher, although still low, level of re-employment than was expected from the official statistics. One explanation for this is that a high proportion of outcomes classified as 'other remedies', the nature of which is not known by the Department, are in fact re-employment.

Table 5.2 shows a comparison of the outcomes reported by applicants in our survey with the Department's statistics for the same period. Of the 145 applicants in our survey who succeeded at tribunal 7.6 per cent claimed to have been awarded re-employment. The comparable proportion in the DE statistics is 4.5 per cent but the difference is not

TABLE 5.2

REMEDIES OBTAINED AT TRIBUNAL: COMPARISON OF DE AND SURVEY

Tribunal Award	DE Statistics		Applicant Sample	
		%		%
Reinstatement	105	2.5	10	6.9
Re-engagement	85	2.0	1	0.7
		4.5		7.6
Compensation	3,387	81.6	133	91.7
Redundancy payment	221	5.3		
Other remedy only	351	8.5	1	0.7
	4,149		145	

SOURCE: IRRU survey; specially prepared DE statistics, using national sample.

statistically significant. Whatever the exact figure, it is clear that re-employment is awarded in only a very small minority of cases where the applicant succeeds and that it forms a declining proportion of the remedies obtained by successful applicants. Thus, before examining the common remedy, compensation, we explore the reasons for the gap between the intention that unfairly dismissed workers should get back their jobs and the reality.

Tribunals and Re-employment

That the tribunals rarely award re-employment is indisputable. Why this is the case is due to a combination of factors which are difficult to weight. Before the legislative changes in 1976 described above the tribunals' lack of power to order rather than just recommend the specific remedies was suggested as one explanation (Williams, 1975: 292). But it is now clear that the explanation lies as much in the operation of the tribunals as in the nature of the statute.

The unfair dismissal law has moved quite far on the question of reinstatement since the introduction of statutory protection in 1971, but the tribunals have not moved with it. As the law now stands, the tribunals have discretion to make an order for reinstatement and in exercising this discretion must take into account

whether the complainant wishes to be reinstated; whether it is practicable for the employer to comply with an order for reinstatement [and] where the complainant caused or contributed to some extent to the dismissal, whether it would be just to order his reinstatement (EP(C)A s.69(5)).

The statute provides that the wishes of the applicant must be taken into account but not the *wishes* of the employer, only whether it is practicable for the employer to comply with a reinstatement order. Similar considerations apply to re-engagement. In practice, however, the wishes of the employer *are* taken into consideration. Indeed, the evidence suggests that the wishes of the employer rather than the employee are heeded more.

Tribunals define practicability in a narrow way. The interpretation is 'capable of being carried into effect with success' and, in determining this, tribunals 'have relied heavily upon the assessment of employers, few of whom have had any personal experience of the remedy in operation' (Williams and Lewis, 1981: 41). In union-supported claims, union arguments for re-employment may be persuasive as the perceived likelihood of workplace support for a re-employed worker may be a factor which enters into tribunal considerations of practicability. In practice tribunals appear to be willing to order re-employment only in cases where there are special circumstances relating to the applicant (such as apprenticeship or physical disability) which serve to underline the inadequacy of compensation as a remedy (Williams and Lewis, 1981:31). Of the eleven people in our applicant sample who obtained a re-employment order from the tribunal, three said that the employer had raised an objection. In thirty-nine of the fifty-six re-employment awards studied by Williams and Lewis practicability was seen by the tribunals almost exclusively in terms of an absence of controversy (1981: 29).

The importance which tribunals give to the views of the employer and their willingness to accept managerial arguments as to the impracticability of the specific remedies is in keeping with their general managerialist approach, discussed earlier in the context of the legal tests of fairness. But it also no doubt owes something to the belief that imposed re-employment will not work. The tribunals and the appeal court certainly have shown that they share other elements of this 'received wisdom' such as the general inappropriateness of ordering re-employment against small employers. In *Enessy Co. SA t/a The Tulchan Estate v Minoprio and Minoprio* [1978] IRLR 490 the EAT made its views *obiter* on the original order for reinstatement, saying:

> It is one thing to make an order for reinstatement where the employee concerned works in a factory or other substantial organisation. It is another to do so in the case of a small employer with few staff . . . Where there must exist a close personal relationship . . . reinstatement can only be appropriate in exceptional circumstances and to enforce it upon a reluctant employer is not a course which an industrial tribunal should pursue unless persuaded by powerful evidence that it would succeed.

It might also be noted at this point that it will be difficult for the typical applicant to begin to counter employer claims of impracticability. Applicants with representation at tribunal may be better able to do this but arguably this aspect of the tribunal's decision-making requires the adoption of an inquisitorial rather than adversarial approach and for the tribunal itself to undertake detailed inquiry as to practicability based on a presumption that unfairly dismissed workers should return to work if they wish. At the moment there appears to be little investigation other than ascertaining the two sides' wishes. Indeed, in some cases the tribunal appeared to be at best perfunctory in actually carrying out its duty of explaining the remedies to the applicant and asking whether re-employment is wanted. Thirty-two per cent of the 133 applicants in our sample who were awarded compensation by a tribunal said the tribunal had not asked them if they wanted their jobs back. Nine (21 per cent) of them said they had wanted their jobs back. Even allowing that some applicants may have forgotten the tribunal's inquiry, it would appear that in some cases exploration of the applicants' wishes did not take place or, and it amounts to the same thing in practice, was not understood as such. In some cases it may be known that the applicant has a new job but in our survey almost two-thirds of successful applicants were still unemployed at the time of the hearing.

Another factor behind the tribunals' reluctance to impose reinstatement may be a hangover from the traditional refusal of courts to order specific performance of a contract of employment. An awareness of this led the Donovan Commission to move away from reinstatement as the prime remedy. This course was later described by one of the Commissioners as 'unfortunate' and exemplifying the 'power of a legal shibboleth' that

> a contract of employment cannot be specifically enforced against either side because Equity does nothing in vain and also because an order for specific performance against the worker would savour of compulsory labour, and the rule of mutuality demands that if no such order can be made against the employee it cannot be made against the employer either (Kahn-Freund, 1978: 316).

This ghost of the common law still haunts judicial thinking about unfair dismissal and yet the basis on which the traditional refusal to order specific performance rests is shaky in respect of an employment contract.[1] As the quotation above indicates, the objections were of two kinds: firstly the view that such orders could not be effectively supervised and thus should not be made, and secondly that mutuality demanded that if a contract could be enforced then it had to be enforceable against either party and in relation to the employee this might amount to involuntary servitude and was therefore ruled out. These objections developed sequentially during the nineteenth century although, as Freedland (1976: 272) notes, they were more strongly felt against reinstatement than against orders to work and the Master and Servant Act 1867 did provide for the making of orders of specific performance against employees.

The personal nature of the contract and the equality of position as between the two parties which the common law presumes are clearly at odds with the real nature of a contract of employment and the realities

---

1. For a discussion of civil remedies for dismissal other than damages and those for unfair dismissal see Bowers, 1984: 2–8.

of the employment relationship. That the termination of the employment contract may have different consequences for employees and employers was recognised by the Donovan Commission (1968: para. 526) which argued:

> In practice there is usually no comparison between the consequences for an employer if an employee terminates the contract of employment and those which will ensue for an employee if he is dismissed. In reality people build much of their lives around their jobs. Their incomes and prospects for the future are inevitably founded in the expectation that their jobs will continue. For workers in many situations dismissal is a disaster.

As noted, however, the Donovan Commission hesitated to make reinstatement the prime remedy. The legislation has attempted to overcome this hesitancy but the tribunals have not.

Another factor which may influence tribunals' thinking about re-employment, given the importance they appear to attach to it being agreed rather than imposed, is the ACAS conciliation stage. As we discuss in the next chapter, the parties to an unfair dismissal case are given the opportunity to settle the case without the issue having to be determined by an industrial tribunal. There may be an unarticulated view that were re-employment possible it would have emerged as an agreed settlement.

It is impossible to quantify the relative importance of these various influences on the tribunals' approach to re-employment. But it is clear that there is a reluctance on the part of tribunals to exercise their discretion in favour of ordering employers to re-employ those whom they dismissed unfairly. At the moment, however, the extent and nature of this reluctance are masked by common assumptions about why there is so little re-employment. These are that applicants do not want to be re-employed; that employers will not accept re-employment and/or that it will not work. These assumptions are often forwarded as explanations for the low level of re-employment and appear to be shared by the tribunals themselves. We therefore shall examine them in some detail.

Applicants' Desire for Re-employment

The commonly held assumption that applicants do not want to be re-employed by their former employers needs to be examined on two levels: first, to what extent is this in fact the case, and, second, why it is that some applicants do not seek the specific remedies of reinstatement and re-engagement. Although the view that employees do not want to return to their former employment is often expressed (see, for example, *Sarvent and others v Central Electricity Generating Board*

[1976] IRLR 66), little is given by way of supporting evidence. One source of information is the tribunal application form (IT1) which, since March 1976, asks applicants which remedy they are seeking. Of the applicants surveyed 24 per cent stated that they had indicated on their application form a preference for reinstatement (22 per cent) or re-engagement (2 per cent) rather than compensation (69 per cent).

The IT1 question by implication encompasses the assumption that applicants are able to make an informed choice between the available remedies and are aware of the implications of their choice. Such an assumption is highly questionable: the typical applicant, unrepresented and often unadvised, is ill-equipped to consider the options properly, even if he or she has read and understood the guidance leaflet. Fifty-seven per cent of applicants were without any form of representation prior to the hearing stage and not all of those with representation will have been advised at the time of application. Each of the two booklets issued by the Department of Employment which applicants are advised to consult has shortcomings. One, 'Unfairly Dismissed', nowhere explains that re-employment is intended to be the prime remedy, that applicants are not necessarily bound by the preferences stated at the time of application, or that employer opposition does not necessarily mean it will be seen as impractical. The other, 'Dismissal – Employee Rights', is more informative in certain areas but does not actually define what the terms 'reinstatement' and 're-engagement' mean.

The IT1 question poses the remedies as an either/or choice. Although ultimately, of course, one remedy has to be chosen, at present some applicants may fear that if they request re-employment and fail to get it they will get nothing. As it is apparently seen as necessary or useful to have applicants indicate their choice of remedy at this early stage, an alternative form of words might be sought. One possibility is:

If it were possible, would you like to go back to work in the company or concern named as respondent, whether in the same job or a different one?	Yes, same job, same place
	Yes, different job, same place
(If for some reason it is not possible for you to go back, or if you change your mind about wanting to, you will still be entitled to money compensation if your dismissal is found unfair.)	Yes, same job, different place
	No, do not want to go back

Change along these lines may produce a higher proportion of applicants 'wanting' re-employment.

It is sometimes suggested that applicants may put reinstatement or re-engagement on the form, not because they actually wish to be re-employed, but because it is seen to be a good starting point in any negotiations with the employer or because they know the employer would not want them back and an unreasonable refusal to re-employ will lead to a higher award of compensation. This tactic, however, demands an understanding of the way the system operates which will be restricted to those applicants who have skilled and experienced representatives at the time of application. Although 44 per cent of those applicants who were union members sought re-employment compared with only 14 per cent of non-members, this does not of itself indicate tactical use of re-employment requests as there are other reasons why union members may opt for this remedy. Re-employment is the usual remedy where dismissals (or decisions to dismiss) are successfully challenged within voluntary procedures and unions and their members may therefore see this remedy as the 'natural' choice. Further, as Table 5.3 shows, applicants appear to view re-employment as more desirable or feasible within larger workplaces and workers in such establishments are more likely to be union members. Union members also may be more likely than non-members to seek re-employment because where re-employment is by a unionised employer the applicant's return will be supervised by the union and there is less likelihood of fear of unpleasantness or victimisation.

Although about three-quarters of the applicants put compensation as the preferred remedy on IT1, an examination of their reasons for so doing reveals that this should not be taken without question as evidence

TABLE 5.3
RE-EMPLOYMENT REQUESTS BY SIZE OF
DISMISSING ESTABLISHMENT

Size of Dismissing Establishment	% of Applicants in Size Band Requesting Re-employment on IT 1
below 10	15
10—19	18
20—99	25
100—499	29
500 and over	48

SOURCE: IRRU survey.

that re-employment is simply not wanted. The reasons given by applicants in the survey for not opting for reinstatement or re-engagement on IT1 indicate that some saw re-employment as physically impossible; others as unlikely because of the employer's attitude; while others gave reasons which could be recast as 'I would have wanted to go back if certain conditions could have been met' but opted for compensation because they had no reason to believe that such conditions would be realised or realisable. Fourteen per cent of the 762 applicants who requested compensation on the IT1 thought that it was impossible for them to return because of their own physical incapacity (1 per cent), because the employer would not agree (5 per cent), or because their particular job was no longer available or because the future of the company was in doubt (8 per cent): in these cases the applicants did not see return as an option and so the question of 'want' does not arise. In some cases, where the previously held job was no longer in existence but the employer continued in business, where the business was taken over, or where there was an associated employer continuing in business, *re-engagement* may have been a possibility but it is likely that most applicants are unaware of the scope of this form of re-employment.

Another 14 per cent (106) of applicants did not put re-employment down as the remedy sought because they apparently thought it would have to be a job they found unacceptable – either the previously held job with new conditions or an inferior one. (This group may include those claiming constructive dismissal who resigned because of unacceptable new conditions.) For example one applicant said: 'I was offered a job as a labourer. I decided that after being in a position of authority for ten months I did not want to go backwards'. Another did not opt for re-employment because 'I was offered a menial job . . . if they had offered my old job back I would have taken it'. Instead of seeing these applicants as saying 'I didn't want re-employment because . . .' their response could be seen as 'I did want re-employment *if* . . . ' (e.g. if I could have my old job back; if management had not been able to impose new requirements, etc.). If these conditions could have been met, re-employment *was* the preferred option.

A similar argument might be applied to the reasons for 'choosing' compensation given by another 21 per cent of applicants. These were people who chose compensation because they were worried about the awkward relationships or bad atmosphere which might exist if they were re-employed. Such fears were expressed as follows: 'it would have been difficult after I'd been sacked in such a way – he had said a lot to other workers'; ' "the atmosphere" would have deteriorated and things generally would have been not very good for obvious reasons'. Except in very small concerns, *re-engagement* might have provided a way of resolving the relationship problem. Again it is likely that some of these applicants did not understand that re-employment does not necessarily mean going back to the same job, working with the same people under the same supervision as before.

Of those applicants who opted for compensation 13 per cent (101) did so because they were afraid of victimisation if they returned to work for the same employer. Some feared they would be badly treated: 'if I'd gone back they'd have given me all the muck of the day. I would have been messed about'; 'if I'd gone back there they'd have made my life a misery — I'd found they were renowned for this sort of thing'. Others feared their re-employment would be followed by another dismissal: 'they would have got me out one way or another if I'd been reinstated'; 'I would never have had a life with them, he would have sacked me for something else'. Although these applicants may have wanted re-employment if they had not feared victimisation, it is difficult to allay such fears and re-engagement provides only limited scope for overcoming the problem. However, it is clearly inadequate to see the question of remedy in such cases as a matter of personal preference on the part of the applicants. What applicants 'want' is often determined by the employer's known or assumed position.

So far 62 per cent of those who did not put re-employment down as the preferred remedy on IT1 have been considered. Their reasons for choosing compensation indicate that to regard the low incidence of the specific remedies as a function of applicants' preference is simplistic and misleading. However, there were various reasons for not opting for re-employment, given by 34 per cent of applicants, which are more readily seen as cases where applicants do not want re-employment. These mainly concern the circumstances, fact or nature of the dismissal itself (14 per cent) or the lack of attractions the job had, or on reflection is seen to have had (18 per cent).

A number of applicants did not want to be re-employed because the way they had been treated destroyed any desire or willingness to work for that employer. One applicant explained he chose compensation as the preferred remedy 'because of what they had done. At the time I wouldn't have gone back at any price — it wasn't what they did — it was the way they did it', and another said 'I didn't want to go back — not after the way I got dismissed'. Others thought that the fact of dismissal itself was enough to make going back undesirable: 'it is a bad step to go back into something where you had been dismissed. Things would not have worked out'; 'I didn't think it was any good. I didn't want to work for a company I had been sacked from'. These comments seem to imply that if the contract could have continued in existence while the dispute was being resolved then remaining in the job might have been acceptable to the applicant, whereas returning to the job after having the contract terminated was seen as unacceptable.

Obviously the circumstances surrounding the dismissal and the fact of dismissal itself lead people to reassess their views of the people they worked with and for and the job they did. For some applicants the lost job had insufficient attractions to lead them to prefer re-employment to compensation: 'it was a cowboy outfit. No trade unions, nowhere to go for help. The proprietor got away with murder'; 'I didn't like the people I was working for – they were a load of crooks'; 'I wasn't making very good money, anyway'. However, this need not mean that these applicants would have left the job had it not been for the dismissal. A large number of people would find faults with their employment if required to consider and earlier research on unfair dismissal applicants indicates that 'the great majority were satisfied with their jobs before dismissal and had not thought of leaving' (Weekes et al., 1975: 17). It may be that a certain amount of *post facto* rationalisation and accommodation to the situation occurs on the part of some dismissed employees.

This examination shows that to dismiss the low and declining incidence of re-employment as unproblematic on the grounds that applicants do not want it is to sidestep the fact that applicants are often ill-equipped to choose between the remedies as they are required to do and, further, that they make their choice on the basis of certain assumptions and within certain constraints which, if changed, might increase the expressed desire for re-employment. Arguably, if re-employment is intended to be the prime remedy it is not enough merely to legislate that this is so; it is also necessary to seek to create a context within which it can be seen as preferable and viable. It is the viability of re-employment which is questioned by the argument that, even if applicants want re-employment, employers will not accept it.

Acceptance and Viability of Re-employment

Although the attitude of the employer may affect the likelihood of re-employment being agreed voluntarily through conciliation, theoretically employer opposition to re-employment should have no legitimacy at the tribunal stage. The matter is not one of voluntary agreement but of compliance with a judicial order. The remedies are enforceable *against* the employer who has acted unlawfully. The importance accorded by tribunals to employer views owes something to notions of employer prerogative in deciding whom to employ but is linked also to the more pragmatic contention that re-employment which has to be imposed by a tribunal 'will not work'. The contention that imposed re-employment will not work is difficult to evaluate partly because of the lack of evidence about re-employment in practice and partly because of the problem of deciding on the criteria by which re-employment should be assessed to adjudge whether it has or has not succeeded.

Re-employment is the usual remedy where dismissal is found un-justified within private appeal procedures both in this country and in the grievance arbitration system found in the unionised sector in the United States. This indicates that in certain circumstances employers are not opposed to re-employment. Also the general consensus is that under these provisions re-employment does work, which at least calls into question assumptions about the impossibility of re-establishing working relationships or the undermining of managerial authority by reinstating dismissed employees.

Both these examples concern union-organised employment, however, and it has already been noted that re-employment may be seen as more viable in such areas. As we noted in Chapter 2, respondents in unfair dismissal cases are generally small, non-unionised employers; almost half the unfair dismissal applications studied involved employers with total labour forces smaller than a hundred. What evidence is available, however, concerning reinstatement ordered by industrial tribunals indicates that, although small employers do pose problems, it would be wrong to assume that re-employment can never be a viable remedy in such cases. The major source of information is the Williams and Lewis study of all tribunal re-employment awards. They note that 'in per-haps a quarter of all cases (where there was an award) there was no return to work, usually because the employer in question simply re-fused to implement the tribunal's decision'. Non-return was associated with small employers but this is not of itself evidence that re-employ-ment will not work in such companies, rather that such employers are unwilling even to give it a try and apparently can ignore tribunal orders to re-employ without penalty as applicants rarely return to the tribunal to complain of non-compliance. Using length of return as one mea-sure of whether re-employment worked, they found that even among firms employing fewer than twenty people, half of the tribunal orders resulted in a period of re-employment lasting at least six months (1981: 24).

This raises the question of how one determines whether a rein-statement or re-engagement has worked. The usual measures are *em-ployer-based* criteria of whether the employee is still with the employer, if not, the length of the return period, and the employer's view of whether the re-employee has been satisfactory. Williams and Lewis suggest that only about a quarter of those who are actually re-employed stay for less than six months before they leave or are dismissed again, with the average length of re-employment being over a year. (This is depressed by the preponderance of cases from later years where the possible length of re-employment is obviously limited.) This would seem to indicate that employment relationships can be re-established successfully in a number of instances.

Even if the return period is short, re-employment might still be seen to 'work' if one adopts more *employee-based* criteria. One positive element in short-period return might be the increased ability to find another job. Re-employees are in a better position to look for another job than they would be if unemployed as a result of (albeit unfair) dismissal. Our survey revealed that 38 per cent (387) of all applicants, regardless of the outcome of their case, felt that their complaint about unfair dismissal made, or was making, it harder for them to find jobs. Of those who won at tribunal 36 per cent felt this. Returning to work and later resigning or even being made redundant may have the advantage of removing the stigma associated with dismissal and again make finding another job less difficult. Williams and Lewis found that resignation was the most common reason for leaving re-employment and that in one-fifth of the cases the re-employed worker was made redundant (1981: 11). From the applicant's point of view re-remployment -- even if only for a short time -- may work if their physical reappearance at the workplace shows workmates that managment cannot 'get away with' arbitrary, unfair behaviour. This may be particularly important in cases where dismissal is on grounds of trade union membership or activity, or race or sex discrimination. An interesting historical example of short-term reinstatement being regarded as satisfactory is provided by Goodrich (1975: 107) who recalls 'the strike of black country colliery enginemen that was settled in June, 1919, on the single condition "that the dismissed engineman be reinstated for an hour" '.

It is this type of consideration, however, which may lead employers to argue that re-employment from their point of view is unsuccessful: managerial authority being undermined by the presence of re-employed sacked workers. There is little evidence that this happens, but even if this might pose a problem for employers it is not clear why re-employment should then be regarded as unsuccessful. Arguably, if managerial authority which is exercised in a manner contrary to statute and industrial 'good practice' is curbed by the reinstatement of someone who was dismissed unfairly, this is a positive aspect of the remedy. It can be seen as negative only if re-employment is evaluated wholly according to the employer's interests.

Tribunals do tend, however, to adopt the employer's definition of success, which is whether the applicant on return would make a satisfactory employee and cause no managerial problems (as in the case of *Nothman v London Borough of Barnet (No. 2)* [1980] IRLR 65, CA), rather than considering the employee interests which might be served by re-employment. Again it should be recalled that the remedies are enforceable against employers and some discomfort to them may necessarily result.

This section has argued that employer opposition to the specific remedies should not be taken as a given or immutable constraint. Even where such opposition does exist its status as a legitimate reason for not implementing re-employment is questionable. Employee interests may be served by re-employment which would be adjudged a failure using employer-based criteria, but even using employer-based criteria what evidence there is cannot be seen as supporting the generalisation that re-employment will not work. It is necessary to distinguish the empirical observation that by some criteria re-employment is not working in certain cases now, from the qualitative judgment that re-employment as a remedy is unworkable. Once it is accepted that re-employment can 'work', steps can be taken to help ensure that it does.

Ultimately, however, as in the case of minimising employer opposition to re-employment in the first place, one comes back to the need to change the way in which re-employment is viewed so that it becomes the inevitable and accepted consequence of unfair dismissal. A pre-requisite for increased acceptability of the remedy would seem to be its greater frequency. This will require the tribunals to adopt a positive presumption in favour of re-employment as a desirable, viable and natural remedy for those who are unfairly dismissed and for them to award more orders for re-employment against unwilling employers. At the moment the employers who have re-employment awards made against them may, not surprisingly, see their position as abnormal, as the vast majority of other employers who have acted unfairly are required to pay compensation to discharge their liabilities. As the next section shows, these payments generally involve relatively low sums of money.

Tribunals and Compensation

In 1982, as shown in Table 5.1 above, compensation accounted for the majority of the remedies awarded by tribunals to successful applicants in unfair dismissal cases. Generally speaking, the compensation awarded by tribunals can have three elements: the basic award, the compensatory award, and an additional award. In cases concerning union membership dismissals a special award applies. The additional award applies only in cases where the employer fails to comply with an order for reinstatement. Given the rarity of such orders, discussed above, most awards consist of the two compulsory elements, basic and compensatory. The basic award, introduced in 1976, relates directly to the length of service of the employee in the job from which he or she was dismissed. The compensatory award concerns the loss sustained by the employee because of the dismissal. The total award is intended to encompass compensation for loss of accrued job rights, actual and potential loss of earnings and expenses incurred as a result of unfair dismissal, including loss of any benefit which might have been expected but for the dismissal, and any additional award for non-compliance with an order for re-employment.

On the face of it, therefore, it is surprising to find that the typical compensation award in 1982, although an increase on previous years, was only about £1,200. Table 5.4 shows the median compensation awards for each year since 1972. The median figures given in the table are approximate because the official statistics give grouped data only. in 1972 half the awards were under £150. In 1973, 1974 and 1975 and for dismissals up to 1 June 1976 about half the awards were under £200. After the introduction of the basic award in June 1976, there was a slight increase in the median amount for the rest of 1976, and in 1977 the median award was £300. In 1978 and 1979 half the awards were under £400 and in 1980 under £600. In 1981 there was a rise in the level of awards with a median of £960 and it reached £1,200 in 1982. The median figures are a better indication of the typical award than the mean average, also given, which is pulled up by a relatively small number of high awards. For example, in 1982 six per cent of awards were more than £5,000, while just over 40 per cent were below £1,000 (DE, 1983a: 449). The table also shows the relationship between tribunal compensation awards and average weekly earnings for all full-time workers. This can only be a rough indication of the 'real' value of compensation awards but it does show that whereas in 1972 and 1973 tribunals were awarding compensation amounting on average to around twelve times the average wage, by 1979 the awards were only eight times the average wage and in 1980, nine times. In 1981 and 1982 the increase in levels of compensation brought the relationship back to its 1972–3 position.

The statute provides the basis on which the compensation calculations must be made and thereby a maximum possible figure. In 1982 the maximum for cases other than those related to trade union membership and activities was £18,050, some fifteen times greater than the typical award of £1,200. This maximum, of course, includes the additional award maximum which in 1982 was £7,000. For an applicant to be awarded this particular maximum would require re-employment to have been ordered by the tribunal against an employer who had dismissed on grounds of sex or race and for that employer to have

TABLE 5.4

COMPENSATION AWARDED BY TRIBUNALS 1972–82

	1972	1973	1974	1975	1976	1977	1978	1979	1980	1981	1982
	£	£	£	£	£	£	£	£	£	£	£
Median compensa-tion amount	150	200	200	200	250	300	400	400	600	960	1,200
Average (mean compensation amount[a]	389	456	463	405	465	582	648	734	1,006	1,478	1,715
Average (mean) weekly earnings of all full-time employees[b]	32.0	36.4	41.6	54.0	64.2	70.2	79.1	89.6	110.2	124.9	136.5
Average compensa-tion divided by average earnings	12	13	11	7.5	7	8	8	8	9	12	13

NOTES:

a. Estimated from mid-points in frequency distribution: known awards. DE statistics. (*Employment Gazettes* 1974–84.)

b. Average weekly pay for all full-time workers. Calculated from NES. Men 21 years and over. Women 18 years and over excluding those whose pay was affected by absence (DE, 1982b: S50; DE, 1983c: S50).

refused unreasonably to comply with such an order. In addition the applicant will have had to have been earning at least £135 per week.[2] The extremely low incidence of re-employment awards has already been noted. Even where an award is made and not complied with, applicants do not appear to seek redress at the tribunal. Thus there is little potential for any additional awards; cases where the maximum might apply are even more unlikely. In most instances, therefore, the maximum possible award will be the basic and compensatory maxima combined. Amounting to £13,050 in 1982 this was still eleven times greater than the median compensation award.

If the question to be asked about the specific remedies is why is there so little re-employment, the question which arises when considering compensation awards is why are the amounts so low. The explanation lies in a combination of the principles underlying the calculation of compensation and the way in which tribunals exercise the discretion granted to them by the statute. This is now examined, with examples being drawn from reported and unreported decisions.

Compensatory Award

The basic approach to unfair dismissal compensation, introduced with the 1971 legislation and continued in the compensatory element of current awards, is that those dismissed unfairly should be recompensed for loss they suffer because of the dismissal but that the unfairness itself attracts no compensation – indeed the employer is not to be penalised. The Donovan Commission's suggestion that compensation be awarded for loss 'in injured feelings and reputation' (1968: para. 553), for example, was not even incorporated in the legislation. In discrimination cases tribunals can award compensation for injury to feelings but they have been discouraged from making other than small awards under this head.[3] The provisions show no awareness that awarding money damages over and above the compensation for demonstrable financial loss could have a broader function in providing a stimulus for change in keeping with the reform intentions of the legislation (discussed further in Chapter 8). This emphasis on compensation, rather than deterrence, is fostered by common law thinking. Lustgarten

2. Employment Protection (Variation of Limits) Order 1982 (SI 1982 No. 77). From February 1983 the limit on the amount of 'a week's pay' was raised to £140 by a similar order, No. 2 (SI 1982 No. 1866).
3. See *Coleman v Skyrail Oceanic Ltd* [1981] IRLR 398 where an Industrial Tribunal award of £1,000 for injury to feelings was reduced to £100 by the Court of Appeal.

(1980: 226) argues those

> steeped in common law see the choices as bounded by the poles of compensation and punishment because they restrict their focus to the plaintiff and the defendant in individual litigation. The deterrent-regulatory view becomes possible only when one's focus shifts to encompass the world beyond the specific case.

The elements that were to be compensated were soon formulated by the courts as loss of wages, the manner of dismissal, future loss of wages, and loss of protection in respect of statutory rights.[4] Loss of pension rights was added later, while the 'loss of protection' head became relatively unimportant with the introduction of the basic award, discussed below. For the most part the size of the compensation award depends on the applicant's loss of net wages pre- and post-hearing.

The main compensation for those successful applicants in heard cases who have found another job before the tribunal hearing will be net loss of earnings during the period between jobs. They will also be compensated for any adverse difference in the rate of pay in the new job for whatever period the tribunal considers just and equitable. For those still without jobs by the time of the hearing the tribunal will make an assessment of future loss of earnings. Because applicants for unfair dismissal come disproportionately from among low wage earners (Dickens et al., 1979: 12–13) the amount of loss of earnings is likely to be low and this will depress the awards.

As Table 5.5 shows, 36 per cent of the 145 successful applicants had found a new job before the date of the hearing. The calculation of their loss of earnings would be relatively simple. In 56 per cent of cases, however, the tribunals would have had to make an assessment of the time likely to elapse before a new job would be secured. Industrial tribunals are expected to draw upon their own knowledge and experience of the local employment situation in determining how long someone is likely to be unemployed and the rate of pay which might be expected in any new job.[5] This can only be informed guesswork partly because, as we observed in Chapter 3, the lay members generally will not come from the same industry as the one in the case they are hearing.

The tribunals are encouraged to adopt a broad approach and, other than where the applicant is approaching retirement age, our examination of decisions revealed that tribunals generally took an optimistic view of the chances of finding new jobs. They did, however, generally

4. *Norton Tool Co. Ltd v Tewson* [1972] IRLR 86, NIRC.
5. For example see *Bateman v British Leyland UK Ltd* [1974] IRLR 101, NIRC.

TABLE 5.5

SUCCESSFUL APPLICANTS AND NEW JOBS

	Number	%	
New job obtained:			
before applying	7	5	
between application and hearing	45	31	
			36
New job obtained after hearing	36	25	
No new job at time of interview, but looking	38	26	
No new job at time of interview, not looking	7	5	
			56
New job, stage not known	1	1	
Tribunal ordered re-employment	11	8	
	N = 145		

SOURCE: IRRU survey.

expect applicants to be flexible in job search and be prepared to move, both occupationally and geographically. A shop assistant in Sheffield was allowed four weeks' future loss which the tribunal felt was sufficient 'provided that the applicant tries hard to get a job in a wide variety of employment'.[6] Geographical mobility was expected particularly in occupations where this is considered common, such as catering. A head-chef dismissed unfairly from a hotel in Pembrokeshire 'where he had bought a home and hoped to settle' but where he had been unable to secure new employment was allowed ten weeks' future loss by a tribunal who did 'not think that he can reasonably object to moving away for the purpose of resuming gainful employment'.[7] A waiter, a man with four children, who had been unsuccessful in finding another job was told by the tribunal that it considered 'there are perfectly reasonable

6. *Challenger v Bambers* (1977) COIT 32605/77.
7. *Sasin v Imperial Hotel (Southcliffe) Ltd* (1977) COIT 28338/77.

prospects of his obtaining a suitable post perhaps out of the district soon'.[8] Perhaps because of the tribunal's view that 'waiters usually move from one job to another in fairly swift succession' there was no allowance in the compensation for anticipated removal expenses. The headchef in the previous case was awarded £100 for this which, given the real cost of moving house, can only be seen as a nominal or token award.

There was no evidence that tribunals, in assessing the length of time it will take to find a new job, saw the unfairly dismissed applicant as being in a position any different from that of other job seekers. However, the survey revealed that 48 (36 per cent) of the 134 applicants who won their cases but were not awarded re-employment felt that their cases made, or were making, it harder for them to find new jobs. The reasons given by these 48 applicants included a shortage of jobs in their particular trade (6 per cent), or their age, health or lack of confidence (8 per cent), or lack of a reference from their former employer (8 per cent). However, 27 per cent of the 48 felt it was harder to find work because having gone to a tribunal was held against them. One applicant said it was harder to find work 'because I've tried for so many jobs and as soon as I tell them I was sacked and took them to a tribunal it goes against me'. Another felt 'very strongly that the fact you have taken an employer to the tribunal does affect future employment. Some employers where I have applied have actually asked if I have been to an industrial tribunal'. Other applicants felt potential employers regarded them as untrustworthy or trouble-makers because they had made unfair dismissal claims against their previous employers. One felt the need 'to go through a hefty explanation' when looking for work as 'people think you are a troublemaker'.

Not all employers are going to take this attitude towards people who exercise their rights as another applicant's comment indicates: 'I had to tell him (the new employer) because he wanted to know why I'd left my previous job. He said *they* wouldn't dream of sacking anyone for being sick'. However, there is some supporting evidence that victimisation of tribunal applicants takes place. In 1978 one of the branches of the National Federation of the Self-Employed circulated to its members a 'blacklist' of employees who had brought cases, while an earlier survey brought forward this unsolicited opinion from one employer: 'A litigant even (especially?) if successful will not be regarded as an ideal recruit by employers and any financial gain will be outweighed by irreparable damage to career prospects' (Dickens, 1978–9: 18).

8. *Martinez v Dorchester Restaurant* (1976) COIT 3294/76,

The National Industrial Relations Court (NIRC), the EAT's prede-cessor, held in 1974 that although dismissed may be a distressing ex-perience it is not itself a matter for compensation. It expressed the hope 'that the decision of the Tribunal vindicating the employee by a finding of unfair dismissal would rectify any temporary mischief that might have occurred as a result of the dismissal whatever its manner may have been' and said it was only where there is cogent evidence that the manner of dismissal caused financial loss, for example by making it more difficult to find a new job, that the 'manner of dismissal' head of compensation becomes relevant. This, it thought, will be only on the very rarest of occasions.[9] The survey findings show that for at least some successful applicants vindication by the tribunal is not sufficient to rectify 'mischief' occasioned by the dismissal but cogent evidence will be almost impossible to produce.

The burden of proof is on the employee to prove how much he or she has lost or stands to lose by the dismissal. The EAT has stressed that 'the tribunal must have something to bite on, and if an applicant produces nothing for it to bite on he will have only himself to thank if he gets no compensation for future loss of earnings'.[10] Providing such evidence may be difficult and even then it is only one element since the tribunal decides future loss on its own assessment of what is likely to happen and on what it thinks might have happened if the employee had not been dismissed. It asks whether he or she would still have been in that employment, and, if the answer is 'no', then the loss which can be seen as arising from the dismissal is less. Thus, for example, where someone is unfairly dismissed on grounds of redundancy, the assess-ment of compensation depends on whether the tribunal finds he or she would have been made redundant fairly at a later date.[11]

As Table 5.6 shows, some successful applicants remained unemployed for quite long periods following their dismissal. Less than half the successful applicants in our survey found new employment within three months. Although we are unable to compare the tribunals' assessment of future loss with actual loss of earnings in individual cases, it seems likely that in some cases at least the tribunal will have underestimated. In others there may have been overestimation. This inaccuracy is un-avoidable given the present system of lump sum compensation rather than, say, a system of periodic payments.

Mistaken estimates of the time an applicant will take to find another job generally cannot be rectified. As tribunals are assumed to have

9. *Vaughan v Weighpack Ltd* [1974] IRLR 105, NIRC.
10. *Adda International Ltd v Curcio* [1976] IRLR 425.
11. *Delanaire Ltd v Mead* [1976] IRLR 340.

TABLE 5.6

SUCCESSFUL APPLICANTS' LENGTH OF TIME BETWEEN JOBS

Time between Jobs	Number	%
4 weeks or less	21	16
Over 4 weeks, less than 8 weeks	23	17
Over 8 weeks, less than 3 months	12	9
Over 3 months, less than 6 months	20	15
Over 6 months, less than 1 year	11	8
Over 1 year	2	1
Still unemployed at time of interview:[a]		
seeking work	38	28
not seeking work	7	5
	N = 134	

SOURCE: IRRU survey.
NOTE:
a. The bulk of interviews took place between January and April 1978. The applications involved had been made between October 1976 and September 1977.

drawn on their knowledge of local conditions in making their estimate, even if on appeal they are shown to have been mistaken, their decisions stand. In upholding a tribunal's refusal to grant a review in a case where an applicant was still unemployed fourteen weeks after the hearing at which the tribunal had decided two weeks would be sufficient for future loss, the NIRC endorsed the tribunal's reasoning that

> the Tribunal had to act upon the information then before it, and as is inevitable in cases where one has to forecast some future event or try to estimate a possibility of some future event occurring, one can be proved wrong by subsequent events. We do not think that we acted upon any false assumption, we assumed that the applicant would in the very near future obtain fresh employment. In the event we were wrong. He did not, or so we are told, but on the other hand if a finding is always open to review, if a fact assumed turns out to be false, it means there can be no finality of decision (*Vaughan v Weighpack Ltd* [1974] IRLR 105, NIRC).

Even if a review were to be granted in such circumstances, there is no guarantee that the tribunal would amend its estimate of future loss to the actual loss incurred. It might consider that the applicant had not shown the required enthusiasm or flexibility in job search that we discussed above.

The common law duty to mitigate loss which is written into the statute in s.74(4) applies equally when actual loss to the time of the hearing is being considered. The fact that an applicant has been unemployed for a certain number of weeks prior to the hearing does not mean that the tribunal will necessarily award the equivalent number of weeks' pay as compensation for loss of earnings. It may take the view that the applicant should have found a job sooner.

Applicants are expected to act as would a 'reasonable person' who had no expectation of any compensation from the dismissing employer. While this may not mean accepting the first job which is offered,[12] it does appear to mean that similar status jobs at similar or slightly lower rates of pay should not be turned down[13] and that some disadvantage may have to be suffered. A nurse, with a handicapped husband and three school age children, found temporary work after her dismissal but as this involved inconvenient travelling she gave it up and in so doing failed to mitigate fully her loss.[14] In another case an unfairly dismissed chargehand aged 58 refused to accept a job involving all-night work and paying £6 less a week. In view of his age and the economic situation the tribunal thought 'that he should have been readier to favourably consider work that he would not normally have considered in order to mitigate his own loss'. The cost of unfairly dismissing a man near retirement age in times of economic difficulty is thus borne not by the employer but by the dismissed employee who, in order to save his ex-employer money, has to accept an inferior job. The compensation would reflect the £6 a week less pay for a specified period but would allow nothing for the fact that it involved all-night work.[15] A quarter of the successful applicants in our survey who had found jobs by the time they were interviewed described their new job as 'worse overall' than the job from which they had been dismissed.

Tribunals may take the initiative in raising and exploring failure to mitigate but, strictly speaking, this is for the employer to prove. The task is easier where the applicant is alleged to have failed to mitigate loss by refusing an offer of re-employment. There are too few reported

12. *Bracey v Iles* [1973] IRLR 210.
13. *Betts v D. Beresford* [1974] IRLR 271.
14. *Hardwick v Leeds Area Health Authority* [1975] IRLR 319.
15. *Lloyd v Standard Pulverised Fuel Co. Ltd* [1976] IRLR 115.

cases where this has occurred to be able to make general statements but it appears that re-engagement rather than reinstatement is what is offered and refused. The tribunals in these cases appear to feel that applicants with long service before the unfair dismissal should not be expected to take too great a drop in salary or status in order to mitigate loss.[16] Given the tribunals' reluctance to force re-employment on unwilling employers it would be unfortunate if they appeared too willing to penalise employees for their unwillingness to accept it. However, some arguments for refusal, such as the economic circumstances of the company not ensuring security of employment, have been rejected[17] and, as we shall discuss below, the Employment Act 1980 increased the penalty (by putting the basic award at risk) for applicants who unreasonably refuse reinstatement offers.

A situation exists, therefore, where an applicant who wants compensation may be penalised for refusing an offer of re-employment under failure to mitigate loss, while an applicant who is seeking reinstatement may be penalised under failure to mitigate loss for not actively seeking a new job elsewhere. Although the duty of those seeking damages to mitigate their loss is a well-established common law rule, its appropriateness can be questioned in a context where the primary remedy is not a financial one but reinstatement.

The statute provides that the compensatory award shall be such amount

> as the tribunal considers just and equitable in all the circumstances having regard to the loss sustained by the complainant in consequence of the dismissal in so far as that loss is attributable to action taken by the employer (EP(C)A s.74(1)).

We have seen how, in deciding whether there has been a failure to mitigate, the tribunal has scope to exercise its discretion to reduce the amount of compensation which would otherwise be awarded. Some of the loss sustained by the applicant is held not to be attributable to the action of the employer in dismissing. Another way in which the tribunal may exercise its discretion to reduce the level of compensation is by finding that the applicant contributed to the dismissal.

Of the 133 applicants in the sample who were awarded compensation by a tribunal, 43 per cent said that a deduction had been made. Of these, 2 per cent said they did not know the reason why a deduction had been made from their compensation. Half of the applicants affected

16. See, for example, *Tiptools Ltd v Curtis* [1973] IRLR 276; *Ramsay v W. B. Anderson & Son Ltd* [1974] IRLR 164.
17. e.g. *Gallear v J. F. Watson & Son* [1979] IRLR 306.

(a fifth of all compensation applicants) said the deduction was made because of contribution to their own dismissal, while the same proportion said the deduction was made for some other reason. This will no doubt include deductions because of failure to mitigate but it is also possible that some applicants may have considered the recoupment of unemployment benefit as a deduction[18] and others may have already received some payment from the employer, the amount of which will have been deducted from any award. It is also possible that some deductions were not seen, or presented, as such. Tribunals used to express failure to mitigate assessments as a percentage or in terms of amounts of money or days etc. They are now encouraged to adopt the latter course. Where an applicant has been unemployed for fifteen weeks but the tribunal feels he or she should have got a job after ten weeks it will award ten weeks' net pay rather than reduce the loss calculation by one third. The applicant may not see this as a 'deduction' and so it will not be included in the figures given.

Reduction in compensation awards because of contribution to own dismissal can have the effect of bringing compensation down to very low levels. In some cases tribunals have regarded it as 'just and equitable' to deny an unfairly dismissed worker any compensation at all. There appear to be cases where the tribunals and courts feel they have no option but to find dismissal unfair and yet are uneasy about it and whittle away the compensation remedy. There are two main kinds of case giving rise to this unease: those where the unfairness comes from the manner of dismissal rather than the reason for it; and those where the applicant's behaviour seems to warrant some sanction, although dismissal is thought by the tribunal too severe and therefore unfair. The attack on compensation in such cases can come through finding that no loss actually resulted from the dismissal and so nothing stands to be compensated for, or by finding that the applicant contributed substantially to his or her own dismissal.

The logic of finding someone was unfairly dismissed and then denying any remedy was questioned by the EAT in England which attempted to prevent deductions greater than 80 per cent. (See *Kemp v Shipton Automation Ltd* [1976] IRLR 305.) It also expressed disquiet over nil compensation awards in cases where the tribunal held that although the employer failed to follow procedure or otherwise act reasonably, the

---

18. Employment Protection (Recoupment of Unemployment Benefit and Supplementary Benefit) Regulations 1977 (SI 1977 No. 674) apply. The tribunal award of compensation includes a prescribed element from which the Department of Employment recoups any unemployment or supplementary benefit from the employer. The applicant receives the rest.

outcome would have been the same even if proper steps had been taken. Such an approach, argued Phillips J., tended to treat 'technical' unfairness as of a lesser order which might undermine the intentions of the legislation and Code to develop good practice.[19] However, the House of Lords in *Devis & Sons Ltd v Atkins* [1977] IRLR 314 maintained that nil awards can be just and equitable where the employee suffered no injustice in being dismissed, an approach followed by the EAT in *Allders International Ltd v Parkins* [1981] IRLR 68.

In private grievance arbitration procedures the possibility normally exists of imposing a lesser sanction where dismissal is found to have been unwarranted. The tribunals would have similar scope to do this were reinstatement in fact the prime remedy by, for example, awarding re-employment without backpay, the equivalent of suspension without pay. However, compensation is in practice the major remedy and therefore the tribunals have only limited scope to substitute a lesser sanction for dismissal. Instead the view that, although dismissal was too severe a sanction in the circumstances, the employee was to some extent deserving of blame, encourages reductions in compensation awards.

Deductions can occur in cases of dismissal for alleged misconduct where the tribunal considers that the dismissal was unfair but some disapproval has to be expressed of the employee's action. But deductions have been made even where the act or omission leading to dismissal could not be termed misconduct as, for example, in the refusal to work non-contractual overtime[20] or in pressing for wage increases.[21] Here tribunals have focused on the manner of refusal or the unreasonableness of refusal. A supervisor who refused to work a new rota contrary to his contract of employment which also stated his agreement was needed before any change could take place was dismissed without warning, having absented himself from work rather than be forced into working the new rota. In so doing, the tribunal held, he had put himself in the wrong. Despite his feeling that to work the new rota under protest would lead inevitably to his having to accept the new arrangements, the tribunal thought he should at least have tried it and reduced the compensation by 75 per cent.[22]

The impression given by this and certain other cases is that there is an onus on the employee not only to avoid acting in a way which might justify dismissal but to do all he or she can to *prevent* dismissal in

---

19. *Trend v Chiltern Hunt Ltd* [1974] IRLR 66, EAT. But see above p. 102, for a discussion of the weakening of procedural standards.
20. *Deegan v Norman & Sons Ltd* [1976] IRLR 139.
21. *Dobson and others v K. P. Morritt Ltd* [1972] IRLR 101.
22. *Gillanders v Riding Hall Carpets* [1974] IRLR 327.

circumstances where it is not justified but where the employer is set upon it. Examples of this were found in our examination of tribunal decisions. For instance, an employee told to leave after a disagreement with the works' manager was held to have contributed to his dismissal because he did leave the premises rather than attempt to bring about some kind of reconciliation beyond telephoning in. The works' manager who had provoked the walking off was described by the tribunal as 'unbending' and indeed the 'walking off can be seen as part of the cooling off period' the works' manager had anticipated. None the less the tribunal put the onus on the applicant to be conciliatory and deducted 50 per cent from his award for not trying harder to prevent being unfairly dismissed.[23] The same proportion was deducted in a case where the applicant, told at 3 o'clock she was being made redundant that day, failed to go to see management before leaving at 5 o'clock, to explain that she was better qualified than the person nominated to take over another job in the company and that she had not previously understood that she was faced with an either/or situation when some time earlier she had been offered another post. That management's failure to make this clear to her or to inform themselves of the relative skills of their workforce had in fact contributed to the finding of unfair dismissal did not prevent the 50 per cent reduction for contribution.[24]

The Court of Appeal in *Nelson v BBC (No. 2)* [1979] IRLR 346 provided some guidance for tribunals in determining whether to make a decision for contributory fault. The degree of contributory fault, however, has been held to be a question of fact, a matter for the tribunal alone to decide; the EAT cannot substitute its own percentage figure.[25]

Basic Award
The low levels of compensation and the fact that the courts saw it as 'just and equitable' that employees who were held to have been dismissed unfairly should not only be denied re-employment but should get little or nothing in the way of compensation prompted the Labour government to institute legislative change in the mid-1970s (DE, 1974a: para. 25). The attempt to increase re-employment has already been noted. The other concern was to increase the level of compensation awards and, in particular, to ensure that everyone who was found to be unfairly dismissed was awarded at least some compensation. The mechanism designed to achieve this was the basic award, to be calculated in the

23. *Brockett v Flender (UK) Ltd* (1977) COIT 33026/77.
24. *Walkey v M. Martin Construction Ltd* (1977) COIT 29551/77.
25. *Hollier v Plysu Ltd* [1983] IRLR 260.

same way as payments for redundancy but with a minimum of two weeks' pay.

The introduction in 1976 of a compulsory basic award did have an effect in slightly increasing the level of tribunal compensation awards. Indeed, if it had not been for the basic award provision in the years 1977 to 1982, 1,782 applicants who won their cases would have been denied a remedy (DE, 1981a: 82; DE, 1981b: 539; DE, 1982a: 520; DE, 1983a: 449). This represents some 13 per cent of those who were awarded compensation by tribunals in this period. Because the basic award is calculated as roughly one week's pay for each year's service, the fact that a high proportion of applicants had fairly short service in low paid jobs tends to reduce the compensation-boosting effect of the basic award and therefore the notion of a minimum was of particular importance. In 1978, the last year for which this statistic is given, 2,477 people were awarded compensation by a tribunal, and in 13.8 per cent of cases the amount of the basic award was the minimum of two weeks' pay (DE, 1979a: 866). A large proportion of these applicants would have received a lesser or no basic award if the calculation had been simply on the basis of calculating a redundancy payment, with no minimum.

The introduction of the minimum level award was an intentional departure from the notion that only financial loss be compensated. As the then Secretary of State for Employment explained,

> the first justification for providing the irreducible basic award in addition to full compensation for financial loss is that unfair dismissal can be a serious event in the life of the individual employee, so much so that compensation for loss will often under present legislation be an inadequate remedy ... The provision to guarantee an irreducible minimum of 2 weeks' pay is no high level of award against elements to be considered such as damage to reputation and effect on one's career – even in circumstances where somebody on being unfairly dismissed can immediately secure another job. It is this type of consideration which leads to the irreducible minimum (7 Parl. Deb HC Standing Committee F, 8 July 1975, col. 1138).

However, the courts were reluctant to accept the notion of a minimum award regardless of loss. The House of Lords decried the minimum basic award as a 'rogues' charter' in the *Devis* case,[26] where an employee had concealed his misconduct until after dismissal, and expressed the hope that the matter would receive the early attention of Parliament. The

26. [1977] IRLR 314.

Employment Act 1980 provided the desired response; the minimum level was abolished.[27] At the same time new grounds were enacted for reducing the level of the basic award. The award can now be reduced for unreasonable refusal of a reinstatement offer and because of the employee's conduct before the dismissal even if not related to the dismissal, as well as for contribution to own dismissal and in respect of any redundancy payment received.

The legislative change in 1976 might have made it clearer that the minimum sum was to compensate for the unfairness of the dismissal per se – an unfairness which existed whenever a tribunal held a dismissal unfair regardless of an element of blameworthiness on the part of the applicant or failure to mitigate etc. This might have been achieved by separating the idea of a minimum level of compensation from the idea of a basic award related to length of service. Because of the method of calculating the basic award the tendency was for the courts to see it as a substitute redundancy payment and for it therefore to be seen as inappropriate for people who would not have been entitled to a redundancy payment, because of their age or service, to obtain the minimum basic award compensation when unfairly dismissed. This is the idea of only compensating actual loss creeping back in despite the conscious departure from it. Because of this view the Conservative government returned in 1979 could 'see no justification in principle why an employee should be paid a minimum of two weeks' pay when by reason of his age and length of service he would have qualified for less than this amount' (DE, 1979b: 875). The justification, however, as the present authors have argued elsewhere (Dickens et al., 1979: 12), is that the basic award is *not* a redundancy payment. Although calculated on the same principle, it is a payment which acknowledges that an employee has suffered an injustice (apart from actual loss) in being unfairly dismissed. By providing some minimum penalty against employers who dismiss unfairly, it underlined the aim of encouraging employers to act reasonably.

This discussion has shown that the statute enables only certain kinds of loss following the dismissal to be compensated. The basis of the compensation calculation, combined with certain characteristics of applicants (low pay, short service), and the tribunals' attitudes towards future loss, together produce rather low awards. These are often further reduced by such extent as the tribunal considers just and equitable on grounds of contribution to own dismissal or failure to mitigate loss. The

---

27. Employment Act 1980 s.8(4) now EP((C)A s.73(7A), (7B). Section 9(5) 410 HL Deb 11 June 1980, 390 makes clear that the Lords' comments were influential.

introduction of an irreducible minimum level of compensation not dependent on financial loss was an important change in principle (the low level of the minimum limited its impact on compensation levels in practice) but one which has been reversed for the general run of dismissal cases. For dismissals on grounds of union membership or activities, or non-membership of a union, however, the minimum award concept has been re-introduced (see below p. 249).

Summary

This chapter began by noting that, despite the statute's emphasis on re-employment as the remedy for unfairly dismissed workers and the strengthening of this remedy in 1976, tribunals have always been reluctant to award it. Lack of desire on the part of applicants for this remedy was seen to be at best a superficial explanation for the low level of re-employment awards, since our research shows that applicants are often ill-equipped to choose between the remedies as they are required to do and that they make their choice on the basis of certain assumptions – some concerning the attitude of the employer – and within certain constraints which if changed might increase the expressed desire for re-employment.

The industrial tribunals pay a lot of attention to the employers' views regarding the acceptability and practicability of re-employment and rarely award the remedy in the face of employer opposition. This is partly because of a view that re-employment which has to be imposed will not work. We argued that employer opposition should not be taken as a given or immutable constraint and noted that enforced re-employment could be seen to work particularly if *employee*- rather than *employer*-based criteria of success were adopted.

In examining the common remedy, compensation, we found that despite an increase in the level of awards made in 1981 and 1982, the average award is still a relatively small amount, falling far short of the statutory maximum. The explanation was found in the statutory principles underlying the calculation of compensation and in the way in which tribunals exercise the discretion granted to them by statute in determining what would be just and equitable. Only certain kinds of loss are compensatable. There is no intention that the employer should be penalised for dismissing unfairly. A deterrent-regulatory view of money awards is not taken and to adopt anything other than *restitutio in integrum* (that is, putting the applicant in the position in which he or she would have been if the wrong had not been sustained) would be seen by the courts to represent 'punishment' of the employer (Lustgarten, 1980: 226). The nature of applicants, low wage earners with short service, depresses the level of awards. They are often reduced further because the tribunals find the applicants contributed to their dismissals or failed to mitigate loss. Taken together, the limited use of the re-employment remedy and the way in which compensation is assessed serve typically to set a low price on the unfair deprivation of a job and can have little deterrent value for most employers.

In Chapter 2 we saw that only a minority of dismissed workers apply to an industrial tribunal to challenge the fairness of their dismissals. Chapter 4 revealed that less than a quarter of those applicants who get to a hearing actually win their cases and in this chapter we have seen that the typical remedy for the successful applicant is a relatively small sum of money. It is, however, only a minority of unfair dismissal claims that are actually determined by the industrial tribunals; 35 per cent in 1982. The remainder are nearly all disposed of as a result of ACAS conciliation. To have a full picture of the industrial tribunal system, therefore, we need to examine this less visible aspect. The importance of the ACAS stage can be demonstrated, in the context of the subject of this chapter, by noting that in 1982 only 11 per cent of all applicants were awarded a remedy by an industrial tribunal, but 32 per cent obtained a remedy through ACAS conciliation.

6

The Invisible Stage: ACAS Conciliation

This chapter looks at the invisible stage in the industrial tribunal system: where ACAS attempts to dispose of unfair dismissal cases without the need for a tribunal hearing in accordance with s.134 of the EP(C)A. This provides, in part, that where an unfair dismissal complaint has been made it shall be the duty of the conciliation officer

(a) if he is requested to do so by the complainant and by the employer against whom it was presented, or

(b) if, in the absence of any such request, the conciliation officer considers that he could act under this section with a reasonable prospect of success,

to endeavour to promote a settlement of the complaint without its being determined by an industrial tribunal.

Only a minority of applications for unfair dismissal are heard by the tribunals, most are disposed of following action by an ACAS conciliation officer. A consideration of how this stage operates and what it achieves is thus crucial to an evaluation of the system and its handling of unfair dismissal cases.

As Table 6.1 shows, only 32 per cent of unfair dismissal applications handled by ACAS in 1982 went on to be determined by a tribunal. The trend is not smooth but over time the proportion of cases going to hearing has declined with more applications being withdrawn without settlement (24 per cent in 1983) or being settled as a result of ACAS conciliation (40 per cent) than being heard.

The importance of the ACAS stage lies not only in the fact that it disposes of more cases than are heard by tribunals but also in the way in which they are disposed: by conciliation rather than judicial adjudication. State provision of conciliation to facilitate dispute settlement has a long history in British industrial relations, with its formal roots in the Conciliation Act 1896 (Dickens, 1979: 290). The essence

TABLE 6.1

ACAS CLEARANCE RATES: UNFAIR DISMISSAL

	1975	1976	1977	1978	1979	1980	1981	1982	1983
	%	%	%	%	%	%	%	%	%
Conciliated settlement	31	32	33	35	36	45	37	39	40
Private settlement	3	4	5	4	4	3	3	3	3
Withdrawn without settlement	24	20	21	23	23	23	25	26	24
Proceeded to tribunal	42	44	41	37	36	30	35	32	33
N[a] =	24,367	36,562	39,168	37,797	39,816	38,154	43,769	41,481	37,123

SOURCE: ACAS *Annual Reports* 1976–83.

NOTE:

a. Number of unfair dismissal cases completed by ACAS during year in question. This does not correspond exactly with the number of cases disposed of by industrial tribunals in the same year.

of conciliation is that the parties voluntarily agree their own settlement to the dispute rather than having one imposed upon them. The inclusion of a conciliation stage in the tribunal system for dealing with unfair dismissal applications reflects the value attached to amicable settlement of disputes between employers and employees in a way conducive to good industrial relations, as well as a desire for some filter mechanism to prevent overloading the tribunals (Donovan, 1968: para. 584; Clark, 1970: 35).

In this chapter we look at why the majority of applicants do not pursue their claims for unfair dismissal to a hearing and discuss the factors which encourage some applicants and employers to settle. The way in which ACAS perceives and undertakes its conciliation function in unfair dismissal cases is then examined and the outcomes of conciliation are discussed. Finally we evaluate ACAS conciliation in terms of its usefulness to the parties and to the administrative efficiency of the system and in terms of its effectiveness with regard to its qualitative results.

Why Applicants do not Proceed to Hearing

Generally speaking, and not surprisingly, applicants withdraw their claims when they feel that there is nothing to gain, or something to lose, in pursuing a case to a tribunal hearing. Their perceptions of what might happen at tribunal and the relative advantages and disadvantages of continuing the case are therefore of major importance. Applicants who do not go to a hearing divide into those who drop their claims (35 per cent of non-heard cases received by ACAS in 1983) and those who agree a settlement (62 per cent of non-heard cases in 1983 (ACAS, 1984: 79)). We look at each of these groups in turn.

Withdrawal without Settlement

In our survey 187 applicants withdrew their unfair dismissal claims without settlement. They constituted 18 per cent of all applicants in the sample (as Table 6.1 indicates this is a smaller proportion than withdrawn applicants constitute of all unfair dismissal applicants) and 29.5 per cent of all those who did not pursue their cases to a tribunal hearing. Their reasons for dropping their claims, given in response to an open-ended question, are shown in Table 6.2.

One would expect that people who apply to a tribunal and later discover that they are not in fact qualified (perhaps because of insufficient service or their age) would drop their claim. This is particularly so as ACAS will tell such people that they appear unqualified and explain that there is the risk of costs being awarded against them if

TABLE 6.2

APPLICANTS' REASONS FOR WITHDRAWAL WITHOUT SETTLEMENT

	No.	% of Applicants
Realised/advised I would lose	72	39
Realised/advised I was not qualified	22	12
Couldn't afford to go on/waste of time and/or money	22	12
Found another job	12	6
Trouble getting evidence/witnesses	11	6
Nervousness/illness	9	5
Fed up with the bother	8	4
Fear of victimisation	6	3
Afraid of the tribunal/of things coming out	2	1
No representative	2	1
Hadn't really wanted to apply	1	—
Other	41	22

N = 187

(Multi-response possible.)

SOURCE: IRRU survey.

they pursue the case to a tribunal. A number of would-be applicants (some 10 per cent) who are unqualified to bring a case will have been filtered out during the process of registration by the Central Office of Industrial Tribunals, but 12 per cent of those applicants withdrawing without remedy gave this reason. A much larger proportion, 39 per cent, withdrew without settlement because they realised or were advised that they would lose at a tribunal hearing or did not have a good case. This category and the former are not necessarily mutually exclusive since the weaknesses of some cases may have related to qualification. But not all of those who thought they would lose saw their cases as weak; in some cases the pessimism arose from perceived difficulties in case preparation and presentation.

Nor does having nothing to gain by going to tribunal mean only that the applicant feels he or she might lose. It may mean that the cost —

in time and effort as well as financial — may be seen to outweigh any potential benefit. Twelve per cent of all applicants who withdrew without settlement did so for this reason. Those applicants who employed a legal representative were likely to incur greater expense than other applicants. Analysis of reasons for withdrawing by representation revealed that 19 per cent of applicants with legal representation withdrew because of the expense, compared with 13 per cent of unrepresented applicants. No applicant represented by a union gave this as a reason for withdrawing — they were more likely than other applicants to withdraw because of advice that they would lose or for 'other' reasons. Quite a large proportion (22 per cent) gave individual reasons for withdrawing their claim which could not be classifed under the coded categories. Among these 'other' reasons were lack of trade union support and withdrawal because the issue was determined through private procedures. The costs involved may relate also to the effort required or the effect on nerves or health; these reasons were given by small numbers of those who withdrew their applications.

Finding a new job may increase the likelihood of withdrawal as not only is actual and potential loss reduced, and hence the level of possible compensation lower, but attending the tribunal would involve loss of time from the new employment and perhaps the necessity of unwelcome explanations. However, the majority (54 per cent) of applicants who did not go to hearing did not find a new job until after the end of their cases. For such applicants therefore this potential reason for withdrawal did not apply. As Table 6.2 shows, only 6 per cent gave 'found a new job' as a reason for dropping their claims.

Agreeing to Settle

Although about a quarter of the cases handled by ACAS do not proceed to tribunal because the application is withdrawn, a higher proportion fail to get to hearing because a settlement is agreed. In our survey 42 per cent of all applicants, or 70.5 per cent of those not pursuing their claims to a hearing, settled their claims.

If an applicant can achieve what is wanted or expected without a tribunal hearing then nothing is to be gained by pursuing the case. As Table 6.3 shows, this underlies the reasons for not proceeding given by the highest proportion of those applicants in our survey who settled their claims. Twenty-two per cent of the 447 settling applicants said they settled rather than go to hearing because they got all they asked for or what they thought was due to them. One applicant typical of this group said he accepted settlement 'because they offered as much as I could have got from a tribunal anyway so there was no point

TABLE 6.3

APPLICANTS' REASONS FOR SETTLING CLAIM

	No.	% of Applicants
Got all I asked for/was due	98	22
Would get no more at tribunal	92	21
Did not want to go to tribunal	70	16
Accepted rather than risk losing	63	14
ACAS advised me to	60	13
Representative advised me to	49	11
Financial difficulty	23	5
Cost of tribunal	23	5
Illness	16	4
Other	73	16
Don't know	13	3

N = 447

(Multi-response possible.)

SOURCE: IRRU survey of applicants.

in going on', and another 'because they offered me the full amount of salary in lieu of notice that I felt was due to me'. This last-quoted comment indicates that applicants may have limited expectations of what is due to them; what is asked for or expected may be substantially less than a tribunal would award if the dismissal was held to be unfair. However, it also indicates that remedies may be achieved through conciliation which cannot be sought directly from the tribunal; for example, the payment of outstanding holiday money, or, perhaps as in this case, the conversion of summary dismissal into dismissal with notice or pay in lieu.

The next highest proportion (21 per cent) of applicants who accepted a settlement did so because they were advised or decided they would get no more at the tribunal than was being offered by the employer. But in weighing up the pros and cons of proceeding to a hearing it is not only financial considerations which are influential. The 16 per cent shown in Table 6.3 as settling because they did not want to go to the tribunal were concerned about the fuss, publicity, stress or strain they thought this would involve. For these people, accepting a settlement appeared to be the easier course.

For others the trade-off was perceived not as between the possibility of an award higher than the settlement and the strain of proceeding but as between the certainty of obtaining something and the risk of getting nothing. Fourteen per cent fell into this category: 'it may have gone against me at the tribunal so I decided to accept the offer rather than risk losing or getting less' was a typical statement here. Some (11 per cent) acted on advice to this effect from representatives: 'my solicitor advised me to take it in case I lost the case, so it was better to take this than nothing'. Others (13 per cent) said they acted on ACAS advice to settle: 'the officer told me to accept the pay offer', said one, while another reported, 'the conciliation man said I should accept. My husband said I shouldn't. I took the conciliation man's advice and signed the paper'.

Obviously applicants cannot consider settling the case rather than proceeding to a hearing unless the respondent employer is prepared to settle as well. In fact very few applicants refuse offers of settlement made to them and so the employers' preparedness to settle appears to be the crucial factor. The vast majority of the 429 applicants we surveyed whose cases were heard by an industrial tribunal had not been offered settlement. Of the remaining 20 per cent who had received offers of settlement, 2 per cent did so only on the actual day of the hearing.

Employers' Preparedness to Settle

It is clear from Table 6.4 that a large proportion of employers who are prepared to settle see it as a way of saving money and time. Forty-two per cent of the 449 employers we surveyed who were involved in settled cases gave 'saving money/settlement the cheaper option' as a reason for preferring to settle the case. One employer preferred to settle 'because of finance. I was advised to offer him a sum to avoid the greater cost of going to tribunal', and another said 'we agreed the £150. The lawyer said it would cost us £200 if we went to tribunal in fees and witnesses, even if we do win, so we just settled for £150. It was cheaper to settle out of court'.

There is a significant cost saving involved in settling rather than going to a hearing. Information on costs incurred was sought from the 1,080 employers surveyed. Some incurred no financial cost. This was particularly so among employers in cases which did not reach a hearing, 59 per cent of whom had no costs to meet. Among those in heard cases only 17 per cent were in this position. Leaving aside these employers, and a further 97 who were unable to provide information about costs

TABLE 6.4

EMPLOYERS' REASONS FOR AGREEING SETTLEMENT

	No.	*% of 449 Employers*
Would cost more to go to hearing	190	42
To save time	122	27
Suggested/advised by representative	45	10
Did not want to go to tribunal (reputation)	46	10
Weak case/fear of losing	42	9
Could lose on 'technicality'/had not followed procedure	39	9
Dismissal was unfair	36	8
To get it over with	30	7
Suggested/advised by ACAS	25	6
Industrial tribunal system favours applicants	19	4
Wanted to be rid of applicant/did not want to reinstate	7	2
Applicant asked for settlement	10	2
Too upset/nervous to go on	3	1
Other	36	8
(Multi-response possible.)		

SOURCE: Survey of employers.

incurred, if any, enables calculation of the average known final cost of the remaining 535 employers. The average known final costs incurred by employers in the survey who were involved in cases withdrawn with settlement was about £50 (at 1977 prices). The average known final cost for those employers in cases which went to a hearing was over £130. For those who had employed legal representation at hearing the average known final cost was over £230. These figures exclude any payment or compensation award to the applicant. They are actual costs incurred in defending the case and do not include any estimate of value of time spent. Time saving was often coupled with financial saving as a reason for settling: as one employer said, 'it would have cost more money and time to go through to tribunal than settle'.

Settlement may appear as the cheaper option not only because any costs in going to tribunal are avoided but also because going to tribunal might result in an award of compensation higher than the settlement figure. The 42 per cent of settling employers who saw settlement as a cheaper option included some who feared they would lose at hearing. As one employer, who said he settled to save legal fees, admitted, 'it is fair to say that I felt we did not have a strong enough case in this instance'. As Table 6.4 shows, about a quarter of settling employers said they settled because they would or might lose at a hearing through substantive or procedural unfairness.

In the main, however, employers tend to take an optimistic view of their chance of having the fairness of a dismissal upheld. This has led to talk of 'nuisance payments': employers having to buy off cases they would win in order to avoid expenditure of time and money in defending at a hearing or just to have done with it. The low applicant success rate discussed in Chapter 4 makes employer optimism seem well founded, but some (although perhaps only a minority) so-called 'nuisance settlements' may allow the employer to escape having to comply with a greater monetary award by a tribunal. An indication of this is provided by looking at those employers who did *not* make any offer of settlement. Of employers who insisted on having the case heard by tribunal because they were sure they would win, 29 per cent in fact lost.

Where the parties do settle the case without a tribunal hearing they normally do so through ACAS conciliation. As Table 6.1 showed, ACAS's statistics show very few settlements being reached privately. The official statistics record as 'conciliated settlements' all cases which are terminated under the auspices of a conciliation officer, usually recorded on an ACAS form, which prevents the case being heard by a tribunal. Because of the special status of agreements reached with the involvement of a conciliation officer, ACAS in fact may be called in after provisional agreements have been reached independently by the parties or their representatives rather than to help initiate such agreements. None the less, ACAS is seen as the major channel through which settlements are arranged. When asked how their settlement was arranged, 60 per cent of applicants and 65 per cent of employers in our survey said it was done through ACAS. Those applicants with trade union or legal representation and those employers who employed external legal representatives generally thought settlement had been achieved via their representative. This does not, of course, mean the representative may not in turn have used ACAS conciliation officers in achieving a settlement. We now examine the characteristics of these officers and the way in which they operate the conciliation stage.

ACAS Organisation for Conciliation

At the time most of the fieldwork for this study was undertaken in 1979, ACAS had 207 people employed on individual conciliation, accounting for approximately 55 per cent of operational staff resources in the nine ACAS regions. Eighteen of the 207 were Senior Industrial Relations Officers (SIROs) who exercise control and management functions, the rest were Industrial Relations Officers (IROs) of the Higher Executive Officer (HEO) civil service grade. The practice was for new recruits to ACAS generally to start on individual conciliation and move from there to other ACAS functions such as advisory work or collective conciliation. The typical conciliation officer was male (only 7 per cent of the IROs were female, and no SIROs), aged 45 (ranging from 27 to 63), with between two and three years' service with ACAS. Generally they would have been recruited to ACAS from within the civil service, probably from within what is known as the 'DE group' which covers areas such as careers advisory services, unemployment benefits, and manpower services. Originally a number of individual conciliation staff would have come from the Department of Employment conciliation service whose duties were transferred to ACAS in the mid-1970s, but by the time of the research these were more likely to have become senior staff working in areas other than individual conciliation. Occasionally recruits came from other civil service areas – such as National Savings – which were contracting. In addition to internal civil service recruitment there were some 'period appointments' – short-term contract staff recruited by open examination. Sixteen of the IROs at the beginning of 1979 were period appointees.

By mid-1982 the number of staff engaged on this work had fallen slightly (169 HEO grade staff plus 14.5 SIROs employed on management/support functions), but the general characteristics were unchanged. The typical conciliation officer is still a 45-year-old man, although as time passes the average length of service of conciliation officers increases. In 1982 the average length of service on this work was five years. Experience in the job is regarded by ACAS as the best training, although some formal training is provided. Following a six-week regional induction and an introduction to individual conciliation in the region to which they are attached, new recruits attended a two-week residential course which instructed them on the unfair dismissal legislation, compensation calculation, tribunal decisions, and the duties and method of operation of the conciliation officer, and gave some guidance on such matters as interviewing technique. They then returned to their regions to handle cases as allocated. On their first visits they were accompanied by more experienced staff. Training in jurisdictions other than unfair dismissal, which make up a relatively small part of ACAS's case load, is given only to a small proportion of conciliation officers, and only after some time spent handling unfair dismissal cases. In 1984 a two-week reinforcement course for experienced conciliators was introduced.

An ACAS conciliation officer is required by statute to 'endeavour to promote a settlement' where requested to do so by a party or where in the absence of such a request the conciliation officer considers there is prospect of a settlement. In practice ACAS tries to offer conciliation in every case where it receives a copy of the tribunal application. How it goes about this varies both between regions and within regions. In some areas the general practice is for the conciliation officer to contact the applicant first. As it is the applicant who is making the claim, the conciliation officer obtains as much information as possible about it before approaching the employer. In others, for example the Midlands region, however, the general practice is for the employer to be contacted first. The conciliation officer will already have details of the applicant's claim as set out on the IT1 but may not have received a copy of the employer's response and so, it is argued, needs to approach the employer first to get his or her side of the story. There is no hard and fast rule on this and to some extent it is a matter of the preference of individual conciliation officers. However, where a representative is specified the conciliation officer makes the initial approach to that representative rather than to the party directly, but permission may be sought from the representative to make a direct approach. ACAS officers prefer to deal with the parties directly if possible and about half the employers and a third of the applicants in our survey who had representatives none the less also had personal contact with the conciliation officer.

Our surveys revealed a high level of ACAS contact, including by telephone and letter as well as in person. Eighty-seven per cent of self-represented applicants and 77 per cent of self-represented employers said they personally (or in the case of employers, the company) had been contacted by ACAS. Nineteen per cent of companies who had no external representative said ACAS had not contacted them, as did 13 per cent of unrepresented applicants. This reported non-contact rate seems high in the light of ACAS policy, but some misreporting may be expected. Within a company the person responding to the survey may not have been aware of ACAS contact with someone else within the company, particularly if conciliation was refused. Or contact may have been by telephone which, after some months and if no settlement occurred, may be forgotten.

Another explanation may be the non-identification or misidentification of the conciliation officer. Applicants, in particular, may not have realised or remembered who the conciliation officer was. As they do not have to contact ACAS themselves but receive a visit as a result of an application to the industrial tribunal, applicants may sometimes have an imprecise view of the ACAS officer. In our survey, for example, reference was made to 'the man from the tribunal' or, even more vaguely, 'a man from Glasgow' (or wherever the ACAS office might be). Having become aware of this problem, ACAS has used, since September 1982, a special leaflet describing the role of the conciliation officer which is handed to unrepresented parties without previous experience of ACAS. An indication that such confusion may not be confined to applicants is given in *Riley and Greater London CAB v Tesco Stores* where the applicant said that she was told by the CAB adviser that 'somebody from the Tribunal would come to see her' ([1979] IRLR 49, EAT).

As might be expected, represented parties often did not know whether there had been any contact between ACAS and their representatives. Where skilled representation is being used ACAS contact may take the form of telephone and letter communication only. This is also the case with some of those employers who have internal specialists handling the case, particularly if they have been involved in other tribunal applications.

The general view among conciliation officers, however, was that applicants, particularly if unrepresented, should be visited and this is still general practice. There are various reasons for this including the fact that, even if the employer is refusing to enter into conciliation, the conciliation officer still has a role to play in giving information which may help the applicant decide whether to withdraw the claim rather than go to a hearing. This difference is reflected in the nature of contact reported by those applicants and employers surveyed who had personal or company contact (as against only through their external representative) with the conciliation officer. Only 9 per cent of applicants reported that no meeting with the conciliation officer had taken place, all communication being by letter or telephone, whereas 22 per cent of employers reported that no meeting occurred. As this shows, however, generally both parties were visited by a conciliation officer at least once in an attempt to dispose of the case without a hearing.

The Conciliation Process

The separation of conciliation from the decision-making of the tribunal, reinforced by the function being given to a different agency and by the confidentiality of the conciliation process, clearly demarcates the role of the conciliator from that of judge. Conciliation and adjudication are seen as alternative rather than linked methods of disposing of applications. The demarcation of the conciliation officer's role from that exercised by the tribunal is emphasised in ACAS's description of what an individual conciliation officer can and cannot do: 'he is not acting as a fact finder for the tribunal'; 'he cannot allow his own views of the merits of the case to intrude'; 'he is not an investigator . . . he does not "take sides" nor does he act as an arbitrator'. However, 'he is ready to provide information and guidance on the legislation, precedents and the tribunal procedure', he 'can help the parties establish the facts and clarify their views . . . he can help the parties to reach their own informed decision about how to proceed' (ACAS, 1979: ch. 10).

The parties' perceptions of what might happen at tribunal and the relative advantages and disadvantages of continuing the case were identified earlier as crucial in their decisions about how to proceed. ACAS plays an important role in shaping these perceptions, particularly where the parties are not represented. As the above examination revealed, applicants' preparedness to withdraw or settle claims will depend on what is being sought, the perceived likelihood of obtaining it, and the financial and other costs involved. Thus they will need to make some assessment of the strengths and weaknesses of their own and the employer's case in order to assess the likelihood of success; they will need to know what remedy, if any, they are likely to achieve and what going to a tribunal will involve. Employers will need to take similar things into account in deciding whether or not to offer a settlement to dispose of a case. Applicants represented by unions and solicitors can address such questions to their representatives, but those who are not represented by specialists (who constituted 57 per cent in our survey) generally seek this information and advice from ACAS. Similarly employers without internal or external specialist representation will turn to ACAS for information on which to base their assesment.

All applicants and respondents who reported having personal (or company) contact with a conciliation officer (that is, excluding cases where contact was solely through an external representative) were asked 'what did you want the conciliation officer to advise you about or to do for you?'. In reply to this open-ended question 15 per cent of the applicants and 21 per cent of the respondents said 'don't know'. In the case of respondents this 'don't know' response can be explained partly by the person being interviewed not having been the person in the company contacted by the conciliation officer. In the case of applicants it is more likely to reflect a lack of understanding as to what one might expect of a conciliation officer, although applicants who had representatives may have thought this was something the representative rather than they themselves should have a view on. This possibility is supported by the higher 'don't know' response among those with union and solicitor representation (25 per cent of whom said 'don't know') than among those without representation (12 per cent). A small proportion of applicants (8 per cent) and a higher proportion of respondents (19 per cent) said they wanted nothing. The conciliation officer was seen as someone who came uninvited and asked about the case. An application to a tribunal seeks a decision on who is right or wrong; the parties may not anticipate being offered the services of a conciliation officer to effect a compromise of the dispute.

The majority of those applicants and respondents who had contact with conciliation officers, and particularly those handling their own cases, did have demands of them. Table 6.5 shows the responses of those self-represented applicants and internally represented employers who had contact with a conciliation officer and wanted something from him. (In other words, those who said they wanted nothing and those who did not know what was wanted are excluded.) A quarter of these employers said they wanted ACAS to arrange a settlement. Eleven per cent of the applicants explicitly said they wanted ACAS to arrange a settlement although 24 per cent of applicants wanted the conciliation officer to obtain the particular remedy they were seeking, be it re-employment, compensation or whatever. Thirteen per cent of employers wanted the conciliation officer to dispose of the matter, not by bringing about a settlement, but by telling the applicant to drop the case.

The two most common demands from applicants (each being made by 27 per cent) were for advice on the strengths and weaknesses of their case and for advice on the law or how the system operated. Typical responses under the first demand included

'I wanted him to explain whether I had a good chance of winning'

'I wanted to hear from him whether I was likely to win the case'

while advice sought under the second demand was expressed as follows:

'I wanted a clear picture of the tribunal system'

'I wanted to know what would be happening at the tribunal — just general advice'.

Similar demands were made by the lay-represented employers. Twenty per cent sought advice on the strength of their own and the applicant's case, while 18 per cent wanted advice on the law and how the system works.

TABLE 6.5

WHAT UNREPRESENTED PARTIES WANTED OF THE CONCILIATION OFFICER

	Self-Represented Applicants		Lay-Represented Employers[a]	
		%		%
To arrange settlement	47	11	59	25
To advise applicant to drop the case	—	—	30	13
To advise applicant to accept offer	—	—	7	3
To get me re-employment, money, wages due, etc. (i.e. specified remedy)	100	24	—	—
To act as a go-between	20	5	9	4
To obtain information from the other side	4	1	8	4
To put facts/explain point of view to other side	12	3	11	5
To comment on/approve what I was doing	12	3	26	11
To give advice (unspecified)	29	7	16	7
To advise whether to settle/ accept settlement or go on	23	6	12	5
To advise on a reasonable settlement figure	16	4	11	5
To advise me whether I had a good case/how good the other side's case was	115	27	47	20
To advise me on law/procedures/ how the system works etc.	112	27	43	18
Other	37	9	15	6
	N = 418		N = 237	

(Multi-response possible.)

SOURCE: IRRU surveys.

NOTE:

a. Employers represented by someone from inside the company who was not a legal or industrial relations specialist.

As Table 6.5 indicates, a number of the demands being made of ACAS conciliation officers appear to be beyond the role which they are meant to perform, requiring them, for instance, to address themselves to the merits of the case or the desirability of settlement. None the less both applicants and respondents generally (60 per cent of each group) expressed satisfaction with the way the conciliation officer did what was wanted, regardless of whether it fell within or outside the role strictly defined.

The ways in which the conciliation officer meets the demands of the parties are indicated in Table 6.6. This shows the frequency with which applicants and employers reported that various specific functions were performed by the conciliation officer with whom they had contact. The responses of the unrepresented applicants and lay-represented employers are shown separately. In each case the function was more likely to be performed where the party was without representation. Seventy-five per cent of applicants who had personal contact with a conciliation officer were unrepresented and 52 per cent of the employers who were in a position to report what the conciliation officer did were lay-represented at conciliation. As noted above, a frequent demand made of conciliation officers concerns advice on how good a party's case is. One way in which a conciliation officer might enable the applicant or employer to evaluate the merit of the case and at the same time satisfy another demand for information about the law is to explain the legal provisions ('i.e. what is meant by 'unfair', what has to be proven, etc.) and to quote precedents or provide examples of cases involving issues similar to those in the case in question. An alternative, more direct, approach is for the conciliation officer to point out to the parties what appear to be the strengths and weaknesses of their and the other side's case. The employer, for example, may not have followed his own disciplinary procedure, or the applicant may be unable to substantiate an alleged reason for absence.

As Table 6.6 shows, conciliation officers appear to opt for this more direct approach. Whereas less than a quarter of applicants said the conciliation officers explained the law or told them about similar cases (with a high 'don't know' proportion), two-thirds said they had pointed out the strengths and weaknesses of their cases and half said they had done the same in regard to the employers' case. More employers reported that ACAS had explained the law on dismissals although, as with applicants, less than a quarter reported that they were told about similar cases. Most employers said that ACAS conciliation officers had pointed out the strengths and weaknesses of each side's case. About half of all applicants (constituting 52 per cent of those not represented) said the conciliation officer had gone further and actually given them

TABLE 6.6
REPORTED FUNCTIONS OF CONCILIATION OFFICERS

| | Applicants[a] | | | | | | Employers[a] | | | | | |
| | All | | | Self-Represented | | | All | | | Lay-Represented | | |
	Yes %	No %	Don't know %	Yes %	No %	Don't know %	Yes %	No %	Don't know %	Yes %	No %	Don't know %
Explained the law about dismissals	20	31	50	18	30	53	56	38	5	64	30	6
Told you about other cases like yours	24	69	7	26	68	6	23	69	8	26	67	7
Advised you about the strengths and weaknesses of your case	67	29	4	71	27	3	59	37	3	64	32	3
Advised you about the strengths and weaknesses of the other party's case	50	43	7	52	44	5	52	44	5	58	38	4
Gave you his opinion on whether you were likely to win or lose	49	45	5	52	44	5	36	60	4	41	55	4
Explained what happens at a tribunal hearing	66	30	5	70	27	3	47	47	6	60	34	5
Advised you or explained about being represented at hearing	56	39	6	56	40	4	40	54	6	47	46	7
Passed messages or information between you and the other party	62	30	8	65	29	5	61	30	9	62	29	9
Tried to arrange a settlement with the other party	76	15	10	80	15	6	72	25	4	79	19	3
	N = 692			N = 521			N = 674			N = 352		

SOURCE: IRRU surveys.

NOTE:
a. Applicants who had personal contact with the conciliation officer; employers who had company contact and were in a position to know what the C.O. did.

an opinion on whether they were likely to win or lose. Thirty-six per cent of employers (41 per cent of those lay-represented) reported this.

ACAS maintains that conciliation officers should not give a direct answer to questions such as 'how good is my case?' or 'what are my chances at the tribunal?' (ACAS, 1979: 78). Our discussions with individual conciliation officers revealed that some do give their own opinions on these matters but make it clear that they are not judges in the case and that the tribunal might take a different view. Even where this is not the case it appears that their indirect answers (pointing out strengths and weaknesses etc.) leave many applicants and respondents in no doubt about the situation. If the parties perceive or interpret what conciliation officers do as giving an opinion as to whether they will win or lose, it is irrelevant (except in the sense of ACAS needing to keep on the right side of the divide between conciliation and judgment) whether they do in fact do so. The outcome is likely to be the same. Of course, applicants and employers can always discount the information given by the conciliation officer or take a different view of the facts presented. This is, however, unlikely in those cases where the party has no other source of information and advice and is looking to the conciliation officer for this. As we have seen, this is the situation for the majority of applicants. Even where other advice is proffered, perhaps by a friend or relation, it may lack the standing of that given by the conciliation officer who is seen to have an 'official' status.

Armed with information and advice from ACAS and, if applicable, their representatives, the parties decide whether or not to go on to a hearing. As noted earlier, one party's choice here is necessarily constrained by the other: an employer who wishes to settle may find the applicant unwilling to do so, while an applicant faced with an employer's refusal to offer a settlement has to go on to a hearing unless willing to drop the case altogether. In practice, the decision on whether to settle the case will be tied to the question of the terms on which a settlement might be reached.

Conciliated Settlements

In our survey, 447 applicants settled their claims, most commonly, as shown in Table 6.7, for monetary payments. Eighty-two per cent of settlements were reported to be of this type, with 8 per cent of applicants obtaining re-employment and 10 per cent obtaining some other remedy alone. The proportion of applicants in our survey reporting that settlement was on the basis of re-employment is higher than reported in the official statistics for all 1977 applications where 4.6 per

TABLE 6.7

SETTLEMENTS OBTAINED BY APPLICANTS

	No.	*% of Applicants*	
Reinstatement	28	6	
Re-engagement	10	2	
Compensation	367	82	
All statutory remedies			90
Pension rights	2	—	
Holiday pay	40	9	
Bonus payment	2	—	
Pay in lieu of notice	40	9	
Back pay	29	6	
Written reference	39	9	
Other	19	4	
	N = 447		

(Multi-response possible.)

SOURCE: IRRU survey.

cent of applicants are shown as obtaining this, and 93 per cent compensation. However, in both cases the level of re-employment is clearly low.

Re-employment

When the unfair dismissal legislation was first introduced re-employment constituted a higher proportion of conciliated settlements than it did of remedies obtained by applicants who succeeded at hearing. For example, in 1972 re-employment accounted for 15.4 per cent of remedies obtained at conciliation and 4.4 per cent of those obtained at tribunals. The following year the proportions were 9 per cent and 6 per cent. However, as the years passed the re-employment proportion of remedies at both stages declined. In 1980 re-employment made up about 3 per cent of the remedies obtained at conciliation, only a fraction higher than the proportion obtained at hearing, while in 1981 a higher level of re-employment was awarded by tribunals (4.8 per cent of remedies) than was achieved at conciliation (3.7 per cent). In 1982 re-employment constituted 4 per cent of tribunal awards and conciliated settlements.

This is so despite the clear duty of the conciliation officer to promote settlements on the basis of the reinstatement or re-engagement of the applicant. The statute (EP(C)A 1978 s.134) instructs that the conciliation officer, in promoting a settlement, should:

> in particular seek to promote the reinstatement or re-engagement of the complainant by the employer, or by a successor of the employer or by an associated employer, on terms appearing to the conciliation officer to be equitable; but

> where the complainant does not wish to be reinstated or re-engaged, or where reinstatement or re-engagement is not practicable, and the parties desire the conciliation officer to act under this section, he shall seek to promote agreement between them as to a sum by way of compensation to be paid by the employer to the complainant.

As at the tribunal hearing, the applicant's wishes and the practicability of re-employment are important considerations and the beliefs explored earlier, namely that applicants do not want re-employment and employers will not accept it, can be influential at the conciliation stage also. The rarity of the re-employment remedy at tribunal puts little pressure on conciliation officers to pursue settlements on this basis, and ACAS (1984: 62) has noted the 'general willingness on the part of employees to exchange employment for a sum of money' as one of a number of factors contributing to the low level of re-employment.

The low level of re-employment *awards* can be pointed to by ACAS as evidence that it is unrealistic to expect this to be a more common remedy where it has to be agreed to. It is argued that, although the obstacle of employer opposition can be surmounted at tribunal, the voluntary nature of conciliated settlements means in fact that employer opposition does make re-employment impracticable.

There would appear to be scope, however, for at least some employers to be reconciled to the idea of re-employment. As we saw earlier, just over a quarter of the employers in the survey who made a settlement did so because they agreed that the dismissal had been unfair or thought their case was weak or admitted that they had not followed procedure. This indicates there is some scope for pursuing the re-employment option: if the employer agrees the dismissal was unfair, or at least 'contrary to statute', why not erase it by reinstatement? Employers who made settlements for other reasons also might be persuaded to consider re-employment. Forty-two per cent of employers who settled rather than go to a hearing did so because it was the cheaper option, but none the less in certain cases this could be an encouragement to employers to offer re-employment where applicants wanted it. The median amount of compensation at tribunals in 1982 was £1,200: the median level of settlement agreed at conciliation was less than half this amount. Reinstatement, of course, merely puts the parties back in the position they would have been in had dismissal not occurred. There is no penalty for any unfairness in the dismissal, merely compensation for loss, and so reinstatement can be cheaper than compensation. The employer will have to pay for loss of earnings between dismissal and reinstatement but no amount has to be paid to cover potential future loss. The employer has to pay wages but obtains the reinstated worker's labour. If re-engagement is agreed the employer may even avoid having to pay loss of earnings, for example return to the job without back pay.

The nature of the case will obviously have a bearing on the employer's willingness to consider re-employment. One might expect re-employment to be more possible in cases where an employee with a good employment record is dismissed for something uncharacteristic or of a one-off kind where the employer might be persuaded that a second chance would be appropriate. Similarly, re-employment might be possible in cases where dismissal was for ill-health absence, lateness or absenteeism resulting from circumstances unlikely to appertain in the future. In cases of alleged constructive dismissal, where the employer is denying there was a dismissal, one might expect re-employment to be the obvious outcome if the applicant can be assured that the circumstances which led to the resignation have changed or will change.

The careful exploration of these possibilities would require ACAS conciliators to adopt a positive approach to the specific remedies in their dealings with both employers and applicants. At present conciliation officers are aware that the question of re-employment has to be raised, but the research evidence indicates that this may be done in such a low-key fashion that the parties fail to recognise it. In their study of cases where tribunals had actually awarded re-employment, Williams and Lewis (1981: 32) found that in only 16 of 39 cases where conciliation officers were known to have made contact with the parties 'could either of the parties recall re-employment having been discussed or suggested at that stage'.

The formal training of conciliation officers which we observed contained little which could be seen as preparing them to identify and handle likely re-employment cases. The emphasis in dealing with remedies was almost wholly on how tribunals calculate compensation and how to bring about settlements on this basis. Given the statutory wording it is legitimate to ask why this was the case. To a large extent the answer lies in the way ACAS interprets its statutory duty which it sees as being, foremost, to promote settlements. The nature of the settlement – re-employment or compensation – is of secondary importance. Although ACAS conciliation officers may pursue re-employment positively where both sides appear predisposed to it or where the applicant or applicant's representative insists on it (and this would apply to union representatives more than others), they are unwilling to pursue enquiries about re-employment where it is thought the prospect of promoting any other form of settlement might be prejudiced (ACAS, 1982: 8). In particular it is felt by ACAS that employers would react badly if ACAS were to pursue the re-employment option with too much vigour as this might imply that they have taken a decision on the fairness or otherwise of the dismissal. The re-employment remedies, therefore, ACAS argues, are best pursued when the employer has realised his actions were to some extent unfair. It is difficult to see how a decision to pursue settlement on the basis of re-employment implies that the conciliation officer has taken a view of the fairness or otherwise of the dismissal while a decision not to pursue re-employment carries no such implication. Indeed, given the clear statutory duty to pursue settlement on the basis of re-employment, not to do so may be thought to carry the greater implication and appear to sanction the employer's view as the objective or 'neutral' one.

Getting the parties to a position where they are willing to consider settlement and actually arranging the settlement are interlinked rather than separate stages in the conciliation process. The information and advice which ACAS provides may act both to make settlement appear a preferable alternative to going to a tribunal and to define what would be a viable or reasonable settlement. This may entail re-definition of the applicant's expectations or demands. If an employer is unwilling to consider a settlement on the basis of reinstatement, then the applicant may be persuaded that such a demand is unrealistic given the infrequency of this remedy at tribunal and the problems which might be entailed by returning in the face of employer reluctance. On the other hand applicants who sought compensation but are offered re-employment may be persuaded to accept on the grounds that not only is this a superior remedy but tribunals can penalise them for unreasonable refusal of such offers. Of the thirty-eight applicants in our survey who obtained a settlement involving their re-employment, twenty-three had put this as the preferred remedy on the application form. The other fifteen had stated compensation. Sixty-one other applicants who had requested re-employment on the application form settled instead for money.

Money and Other Settlements

Some applicants, in applying to tribunal, will be seeking things which are not necessarily or only satisfied by the tribunal remedies of re-instatement, re-engagement or compensation, and settlements reached through conciliation can be more flexible than tribunal awards. Some applicants may be aggrieved that holiday money or back pay owing at the time of dismissal has not been paid and want what is 'owing to them' rather than compensation in the sense of recompense for loss arising from dismissal. Other applicants may request compensation because they see such payment as symbolic of the fact that the employer was wrong; and are concerned to 'clear their name'. In such cases it may be pointed out in conciliation that perhaps the best way of achieving this is not through the publicity of an industrial tribunal hearing but by obtaining a reference from the employer in return for withdrawing the claim. In such cases there may be no demand for compensation as such and settlement is likely. As Table 6.7 showed, 10 per cent of applicants settled for something other than one of the three stated remedies and 9 per cent of all settling applicants obtained a written reference from the dismissing employer.

Where compensation is demanded the likelihood of settlement increases as the amount the applicant wants or is willing to accept decreases, partly because employers can then be persuaded to make an offer on the basis that settlement would be cheaper or cost no more than defending the case. It was noted in Chapter 5 that compensation awards made by industrial tribunals are relatively low. However, they are on average almost twice as high as those agreed at conciliation. The conciliation officer is required to take account of the equity of the settlement only where re-employment is involved; there is no such requirement in the case of a monetary settlement. Unlike tribunal awards of compensation, settlements are not meant actually to compensate loss, they are merely sums agreed between the parties.

The conciliation officer is not meant to take a view as to the reasonableness or sufficiency of settlements; if one side is prepared to offer a sum of money and the other side accepts it, then the amount agreed is immaterial. What the officer can do is to inform each side how the tribunal would assess compensation if it were making an award in the case in question, pointing out the uncertainty of future loss calculations and the possibility of deductions for contribution or failure to mitigate. This gives the parties a rough yardstick against which offers and requests may be measured and means the approach to compensation laid down in the statute and the manner in which tribunals act in making awards have a direct influence on the parties' expectations. But

TABLE 6.8

HOW APPLICANTS CALCULATED WHAT WOULD BE A REASONABLE AMOUNT TO SETTLE FOR

	No.	*% of Applicants*
'Redundancy formula'/actual loss	94	26
ACAS advice/suggestion	58	16
Amount of holiday pay/sick pay owing	42	11
Took what was offered — needed money	36	10
Union/solicitor/representative advice	38	10
Lump sum/round figure/reasonable amount	22	6
Let other side decide	15	4
What tribunal might award	5	1
Other	45	12
Don't know	12	3
	N = 367	

SOURCE: IRRU survey.

conciliation officers are not required by the statute to go through the heads of compensation in every case and do not always do so.[1] Sometimes an applicant or employer will already have a figure in mind which provides the grounds for a settlement. It may be considerably out of line with any possible tribunal award, but the conciliation officer is not required to be concerned with obtaining 'fair' money settlements, or settlements in line with tribunal compensation awards but only settlements per se.

The 367 applicants in the sample who settled for a money payment were asked how they decided what would be a reasonable amount to settle for. Table 6.8 shows that 26 per cent mentioned some calculation based on years worked or their actual loss, generally meaning the number of weeks out of work rather than other elements of compensation, and 16 per cent said they accepted what ACAS advised or suggested. The replies indicate that few applicants take the likely tribunal award if they should win as indicating the size of a reasonable settlement sum, although elements of the tribunal's calculation — actual loss of wages

---

1. *Slack v Greenham (Plant Hire) Ltd* [1983] IRLR 271.

or length of service — may be considered. Some applicants (11 per cent) regard it as reasonable to obtain merely what they consider owing to them, holiday pay, for example, while others (10 per cent), in need of money, accept whatever is offered.

Of course applicants settling at conciliation could argue that things which tribunals cannot consider — such as injury to feelings — should be compensated for or that, rather than attempt any loss calculations, some representative or symbolic lump sum is what is required. The situation in which this latter approach is most likely is where the applicant has a skilled representative acting on his or her behalf at conciliation. However, although some union officers reported that they adopted a straightforward negotiating stance when discussing settlement, the majority appear to use the tribunal calculation as a guide and seek compensation under similar heads.

Employers also use the tribunal approach to compensation as a yardstick, although again only certain aspects may be considered. Of the 352 employers in our survey who paid money in settlement, 16 per cent said ACAS calculated the settlement sum for them or told them how to calculate it. Twenty per cent mentioned a calculation based on the number of years the applicant had worked for them or 'redundancy formula'. The way an employer determines what might be a reasonable settlement will clearly be influenced by the assessment of the likely outcome of the case; the level of compensation a tribunal would award if the applicant succeeded; and the cost in defending the case. Employers who see settlement as a way of minimising expense will pay particular attention to this last mentioned factor. Seven per cent offered a sum in settlement which was equivalent to or less than the anticipated legal and other costs. Table 6.9 shows also that in 10 per cent of cases the employer agreed to a figure stated by the applicant.

Evaluation of Conciliation

The ACAS conciliation stage can be evaluated from a number of perspectives. First the assessment made by the parties and representatives is discussed and then a wider perspective is adopted which enables the process to be examined in terms of the intentions and expectations behind its inclusion as part of the industrial tribunal system.

The Users' View
The parties' assessment of ACAS conciliation was obtained by seeking whether they regarded the conciliation officers' intervention as helpful and to what extent they thought that the same outcome could have been achieved without such intervention. Also, partly because of the

TABLE 6.9

HOW EMPLOYERS CALCULATED WHAT WOULD BE A SUITABLE SUM FOR A CONCILIATED SETTLEMENT

	No.	*% of Employers*
'Redundancy formula'	71	20
ACAS calculation	55	16
Offered the least/what we thought applicant would accept	35	10
Agreed to applicant's request	36	10
Representative's advice	25	7
Sum equivalent to or less than cost of legal representation	25	7
Pay in lieu of notice/holiday pay/ sick pay owing	24	7
What industrial tribunal might have awarded	11	3
Other	56	16
Don't know	27	7
	N = 352	

(Multi-response possible.)

SOURCE: IRRU survey.

emphasis ACAS itself places on the need for its officers to be, and be seen to be, neutral as between the parties, the parties were asked about the impartiality of the conciliation officer with whom they had contact, that is whether he or she was more on the employer's side, more on the applicant's side or not on one side or the other.

There is no doubt that the general view of both applicants and respondents is that ACAS conciliation officers are impartial and helpful. It is also clear that, not surprisingly, the parties' assessments are to some extent influenced by the outcome of their particular case. About two-thirds of all applicants and employers who had contact with a conciliation officer considered he or she was 'not on one side or the other'. Although the proportion of applicants regarding the conciliation officer as neutral remains at 66 per cent, the distribution of perceived bias varies according to outcome. Among applicants who settled their claims where the conciliation officers are not described as neutral, they are seen as more on the applicants' side and among those withdrawing without settlement the bias is seen to be towards the employer. Employers are less likely than applicants to see an outcome which is favourable to them as indicating any bias on the part of the conciliation officer. Rather they see this as evidence of neutrality. Thus, among employers where the case was withdrawn without settlement it is the neutrality score (i.e. not on one side or the other) which increases (to 80 per cent), and where a settlement was made or the employer lost at the hearing, the neutrality score declines slightly (to 66 per cent), with a consequent increase in the perceived bias towards applicants.

Those applicants and respondents who had settlements arranged through ACAS were most likely to find the conciliation officer 'very helpful' or 'fairly helpful'. Fifty per cent of applicants in settled cases said the conciliation officer was very helpful, a further 34 per cent said he or she was fairly helpful. Among employers in settled cases in a position to answer, 54 per cent found the conciliation officer very helpful and 32 per cent fairly helpful. High helpfulness scores were also recorded among employers in cases which were withdrawn without hearing (53 per cent 'very' and 28 per cent 'fairly'). Although the perceived helpfulness varies with outcome, in no case does the proportion of applicants or of employers saying the ACAS conciliation officer was helpful fall below 50 per cent.

Given the range of functions which the parties reported were performed by the conciliation officer, encompassing the giving of information about the tribunal system, advice on the strengths and weaknesses of the case and the conveying of information and messages between the parties (see p. 156, above), it was not expected that many would find the conciliation officer's intervention 'not at all helpful' or 'not very helpful'. In fact the responses indicate that conciliation officers may not have to do very much before they are seen as helpful, especially when dealing with unrepresented parties. Applicants, particularly, greatly appreciate the fact that someone calls at their home prepared to listen to and discuss their case. One applicant described the conciliation officer as helpful because 'he came and sat in your own home — he was a fatherly sort of person, you felt confidence in him; he was sympathetic and didn't make you feel a nuisance or anything'. Those with representation have an alternative source of help and advice, and if they require anything of conciliation officers, it is likely to exceed the often simple requirements and expectations which the unrepresented have of them. This is reflected in the fact that represented applicants are less likely to see the conciliation officer as helpful, particularly where they have legal representation. Within each group the majority found the conciliation officer helpful, but the size of the majority declines where legal representation was used, as does the distribution of the majority response between 'very helpful' and 'fairly helpful'. Three-quarters of self-represented applicants found the conciliation officer helpful compared with 59 per cent of those who had legal representation and personal contact with the conciliation officer. A similar picture is found among employers, with 73 per cent of lay-represented employers finding the conciliation officer helpful compared with 58 per cent of those with external legal representation.

Those applicants and employers in settled cases who said settlement was arranged through ACAS (60 per cent and 65 per cent respectively) were asked about the possibility of obtaining the same outcome without ACAS intervention. Table 6.10 shows that employers whose settlements were arranged through ACAS were less inclined than applicants to think settlement could not have been otherwise arranged. Various explanations may be suggested. It may be that applicants seeking judgment on the

TABLE 6.10

POSSIBILITY OF SETTLEMENT WITHOUT ACAS

	Applicants[a]	*Respondents*[a]
	%	%
Definitely not possible	52	16
Probably not possible	27	26
Total not possible	79	42
Probably possible	13	33
Definitely possible	3	11
Total possible	16	44
Don't know/can't say	4	14
	N = 267	N = 290

SOURCE: IRRU surveys.

NOTE:

a. Applicants and respondents who said settlement was arranged through ACAS.

fairness of their dismissal may not have considered the option of voluntary settlement without ACAS intervention. Or, if it was thought of,
unrepresented applicants may have been unwilling or unable to initiate
any contact with the employer to explore the possibility of a settlement,
whereas the respondent employers appear to think that in the absence
of ACAS another intermediary could have been found. Whether any
attempt at settlement would in fact have been made is, of course, not
known. It seems reasonable to suppose that without ACAS intervention
some employers at least may not have seen this as a course open to
them and that even if they did approach the applicant, an offer of
settlement may have been regarded with more suspicion than one
transmitted via a neutral third party of some official standing who
thereby sanctions this way of ending the case.

As noted earlier, represented parties tended to see any settlement
as achieved through their own representatives rather than ACAS, and to
be less likely than unrepresented or lay-represented parties to find
the conciliation officer helpful to them. However, it is possible that
the representatives concerned will have found ACAS useful to them,
although representatives' demands and expectations of the conciliation
officer will differ from those of the unrepresented applicant or respondent. The extent and way in which they differ will depend in part on
the identity, skill and experience of the representative in question as
well as on his or her perception of the conciliation function. Some
functions which unrepresented parties consider it useful for the conciliation officer to perform will have less utility for representatives:
trade union and employers' association officials and solicitors are now
likely to know as much as the conciliation officer about such matters
as how tribunals operate.

Representatives are also likely to have their own informed view of
the strengths and weaknesses of the case. However, to make an accurate
assessment they need to know something about the other side's case.
Where there is direct contact between the two sides or their representatives or where use is made of the interlocutory steps, this may not be a
problem. Where not, the conciliation officer may be a useful source of
such information. Communication via the conciliation officer may also
be seen as a preliminary to direct contact, enabling the representative
to ascertain whether such direct contact would be fruitful. Where one
party, or representative, simply refuses to deal with the other, then the
conciliation officer may be valuable as a method of establishing communication and acting as a channel. For example, where the dismissed
employee is a union member and has union representation but the employer does not recognise the union, the conciliation officer may be
able to facilitate indirect communication and perhaps bring about

direct contact. An ACAS conciliation officer may also be useful to representatives as an independent authority. For example, an employer who refuses to accept what the union representative says concerning the provisions of the law or procedural requirements may more readily accept it from a conciliation officer. Similarly, the conciliation officer can be useful to representatives in this role vis-à-vis members or clients. A representative who is trying to convince the member or client that the case is weak and should be withdrawn may be more likely to succeed in this if the conciliation officer concurs in this assessment of the position and so informs the member or client.

Where representatives can use the conciliation officer in the ways just outlined they are likely to consider the conciliation function useful. However, interviews with trade union and employers' association officials who represent their members in tribunal cases revealed a certain amount of criticism. Often union and employer officials were using their experience of other forms of conciliation – notably that provided by ACAS in collective disputes – as a yardstick against which the individual conciliation was measured and, in certain respects, found wanting. One official argued that 'conciliation officers do not take enough initiative. They are only good listeners and messenger boys', while another dismissed ACAS conciliation 'because it doesn't exist, [the conciliation officer] just conveys one side's position to the other side'.

Some criticism arose because the narrowly defined function of the conciliation officer was seen by the specialist representative as inadequate in that the conciliation officer undertook no independent investigation of the facts and did not take the initiative in trying to bring about a resolution. One union official argued that 'they don't take initiatives and seem to spend most of their time agreeing with both sides', while another official who made this criticism said it arose because the conciliation officer was 'far too interested in appearing impartial'. Another union representative wanted the conciliation officer to 'have more time to go into the case more fully', whereas 'he only wants to know what the union is prepared to settle for'. Comments made by union and employers' association representatives indicated that, as one would expect, there is a variation among ACAS individual conciliation officers in their personal qualities and approach to the job. But similarly representatives themselves vary in the way they perform their duty. There was a tendency for those officials – particularly in employers' associations – who spent a lot of time investigating the facts of the case to describe ACAS conciliation as shallow and perfunctory and to be more favourably inclined to conciliation officers who did spend time finding out a lot about the case.

Although representatives may be seeking a form of intervention which differs from that which apparently satisfies unrepresented parties, ACAS's *modus operandi* has been evolved mainly with unrepresented parties in mind and 'the involvement of representatives makes no difference to the conciliation officer's task, approach or methods' (ACAS, 1979: 82). Where the involvement of representatives does make a difference to ACAS is in making 'conciliation more cumbersome and time-consuming' (ibid.). Unlike the position of unfair dismissal applicants, those who apply to tribunals complaining of race or sex discrimination may call on the services of agencies designed to help them achieve favourable outcomes, the Commission for Racial Equality and the Equal Opportunities Commission. In our discussions with ACAS officials it was stated that the wider duties and interests of these bodies in promoting equal treatment can mean that in any particular individual case where they act as representatives they may pursue a strategy which minimises the likelihood of settlement. This may involve a demand that any acceptable settlement must include an admission from the employer that discrimination did occur, or a desire to have a public tribunal hearing or judicial ruling on a particular case. Such strategies obviously make it harder for ACAS to promote a settlement and so conciliation officers prefer to deal directly with applicants if possible.

The parties' assessment of ACAS conciliation which emerged from our survey is largely favourable. However, we did not solicit complaints about conciliation and the opportunities for complaints about ACAS to emerge in the course of our interviews were limited to those of irrelevance, bias or unspecified unhelpfulness. Other complaints have been made at various times about the role played by ACAS conciliation officers, particularly in the discrimination jurisdictions. These complaints centre on what is seen as unwarranted or misplaced encouragement to withdraw or settle complaints, attitudes unsympathetic to applicants, and a failure to provide support to applicants which would help redress their disadvantaged position vis-à-vis the employer (Gregory, 1982: 81, 82). However, some of these criticisms arise because the performance of conciliation officers is being measured, implicitly or explicitly, against a model or expectation of conciliation which differs from that of ACAS itself. Such criticism is seen most appropriately as directed at the statutory function, as interpreted by ACAS, rather than at the way conciliation officers perform that function.

A Wider View

This brings us to a consideration of the intentions and expectations which lay behind giving ACAS a statutory duty in unfair dismissal cases in order to judge whether the statute satisfactorily embodies the intentions and whether ACAS is fulfilling its statutory duty. Two kinds of reason can be suggested to explain why it was considered necessary or desirable to provide an opportunity whereby unfair dismissal cases might be settled without their being heard by the bodies given jurisdiction to determine such issues. The first kind is pragmatic, being concerned with administrative efficiency; the second kind concerns the effectiveness of the system in terms of its qualitative results.

It would not be cost-effective to set up tribunals to hear cases which, with help, could be disposed of satisfactorily by mutual agreement between parties, nor to hear cases which should not have been brought, because of lack of qualification or merit. Thus behind the inclusion of a conciliation stage was the pragmatic consideration that ACAS would provide a filter which would ease the case load of the tribunals and help prevent long delays and additional public expenditure. The 'filtering out' of meritless cases, as opposed to assisting the achievement of settlements, is not mentioned explicitly in the statute and other filter mechanisms do exist, the COIT registration and the pre-hearing assessment procedure. Applicants can withdraw their applications at any time, however, and ACAS sees its s.134 duty to endeavour to settle cases without a hearing as encompassing the obtaining of withdrawals. It is felt that although conciliation officers should not seek to persuade applicants to withdraw, they would

> be failing in their responsibilities to some complainants if they did not draw attention to such matters as the relevant qualifying conditions for presenting a complaint; appropriate case law and precedent; the strong points in the respondent's case. Applicants' attention must also be drawn to the risk of costs being awarded if a tribunal were to decide that either party had acted in a frivolous, vexatious or unreasonable manner (ACAS, 1982: 6).

With some 60 to 70 per cent of cases being disposed of without a hearing each year, almost half of them by withdrawal of the application, there is little doubt that the ACAS conciliation stage helps the tribunal system operate efficiently as far as the disposition of cases is concerned.

In the debate prior to the introduction of the statutory right, however, importance was placed on considerations other than administrative efficiency. A conciliation stage was seen as valuable and desirable because it was considered that outcomes reached in this way would be qualitatively superior to those obtained at tribunal both because of the method by which they were achieved — voluntary, bargained agreement rather than external imposition — and in their nature.

Taking first the nature of settlements, it might be thought in particular that successful re-employment would result more probably from a mutually agreed conciliated settlement than from an externally imposed tribunal award. Firstly, less time will have elapsed since the date of dismissal and the employer will not have had to justify the dismissal at a public hearing — something which can be expected to exacerbate the breakdown in relationship with the applicant. Secondly, applicants may be more willing to return where the employer is agreeing to their re-employment, being less afraid of hostility or victimisation, than where a tribunal has to order the employer to take them back. Thirdly, a skilled conciliator should be able to reconcile the parties in some cases, help smooth the differences between them and create a climate in which re-employment is seen as a viable and preferred option. As we have seen, however, the level of re-employment achieved through conciliation does not exceed the low level awarded by tribunals. ACAS conciliators see their prime duty as encouraging the parties to settle; they do not see their statutory duty as requiring them to pursue vigorously the re-employment options. Indeed in some cases, for instance when the parties have already reached some agreement on a money payment, it is seen as inappropriate to pursue the question of re-employment at all.

One construction of the statutory duty is that in order to take action in accordance with s.134 the conciliation officer has to seek to promote the re-employment of the applicant and this requires some positive initiative (Upex, 1982: 125). However, the courts have rejected this interpretation and supported the approach followed by ACAS which implies into the statutory duty the words 'so far as applicable in the circumstances of the particular case' (Lord Brandon in *Moore v Duport Furniture Products Ltd* [1982] IRLR 31, HL). In most cases, therefore, the conciliation officer operates on the basis that there is, and will be, no continuing relationship between the parties. Few attempts are made to discover, and if possible allay, the fears which may underlie an applicant's reluctance to return or to examine and probe the employer's arguments of impracticality of re-employment. The emphasis is not on reconciliation and re-establishing the relationship but on the terms of ending it.

Although no more re-employment is achieved via conciliation than is awarded by tribunals, it is possible that the settlements achieved could none the less be qualitatively better than tribunal awards in that, for example, the re-employment is more 'satisfactory'. The small number of people in the sample who got re-employment makes it difficult to assess this satisfactorily — eleven said they were awarded a re-employment by a tribunal, thirty-seven said they achieved it by settle-ment. However, four of the thirty-seven (11 per cent) did not in fact return to work. All of those awarded re-employment by the tribunal did in fact return, although the gap between the decision and return was longer than that between agreement at conciliation and return. Our sample does not appear typical in this respect, however, since follow-up work on all tribunal-awarded re-employment during the first five years of the jurisdiction found a non-return rate of a least 20 per cent (Williams and Lewis, 1981: 5).

At the time of the interview, which took place from approximately six months to fifteen months after the case had finished, eight of the eleven (73 per cent) who went back after a hearing and twenty-two of the thirty-three (67 per cent) who went back after settlement were still working at that company. The slightly less successful stay rate among those who settled on the basis of re-employment is even lower if the four who did not return are included, giving 59 per cent of settled re-employees who were still at work at the time of the interview. Of the fourteen applicants who were no longer at work after being re-employed, eight resigned (including two re-employed after a tribunal award), three were made redundant (all of whom had gone back by con-ciliated agreement), and two were dismissed (one of whom had been awarded re-employment by the tribunal). One other left for some 'other' reason. What limited data there are, therefore, do not suggest that, taking length of return as a yardstick, re-employment obtained by settlement is qualitatively superior to that awarded by tribunal.

In settling on the basis of a monetary payment, employers may make payments to applicants who would have received nothing or far less from the tribunal. Conversely applicants may accept offers below what a tribunal would have awarded them. Any qualitative superiority of conciliated settlements on the basis of compensation, therefore, cannot be sought in the size of the amounts agreed. It appears from the survey that applicants agreeing to a monetary settlement are more likely to receive it, and to receive it sooner, than those awarded compensation by a tribunal. Of the 367 applicants who agreed to money in settlement, most (81 per cent) received it within six weeks from the time of the agreement, whereas only 37 per cent of those 133 who were awarded compensation by tribunals received their money within this time period after the award. Employers in heard cases appear, not unreasonably, to wait until they receive the written decision from the tribunal before paying the applicant. Written decisions are generally sent to the parties within four weeks to six weeks of the hearing. However, 35 per cent of applicants in heard cases had to wait over eight weeks (compared with

7 per cent of those who settled) and 12 per cent (fifteen people) had not received the money by the time of the interview. Two per cent of applicants who settled were similarly still waiting for payment.

The main argument for the qualitative superiority of monetary settlements at conciliation, as indicated earlier, lies in the method by which they are achieved. Rather than being imposed on the parties they are the voluntarily agreed outcome of a bargaining process aided by ACAS. This is the essence of conciliation as a form of third-party intervention: 'Conciliation is a process in which a third party – the conciliation officer – tries to help two others reach a voluntary settlement of a matter in dispute between them' (ACAS, 1982: 2). It is often described as 'assisted bargaining': the parties to the dispute are helped towards a solution but it is not imposed on them; they decide themselves whether or not to settle and on what terms.

However, an examination of conciliation arising from unfair dismissal applications shows it to be a bargaining process of a rather peculiar kind. The first peculiarity of individual conciliation as a bargaining process is that the parties do not actually meet. Whereas joint meetings are seen almost as a *sine qua non* for successful conciliation in collective disputes (those between unions and employers), individual conciliation officers feel they can perform their function satisfactorily without bringing the disputing parties together; indeed they feel that to do so may hamper the chances of a conciliated settlement. Any bargaining therefore occurs at one remove. Only 1 per cent of applicants (nine) who had a meeting with the conciliation officer reported that the employer or his or her representative was also present. Such an approach reflects the concern of individual, as opposed to collective, conciliation which, as noted earlier, is not with the reconciliation of the parties and the re-establishment of their relationship but with arranging severance terms. Individual conciliation is conducted by the ACAS officer going from one party to the other, either physically or, especially with regard to employers, by telephone.

The second peculiarity of individual conciliation as a bargaining process is that first offers are generally accepted. Seventy per cent of employers in settled cases surveyed said that the settlement terms were what they had first offered. Sixty-four per cent of self-represented applicants who settled said the first offer from the employer was accepted. A higher proportion of those with representation said the settlement was a result of negotiation Forty-three per cent of those represented by trade unions and 45 per cent of those represented by solicitors said the settlement was the result of negotiations. One explanation for ready acceptance of employers' first offers by unrepresented applicants is that such offers are seen as ideal. However, this has to be rejected in most cases. Although, as we have seen, applicants' expectations are generally low, half of the applicants who accepted monetary settlement regarded the amount as too little. It would appear that unrepresented applicants are either unaware that conciliation 'is by its very nature a negotiation and bargaining process' (ACAS, 1979: 85) or that they do not see themselves in any position to haggle over the employer's offer as their bargaining position is weak.

The inequality in the relationship between the individual worker and the employer is implicitly recognised by the unfair dismissal legislation itself which sought to improve the worker's position by providing a right to challenge the employer's decision to dismiss. Rather than the will of the stronger party prevailing, appeal can be made to an external standard — the concept of fairness as embodied in statute and case law. The statutory formulation of the protection against unfair dismissal is in the form of a dispute of right, the essence of which is that there is some more or less definite standard against which the alleged infringement can be judged. Adjudication on who is 'right' is being sought by unfair dismissal applicants. First, however, they are offered conciliation which has at its core not adjudication but haggling and compromise — features associated with disputes of interest where no external standards prevail, where the relative strengths of the parties are crucial and where the only 'right' solution is the one the parties agree to.

The existence of the right does give the individual worker some bargaining strength which would not otherwise exist in most non-unionised employments. Prior to the legislation, the non-union employee sacked from a small firm may have had a grievance but he or she will have lacked a means of expressing and resolving it and hence cannot really be said to have been 'in dispute' with the employer. The unfair dismissal legislation and the industrial tribunal system provide both the vehicle whereby the grievance can be articulated as a dispute over dismissal and a mechanism through which the dispute may be resolved. The right (or the threat to exercise it) is therefore a bargaining counter for the employee. But how strong a counter is it? As noted earlier, the cost and inconvenience which the exercise of the right cause the employer in having to defend an unfair dismissal application may lead to a small 'nuisance value' sum being offered in settlement. As ACAS points out (1979: 81), in response to criticism that conciliation encourages the making of such offers,

The fact that a respondent may find it cheaper to make such a payment than to contest a case at a tribunal, even if convinced of winning, is an inevitable consequence of giving a statutory right of complaint and has nothing to do with the role of the conciliation officer.

Potential cost saving through settlement is therefore 'a fact of the situation'; part of the context within which the decision to settle has to be taken. This particular fact works to the advantage of the applicant. However, there are other facts of the situation which serve to weaken the applicant's bargaining position. These have been discussed in earlier chapters and concern the nature of the system, its operation and its outcomes. Information about the operation of the system which may be conveyed includes: employers win two out of three cases; even if the applicant wins, re-employment is unlikely and any compensation generally is not high and may be subject to deductions; chances of succeeding at tribunal are enhanced by supporting the case with documentation and witness testimony and employers are better placed to maximise their chances of success in this way; tribunals may award costs against those pursuing cases frivolously, vexatiously or unreasonably.

An applicant faced with this information, usually provided by the conciliation officer, not surprisingly is likely to be predisposed towards accepting an offer of settlement. In addition information conveyed from the employer – that legal representation will be used or costs will be asked for – may increase the reluctance to proceed to tribunal. The giving and conveying of information is quite a legitimate technique of conciliation but in the context of individual conciliation it may have a significance and impact greater than that in a collective dispute. This is because the parties – particularly applicants – may lack any external reference point, any alternative source of knowledge or any experience against which the information can be assessed.

Although ACAS, in individual conciliation as in collective, theoretically leaves the parties to assess the merits of the case themselves and to arrive at their own settlement terms, in individual conciliation the parties, particularly unrepresented applicants, do so largely on the basis of the information, advice and guidance ACAS itself provides. Furthermore, as we have argued, the information which ACAS transmits tends to depress applicant expectations and demands. In short, the industrial tribunal system provides a context within which conciliated settlements of whatever nature will often appear preferable to a tribunal hearing. Although the marshalling and channelling of pressures inherent in the situation is again a legitimate tool for a conciliator to use, the nature of the tribunal system means this generally places the applicant at a disadvantage vis-à-vis the employer.

Because ACAS is generally the means whereby the various pressures towards settlement which are in the system are made known to the parties, conciliation officers have been criticised for putting pressure on one or both parties in a case in order to secure withdrawal or get a settlement. However, fewer than a third of applicants and employers in our survey who settled their cases reported that they felt under pressure to do so and only twelve employers (3 per cent) and twenty-three applicants (5 per cent) identified ACAS as the source of pressure. It appears, therefore, that learning the 'facts of the situation' is not felt as pressure and in this sense the parties generally affirm that the settlements were reached voluntarily.

The parties can always reject conciliation or refuse to settle the case. Where agreements are reached, therefore, they are voluntary settlements. But the freedom of choice implied in this description is quite clearly constrained by the particular context within which it has to be exercised, a context which generally works to encourage the applicant to settle. As the survey revealed, employers often see settlement as a cheaper option and where employers are prepared to make a settlement offer applicants hardly ever refuse.

ACAS can be seen, therefore, to transmit pressures to settle which the system contains but not necessarily to create them. But nor does ACAS in any way seek to ameliorate them. Thus, for example, a conciliation officer may tell an applicant that the tribunal can award costs against applicants in certain circumstances but cannot give an opinion on whether this would happen in the case in question 'since only a tribunal can form such a view' (ACAS, 1982: 6). Similarly ACAS will convey a settlement offer regardless of its nature. Its presentation by the conciliation officer may appear to give an offer some kind of standing, but an applicant or employer who thought that the conveying of an offer implied any view by the conciliation officer that it was a suitable or reasonable offer would be mistaken. As we have seen, ACAS does not see it as part of the conciliation officer's duty to take a view on the fairness of monetary settlements. Section 134(2)(a) of the EP(C)A 1978 requires the conciliation officer to promote re-employment of the applicant 'on terms appearing to the conciliation officer to be equitable', but no such phrase appears in s.134(2)(b) which concerns promoting agreement as to a sum of compensation and an attempt by tribunal lay members to imply it was thwarted by the higher courts.[2]

The unfair dismissal legislation gives employees a right which seeks to adjust the inequality in the employer-employee relationship. This same inequality could, however, be used to prevent workers exercising

2. *Moore v Duport Furniture Products Ltd* [1982] IRLR 31, HL.

that right. Thus s.140 of the EP(C)A 1978 makes void any agreement which attempts to preclude any person from bringing a complaint to an industrial tribunal. This protection is lost, however, where the agreement is reached by circumstances where ACAS has 'taken action'. A change to s.134 of the EP(C)A, made by the Employment Act 1980 requires a conciliation officer to endeavour to promote settlement where

> a person claims that action has been taken in respect of which a complaint could be presented by him [to an industrial tribunal] and before any complaint relating to that action has been so presented, a request is made to a conciliation officer (whether by that person or by the employer) to make his services available to them.

This provision enables agreements reached at the time of dismissal, and not just those following an application to a tribunal, to act as a legal barrier to an unfair dismissal claim being heard, if ACAS has been involved. Employers are making increasing use of the provision to bar possible applications (ACAS, 1984: 61). ACAS conciliators see it as their duty to ensure not only that the employees concerned are claiming that action has been taken in respect of which they could complain to an industrial tribunal, but that they understand what is going on. ACAS is concerned that the conciliation officer should not be called in merely to 'rubber stamp' an agreement already reached independently by the parties.

The statute gives little guidance as to what a conciliation officer actually need do in taking action under s.134 to endeavour to promote a settlement, although the implication of s.140 is that agreements reached under ACAS supervision are distinct from those the parties might reach without such intervention. But, because ACAS is not concerned with equity, it has been held that a conciliation officer need do no more than record settlement terms already agreed by the parties, having ensured they understand them, in order to have taken action under s. 134.[3] Nor need the agreed settlement be reduced to writing for it to be binding on the parties.[4] Unless a conciliation officer were to act in bad faith or adopt unfair methods when promoting a settlement, it appears that any agreement reached with ACAS involvement will act as a bar to proceedings.[5]

The protection afforded by s.140 thus may be lost relatively easily

3. *Moore v Duport Furniture Products Ltd* [1982] IRLR 31, HL.
4. *Gilbert v Kembridge Fibres Ltd* [1984] IRLR 52.
5. *Slack v Greenham (Plant Hire) Ltd* [1983] IRLR 271.

and the nature of the settlement reached where ACAS takes action may be identical to that which would have been reached without such action. The difference lies only in the loss of the s.140 protection so the applicant cannot change his or her mind about the acceptability of the terms and continue to a tribunal hearing (cf. *Council of Engineering Institutions v Maddison* [1976] IRLR 389). It has been argued that the statute could be construed to require ACAS to take a view of the fairness of any settlement (McIlroy, 1980; Upex, 1982) but ACAS's interpretation of its role has been upheld by the courts as the correct one. None the less, at times it seems to sit uneasily in the context of a statutory right designed to improve the position of employees vis-à-vis the employer. In practice, by acting in a neutral way in a situation of inequality, ACAS conciliation officers perpetuate that inequality rather than redressing it.

Summary

The previous section evaluated ACAS conciliation in terms of its contribution, as a filter, to the administrative efficiency of the industrial tribunal system and then assessed it in the light of other intentions and expectations concerned with its qualitative outcomes.

ACAS operates as an effective filter, disposing of about two-thirds of tribunal applications for unfair dismissal without a tribunal hearing and does so in a way generally perceived by the parties as impartial and helpful. The parties' perceptions of what might happen at a tribunal hearing and how they weigh the relative advantages and disadvantages of proceeding to that stage are important determinants of their preparedness to settle the case. Conciliation, unlike adjudication, theoretically leaves the decision on whether to settle and on what terms to the parties themselves. Applicants and employers in unfair dismissal cases, however, particularly if unrepresented (or lay-represented) reach these decisions largely on the basis of information, advice and guidance provided by ACAS itself.

In performing their conciliation role, ACAS officers inevitably marshal and channel to the parties pressures in the industrial tribunal system which tend to encourage settlement. Some of these 'facts of the situation' dictated by the tribunal context, and often conveyed to the parties by the conciliation officer, incline the employer towards settling. Generally, however, the nature of the tribunal system places applicants at a disadvantage, predisposing them to accept offers which employers may choose to make.

Settlements are reached rarely on the basis of re-employment of the applicant. ACAS sees its statutory duty as being primarily the promotion of settlements, with the nature of the settlement — re-employment or compensation – as of secondary importance. Settlements are commonly for money. ACAS is not required to take a view as to the equity of any monetary settlements it conciliates and generally relatively small sums of money are involved.

Very few offers of settlement conveyed by the conciliation officer are refused by applicants. The inequality in the employer/employee relationship and the relative disadvantage of an unfair dismissal applicant within the industrial tribunal system is perpetuated, not ameliorated, by the neutral stance required of ACAS in conciliation. In the context of a tribunal system used by unaided and unrepresented applicants the description of conciliated settlements as voluntary agreed outcomes of an assisted bargaining process, qualitatively superior to tribunal-imposed awards, is inappropriate. The description might have more applicability if there were rights enforcement officers to aid unrepresented applicants. Inherent in some of the criticism made of ACAS conciliators discussed above (p. 170) is the assumption that they should take a more positive, rights-enforcing, stance.

The rhetoric of conciliation emphasises the responsibility of the parties for any settlement reached and in collective disputes ACAS's refusal to involve itself in the merits of any outcome is seen as crucial (Jones et al., 1983). There is, however, some precedent for a form of conciliation which might be thought more appropriate in individual rights cases which may be called 'committed conciliation'. That is, conciliation designed to bring about agreed settlements promoting certain desired substantive ends. Under the Employment Protection Act 1975 trade unions seeking recognition from an employer for collective bargaining purposes could invoke a procedure involving ACAS (Dickens, 1978). ACAS had a duty to conciliate in such cases in an attempt to resolve them without the need for a report to be issued following an inquiry. This conciliation took place within the context of the general duty which s.1 of the Act placed on ACAS 'of encouraging the extension of collective bargaining'. As collective bargaining requires the recognition of trade unions, ACAS was required to adopt a positive approach when conciliating in recognition claims. By analogy one might argue that conciliation in cases where individuals are seeking to pursue their legal rights could seek to promote those rights, ensuring they are not abandoned or compromised below their value.

In effect this would move the role of ACAS in such cases away from conciliation as it understands it now towards rights enforcement. The recognition provisions referred to above provide an example of a requirement of committed conciliation but also illustrate the problems such a role may cause for a body which strives to maintain an impartial stance. The operation of the recognition procedure ran into a variety of problems which finally led the Council of the Service to inform the Secretary of State that it could not 'satisfactorily operate the statutory recognition procedures as they stand' (ACAS, 1981: 138). One among many problems identified by ACAS was that its role in the recognition procedure led to perceptions among some organisations that it was biased in favour of trade unions, which ACAS thought undermined its acceptability to employers as a provider of voluntary third-party services (ACAS, 1981: 89). Although a committed conciliation stance might improve the quality of settlements reached from the applicant's point of view, it seems likely that it would result in fewer settlements being reached, thereby lessening ACAS's success as a filter. If a more positive rights enforcement role is seen as necessary at this stage, therefore, ACAS does not appear the appropriate body to provide it.

The discussion in this chapter has looked at the effectiveness of conciliation as a filter, aiding the administrative efficiency of the tribunal system, and in terms of the outcomes achieved. A similar, efficiency evaluation can now be made of the tribunal system more generally.

7

The Efficiency of the Industrial Tribunal System

In selecting the criteria by which the industrial tribunal system should be evaluated, an obvious starting point is the advantages claimed for tribunals over the ordinary courts by the Franks Committee on Administrative Tribunals. The Franks Committee's view (1957: para. 406) was that, compared with the ordinary courts, tribunals offered 'cheapness, accessibility, freedom from technicality, expedition and expert knowledge of a particular subject'. One evaluative measure of industrial tribunals, therefore, is the extent to which they display these characteristics. The first four concern the mode of operation, the efficiency of the machinery. Expertness, however, moves the focus of attention towards the output of the machinery, the nature of the decisions reached. It has been suggested that part of the expertness of tribunals compared to the ordinary courts is their ability to display doctrinal flexibility and policy consciousness in their decision-making (Abel-Smith and Stevens, 1968: 220).

In this chapter we examine whether the industrial tribunal system does offer a cheap, accessible and expert way of resolving unfair dismissal disputes in a way that is also free from technicality. We thus explore the efficiency of the tribunals in dispute settlement compared with the courts but, in the final section, we also raise the question of their efficiency when judged by the needs of different parties and in terms of what is demanded by the type of dispute they are handling.

The characteristics listed by Franks are not distinct but interrelated. In particular cheapness may be seen as an aspect of accessibility. It also concerns awareness on the part of those who might apply, and their ability to obtain advice and help in so doing or to manage without it.

Accessibility

Knowledge

The first stage at which a barrier to access may be encountered is in knowledge of the right to apply. There is no duty placed on employers to notify workers whom they dismiss that they may have the right to challenge the fairness of the decision at an industrial tribunal, although this would seem to be the best way of ensuring that non-application is not the result of ignorance. In fact there is no general duty on employers to give workers reasons for their dismissals although the Employment Protection Act 1975 (now EP(C)A 1978 s.53) did provide employees with the right to a statement of the reasons for dismissal *on request.*

We noted earlier (Chapter 2) that only a small minority of dismissed workers seek to challenge the fairness of their dismissals at industrial tribunals but that it is impossible to know what proportion of non-applicants are ignorant of their rights. As the law on unfair dismissal has now been in existence for over a decade and the media publicise the more newsworthy cases, it is unlikely that workers are unaware that there is some provision for challenging dismissal. But a general awareness may be insufficient to bring about an application. Knowledge that a law exists is of little use without some understanding of who can use it and how.

Applicants in our survey, as detailed in Chapter 2, generally found out about industrial tribunals from friends and relatives, the media, and local job centres and unemployment benefit offices. These offices generally display posters and have leaflets available advising employees about unfair dismissal but the staff do not have a duty to take the initiative in informing potential applicants of their rights.

Cost

So that dismissed workers should not be deterred from seeking redress through an industrial tribunal by the cost of pursuing a case, no application fee or court fees are payable, direct costs are met from public funds and the losing party does not generally have to bear the other party's costs. The estimated expenditure on salaries, fees and directly related expenses for 1982–3 was over £9 million, with additional expenditure to cover superannuation, printing, stationery, etc. (COIT, 1984: 2; SCOIT, 1984: 1). It was estimated that, in 1979–80, the average cost of a day's hearing was £266 (COIT, 1981a: 2). Industrial tribunals operate in twenty-five centres in England and Wales and six in Scotland. Additional premises are hired if necessary to meet the demand. This attempt to make the tribunals geographically accessible helps reduce the amount of time and money which would have to be expended otherwise in going to a hearing. Travelling and subsistence costs incurred by the parties and witnesses in attending hearings are reimbursed and actual loss of earnings are recoverable up to a daily maximum. This approach is in keeping with the Franks Committee view that 'if tribunals are to be truly accessible the citizen must be able to have recourse to them without running the risk of being out of pocket his reasonable expenses' (1957: para. 94). The 'reasonable expenses' do not, however, include the cost of representation which has to be borne by the represented party. Nor is there any reimbursement of expenses incurred by lawyers, full-time trade union officers or officials of employers' associations who act as representatives. Unlike the costs incurred in travelling to the tribunal hearing, the cost of engaging a representative is seen as optional since the parties are permitted to represent themselves.

Whether, and to what extent, costs were incurred in going to a tribunal hearing by those parties we surveyed depended to a large extent on the type of representation used. As Table 7.1 shows, just over half of the 429 applicants whose cases went to a hearing and just under three-quarters of the 443 employers involved in heard cases said they incurred some net cost. Those employers using company specialist representation and applicants represented by trade unions were the two groups least likely to incur any cost. Next came employers with company lay representation and applicants who represented themselves. The average cost incurred by employers ranged from £50 where company lay representation was used to around £240 where external legal representation was engaged. Among applicants average costs incurred ranged from £10, the average for those representing themselves, to £130, the average for those engaging lawyers. At present prices these 1977 figures would double.

Applicants and employers who incurred costs in bringing or defending a case at a tribunal hearing were asked whether they considered the amount expended was on the whole reasonable or unreasonable. Fifty-nine per cent of those applicants who incurred costs in going to a hearing of their case considered them reasonable, 39 per cent did not. Among employers who incurred costs, 48 per cent considered them reasonable and 49 per cent did not. Views on reasonableness will obviously depend on the amount of expenditure involved. The average cost (1977 figure) incurred by applicants who thought their costs reasonable was £40 and among those saying unreasonable £140. The average cost which had to be met by employers who felt costs incurred were reasonable was £110 and twice that amount among those employers who felt they were unreasonable. The outcome of the case made only a slight difference to views on reasonableness.

TABLE 7.1

THE COST OF GOING TO TRIBUNAL HEARING

APPLICANTS

	All Heard	%	Self	%	Representation at Hearing: TU	%	Sol.	%	Other	%
Costs incurred	231	54	103	54	24	26	85	88	20	45
No net costs	194	45	88	46	72	75	10	10	24	54
Don't know whether costs incurred	3	1	1	1	–	–	2	2	–	–
Average known total cost (£)a	40		10		30		130		10	
	N = 429		N = 192		N = 96		N = 97		N = 44	

EMPLOYERS

	All Heard	%	Co. Lay	%	Representation at Hearing: Co. Spec.	%	Ext. Legal	%	Empl. Assoc.	%
Costs incurred	326	74	98	66	47	57	161	88	14	70
No net costs	78	17	40	27	29	35	1	1	4	20
Don't know whether costs incurred	39	9	10	7	6	7	21	11	2	10
Average known total cost (£)a	130		50		60		340		70	
	N = 433		N = 148		N = 82		N = 183		N = 20	

SOURCE: IRRU surveys.

NOTE:
a. Includes those incurring no cost; excludes those not knowing whether costs were incurred or what level. Prices at 1977 level rounded to nearest £10.

Cheapness as a characteristic of an accessible system appears to be concerned more with the costs likely to be incurred by the applicant as the initiator of the action. To some extent this probably reflects the fact that the Franks Committee was concerned mainly with administrative tribunals at which the respondent is the state or a government agency. Where this is not the case it is arguable that costs which have to be incurred by the respondent in defending the case should be considered also. We have indicated above the amounts actually expended by employers on legal advice and representation and travel and other direct costs incurred in attending the tribunal hearing. But it is necessary also to take some account of less easily quantifiable 'expenditure' such as managerial and other time taken in the preparation and presentation of a case. For example, a small company in particular may find the necessity for certain key personnel to attend as witnesses at a hearing very disruptive to business.

Sixty per cent of the 443 employers in cases heard by a tribunal considered the amount of working time spent on the case was unreasonable. Again, the outcome of the case made no significant difference to the employers' view. Engaging an external lawyer to handle the case does not appear to obviate the need for internal personnel to spend time on it. Sixty-four per cent of employers who were represented at the hearing by external lawyers said they thought the amount of working time expended was unreasonable compared with 51 per cent of those represented by internal company specialists. Of course part of the job function of internal company specialists is handling cases of this kind and time spent so doing is, therefore, less likely to be seen as unreasonable. Although employers may feel aggrieved at the time required to deal with an industrial tribunal case, it is difficult to envisage how the right to apply to a tribunal can be invoked by dismissed workers without causing some inconvenience to the dismissing employers. Perhaps it might be noted that a 'reasonable' employer will have taken various steps prior to dismissing (for example ensuring that a proper investigation of alleged misconduct has been undertaken or performance has been monitored adequately and proper warnings have been given and recorded) which will facilitate the production of evidence and reduce the time which has to be expended.

As noted, one element in the cheapness/accessibility of industrial tribunals compared with the courts is that the losing party does not have to pay the costs of the winner. There is a provision for the awarding of costs but such awards have been infrequent. In 1980 the grounds on which costs could be awarded were widened but it is too soon to evaluate the effect of this change.

The 1980 Regulations provide that

> a tribunal shall not normally make an award in respect of the
> costs and expenses incurred by a party to the proceedings but
> where in its opinion a party . . . has in bringing or conducting the
> proceedings acted frivolously, vexatiously or otherwise unreason-
> ably the tribunal may make an order (r.11(1)).[1]

'Or otherwise unreasonably' was added as part of the 1980 changes
which also clarified that the rule covered action both in bringing and
in conducting the proceedings. This view had already been expressed
by the EAT in *Cartiers Superfoods Ltd v Laws* ([1978] IRLR 315). In
this case the award of costs was made against the employers. The
applicant had been summarily dismissed without any opportunity
to offer an explanation for her conduct; the employers had threat-
ened her with a suit for damages if she took legal advice, had described her as a criminal in their notice of appearance to the tribunal
and then failed to call evidence at the hearing to support their case.
Although the EAT found the employer had acted frivolously in attempting to defend a manifestly hopeless case, it noted that ' a finding of
that character, particularly in the case of a respondent, is a strong
finding to make because the respondent is obviously brought to Court
even though the onus of proof is on him and, therefore, must not lightly
be said to be frivolous'.

This case is of further interest because it extended the meaning of
vexatious and frivolous action to cover not only situations where the
parties know there is no substance to their claims or defences but also
situations where they *ought* to have known if they had gone about the
matter sensibly. This widened the possibility of costs being awarded
beyond cases where a party could be seen to be acting in bad faith although in *Lothian Health Board v Johnstone* ([1981] IRLR 321) the
EAT reminded tribunals that the circumstances of the *Cartiers* case
were rather exceptional and that 'frivolous' should not be interpreted
too widely. The 1980 changes remove the necessity for tribunals to try
to widen the interpretation of vexatious and frivolous in order to award

---

1. Under r.11 tribunals may also award any costs or expenses incurred as a result
of a postponement or adjournment. Where the postponement or adjournment
is caused by the employer's failure to provide information on job availability in
cases where notice has been given that re-employment is being sought, or where
the case involves return to work after pregnancy or confinement absence, then the
tribunal has to order the employer to pay costs or expenses incurred by the
applicant as a result of the postponement or adjournment.

costs by providing the potentially wide ground of 'otherwise unreasonable' action.

Unlike tribunals, the EAT has always had the power, under its r.21(1), to award costs for unreasonable action and it has done so where cases have been held to have been non-starters and where claims have been withdrawn at the last minute, after the other side incurred expense in preparation. There are good reasons why the tribunals should not follow this example too closely. Firstly, the listing of a case for a tribunal hearing is not delayed while conciliation takes place and it may be that a settlement is agreed or a case dropped very near the time of hearing. As the efficient operation of the system benefits from a proportion of cases being disposed of without a hearing, it would be unfortunate if tribunals started awarding costs against applicants or employers for agreeing to or offering last-minute settlements. Secondly, with regard to cases which are held to have been non-starters, there is the problem of knowing this before the event. As Abel-Smith and Stevens point out (1968: 66), while the principle of having the winner's costs paid by the loser:

> helps the poorer litigant with a cast iron case, it is all too often possible to know that a case is cast iron only after it has been tried. Thus the risk, however small, of having to pay one's opponent's 'taxed' costs makes litigation even less attractive for those with modest means.

The EAT, which can only hear appeals on points of law, has taken the view that to bring an appeal where there is no point of law may be unreasonable behaviour and result in an award of costs. In *Redland Roof Tiles Ltd v Eveleigh* ([1979] IRLR 11) the EAT held that had counsel's opinion been sought the party would have been advised that the appeal would be a non-starter. Although ascertaining whether there is a point of law requires legal advice, the EAT did not regard counsel's opinion as a luxury at the appeal stage in this case. As we have noted earlier, it is more difficult for parties at first instance to know whether their cases are likely to succeed. What then is unreasonable action? It might be argued that a reasonable applicant or employer would seek expert advice where the merit of the case was not clear. In many cases this will mean engaging the services of a private lawyer which would contradict and undermine the desired cheapness and accessibility of tribunals. Other problems might also arise. For example, unions and their members may be concerned with collective interests in pursuing a particular unfair dismissal case which itself has little chance of success. While perfectly reasonable from the collective point of view (for example as a way of putting pressure on an employer to adopt a discipline procedure or to demonstrate a preparedness to challenge management decisions as a way of encouraging unionisation), bringing such a case may be held to be unreasonable by a tribunal concerned with the *individual* dismissal.

The parallel circumstances at first instance to bringing an appeal which lacks a point of law is bringing a case which is out of scope (for example because the applicant is too old) and which could have been seen easily to have been out of scope. However, the tribunals are not limiting themselves to this type of case. In *Stein v Associated Dairies Ltd* ((1982) EAT 67/82; see IRLIB 1982: 10) one of the first decisions under the new costs rule, an applicant who was 67 minutes late the morning after receiving a final warning was held to have been fairly dismissed and to have acted unreasonably in bringing the application. This decision to award costs was allowed to stand by the EAT on appeal.

The tribunal has discretion as to the amount of costs which it awards. It can award a specified sum or that costs are 'taxed', that is assessed by the county court if the parties themselves cannot agree an appropriate sum. The tribunal may take account of the party's ability to pay in determining an appropriate sum or whether to award costs. Thus, in *Wiggin Alloys Ltd v Jenkins* [1981] IRLR 275, a tribunal refused to award costs against someone in prison who brought an unfair dismissal application frivolously. The amount of costs awarded is generally not high. Because of their lesser ability to bear and spread costs and because of the greater use of specialist representation by employers, the threat of costs can be seen to weigh more heavily on applicants than respondents. This is in keeping with the rationale behind the new costs rule. The rule change making costs more likely was not to ensure that fewer successful parties were out of pocket but to deter applications (DE, 1979b: 876).

Although the rule on costs makes it clear that awards are still to be abnormal, the 1980 changes may be expected to increase their likelihood. The proportion of heard cases in which costs were awarded may not increase above the 1980 level of 4 per cent, however, since the pre-hearing assessment system is leading to the withdrawal of many cases where the possibility of costs is raised (see above, p. 104). As we discussed earlier, the tribunal system was seen as almost too accessible – dismissed workers had 'nothing to lose' by applying. The threat of costs was seen as a deterrent which would act both to reduce applications and, coupled with the pre-hearing assessment, to reduce the number of cases proceeded with. The introduction of this additional filter, although limiting accessibility and potentially increasing the cost of going to tribunal, was seen as functional in ensuring that only 'worth-while' cases took up valuable tribunal time.

Representation

One access barrier in the ordinary courts is the need to employ a lawyer or, in some lower courts, to obtain permission of the court to dispense with legal representation. The tribunals allow, even formally encourage, parties to present their own cases but it is questionable whether this completely removes the barrier of representation. While representation at tribunals is not *necessary* in formal terms, we have seen that it is perceived by operators and users of tribunals alike to be beneficial. As the Benson Commission on Legal Services concluded (1979: para. 2.17): 'whatever the tribunal and however informal its procedure, representation, whether by a lawyer or skilled layman, in the majority of cases confers an advantage on the represented party'.

Where representation is seen as beneficial, problems experienced or anticipated in obtaining skilled advice and help in preparing and present-ing a case may deter application or lead to withdrawal of claims, in short reduce the accessibility of tribunals. Two, not mutually exclusive, approaches to remedy this are possible: one is to attempt to provide a system where representation confers no advantage, the other is to at-tempt to achieve equality of representation.

The ideology of the tribunal system, as we have seen, is that unrepre-sented parties are not disadvantaged and that the nature of tribunal hearings is such that the parties can present their own cases without prejudicing their chances of success. The evidence presented earlier, however, suggests that this is not the case in practice. There have been changes to the tribunal regulations and occasional reminders to the tribunals designed to combat what is seen as creeping legalism and no doubt more changes could be introduced to emphasise the informal, flexible approach which is the model for tribunal behaviour. But the characteristics of the parties and the context in which the tribunals have to operate, the fact that they are court-substitute bodies applying complex law rather than non-court bodies, constrains the extent to which skilled advice and representation will ever be seen as irrelevant or unimportant.

Unless the system is to be revised radically, therefore, the second ap-proach, attempting to achieve equality of representation, seems poten-tially more fruitful. Banning legal representation and insisting that both parties represent themselves would help procure a superficial equality. But it would be only superficial because it ignores the fact that the parties do not start from equal positions in their ability to prepare and present their cases and that employer self-representation often means the use of internal specialists and is superior to the usual applicant self-representation. It also ignores the fact that representation may be beneficial at two stages: advice and assistance prior to the hearing and advocacy at the hearing. Banning legal representation at hearing would not address the inequality at the stage prior to the hearing, the stage which the first President of Tribunals in England and Wales considered the more important. Commenting shortly before the tribunals received the unfair dismissal jurisdiction, Sir Diarmaid Conroy noted (1971b: 1070):

> My experience is that legal representation at the hearing of a case does not normally make any difference — with or without it, we will reach the same decision. What often troubles me is that if the employee or the employer had had better advice in getting his papers together and in preparing the evidence then the result might well have been different.

Disadvantage through lack of representation, therefore, has to be tackled at both stages. Rather than banning legal representation at hearing, skilled advice and representation at hearing and prior to hearing should be made more accessible.

The best way of doing this would be to make the availability of skilled lay advice and representation more widespread. As we saw in Chapter 2, at the moment the most common skilled lay (non-legal) representation is that provided by industrial relations officers and similar specialists within larger companies, by employers' associations and by trade unions. None of these forms of representation is generally publicly available. Increased membership of employers' associations and trade unions and an increase in the services such bodies provide for their members would, or course, increase the possibility of this kind of assistance. However, membership of an employers' association might bring with it certain obligations for employers such as recognition of trade unions, or having to follow certain wage rates which may be seen as unacceptable. For applicants union membership may appear to offer a solution but, as we have seen, many unfair dismissal applicants come from areas of employment where unions have found it difficult to organise. Although this does not prevent any individual from joining a union this is less likely in circumstances where the employer does not recognise one.

The skilled lay advice and representation which is theoretically available to everyone is that provided by such bodies as Citizens Advice Bureaux and Law Centres. As we have seen, such provision is patchy and variable but these bodies provide a nucleus which could be extended with the aid of grants and public funding to provide an easily accessible, free or cheap source of skilled advice and representation. An additional or alternative measure would be to establish rights enforcement officers to advise applicants. As we saw in the previous chapter, this is a role which some expect of ACAS conciliators but one which they are not able to perform.

Encouraging the growth of sources of skilled lay advice and representation provides a better approach than simply extending legal aid to tribunals, an approach which has been advocated by the Lord Chancellor's Legal Aid Advisory Committee and the Council on Tribunals among others, although perhaps ideally both approaches might be adopted. Extending legal aid to tribunals, designed to address the problem of disadvantage at the hearing stage, would help remove the cost barrier for those who qualified for aid but this is only one of the barriers to using legal representation. Any extension of legal aid would need to be accompanied by extensive publicity and information so that those who might be entitled to it were aware of its existence. A survey undertaken in Scotland to investigate public attitudes and experiences with regard to legal problems and legal services found that, even using a generous definition of what constitutes accurate information, there was an extensive lack of knowledge on the part of the public about such schemes as legal aid and legal advice and assistance. The lack of information was not spread randomly throughout the population: information about legal aid, for example, was least among those in lower socio-economic groups who are most likely to be eligible for it (Hughes, 1980: 84). Even where the availability of legal aid is known, other barriers may exist. These include access to solicitors operating the scheme: they need to be in convenient locations at convenient times and to appear approachable to groups in society who are at present wary of using them.

A combination of more easily available legal advice and representation and skilled lay advice and representation would appear to offer a way of meeting the needs of tribunal applicants more accurately than would be achieved by the extension of legal aid alone. Defining unfair dismissal as a legal problem and providing a court body to adjudicate appears to signpost legal advice and representation as the most appropriate form. But, although the nature of the system demands some knowledge of statute and case law for effective representation, applicants, as we suggested in Chapter 2, have a range of needs wider than for specifically legal skills and they look to representation to meet them.

Reasons given by applicants in our survey for employing legal representation give an indication of this. One applicant who employed a solicitor explained this was 'because when you go to court you can't put into words what you want to say where a solicitor can', a feeling echoed by another applicant who said 'my solicitor did well, he was able to talk – I could never have managed'. Verbal skills can of course be provided by lay representatives but where, as at present, these are not easily available, applicants will have to turn to solicitors. The same applies to other functions which applicants explicitly or implicitly want representatives to perform, such as providing moral support and reassurance, interpreting what is going on, and bridging the social and educational gap which can exist between themselves and the tribunal (Frost and Howard, 1977: 64). The reasons given by the 97 applicants in our survey who were legally represented at the hearing for choosing that kind of representation show that a quarter of them were seeking specifically legal advice and help, or thought that a lawyer was the best person for the job. Almost as many (23 per cent of legally represented applicants) chose this kind of representative, however, because they felt unable to manage on their own and 16 per cent of the 97 wanted expert, but not specifically legal, help. Skilled lay representation would perhaps be more appropriate and less costly for some applicants who at present engage lawyers because there is no other alternative to self-representation.

The wider provision of skilled lay representation would mean that the applicants who present their own cases to tribunal are those who want to do so. Most of the 192 applicants in our survey who represented themselves at hearing had not made a positive choice to do so. Two-thirds of them said they presented their own cases because there was no real alternative, either because they could not afford to employ a lawyer (43 per cent of self-represented applicants said this) or because representation had been refused (11 per cent) or because they were unaware that any other form of representation was possible (11 per cent) or because they had no one to ask to represent them (4 per cent).

The main argument usually made against the extension of legal aid to the industrial tribunals is that of cost, but other objections may also be raised which have to do with the consequences of increased legal representation. These might be avoided in the case of skilled lay representation. It can be argued that the specific legal skills of a lawyer are only occasionally necessary at hearings but that an increase in legal representation would follow from an extension of legal aid. This in turn would lead to more delay in the system, and increase the likelihood of formality and legalism at hearings by, for example, increasing the frequency of case citation and the insistence on strict adherence to rules of procedure and would serve to emphasise the court-like features of tribunals, such as the adversarial nature of hearings, rather than encourage the development of a more inquisitorial approach. In short, increased frequency of legal representation would make it harder for tribunals to display freedom from technicality.

Freedom from Technicality

This aspect of accessibility is often expressed as the informality of tribunals. The 1980 Industrial Tribunal Regulations instruct (r.8(1)):

> The tribunal shall conduct the hearing in such manner as it con-
> siders most suitable to the clarification of the issues before it
> and generally to the just handling of the proceedings: it shall so far
> as appears to it appropriate seek to avoid formality in its pro-
> ceedings and it shall not be bound by any enactment or rule of
> law relating to the admissibility of evidence in proceedings before
> the courts of law.

Strict adherence to rules of evidence, therefore, is one aspect of technicality which the tribunals can dispense with in attempting to achieve the desired informality. But, as the rule implies, there are limits as to how much informality is appropriate or possible. Certain aspects of formality may be functional in that they provide a reasonably efficient solution to a particular problem and certain technicalities may be unavoidable given the context in which tribunals have to operate.

Two main sources of technicality may be identified: the nature and importance of the law and the procedure adopted. Various factors arise from the nature of the system which help foster legalism and formality. Among them is the law itself as enacted and as developed by case law. As Phillips J has noted (1978: 137, 140), tribunals operate 'under the handicap that they are enjoined to be informal and to eschew technicalities and legalism but are at the same time required to cope with ever increasing complexity of subject matter'. The statutory concept of dismissal itself, which is a contractual definition, inevitably opened the way for the principles of common law to be brought into industrial tribunal determination, particularly in cases concerning constructive dismissal. The existence of the right to appeal has inevitably led to legalism in that case law is reported and cited and, together with the court-substitute nature of the tribunals, has meant that tribunal rulings need to be consistent and reasoned. Allowed discretion as to the way the hearing is conducted, the tribunals, with lawyers in the chair and with the underlying accusatorial model of hearings, have, not surprisingly, echoed many court practices. These are seen, particularly by those trained in court procedures and practices, as the best, or sometimes the only, way of arriving at the facts of the case and of ensuring a just and orderly procedure. The nature of the legislation and the procedures adopted have reinforced the apparent appropriateness of legal representation and, in turn, increased use of legal representation has emphasised and reinforced some of the court-like features of tribunal procedure, increased legalism and so reduced the informality.

We would agree with Munday (1981: 151) that industrial tribunal hearings 'are conducted in an environment from which some conventional legal technicalities cannot reasonably be banished' and recognise that ultimately severe limitations are placed on the potential informality of tribunals. It is necessary, however, to look more closely at what is meant by formality and when formality might be functional in order to know what degree of informality and freedom from technicality might be achievable.

Atkinson has argued that conversation is a basic comparative reference point in the categorisation of actions as formal. That is to say, the more interactional details depart from conversational ways of talking the more the situation will be perceived as formal (1982: 90). Thus features found in court settings, like rules of evidence and procedure, can be seen as exerting special constraints on what may be talked about and at which point in the proceedings. These are counterproductive to conversational interaction and are therefore formal. Attempts to bring about greater informality are likely to involve the elimination of such constraints. But Atkinson argues (1982: 114) that specialised and legal procedures have developed because they perform certain functions and that

> policy recommendations designed to eliminate or reduce 'formality' from various settings may have the effect of reducing the chances of certain sorts of practical tasks being accomplished at all.

This tension is implicit in the Franks view that:

> the object to be aimed at in most tribunals is the combination of a formal procedure with an informal atmosphere . . . it means a manifestly sympathetic attitude on the part of the tribunal and the absence of the trappings of a court, but on the other hand such prescription of procedure as makes the procedure clear and orderly (1957: para. 64).

A line needs to be drawn therefore between trappings and useful features. Abel-Smith and Stevens criticise the excessive formality of dress and ritual of the courts (1968: 206–7):

> for a party or witness unused to them they may well add considerably to what is already an ordeal and thus act as a barrier to

communication, or even to the willingness of persons with good cases to take them to court at all. The traditional modes of address may have a similar effect. Even the layout of the court room may have certain inhibiting effects. It might be possible to indicate the role of the judge without raising his chair too far from the floor as if it were a throne.

Atkinson argues that formal language and formalities such as standing up when addressing the court, the wearing of robes and so on may not be trappings but functional aspects of court proceedings. The wearing of robes etc. may be 'extremely effective in providing for the instant and unambiguous identification of particular individuals even from quite considerable distances' (1982: 106) while standing up to speak is necessary for visibility, for seeing and monitoring audience reaction and attentiveness, and the use of formal language and procedure is a solution to a 'general interactional problem' of 'achieving and sustaining the shared attentiveness of co-present parties to a single sequence of actions'. He also notes that the form of speech characteristic of lawyers in court – greater volume, slower pace, longer pauses than in normal conversation – is necessary for them to be heard and followed.

A number of the functional characteristics of the features discussed by Atkinson do not apply to the industrial tribunals in the way they do to the traditional courts, not least because the tribunals operate on a smaller scale. The dozen, often fewer, people at a tribunal hearing do not call for the same aids to visibility and hearing as do large numbers of people gathered in cavernous court rooms. Following a procedure which governs the order of giving evidence, when questions may be asked, and what is permitted cross-examination etc. may be necessary to ensure everyone gets a fair turn and that the facts of the case are brought out in an orderly way. But this is not necessarily the only way of achieving this and insistence on the procedure being followed by parties unused to it may be inimical to these ends. During our observation exercise we came across instances where unrepresented parties were inhibited and constrained in presenting their cases by being criticised and stopped when, for example, they made statements instead of asking questions, tried to introduce new information at 'inappropriate' points in the hearing or tried to contribute information while not in the witness chair.

Procedures and ways of doing things which have proved functional in the court context may well come to be taken for granted as 'the best way' of doing things even out of that context and it requires vigilance on the part of the tribunal, particularly the legal chairperson, to ensure that only those aspects of formality which are still functional and not counterproductive in the tribunal context are insisted upon. A recent case provides an example of what is meant here. The chairperson in this case insisted that an unrepresented applicant give her evidence by word of mouth after the employer's counsel objected to her reading from a prepared statement. She was stopped again when she tried to give evidence with the help of a note she had made the previous day when the employer had given evidence. It is normal court practice for witnesses to be allowed to refer only to notes made at the time of, or shortly after, the incident referred to. However, the EAT, in allowing the applicant's appeal and remitting the case, held that such an approach was inappropriate where there is no advocate to take the person through their evidence. The effect of the tribunal's ruling had been to deprive the applicant 'of the props which are necessary to enable even the professional applicant to elicit evidence properly . . . (which) put her at the gravest disadvantage in the presentation of her case' (*Watson-Smith v Tagol Ltd t/a Alangate Personnel* (1981) EAT 611/81; see IRLIB 312, 20 July 1982).

An approach to eliminating undue formality in tribunal hearings, therefore, is to ask of a particular feature why is this done, what function does it serve? Is the function necessary? If so, is this the only or best way of achieving it? If it serves no function or is counterproductive in the tribunal context, or if it performs a function which could be performed by other, less formal means, then it could be dispensed with. This provides one way of separating those aspects of formality which are useful from those which owe more to legal tradition or mystification. But there may be no single 'right' answer to some of these questions. For example, the Franks Committee felt that tribunals should have the power to administer the oath but thought it would be counterproductive to the 'preservation of informality of atmosphere before many tribunals . . . ordinarily to require the oath to be administered' (1957: para. 91). Industrial tribunals have the power, under r.8(4) of the 1980 Regulations, to require witnesses to give evidence on oath or affirmation and, from our observation, do so invariably. This is clearly a formal feature of hearings but one which the industrial tribunals, unlike Franks, consider functional in obtaining the truth of the matter, even though it may jeopardise the non-court atmosphere they strive to obtain.

There are also likely to be different views on the level of formality which is functional in upholding the status of the tribunal, an important factor if its decisions are to be heeded. This may help account for different practices between tribunal regions as to whether those present are required to stand as the tribunal members enter and leave the room. Another aspect of this is referred to by Atkinson (1982: 173) who comments that were professionals to forsake formal language and to adopt normal conversational conventions, for example, saying 'oh' on receiving new information, then their specialist competence or expertise might be put seriously in doubt.

This raises the linked question of the expectations of the parties. Applicants and employers do not generally see their tribunal hearing as an everyday event and some formality may be expected and taken for granted. For example, our observations revealed that most, probably all, people attending tribunals had 'dressed-up' for the occasion and would no doubt have been surprised if the members of the tribunal had dressed casually. The guidance literature provided for parties says that 'the procedure during the hearing is orderly, but simple and flexible' (COIT, 1981b: 10) and that 'the atmosphere of a tribunal is not that of a law court' (Henderson, 1982: 7). This advice creates certain expectations which may or may not be met. It partly depends on the criteria against which the tribunal is measured.

To lawyers and others using the traditional courts, implicitly or explicitly, as a yardstick, the tribunals will appear informal and procedurally flexible. But this may not be how they are seen by those without experience of courts. Seventy-one per cent of the 429 applicants we surveyed whose cases went to a hearing had never previously taken part in tribunal or court proceedings of any kind. As Table 7.2 shows, applicants were less likely than other participants to find their tribunal hearings 'relaxed and informal'. Fifty-five per cent agreed that they were, a smaller proportion than among employers, 60 per cent of whom agreed with this statement. Over 80 per cent of those who chair tribunals and sit as lay members thought that hearings were relaxed and informal.

That different people assess tribunal hearings from different perspectives helps explain variations in reactions to other statements about tribunal hearings which were put to the various groups surveyed. As Table 7.2 indicates, what lawyers and certain others may regard as normal or acceptable vocabulary may be seen by different people as 'legal jargon'. Only 3 per cent of the chairpersons surveyed agreed that 'tribunal hearings have too much legal jargon', a view shared by 10 per cent of employer-nominated lay members and 14 per cent of respondent employers. A higher rate of agreement came from trade-union-nominated lay members and from applicants who went to a hearing, 45 per cent of whom thought there was too much legal jargon at their hearing.

Inasmuch as 'legal jargon' is an aspect of technicality, then whether tribunals exhibit freedom from technicality may be thought to be in the eye of the beholder. However, it is the applicants' perceptions

TABLE 7.2

VIEWS OF TRIBUNAL HEARING

	Chair	TU Lay Member	Employer Lay Member	Respondent Employer	Applicant
			Percentage Agreeing with Statement[a]		
Tribunal hearings are relaxed and informal	80	82	85	60	55
Tribunal hearings have too much 'legal jargon'	3	30	10	14	45
	N = 35[b]	N = 101	N = 107	N = 389	N = 417

SOURCE: IRRU surveys.

NOTES:
a. The statements are recorded as put to tribunal members, the parties were asked about their particular hearing.
b. Percentages relate to those giving an answer; 'don't knows' are excluded.

which are the key ones if freedom from technicality and informality are seen as crucial aspects in the willingness and ability of people to apply to a tribunal without representation on which the cheapness and accessibility of the tribunal largely rest. It may be, however, that the degree of informality and freedom from technicality which would be necessary to satisfy the needs of unrepresented applicants is impossible for tribunals operating within the present context, as discussed above.

This section has been concerned with freedom from technicality in tribunal hearings, and this is the stage of proceedings on which attention is usually focused. However, it is important that undue formality is also avoided in dealings prior to the hearing. The communications from the tribunal office and the forms which are used, particularly when judged by the standards of other official documents, do appear to have been designed to avoid technicalities, although still demanding quite a high standard of literacy.

Expedition

A major advantage which the tribunals have over the ordinary courts is the short time which elapses between application and hearing. The tribunal regulations contain some time requirements which help determine the minimum possible time: the employer is allowed up to fourteen days to make a notice of appearance in response to the application, and the parties have to be given fourteen days' notice of the hearing. Adding on time for the processing of forms and arranging the hearing, it seems that the practical base line is around six weeks. As Table 7.3 shows, a fifth of cases came to hearing in this time and 39 per cent were heard within eight weeks from application. It has also to be borne in mind that, through ACAS conciliation, the majority of cases come to an end within an even shorter period.

As would be expected, applicants bringing their own cases came to hearing more quickly than those represented by solicitors or those in cases where the employer had legal representation. Legal representatives, as we have seen, are more likely to take interlocutory steps and thus require more time to prepare. They are also likely to have other court commitments. Only 15 per cent of employers in cases heard by the tribunal had to wait more than three months after receiving notice of the claim against them before the hearing of the case. Among those with external legal representation, however, a quarter waited more than three months. Similarly with applicants employing solicitors: while a quarter of the 192 self-represented applicants in heard cases waited over three months from the time of application to the hearing, a third of those with legal representation waited this long. A quarter of self-

TABLE 7.3

TIME FROM APPLICATION TO HEARING

	All Heard Applicants %	Self-Representation %	Specialist Representation %
4 weeks or less	6	6	6
Over 4 weeks, less than 6 weeks	14	18	11
Over 6 weeks, less than 8 weeks	19	23	15
	39	47	32
Over 8 weeks, less than 3 months	31	29	35
Over 3 months, less than 4 months	17	14	19
Over 4 months, less than 6 months	10	8	11
Over 6 months, less than 9 months	3	2	3
Don't know	1	1	—
	N = 429	N = 192	N = 193

SOURCE: IRRU survey. (There are no comparable official statistics published.)

represented applicants had their case heard within six weeks, while only 16 per cent of those represented by solicitors got to hearing within this time. To some extent the time taken to get to hearing reflects the listing practices of the regional offices rather than solicitors actually requesting postponement. But the listing practices are themselves based on experience and the knowledge that legal representatives require more time for case preparation than self-represented parties and are likely to have other commitments preventing attendance at short notice.

Tribunals can grant postponements and 30 per cent of the applicants surveyed said their hearing had been postponed, generally at the request of the employer. In Scotland the practice is to ask both parties about their availability before listing the case for hearing and to be reluctant to change the date once notified. Fewer applicants (20 per cent) in Scotland than in other regions reported postponement of hearing. This practice is now being adopted by some regions in England and Wales.

About two-thirds of applicants in cases taking six to eight weeks to be heard thought this time period 'about right'; just over half of those whose case took three to four months to come to hearing also thought this. Among those whose case took over four months the majority thought the time 'too long'. Table 7.4 shows the overall response of applicants and respondents when asked about the time between application (or, for employers, notification of the application) and the hearing. It should be borne in mind that application may be made up to three months after dismissal.

Employers were generally satisfied with the time taken for cases to get to hearing. Of course, they can exercise more control over this than the applicant by the speed with which they respond to the application. Where there was dissatisfaction it was felt that the time taken was 'too long'. A higher proportion of applicants (39 per cent) than employers (23 per cent) considered the time taken was too long but the reasons given by the two sides for thinking this were very similar. The most common reason for considering the time taken too long, given by 30 per cent of the employers who thought this and 28 per cent of applicants, was that the memory becomes unreliable and one forgets facts. Next came the desire to get the matter over with (22 per cent of applicants and 19 per cent of employers) followed by financial considerations. Sixteen per cent of applicants thinking the time was too long thought this because they were receiving no income and were finding it difficult to find a job. The same proportion of employers thought delay meant they risked paying higher compensation. Fourteen per cent of applicants and of employers thought the time taken was too long because of the stress and strain thereby occasioned.

TABLE 7.4

PARTIES' VIEW OF TIME TAKEN TO GET TO HEARING

	Applicants	*Respondent Employers*
	%	%
Too long	39	23
Too short	2	4
About right	59	70
	N = 429	N = 443

SOURCE: IRRU survey.

The parties' own evaluation of the length of time and reasons why it is considered too long, in a minority of cases, makes no mention of remedies, other than the fear of some employers that the more time which elapses before the case is heard the higher any compensation award would be. There is, however, an argument that the time between application and tribunal hearing reduces applicants' desire for re-employment (Lewis, 1981: 323). But, as we argued in Chapter 5 and as Lewis acknowledges (1983: 233), lack of desire for the remedy is not an adequate explanation for the low level of re-employment awards. In fact arguments can be made to support the opposite view, that is, that some lapse of time may make re-employment *more* likely, for example by in effect imposing a 'cooling off' period. In their study of reinstatement awards made by tribunals, Williams and Lewis (1981: 361) found that

> it was often the case, however, that neither of the parties had made an informed judgement prior to the hearing about the suitability of re-employment. The case studies suggest that more than half the employees who ultimately secured a tribunal decision had not been seeking re-employment when they first lodged their complaint. Indeed some had not considered re-employment until the day of the tribunal hearing.

We do not wish to suggest that the time between date of dismissal and resolution of the question may not be important in determining the likelihood of re-employment being achieved. But we would argue that what is more important is the status of the contractual relationship during that period. Some reasons given by applicants in our survey for not requesting their jobs back when applying to the tribunal, which were detailed in Chapter 5, indicate that *remaining* in the job might be more acceptable to applicants than *returning* to a job after the employment contract had been terminated.

In theory all dismissal disputes other than summary dismissal could be resolved prior to the actual dismissal without changing the existing unfair dismissal provisions as application for unfair dismissal can be made by an employee under notice of dismissal. This happens infrequently but the main obstacle is that, even if application were made as soon as notice of dismissal was received, the relatively short periods of notice to which British workers are statutorily entitled under EP(C)A s.49 allow little time for conciliation, let alone a hearing, to take place. Even if tribunals could hear cases within four weeks of application, only applicants who have at least five years' service are entitled to a long enough statutory minimum notice to allow for this and only a quarter of applicants in the survey came into this category. A large proportion of applicants have relatively short service and the statutory minimum notice period for those with under two years' service is only one week.

The special interim relief provisions in s.77 of the EP(C)A 1978 overcome this problem to some extent for applicants claiming unfair dismissal on the grounds of trade union membership or activity or non-membership. If, at an expedited hearing, a tribunal feels that the likely outcome of a full hearing will be a finding that dismissal was unfair on these grounds it can order the revival of the employee's contract, if terminated, or its continuation until the full hearing. These provisions can amount in effect to status quo pending the full hearing of the case although they do allow for interim re-engagement, if agreed, instead of reinstatement. There is, of course, no certainty that the tribunal will order re-employment at the full hearing.

This discussion has started to switch the yardstick by which the expedition of the tribunals is measured from comparison with the ordinary courts to criteria concerned with what is required by the nature of the dispute and the intentions of the legislation. This will be explored further later. Here we may note that, operating within the current framework, industrial tribunals appear to display the expedition in bringing cases to a hearing which the Franks Committee looked for.

Once at a hearing cases are disposed of relatively speedily. As Table 7.5 shows, according to both applicants and employers who attended their hearings, the vast majority of cases were heard in less than one day and over half took less than half a day. Sixty-one per cent of appli-

TABLE 7.5

DURATION OF TRIBUNAL HEARING

	Applicants %	Respondent Employers %
Half a day or less	61	51
One day	29	34
	90	85
1½ days to 2 days	8	10
More than 2 days	3	2
	N = 417	N = 443

SOURCE: IRRU survey.

cants surveyed said their cases were heard in a half a day or less and 29 per cent said the hearing took between a half and one day.

As with getting to a hearing, legal representation is associated with more time being taken. Twenty-three per cent of applicants had legal representation at the hearing but in those cases lasting longer than a day 43 per cent of applicants were so represented. Similarly with employers: in 41 per cent of heard cases the employer had external legal representation but 55 per cent of the cases taking longer than one day to be heard had solicitors or barristers representing the employer. While in part this is possibly a result of more complex cases being handled by legal representatives (although the causal link between complexity of a case and legal representation is not one way), the time taken also reflects the manner in which legal representatives choose to present cases, often with detailed opening and closing statements, calling of several witnesses, and citing of case law. Where a case is not completed by the tribunal within a day, long delays may occur between the first hearing date and the continued hearing. To a large extent this is a function of having a system which uses part-time chairpersons and lay members on an ad hoc rather than, for example, a seconded basis, as in such circumstances it may be difficult for the tribunal members to find a mutually acceptable date for the adjourned hearing at short notice.

The third element of expedition which needs to be considered, along with time taken to get a hearing and time taken for the case to be heard, is the time taken to receive any remedy awarded. Only eleven applicants surveyed were awarded re-employment by a tribunal and so Table 7.6 shows the assessment of time taken to receive their remedy made by only those 133 applicants who were awarded compensation for unfair dismissal by a tribunal. That only a fifth of these applicants received their compensation from the employer within four weeks of the hearing may indicate that employers generally wait until they have received the written decision from the tribunal before authorising payment. Over a third of applicants had to wait more than eight weeks before receiving any money, however, and a further 12 per cent had still received nothing by the time of the interview which generally was conducted some six months or more after the hearing. At present no interest is payable on tribunal awards, even those delayed when an appeal is lodged, although the Lord Chancellor's Department recently suggested a scheme whereby simple interest could be sought on awards over £500 (LCD, 1983: 1). The Employment Act 1980 inserted a provision into the EP(C)A (Sch. 9, para. 6A) giving the Secretary of State power to provide for payment of interest but this has not yet been used.

Any sum of money payable in pursuance of a tribunal decision in England and Wales is recoverable by execution issued from the county court after the making of an order by that court. In Scotland the sum is recoverable by Sheriff Officers provided with a copy of the decision. The information booklet, ITL1, provided to applicants informs them that in England and Wales awards are enforceable by application to the county court and notes that 'information about enforcement is given in a covering note issued with each tribunal decision' (p. 10). The covering note says that:

> Enforcement of awards by Industrial Tribunals is a matter for the County Court, under the provisions of the Employment Protection (Consolidation) Act 1978 Schedule 9 paragraph 7(1). If a sum of money awarded by an Industrial Tribunal is not paid when due, a request that enforcement action should be taken may be made by the person entitled to receive it to the nearest County Court. The Court staff will need to be shown (a) the decision of the tribunal and (b) any recoupment notice that may have been served by the Department of Employment in respect of unemployment or supplementary benefit received. They will explain the methods of enforcement that are available and the award may be enforced accordingly (para. 20, Notes on Tribunal Decisions IT9A, October 1980).

TABLE 7.6

TIME TAKEN TO RECEIVE COMPENSATION

	Number	% of Applicants Awarded Compensation
Less than 4 weeks	27	20
Over 4 weeks, less than 6	23	17
Over 6 weeks, less than 8	21	16
Over 8 weeks	46	35
Not answered	1	1
Not yet received by time of interview	15	12
	133	

SOURCE: IRRU survey.

Although obviously intended to be helpful, the covering note does not actually tell the applicant how to get in touch with a county court or give much indication of what is involved in so doing. Given that part of the rationale for giving unfair dismissal jurisdiction to the industrial tribunal system was the fact that ordinary people had a fear of 'going to court', it is perhaps to be regretted that in England and Wales they find this is where they have to end up should the employer not comply with the tribunal award.

Expertise

'Expert knowledge of a particular subject', the last of Franks's criteria, is rather harder to define than the others. The expertness of the industrial tribunals can be seen to consist of two elements: jurisdictional specialisation and the presence of lay judges with relevant knowledge or experience of that particular area. This lay member predominance should help ensure that tribunal decisions are not based purely on the 'black letter of the law' but show an awareness of wider industrial relations considerations.

Jurisdictional specialisation is one element of expertness of tribunals compared with the courts, but what exactly is the industrial tribunal's 'particular subject'? Since industrial tribunals were set up under the Industrial Training Act 1964 to hear appeals against training levies they have attracted more and more jurisdictions. Many of these concern disputes between individuals and their employers: for example over dismissal, sex and race discrimination, and various employment rights contained in the Employment Protection (Consolidation) Act 1978, such as time off for public duties or the right to maternity pay. However, there remain jurisdictions, such as that under the Industrial Training Act, where the state is the respondent and the employer the applicant. This is the case, for example, where there are disputes concerning rebates in respect of maternity or redundancy payments. More recently, under the Employment Act 1980, tribunals have been given jurisdiction over certain disputes between individuals and trade unions concerning unreasonable exclusion or expulsion from membership.

The industrial tribunals are in the main concerned with what are termed 'individual employment rights'. The distinction between individual and collective issues is a blurred one, but employment rights have generally been framed in such a way that a remedy can be sought only by an individual. In the case of lack of consultation over proposed redundancy, however, the situation is rather different in that the Employment Protection Act 1975 enables the union to apply to a tribunal citing the employer as respondent. If the tribunal finds the complaint well founded, however, the remedy is a declaration and monetary payment to the individuals made redundant.

Although tribunals deal with disputes between the state and employers, between individuals and their unions, and between unions and employers, the major jurisdictions in terms of case load are undoubtedly those concerning disputes between individuals and their employers. As we noted earlier, unfair dismissal alone accounts for some 75 per cent of tribunal applications. Not all disputes arising from the individual employment relation, however, can be taken to industrial tribunals. The Lord Chancellor (and Secretary of State in Scotland) has the power under s.131 of the EP(C)A 1978 to confer jurisdiction upon tribunals in respect of claims for damages for breach of the contract of employment and other contracts connected with employment, but this power has not yet been exercised.

The 'particular subject' of the industrial tribunals, therefore, can be seen to be disputes arising from the employment relation. The tribunals' expert knowledge of this area is obtained through their composition. As we discussed in Chapter 3, the tribunal consists of a legally qualified chairperson and two lay members, one nominated via employee organisations and one via employer organisations. The format of the tribunal is intended to bring both legal and industrial or commercial expertise to bear in deciding employment cases.

As we identified earlier, however, there are a number of constraints on the ability of lay members to make an expert contribution when deciding unfair dismissal cases. For instance the practice of not matching lay member background to the case when listing for hearings means the lay member can make only a general contribution of industrial or commercial knowledge rather than a specific expert contribution, based on detailed knowledge of the industry or occupation in question. This is a weaker, less specialised notion of expertise. At present the industrial background of lay members appears to differ significantly from the industrial distribution of unfair dismissal applicants. The construction industry, miscellaneous services, and distributive trades produced almost half the applications in 1976, the last year for which national figures on characteristics of the parties were provided (DE, 1977b: 1214). Only 12 per cent of the 102 employer-nominated lay members surveyed, however, came from these industries. The largest proportion of employer-nominated lay members, 30 per cent, came from engineering-based industries which produced some 17 per cent of applicants.

Although changes could be made to enhance the status of lay members within the tribunal, for example lay member chairing of hearings and closer matching of expertise to cases, these would not address the major constraints on the lay member expert contribution. These constraints derive from the legal framework, in particular the right of appeal to the courts. The existence of the appellate structure acts to accentuate the differential position of lay and legal members, but its main impact is on the tribunal as a whole which is constrained in its ability to act in a discretionary way as an expert body. The legislators appealed to a deliberately undefined notion of justice which would be worked out by industrial tribunals on a case by case basis (Davies and Freedland, 1979: 349) but the appelate courts have handed down their own conceptions of justice which the tribunals have to follow.

In discussing the limits imposed by the appellate courts on the industrial tribunals' exercise of expertise, it is necessary to distinguish the first level of appeal, the Employment Appeal Tribunal, from the higher levels, in practice normally the Court of Appeal. The distinction lies in the fact that the EAT is itself a body of specialised jurisdiction and mixed lay/legal composition: it is an expert body.[2] Precedents provided by the EAT, therefore, although constraining the discretion of the industrial tribunals, need not necessarily reduce the extent to which the industrial tribunal system as a whole can be viewed as expert. Certainly the recently retired EAT President saw the EAT as emphasising, rather than reducing, the importance of industrial relations considerations in determining unfair dismissal cases and saw the notion of fairness embodied not just in the statute but in 'good industrial practice' (Browne-Wilkinson, 1982: 75).

The EAT adopted the role of developing and laying down the principles of fair industrial practice which 'reasonable employers' can be expected to adopt. This was seen as important both in ensuring consistency per se in the decision-making of some 60 tribunals up and down the country (Phillips, 1978: 139) and in enabling employers and others to predict the likely outcome of their actions in terms of the consequences at law; a development seen to be in the best interests of orderly industrial relations. What the EAT saw itself as doing in drawing on the knowledge and expertise of its own lay members in drawing up guidelines for the industrial tribunals (as for example in the redundancy case of *Williams and others v Compair Maxam Ltd* [1982] IRLR 83) was developing a code of practice for handling dismissal. The Code of Practice provided for by statute is seen as inadequate and out of date (Browne-Wilkinson, 1982: 74).

The EAT in dismissal cases hears appeals on points of law and its ability to act in the way just described rests on a broad interpretation of what constitutes an error of law enabling it to intervene in a tribunal decision. The use of an appellate jurisdiction to lay down guidelines on

2. EPC(C)A 1978 s.135.

industrial practice, however, does not accord with the lawyer's usual conception of the role of an appeal court (Browne-Wilkinson, 1982: 76) and, as we indicated in Chapter 3, the Court of Appeal in a number of decisions has been concerned to curb the EAT's activity. It has advised the EAT that it is wrong to make rules and establish presumptions for industrial tribunals (for example Lawton LJ in *Bailey v BP Oil Kent Refinery Ltd* [1980] IRLR 287) and is increasingly finding issues to be questions of fact and not of law and thus issues for the industrial tribunal to decide free from interference by the EAT (for example, *O'Kelly v Trust House Forte plc* [1983] IRLR 369). The view expressed in this and other cases is that decisions of industrial tribunals in such areas should not be disturbed unless the tribunal has either misdirected itself in law or reached a decision which no reasonable tribunal, directing itself properly on the law, could have reached.

On the face of it the Court of Appeal, in seeking to curb the EAT's guidance activity appears as defender of industrial tribunal discretion; upholder of expertise at first instance. It is, however, the Court of Appeal itself which has placed perhaps the greatest constraint on the ability of the industrial tribunal to operate as an expert body by laying down the 'reasonable employer' test discussed in Chapter 4. This requires an industrial tribunal, despite its expert nature, to judge an employer's action in dismissing not by its *own* view of what would have been reasonable in the circumstances but by the standards of the 'reasonable employer'. They must be norm reflecting not norm setting. Although characterised as industrial juries applying the accepted standards of industry operating at the relevant time and place (Anderman, 1978: 67) the tribunals, having heard the evidence, are not allowed to say 'if we had been the employer we would have done it this way'. The tribunal is not allowed to act as an expert body and impose its own independent solution in the way an industrial arbitration body would. To do so is to err in law.

This discussion suggests that where the right of appeal is to another expert body, although the discretion of the first instance body may be curbed, the degree to which the system displays expertness may be undiminished. When appeal is to the ordinary courts, however, the limitation on the discretion of the lower courts may also be a limitation on expertness in the system. Set against the ordinary courts, the industrial tribunals are expert bodies. Because they are not divorced from the ordinary court structure, however, the exercise of their expertise is constrained. As Ewing has noted in another context (1982b: 227):

It is one of the inexplicable facts of life of the post-Franks era that an appeal will lie from a specialist jurisdiction to a body with little or no experience in the subject matter of the dispute. It is all the more remarkable when the degree of expertise often exists in inverse proportion to the position of the appeal body in the hierarchy of courts.

The extent to which the expert industrial tribunal system can display 'doctrinal flexibility' or 'policy-consciousness' (Abel-Smith and Stevens, 1968: 220) is reduced by the appellate structure. That this would have been the case in operating the unfair dismissal legislation might have been foreseen from the experience of tribunals and the Redundancy Payments Act in the late 1960s. In their early discussion of how the tribunals were dealing with redundancy payment cases, Wedderburn and Davies noted (1969: 258–9) that the higher courts in many of the appeals had 'curbed the liberal spirit of the tribunals, imposing both a strict adherence to the black letter of the statute and . . . to more general legal doctrines'. They provide examples of cases where tribunal decisions 'plainly sound in policy' were overturned on appeal (ibid.: 267) and where 'the High Court can only be said to have replaced the tribunal's policy with its own'.

Cases involving alleged trade union membership dismissals provide an illustration of this process in respect of the unfair dismissal legislation. The policy intention behind part of the legislation (s.58 of EP(C)A 1978) is that workers should be free to exercise their rights to be members of a trade union and to take part in its activities without fear of dismissal. As the Donovan Commission emphasised, to sanction dismissal in such circumstances is to undermine trade unionism and the development of collective bargaining (1968: para. 527). The policy intention therefore was both to protect individuals and to underpin trade unionism and collective bargaining. The importance attached by the legislators to this aspect of policy is underlined by the fact that dismissal for these reasons is automatically unfair (the question of reasonableness does not arise); the usual service and age qualifications do not apply and a special, expedited procedure for interim relief is provided.

The EAT demonstrated its awareness of the policy intentions underlying the rights embodied in s.58 of the EP(C)A in the case of *Therm A Stor Ltd*, but its decision was not upheld by the Court of Appeal ([1983] IRLR 78). Within six months of the Therm A Stor factory opening in Peterborough, some 60 of the 70 employees had joined the Transport and General Workers' Union and, in April 1980, the union's district secretary was asked by employees at the factory to apply to the company for recognition. The district secretary wrote to the company's managing director claiming recognition and the company responded by dismissing twenty employees immediately. The four workers in the EAT case were among those selected for dismissal by chargehands. Lacking fifty-two weeks' service their claim for unfair dismissal could only be heard if they could show they had been dismissed on grounds of union membership or activities within the meaning of s.58. The EAT considered that since the reason for dismissal was by way of reprisal for the involvement of the Transport and General Workers' Union, where the employee was a union member then 'it can be said of him that the reason for his dismissal was that he was, or proposed to become, a member of a trade union or had taken, or proposed to take, part in the activities of a trade union'. This is the wording of s.58 and the EAT noted that 'any other conclusion would put an extraordinarily narrow construction upon s.58 and render it wholly inoperative in many instances where it must have been intended to apply'.

The Court of Appeal, however, was not prepared to construe s.58 to recognise the collective dimension of the individual right, so that, as the dismissed workers were members of a wider group, the union, and the reason for the dismissals was the activities of that group, the reason for their dismissal was their union membership and activities, albeit with others. Rather it held that s.58 is not concerned with an employer's reactions to a trade union's activities but with his reaction to an individual employee's activities in a trade union context. The reason why each of the employees had been dismissed, said the Court of Appeal, had nothing to do with anything which the worker concerned had personally done or proposed to do and so s. 58 had no application. The Editor of *Industrial Relations Law Reports* (IRLR) comments (1983: 88):

> The reasoning that the retaliation against the union 'had nothing to do' with anything which the employees had personally done appears based on the premise that in seeking recognition the union was acting of its own accord, in some sort of legal vacuum, and was not simply acting as the spokesman for the employees concerned. Since it is beyond doubt that the pursuit of recognition is a fundamental trade union activity, it seems inconceivable that if the employees themselves had presented the recognition claim in person and were dismissed for that reason, that their dismissals would not have fallen within the protected grounds. But to distinguish between a demand for trade union recognition directly by the employees and a recognition claim on their behalf by the union's official is to elevate a mode of communication into a principle of law.

> Although at first instance the tribunal had construed the statute

narrowly, the EAT had paid attention to the social policy underlying the statutory provisions. The Court of Appeal, however, stressed that effect should be given only 'to the intentions of Parliament as expressed in the statute'. In a judicial system the scope for operationalising social policy will depend on how well that policy has been encapsulated in the legal provisions, but statutory interpretation is not purely a deductive mechanical process; it is influenced by the 'social-moral or economic norms' of those making the interpretation (Kahn-Freund, 1931: 109).

Even where the policy objectives are clear in the legislation, however, they may not be realised in decision-making. This is shown by considering the tribunal remedies. The intention of the legislators, reinforced by changes effective from 1976, is that workers dismissed unfairly should get back their jobs. Re-employment is awarded rarely, as Chapter 5 noted, but there is little, if any, evidence that this is because the legislation does not promote it clearly or because it is feared that such awards would be put to one side on appeal. Rather the tribunals' reluctance to award the intended primary remedy comes from those factors discussed in Chapter 5 which, in addition to the influence of common law thinking, include assumptions about the desirability and viability of the remedy and a sensitivity on the part of the tribunals to the interests and views of employers regarding re-employment.

The discussion of re-employment is not intended to imply that legislative change might not achieve a greater incidence of continued employment. As we have noted elsewhere (Dickens et al., 1981: 174) the need for re-employment arises only because the employment contract is terminated. A new approach would be to give the employee priority of interpretation. This would mean no dismissal, if challenged, could be implemented until and unless the reasons forwarded by the employer were upheld as justifying dismissal. If they were not so upheld then the notice of dismissal would be declared invalid. Alternatively a tribunal could be empowered to declare a dismissal ineffective. Legislative change of this kind would create more of a positive presumption in favour of continued employment (or at least a continuing right to wages). While this could be expected to result in more people keeping their jobs than achieve re-employment under the present system of challenging dismissal post hoc, its effectiveness would depend as now on the willingness and ability of the tribunal to put aside employers' decisions. Legislative change of itself will not necessarily affect the attitude of tribunal members. The point here is that effectiveness in promoting policy objectives through legislation depends both on the provisions of the legislation and their interpretation in a way sympathetic to those objectives.

The question of the objectives underlying the unfair dismissal legislation and the extent of their achievement is picked up again in the next chapter. Here we have sought to demonstrate that the attempt to use expert tribunals to temper judicial determination of unfair dismissal disputes with industrial relations considerations, and to permit attention to be paid to the spirit of the law as well as to the black letter of it, has been constrained by the framework within which the tribunals operate, in particular the right of appeal to the ordinary courts.

Other Measures of Efficiency

The Franks characteristics which have been used as evaluative measures in the chapter so far are comparative characteristics and the point of comparison is the ordinary courts. Tribunals, with the reservations noted, are cheap, accessible, free from technicality, speedy and expert *in comparison with the ordinary courts.* In assessing the extent of their superiority, however, we need to consider the particular reasons why the unfair dismissal jurisdiction was entrusted to them.

The desirable characteristics identified by Franks were seen as necessary in the determination of dismissal disputes for two reasons. Firstly, the right not to be unfairly dismissed was a general right and the enforcement system had to be usable by individual non-union workers who generally would not have representation. Secondly, the system had to appear as a realistic option for organised workers and their unions who otherwise might seek to challenge employer dismissal decisions by collective action. The Donovan Commission (1968: 143) suggested that 'the right to secure a speedy and impartial decision on the justification for a dismissal' might avert many of the two hundred or so strikes which on average then arose each year out of non-redundancy dismissals. This view was echoed in the Consultative Document on the Bill which first introduced the unfair dismissal provisions (DE, 1970: 7) where it was noted:

> Britain is one of the few countries where dismissals are a frequent cause of strike action. It seems reasonable to link this with the fact that in this country, unlike most others, the law provides no redress for the employee who suffers unfair or arbitrary dismissal.

To be efficient in minimising the risk of strike action over a dismissal the tribunals had to offer the advantages listed by Franks. In particular they had to be speedy since dismissal is seen as a 'perishable' issue, one demanding instant action. But, as Donovan recognised, efficiency in reaching a decision was only one aspect; the nature of the decisions reached – the extent to which the law was seen to safeguard against unfair dismissal – would be crucial in determining the efficicacy of the statutory provisions in contributing to a reduction in strikes (1968: para. 537).

We can widen our consideration of the efficiency of the industrial tribunal system, therefore, from considering whether the system is administratively efficient to asking in whose interests is it efficient. In particular, is it efficient when judged by the needs of those expected to initiate action: unrepresented applicants and organised workers and their unions.

The examination in this and earlier chapters has shown that although the tribunal system is relatively accessible and informal, the unrepresented applicant still encounters difficulties in case preparation and presentation, in knowing what course to take at conciliation, and is likely to be deterred by any expense (or threat of it) which use of the system entails. In discussing the Franks criteria above, we suggested that the degree of informality and freedom from technicality which would be necessary to satisfy the needs of unrepresented applicants in fact might be impossible to achieve in a quasi-court system like the industrial tribunals. But, at the same time, we have pointed to ways in which the tribunals are becoming more legalistic with increasing use of lawyers and less accessible through the introduction of an additional filter and increased risk of costs. We have also, in Chapter 5, described the declining rate of applicant success. Such trends reduce the efficiency of the industrial tribunal system when seen from the point of view of the unrepresented applicant.

The efficiency of the tribunal system in meeting the needs of applicants can also be questioned in a different way. The dismissed worker may have a range of problems arising from his or her dismissal: the need to find new employment, the loss of income and consequent housing problems, strain on personal relationships, loss of self-esteem and so on. The tribunal system as a mechanism for applying and enforcing law is designed to address only those needs which are defined as a legal problem. The fairness of the dismissal can be challenged but the social needs may be wider than this individual legal problem. The capacity of the tribunal system to meet the needs of dismissed workers is, therefore, in this sense limited at the outset.

As we discuss in the next chapter, it was hoped that the introduction of statutory protection would lead to a reduction in industrial action. In part this necessitated the tribunal system appearing attractive to organised workers and their unions. In considering the efficiency of the tribunals from this particular point of view, the ordinary courts are no longer the point of comparison for the characteristics listed by Franks. Rather, the yardstick is what might be attained through negotiation backed by industrial action. This is not to imply that collective action is a viable course of action or necessarily would be considered in every dismissal. Where it is used, however, it is immediate and aimed at securing the re-employment of the dismissed worker. The arguments used in such negotiation are not restricted necessarily to the question of fairness in the individual case and are made in a context where union officials are most able to be effective.

By contrast, the tribunal system, although quicker than the ordinary courts, has a practical minimum time of six weeks from application to dismissal, which is achieved in a fifth of heard cases, rarely provides re-employment as a remedy in the minority of claims that succeed, and, although allowing representation by union officials, is concerned to apply the law and, in the words of one chairperson responding to our survey, 'to discover the truth, not negotiate about it'.

The legislators in introducing interim relief, as part of the Employment Protection Act 1975, to some extent recognised the fact that a system which is expeditious compared to the ordinary courts may still not be speedy enough when the point of comparison is an immediate challenge through collective action. An analysis in 1975 showed that a high proportion of the working days lost through strikes about dismissal were accounted for by challenges to the dismissal of workers' representatives (8 HC Deb Standing Committee F 22 July 1975, 1632–3). This helped stimulate the introduction of the interim relief provisions for cases where dismissal was alleged to be for trade union reasons.

The interim relief procedure is the nearest the legislation goes towards instituting status quo in dismissal cases, that is, giving the worker priority of interpretation pending the resolution of the dispute. Even an expedited hearing may not take place, however, until two or three weeks after the dismissal and if the case is appealed after the full hearing then it may take months to be resolved. Further, status quo applies only if the employer agrees to reinstatement where the interim relief tribunal finds it is 'likely' that the claim will succeed at full hearing. This is interpreted as a 'pretty good' chance of winning and not just a reasonable prospect of success (*Taplin v Shippam Ltd* [1978] IRLR 450). If the claim is upheld at full hearing there is no guarantee that re-employment will be awarded. If an order is made and not complied with the remedy is a level of compensation higher than in other dismissal cases but ultimately union activists can still be 'bought out'.

The constraints on the expertness of the tribunal system and the context in which the contribution of lay members has to be made, which we discussed earlier, are particularly relevant in considering how efficient the system is when judged by organised workers and their trade unions. The more tribunals have to treat a dismissal as an issue between an individual worker and an individual employer without regard to the industrial relations context of the dispute and the possible collective implications of it, the less attractive will the system be to the organised sector. The more reluctant tribunals are to overturn employers' decisions because of the broad nature of the 'range of reasonable employer responses' test, discussed in Chapter 4, the less likely are they to be seen as efficient from the point of view of dismissed workers.

Employers also have an interest in achieving a peaceful, low cost and quick means of resolving dismissal disputes. The more likely employers are to have their decisions challenged by collective action, the more willing they may be to accept some limitation on managerial freedom and the legal review of their decisions which the unfair dismissal legislation entails. As we discussed earlier (p. 175), however, in some situations, notably small company non-union employment, the unfair dismissal legislation and the industrial tribunal system not only provide a mechanism whereby dismissal disputes may be resolved, they are actually the vehicle whereby an employee's *grievance* over dismissal can be articulated as a *dispute* in the first place.

For employers whose workers are unorganised or weakly organised, therefore, the existence of the system appears to offer few advantages. Given that the legal right to challenge a dismissal exists, however, they do have an interest in obtaining a cheap, speedy, informal adjudication system, and one which does not go too far in impinging on managerial prerogative in dismissal questions. As employers generally speaking are better able than applicants to bear costs and employ assistance, and as most dismissal decisions are upheld by tribunals, their needs appear to be met to a greater extent than those of applicants by the existing operation of the industrial tribunal system. Unlike applicants, employers have an interest in reducing accessibility and so developments such as pre-hearing assessment improve the efficiency of the system from the employers' point of view. Pre-hearing assessment sessions take about half an hour on average where a warning is given and generally result in the application not being pursued to a full hearing (COIT, 1984: 5).

The balance which the system needs to strike for employers is between appearing attractive enough to organised workers and their unions to minimise the likelihood of industrial action, and not going further than necessary in limiting managerial freedom to achieve this, particularly as any benefits which the system provides for employees apply to *all* employees and not just those capable of mounting a collective challenge. Where employers think the balance should be struck depends not only on the nature of the individual employer, as discussed above, but also on other factors affecting the likelihood of collective challenges to individual dismissals. The circumstances of the individual dismissal is one factor but industrial action and union bargaining power will be affected by other considerations also.

In the 'full employment' economy of the 1960s, workers insisted on fair and reasonable treatment by taking industrial action (Donovan, 1968: 105). When the unfair dismissal provisions were introduced, some legal restriction on employer freedom of action was seen as necessary and desirable in order to obtain other desired ends, subsumed under the rubric of improving industrial relations or obtaining industrial peace (see below, Chapter 8). What was involved in many cases by reform was not new restrictions on employers but a *de jure* recognition of the restrictions which growing workshop organisation and influence had *de facto* placed on them. This was the base against which the efficiency of the industrial tribunals in their operation of the unfair dismissal provisions would be judged. But the base has shifted. In the different labour market conditions of the 1980s, government and certain managerial strategies appear to be concerned more directly with reducing workshop organisation or influence than formalising the ways in which it may be exercised (see for example Terry, 1983: 90). The less likely it appears that successful industrial action will be taken over employers' dismissal decisions, the more likely it is that the constraints which the system imposes on managerial freedom will be seen as too high a price to pay. In changed circumstances, a new balance may need to be struck for the system to be viewed as efficient by employers.

Summary

This chapter evaluated the industrial tribunals by the extent to which they display the characteristics identified by the Franks Committee, namely cheapness, accessibility, freedom from technicality, expedition and expertness. The tribunals were found to be accessible in that it costs nothing in financial terms to apply, some expenses are refunded and the loser only rarely is required to pay the winner's costs. Formally representation is optional and tribunals attempt to achieve a freedom from technicality in order that lay case presentation will be possible and not disadvantageous. This is done in part by dispensing with certain court procedures. Expedition was displayed in tribunals getting cases to a hearing generally within three months of application and usually hearing them in a day or less. The expertness of tribunals was found in their specialised jurisdiction, dealing with disputes arising from the employment relation, and in their mixed composition.

Although the tribunals were found to display the Franks characteristics, the *extent* to which they were displayed was found to be constrained by the quasi-court nature of the industrial tribunals and their location within a legal framework involving the ordinary courts. Thus, for example, although tribunals acknowledged the ideal of freedom from technicality, various factors arising from the nature of the system were noted which helped foster legalism and formality. Similarly, although part of the tribunals' accessibility lies in the provision for parties to present their own cases, legal representation is seen as beneficial and is used. The presence of lawyers tends to make the industrial tribunals more court-like and is associated with less expedition, more expense and greater technicality – in short a reduction in the extent to which the Franks characteristics are displayed.

The constraints imposed by the framework within which the tribunals operate were seen particularly in the way the tribunals' ability to pay attention to considerations wider than the black letter of the law was limited by the right of appeal from the 'experts' to the ordinary courts.

The discussion in this chapter indicates that while tribunals are displaying certain advantages over the ordinary courts in the efficiency of their operation,they are tending to be more like courts than originally hoped. The use of legal representation is a major factor explaining the tendency towards court-like industrial tribunals, but, as we have seen, the perceived need for and use of legal representation is itself partly a result of the judicial, quasi-court nature of the tribunal system with, for example, the underlying accusatorial model of hearings which helps make such representation appear appropriate; the lack of other sources of skilled advice and representation, and the complexity and quantity of statute and case law.

The inevitability of legalism is such circumstances is pointed to by Munday who argues that 'the underlying problem which has led to charges of legalism being levelled against tribunals is that there exists a wide gulf between what is preached and what *has* to be practised, between what is postulated and what is possible' (1981: 158). He points to the 'recurrent chimera that somehow it is possible to create areas of layman's law within a system where lawyers are active, where there is a highly accessible system of appeal to the High Court and, finally, where there exists a prolific law reporting industry' (ibid.: 156).

Having determined that industrial tribunals generally can be seen as efficient in providing adjudication machinery which is cheap, accessible, free from technicality, speedy and expert when *compared with the ordinary courts*, we introduced other measures of efficiency. As the industrial tribunal system was intended to be used by individual non-union workers who would lack representation and was meant to appear attractive to organised workers and their unions who might otherwise challenge dismissal by collective action, we judged the efficiency of the system by the needs of these two groups. By these measures, the industrial tribunal system appeared less efficient than it did when simply compared with the ordinary courts.

The 'inefficiency' of the tribunal system from the point of view of organised workers was seen to arise from its quasi-court nature, where, for example, legal considerations imposed constraints on industrial relations expertise, and from the inadequacies of its decisions both in terms of applicant success rate and the remedies awarded. To the extent that employers have an interest in obtaining a system which unionised workers will use rather than resort to collective action, it was argued these factors might constitute a source of inefficiency from the employers' point of view as well. We noted, however, that the likelihood of employers' dismissal decisions being challenged by successful collective action is neither a universal nor a constant factor. Thus, the extent to which limitations on managerial freedom will be accepted as the price to pay for the possibility of peaceful dispute settlement will vary as between employers and at different points in time (see also below, pp. 263–8).

The employers who are most involved in tribunal applications, as we saw in Chapter 2, are those whose workers have no other means of challenging their dismissal. Given that the legal right to challenge dismissal exists, the needs of these employers is for a system which has limited accessibility, disposes of applications quickly and at little or no cost to them by deterring applicants from continuing to a hearing and which, where determination is made, sanctions their dismissal decisions. This kind of employer-efficient system has not been achieved fully but the evidence shows that the trend is in that direction.

8

The Impact of the Unfair Dismissal Provisions

Earlier chapters have examined and discussed the direct impact of the unfair dismissal provisions in terms of the outcomes of applications to industrial tribunals. In this chapter we look at the wider impact which the existence and operation of the provisions has had.

In deciding where to seek any impact we turn to the effects expected or hoped for by those advocating and introducing the right not to be unfairly dismissed. As we noted in the previous chapter, one expected impact was on the level of industrial action over individual dismissal. It was thought a reduction would occur through the use of the alternative means of challenging employers' decisions – the industrial tribunals – and through the development and reform of voluntary procedures for handling discipline and dismissal questions in the workplace. The lack of 'clear, speedy, comprehensive and effective procedures for the settlement of grievances and other disputes' was identified by the Donovan Commission as an important explanation of unofficial and unconstitutional strikes (1968: para. 501).

The emphasis on procedural reform and development was an important part of Donovan's endorsement of voluntarism. The 'voluntary principle' had been identified by Flanders, in his influential submission to the Commission, as the basis of the merits of the British system preventing 'the conduct of industrial relations – and especially the settlement of disputes – from becoming entangled with legal process' (1975: 164). The introduction of unfair dismissal legislation was expected to stimulate rather than to replace or undermine voluntary action. Statutory protection, argued the majority of the Donovan Commission (1968: para. 533), would encourage the development of voluntary procedures:

if employers know that employees have the right to challenge dismissal in a statutory tribunal then there is a clear incentive for them to see that dismissals are carried out under a proper and orderly procedure, so as to ensure that as many cases as possible are settled satisfactorily without recourse to an outside appeal and that in those cases where appeal is made it can be shown that the dismissal was fair and justified.

As a further incentive to procedural development and reform, the Commission argued that there should be provision for satisfactory procedures to be exempted from the statutory machinery (ibid.: para. 559). This kind of exemption, contained in the legislation, recognises what Kahn-Freund referred to as the 'primacy' of collective bargaining in the British system. British protective legislation 'permits the trade union and the employer to take a group of workers outside the application of its standards, if certain conditions are met, and to place them under a regime of "voluntary" but superior conditions' (Wedderburn, 1983: 36).

The Ministry of Labour's National Joint Advisory Council, reporting on the question of dismissal in 1965, did not favour the introduction of protective legislation. It envisaged that instead of encouraging voluntary action, it might deter it and foster a legalistic element in relations in the workplace (Donovan, 1968: para. 535). The development whereby the conduct of day-to-day industrial relations becomes increasingly affected by legal norms and process is sometimes termed the juridification of industrial relations.

Although arguing that legislation would help quicken the pace of procedural reform, the Donovan Commission acknowledged that there were some areas where the voluntary measures were 'unlikely to be effective within the measurable future' (ibid.: para. 541). These were areas which trade unions found difficult to organise. Here statutory protection would provide workers with minimum rights. The Commission was concerned, however, that collective bargaining should extend to such areas and saw the unfair dismissal provisions as an important part of its strategy of promoting 'the growth of collective bargaining machinery on sound lines' (ibid.: para. 527). An essential element of freedom of association and the right to organise, upon which collective bargaining rests, was seen to be that employees should be protected from dismissal for joining a union or because, having joined, they took part in legitimate trade union activities.

The possibility of having dismissal decisions challenged via an industrial tribunal, which could award payment of compensation or re-employment, was also expected to affect employers' practices and policies in a way which would improve individual job security.

Assessing the wider impact of a piece of legislation cannot be a matter of exact quantification. There are, for example, problems in isolating the impact of the law from that of other factors and of knowing what importance to attach to a range of mediating factors which may come into play. Further, examining the precise impact in some areas we have identified would have required detailed, large-scale longitudinal case study work which was outside the scope of this research. Although it is not possible, therefore, to measure exactly the impact of the legislation, we identify and discuss where, in what direction, and why, change is likely to have occurred because of the existence of the right not to be unfairly dismissed.

We examine in turn each of the areas where an impact was intended or expected: reduction of industrial action; stimulating voluntary reform; support for the establishment of collective bargaining; juridification of industrial relations and, finally, employers' policies and security against job loss. After this we discuss the more general impact of the unfair dismissal provisions on employers.

Reduction of Industrial Action

The statutory provisions, in extending protection from unfair dismissal to those not covered by collective bargaining, provided a means of challenging management decisions to many who previously had none. For the worker in a non-unionised firm, industrial action over a discipline/dismissal issue is not a real option. This, and the fact that strikes over dismissal were not made unlawful on the introduction of statutory protection, meant any reduction in industrial action had to be obtained by persuading those who were in a position to take it that it was not necessary.

This was to be achieved in two ways: firstly, by ensuring that dismissal decisions would be seen as fair and reasonable and, therefore, would not be challenged. Secondly, by providing an alternative means of challenging peacefully any decision not thought to be fair and reasonable. Ideally the first objective would be achieved by 'clarifying' management's right to dismiss in certain circumstances and by obtaining union participation in the formulation and administration of disciplinary rules and procedures, thereby legitimising the imposition of sanctions and removing any potential challenge. The second would be achieved by providing an acceptable, accessible channel whereby contested decisions could be challenged without the need for industrial action.

The strike statistics compiled by the Department of Employment provide some indication whether strikes over dismissals have become less common since the introduction of statutory protection against unfair dismissal. For a number of reasons, however, they cannot provide a complete answer. The way in which strikes are categorised and changes in categorisation over time is one limitation; problems of labelling the 'cause' of a strike another. The Department also does not record stoppages lasting less than a day or involving fewer than ten workers unless the aggregate days lost exceeds a hundred. Furthermore, comparison of number of stoppages, although a better guide than number of days lost, tells us nothing about the *proportion* of disputes which resulted in strike action being taken and of course it is difficult to isolate any effect which the unfair dismissal legislation may have had on the level of industrial action from other factors, such as economic decline.

From the available evidence, with the reservations expressed above, it appears that the introduction of statutory protection has not reduced the level of strikes over dismissal. The Donovan Commission (1968: 143) noted that over the period 1964–6 there were on average 203 stoppages a year over dismissals other than redundancies. This constituted around 10 per cent of the number of stoppages. For 1982, the Department of Employment recorded 143 stoppages over 'dismissal and other disciplinary measures' excluding redundancy strikes and stoppages arising from the dismissal of worker representatives. This accounted for 9 per cent of stoppages (DE, 1983b: 298).

Information on what happened in some intervening years is provided by Department of Employment research into strikes in the period 1977–76 (Smith et al., 1978). Table 8.1 gives the number of stoppages for each year over 'dismissal and other disciplinary matters', other than redundancy dismissals, and over 'trade union matters'. This second category includes dismissal of worker representatives as well as such issues as union recognition and demarcation. Dismissal of worker representatives accounted for 18.9 per cent of the stoppages under this heading in the period.

Although pay is the issue which dominated stoppages throughout the period studied, the authors comment that 'job security emerges as another very important issue, despite the alleged increase in worker security in the post-war period' (ibid.: 53). The unfair dismissal provisions came into effect at the beginning of 1972 and so the 1966 to 1976 period spans the pre- and post-legislation period. The research indicated, however, that the 'cause structure' over the whole period, that is, the reasons given for striking by the parties involved, 'is broadly a fairly stable one; there were no large year-on-year variations in the major cause categories over the time period studied' (ibid.: 46). The category showing the most variation over the period was redundancy. If the introduction of statutory protection had led to a reduction in

TABLE 8.1

STOPPAGES OVER DISMISSAL 1966—76

	1966	1967	1968	1969	1970	1971	1972	1973	1974	1975	1976
Dismissal and other disciplinary matters	254	293	314	327	365	316	260	384	259	248	210
TU matters[a]	149	179	227	266	317	177	164	235	184	142	166

SOURCE: Extracted from Table 27 (Smith et al., 1978: 131) Revised classification.

NOTE:

a. Includes dismissal of worker representatives.

strike activity over dismissals, some variation in the cause structure to reflect this would have been expected.

There are various reasons why the hope of a reduced level of industrial action over discipline/dismissal because of the existence of the statutory provisions may not have been realised. As indicated earlier, the majority of those who seek redress through the statutory machinery are not trade unionists and thus for them collective action was not an option. Although about one third of applicants are trade union members, this need not indicate that the legal route is being used instead of collective action since a collective response in their cases may not have been possible. Some trade union members apply to an industrial tribunal because industrial action is not an option, perhaps because they work in weakly organised or unorganised workplaces or did not seek or receive support from their fellow workers or union.

Where collective action is a viable option the legal route is likely to be used only if the industrial tribunal system is seen as offering the possibility of an outcome as favourable as that which could be obtained by exerting pressure on the employer through a stoppage or, perhaps, provides some trade-off in terms of less cost in obtaining a remedy. The low applicant success rate at tribunal, the rarity of re-employment awards, the primacy of legal over industrial relations considerations, the individualist, managerialist approach of the tribunals and courts, all discussed in earlier chapters, combine to reduce the attractiveness of the legal route. Industrial action has an immediacy which the statutory procedure lacks and offers the chance to impose workers' definitions of 'fairness' or to negotiate such definitions rather than accept those of 'reasonable' management backed by law. If successful, it results in re-employment.

Industrial action is a way of attempting to induce the employer to withdraw the dismissal or to negotiate over the issue. In bringing about negotiation, it allows union officials to operate in the forum where their skills and experience are most valuable — bargaining rather than legal advocacy. Treating an individual dismissal as an industrial relations matter rather than a question of individual legal right gives it a collective dimension. Where the issue is not resolved through industrial action or subsequent negotiation, then, as with other collective disputes, a non-legal form of impartial adjudication or inquiry may be set up voluntarily at the request of the parties. In each year of the period 1975 to 1983, ACAS was called in to conciliate on average more than 200 *collective* disputes over dismissal. In the same period an average 46 dismissal cases a year were referred to arbitration, mediation or inquiry set up by the Service (ACAS, 1977–84). ACAS deals with collective conciliation cases quite separately from industrial tribunal conciliation: different staff are used and generally different techniques are employed. Joint meetings, for example, are more likely to be set up than in individual conciliation (see Chapter 6). Where conciliation fails to resolve the issue and it goes to an independent arbitrator or mediator the parties themselves select the third party from ACAS's list of academics, retired industrial relations practitioners and others and they agree the terms of reference.

That cases may end up with independent adjudication does not indicate necessarily that industrial action was 'unnecessary' as a stoppage may be instrumental in getting the employer to agree to such adjudication. It also affects the definition of the issue to be determined. A study of dismissal cases handled by arbitration through ACAS between 1972 and 1977 found they 'consistently showed the importance attached to an industrial action context by arbitrators' (Concannon, 1980: 17). As we shall discuss in more detail in the next chapter, consideration of a dismissal by an arbitral body differs from that of an industrial tribunal. While the tribunal is concerned to find who is legally right and focuses on the reasonableness of the employer's action in the circumstances of the individual dismissal, in voluntary arbitration the problem is seen as an industrial relations one, not a legal one, and the search is for a workable and acceptable solution which takes account of the wider context. Thus importance may be placed on issues not relevant to determination of the matter at law.

In the Ford dispute referred to in Chapter 1, the arbitration panel's report noted that the parties, particularly at the insistence of the union, chose a panel of arbitration as the best method of dealing with the problem, rather than an industrial tribunal because they felt that there were wider issues involved (ACAS, 1983b: 8). The terms of reference for the arbitration asked the panel to consider 'background events' and their ability and willingness to do so helped produce a result more favourable for the dismissed worker than might be expected from the industrial tribunal system. The panel was satisfied that the company had ample evidence to conclude that there was a case of vandalism to answer and that the worker concerned was responsible for the damage in question. It was further satisfied that the company had followed its procedure in the usual manner, with regard to the principles of fairness. In view of the legal tests discussed in Chapter 4, it seems likely that in these circumstances an industrial tribunal would have upheld the dismissal as fair. The union's arguments to the arbitration panel that the company had only circumstantial evidence and should provide more positive proof that the worker had committed the act of vandalism, for example, would not have been pertinent before a tribunal given that it would have needed only to satisfy itself that the employer honestly believed, on reasonable grounds, that the individual was responsible and not that the company could prove it beyond reasonable doubt (see p. 100).

The arbitration panel went on to assess whether the dismissal penalty was appropriate and reasonable and did so in the light of various contextual factors, including the company's agitation about vandalism in the plant and the fact of an anonymous telephone call about the worker involved. The industrial conflict occasioned by the dismissal was an unacknowledged background factor. The arbitration panel concluded that a more appropriate decision for management to have reached in the circumstances was a ten-day disciplinary suspension, a written warning and transfer to another area. At times tribunals have challenged managements' classification of offences as gross misconduct, thereby warranting instant dismissal under their disciplinary rules, but generally they endorse managerial rules 'without testing the seriousness of the deviant behaviour against the exigencies of the company's interests in having the instruction carried out' (Collins, 1982: 171–2) and rarely seek to assess or criticise the appropriateness of dismissal as a sanction. This is because dismissal, even if a somewhat harsh penalty in the particular circumstances, generally will fall within the range of 'reasonable employer' responses (see, for example, *British Leyland UK Ltd v Swift* [1981] IRLR 91, CA). For unions and their members seeking to contest the fairness of dismissal by challenging management's definition of a matter as a disciplinary offence warranting the sanction of dismissal, therefore, the industrial tribunals will not appear an ideal vehicle.

In examining why the legislation has not apparently reduced the number of strikes over dismissal we should note also that the analysis of unofficial strike action forwarded by the Donovan Commission, and thus the potential efficacy of its proposals for reducing it, can be questioned (Edwards, 1982). Donovan saw the inadequate conduct of industrial relations at company and plant level as the cause of unofficial strikes which at the time were defined as *the* industrial relations problem. As we noted, the development and reform of procedures for handling disputes was seen as a way of helping establish 'order' on the shopfloor and reducing industrial action. Surveys have revealed, however, that there is no tendency for establishments with formal, agreed procedures to be less prone to industrial action than those without such procedures (Brown, 1981: 44; Daniel and Millward, 1983: 226). Indeed, partly because both are correlated with size, strikes are more common where formal procedures for handling disputes exist than where there are no such procedures.

This is not to argue that the introduction or improvement of procedures for handling dismissal may not affect the likelihood of industrial action over this question. It can do, but not always in the direction expected as in some circumstances it may increase it. Management response to the legislation in developing and reforming disciplinary rules and procedures (see below, p. 233). may provide unions with new opportunities to bargain over disciplinary issues and the breakdown in such bargaining may lead to industrial action. It has been suggested also (Hyman, 1977: 183) that the actual introduction of reform of the kind advocated by the Donovan Commission was itself a potential source of conflict.

The intention was that the introduction of agreed rules and procedures would help make dismissal decisions taken in accordance with them appear fair and reasonable and, therefore, less open to challenge. The nature of the procedures which have been developed, discussed in the next section, lessens the extent to which management decisions are likely to be regarded in this way. But adherence to even unilateral managerial procedures removes the apparent arbitrariness from some dismissals and should provide the opportunity for the grievance to be aired and the dismissal decision to be reconsidered. This may serve to take the steam or momentum out of the issue which otherwise might have found expression in industrial action.

Another way in which the existence of statutory protection and machinery may affect industrial action is at the level of legitimation. The introduction of the legislation can be seen to legitimise a challenge to management's exercise of its 'right to dismiss'. The right is seen as subject to limits: a dismissal may be unfair. This may assist the mobilisation of collective action in support of a dismissed worker. But, conversely, the existence of the statutory machinery also provides grounds for challenging the legitimacy or rationality of industrial action over individual dismissals.

The existence of a legal route whereby management's decisions can be challenged before an independent body enables industrial challenges to be labelled unnecessary. The argument that if the decision is disputed it should be challenged 'responsibly' in front of the tribunal established for that very purpose has been used on various occasions by management, and also by union officials, seeking to portray industrial action as unreasonable or unnecessary.

Although the chance of success at tribunal is slight and the remedies limited, the statutory channel does provide the union with a means of meeting demands from the membership to 'do something' about a dismissal in circumstances where it is reluctant to initiate or sanction industrial action but where this would occur unless an alternative form of action existed. Where there is already some reluctance on the part of workers or their unions to take industrial action over a dismissal issue but where some token protest at least is necessary, the existence of a 'responsible', 'rational' legal route provides a convenient means of justifying industrial inaction. Where workers and/or unions are willing to take action the labelling of that action as irresponsible and unnecessary by management and media may serve to undermine their chance of mobilising support or sustaining the action.

The challenge to the rationality of collective action over individual dismissal when an independent legal channel is available reflects the concept of dismissal which the statutory provisions embody. Discipline/dismissal is seen as an individual rather than a collective issue; a question of individual rights calling for judicial adjudication rather than part of a wider struggle over job control. Not all dismissals will be seen by workers and their unions as raising collective issues; unions can be found helping enforce discipline and sanctioning dismissals of certain workers, notably those 'mavericks' or 'cowboys' who themselves may be seen as threatening the collective interest. But other dismissals will be seen as challenges to the collectivity itself, such as the victimisation of a shop steward, or to the collective interest in, for example, maintaining certain work practices.

Management may seek to treat a certain action – say, the refusal by a worker to operate new working practices – as individual misconduct and thus an individual disciplinary issue, whereas the union may define it as a collective issue concerning the negotiation of change on the shopfloor. Similarly a dismissal may be perceived by workers not as individual misfortune but as a breach of agreed 'rules of the game' embodied in custom and practice or as an instance of arbitrary management action which if unchallenged might be repeated. Where the issue is defined in this way collective action rather than a legal action is a rational response, not least because an industrial tribunal would adopt the individual indiscipline perspective.

Thus strike action over individual dismissals continues. Among the 'prominent stoppages' of 1981 (that is those involving at least 5,000 working days lost) was a strike in support of a worker dismissed for alleged clocking offences; a strike in protest at the dismissal of workers for allegedly failing to meet requirements of a new productivity scheme; and another over disciplinary action taken against workers for refusing to change jobs (DE, 1982c: 291). Although management sought to treat these cases as instances of individual indiscipline, as transgression of accepted or imposed standards, the workers concerned perceived them as issues of collective interest. It is not the nature of the issue which defines this – clocking offences in other circumstances may lead to uncontested or even union-supported dismissal – but the whole context within which the issue arises (see, for example, Mellish and

Collis-Squires, 1976: 175). Where the context calls for and enables a collective response, the industrial tribunal system operating individual rights will not be preferred to bargaining backed by the threat or taking of industrial action.

Stimulating Voluntary Reform

Procedural Growth

The main area in which the Donovan Commission thought the introduction of the legal right not to be unfairly dismissed would stimulate voluntary action was in the extension and improvement of procedures for handling discipline and dismissal. There is no doubt that, since the statutory provisions were enacted, there has been a great increase in the incidence of formal procedures in this area.

The main sources of information on the existence of formal discipline/ dismissal procedures before the introduction of the unfair dismissal legislation are a survey undertaken by the Ministry of Labour's National Joint Advisory Council in 1965 and a Government Social Survey of 1969. The former drew on three enquiries: visits by Ministry of Labour officials to 373 firms, written enquiries to 38 firms thought to have good personnel records, and information on 45 large engineering firms provided by the Engineering Employers' Federation. The proportion of companies in each category reporting the existence of formal procedures was 17 per cent, 55 per cent and 73 per cent. The NJAC concluded that the proportion of all firms which had formal procedures was probably well below 20 per cent (Anderman, 1972: 21). The 1969 survey of 1,100 private sector establishments employing over 25 workers found that only 8 per cent claimed to have a formal procedure (ibid.: 22).

When the unfair dismissal protection was enacted there was, as Donovan had urged, provision for satisfactory procedures to gain exemption from the statutory machinery. Further, as we noted in Chapter 4, the concept of 'unfair' encompasses procedural as well as substantive fairness. The early industrial tribunal and court decisions emphasised the importance of handling dismissals in a procedurally fair manner, looking to the Code of Practice for guidance as to what this might entail.

The first Code of Practice, which accompanied the Industrial Relations Act, stated that except in very small establishments there should be a formal procedure on discipline and dismissal (DE, 1972: 28). The ACAS Code published in 1977 expanded on the earlier code, which it replaced, but both set out standards of reasonable procedure. These included the giving of oral and written warnings in the case of minor offences, stating the nature of the offence and allowing time for improvement; the right of the employee to state his or her case before dismissal; the right of appeal to a higher level of management or appeals body, and the need for the employer to undertake proper investigation of alleged breaches of rules or poor performance before taking disciplinary action.

The provisions of the Code are not absolute requirements in that they are not enforceable at law but, as we noted in Chapter 4, they may be taken into account by the tribunals and courts. In an early case,[1] the House of Lords held that 'a failure to follow the procedure in the Code may lead to the conclusion that a dismissal was unfair which if that procedure had been followed would have been fair'. As well as this early judicial encouragement to develop procedures, impetus was given by changes to the Contracts of Employment Act 1972 made by the Employment Protection Act 1975, now EP(C)A s.1(4). These require that any disciplinary rules be set out in the employee's written statement of terms and conditions of employment which must also refer to the initial stage of any disciplinary or grievance procedure and any further steps beyond that stage.

Evidence of procedural development and change since the introduction of the unfair dismissal provisions is provided by a number of surveys. A survey of one in ten drawn from *The Times* 1,000 Companies list, undertaken shortly after the introduction of the legislation, found almost two in three had formal procedures for discipline/dismissal. Although less than a quarter said they had initiated procedures because of the Act, 30 per cent had changed responsibility for dismissal (usually giving it to a higher level of management) as a result of the legislation. Among medium-sized companies employing between 100 and 500 workers, 53 per cent claimed to have written procedures covering manual workers. Over a third of these procedures had been initiated or modified as a result of the legislation. The same research found little change in the nationalised industry sector where formal procedures had existed before the introduction of the legislation (Weekes et al., 1975: ch. 1).

Later surveys confirmed these findings of procedural initiation, formalisation and modification with the legislative provisions identified as a major stimulus. A random sample survey undertaken by the Institute of Personnel Management (IPM) in 1979, covering both the private and public sectors, reported an extremely high rate of procedural provision for both manual and non-manual workers (1979: 7). These findings were echoed by the 1977–8 survey of manufacturing establishments employing over 50 workers (Brown, 1981: 44) and the 1980 survey

1. *Devis & Sons Ltd v Atkins* [1977] IRLR 314.

of over 2,000 establishments employing at least 25 workers in most of the private and public sectors (Daniel and Millward, 1983: 159). This last mentioned survey found that 83 per cent of establishments had dismissal procedures and that the vast majority of written procedures were less than ten years old.

These various findings are summarised in Table 8.2 which shows the increase in formal procedural provision since 1965. Another survey referred to in the table is that of employers we surveyed in 1978 as respondents in unfair dismissal cases. Included in this group were establishments smaller than those covered by other surveys and the data reveal that, although 72 per cent of those employers interviewed claimed to have a formal discipline/dismissal procedure, this was more likely to be the case the larger the establishment. Table 8.3 shows that just over half of the establishments with fewer than ten workers in the respondent employer survey reported the existence of a written procedure at the time of the interview, whereas at the 500 or more size such procedures were universal. Many employers will have taken steps to develop or modify procedures without actually having experienced a claim for unfair dismissal, but this survey also shows that 95 (12 per cent) of the establishments with a procedure at the time of the interview had not had one at the time the dismissal claim was brought against them.

The absence of a formal procedure, generally defined as a written procedure, does not mean necessarily that no organised or recognised method exists for dealing with discipline and dismissal questions. To some extent, therefore, the increase in the number of procedures indicated by Table 8.2 may represent a codification and formalisation of already existing arrangements rather than a new development. But it is unlikely that this would explain all the apparent increase. The survey undertaken in 1969, for example, which found only 8 per cent of companies reporting formal procedures, found that a further 34 per cent had less formal 'normal' procedures but that over half, 52 per cent, had 'no organised methods of dealing with appeals from dismissal or disciplinary action and every case was treated in a completely ad hoc way' (Anderman, 1972: 22).

Joint Procedures

Donovan wanted managers to review their own procedures (1968: para. 535) but also suggested that effective voluntary procedures could not be developed without the involvement of unions (ibid.: para. 540). The decisions of the industrial tribunals and courts, however, did not give particular emphasis to the desirability of joint procedures. An early decision saw the fact that a procedure did not involve, and had

TABLE 8.2

REPORTED EXISTENCE OF FORMAL DISCIPLINE/DISMISSAL PROCEDURES 1964–80

	1964	1969	1974[a]	1974[b]	1977/8	1978	1979	1980
	%	%	%	%	%	%	%	%
	17	8	65	53	89	72	98	83
	N = 373	N = 1,100	N = 77	N = 76	N = 970	N = 1,080	N = 273	N = 2,040

SOURCES:

1964 — NJAC; Ministry of Labour officials visits
1969 — Government Social Survey of private sector establishments
1974a — Weekes et al., 1975, *Times* Top Thousand survey
1974b — Weekes et al., 1975. Medium-sized firms survey, manual workers
1977/8 — Brown (ed.), 1981. Survey of manufacturing industry establishments employing over 50
1978 — IRRU survey of unfair dismissal respondents
1979 — IPM survey: manual workers
1980 — Daniel and Millward, 1983. DE/PSI/SSRC survey of all industries excluding coal and agriculture, establishments employing at least 25.

TABLE 8.3

**EXISTENCE OF PROCEDURES BY SIZE OF ESTABLISHMENT
RESPONDENTS IN UNFAIR DISMISSAL CASES**

Establishment Size (No. of Employees)	No. of Establishments in Size Band	Percentage with Written Discipline/Dismissal Procedure at Time of Interview
less than 10	285	51
10—19	174	59
20—99	327	78
100—499	185	94
500 or more	81	99
Don't know	27	74
All	1,080	72

SOURCE: IRRU survey.

not been agreed with unions as 'a mere detail' (*Neefies v Crystal Products* [1972] IRLR 118). As an early study of dismissal decisions concluded, the legislation as operated by the tribunals and courts 'offered less inducement to employers and unions to negotiate disciplinary and dismissal procedures than some said it did when it was fresh on the statute books' (Weekes et al., 1975: 31).

Agreeing the procedure with a trade union is perhaps the minimum level of union involvement enabling it to be called a 'joint' procedure. The various surveys referred to above, although having different bases and using slightly different definitions, do appear to indicate that on this definition there has been an increase in the incidence of joint procedures. The Government Social Survey of 1969 reported that 20 per cent of dismissal procedures had resulted from consultation and negotiation with trade unions (Anderman, 1972: 31). The survey of manufacturing establishments in 1977–8 reported 64 per cent of dismissal procedures had been negotiated with trade unions (Brown, 1981: 47). In 1980, 64 per cent of the establishments covered by the DE/PSI/SSRC survey reported dismissal procedures agreed with a union or staff association (Daniel and Millward, 1983: 167). In establishments where employees covered by the procedure were represented by unions or staff associations, managers reported that the procedure had been agreed with those bodies in 91 per cent of cases.

The most common form of union involvement in the operation of dismissal procedures is as advocate, representing members who are being disciplined. This is virtually universal where unions are recognised. Indeed, the granting of representational rights is often the first step on the way to full recognition of the union. The right of employees to be represented by, or 'accompanied by', their union representative when appearing at disciplinary hearings etc. is generally now formally recorded in procedures, but this practice predates the procedural development documented above (McCarthy, 1967: 12). In voluntary procedures unions are more willing to take on the role of advocate than judge.

The highest level of union involvement in employers' discipline/dismissal procedures is as judge, that is participation in determining the issue and applying sanctions normally through membership of a joint body. It is, however, very rare to find this kind of joint procedure. The DE/PSI/SSRC workplace survey in 1980 found that only 3 per cent of all establishments surveyed had a procedure with a right to appeal to a joint body within the establishment and 8 per cent with provision for appeal to a joint body within the organisation. The IPM survey the year before had found a similar picture with 11 per cent of the procedures covering manual workers having provision for appeal to a union/management joint body (1979: 43).

An improvement in voluntary procedures which was looked for by the Donovan Commission was the right to challenge management's decisions and ideally the right to do so ultimately to an independent appeal body. Although there has been some development, the provision of independent appeal has not become at all widespread since the introduction of statutory protection. The survey of manufacturing industry in 1977–8 found that 21 per cent of procedures provided for reference to an independent outside body, generally ACAS, as the last stage in procedure. It was the large unionised establishments which were most likely to report such a provision. The right to appeal against a dismissal decision is present in almost all procedures now, but this is usually to a higher level of management within the organisation (Daniel and Millward, 1983: 167).

There has been a large increase in the incidence of formal, written discipline/dismissal procedures and some increase in union involvement in agreeing them since the unfair dismissal provisions were enacted. But the procedures remain for the most part managerial procedures, devised and operated by management, without an independent appeal stage. Very few, therefore, approach the ideal voluntary procedure which would qualify for exemption from the statutory provisions and thus prevent those covered from having dismissal claims heard by the industrial tribunals.

Statutory Exemption

Two essential characteristics for exemption are that the procedure be jointly agreed between the employer and an independent trade union and that it have an independent appeal provision. Another is that it must provide remedies on the whole as beneficial as, but not necessarily identicial with, those provided by statute.[2] The parties to the procedure have to make a joint application for exemption to the Secretary of State.

Only one procedure has been exempted, that of the Electrical Contracting Industry. The parties to the agreement are the Electrical Electronic Telecommunication and Plumbing Union (EETPU) and the Electrical Contractors' Association (ECA) who together form the Joint Industrial Board (JIB) of the industry.

In the late 1960s the JIB decided that in order to settle any disputes which arose on sites in a quick simple way, without loss of work through industrial action, Dispute Committees would be set up con-

2. EP(C)A 1978 s.65.

sisting of representatives from the EETPU and representatives from the ECA who would attempt to resolve the matter. If they failed there would be recourse to a National Appeals Committee, also with representatives of the union and employers' association, and, ultimately the matter could be determined by the JIB chairperson.

In practice this domestic procedure rather than the industrial tribunals came to be used for handling dismissal disputes and so the JIB thought it sensible to prevent duplication by seeking exemption for a procedure based on that described above. It was thought also that the principle of joint collective responsibility, on which the JIB rests, could be undermined by tribunal adjudication of individual cases (IRRR, 1976: 8). Exemption was finally obtained with effect from 1 October 1979.

In the event of a dismissal complaint by an EETPU member not being resolved within the firm in membership of the ECA, it is referred to the JIB Regional Board whose Secretary attempts to conciliate. If this fails an investigation is undertaken within ten days by the Regional Board which ascertains facts and reaches a decision. The decision may be appealed to the National Board within ten days. These two stages involve union and employer representatives not concerned directly with the dispute. The final stage allows appeal to a legally qualified arbitrator appointed by ACAS and assisted by a representative of the union and one of the ECA, acting as advisers. The appeal from the National Board has to be lodged within ten days and must seek to show that in reaching a decision the Regional or National Board, or both, made an error of interpretation or application of the Dismissal Procedure Agreement.

The Dismissal Procedure Agreement is extensive, covering the range of matters dealt with in the statutory provisions, in many respects mirroring them closely. Where the procedure is silent on any matter it provides that decision-makers should be guided by the statutory provisions. A particular difference from the statutory provisions is that there is no length of service qualification. The Electrical Contracting JIB procedure provides a quicker determination than that of the industrial tribunal system – the full procedure, including appeal, can be exhausted within six weeks – and in practice leaves determination in the hands of those who know and work in the industry who seek to find a workable settlement to a particular dispute (Cairns, 1980: 28).

Some procedures in the public sector and in some large private corporations could, with modification, come near to fulfilling the requirements for exemption. But the Electrical Contracting JIB is alone in formally applying for exemption. In seeking to explain this lack of interest in exemption, Bourn (1979: 92) points to the fact that when the exemption provisions were introduced, the majority of dismissal procedures lacked provision for independent appeal and for compensation as a remedy, and discusses the reasons for this. But, as we argued above, the existence of the exemption was meant to encourage change in procedures so they could qualify. It is not sufficient, therefore, to point to the existing inadequacy of procedures as an explanation. We have to ask also why the statutory provisions failed to stimulate interest in changing procedures so they *would* qualify for exemption.

One inducement to change in order to gain exemption would be if the statutory provisions were seen to undermine a valued voluntary procedure or practice. For instance, before the Electrical Contracting procedure gained exemption, an industrial tribunal had ordered an 'approved electrician' to be re-employed as an 'electrician' which cut across the JIB National Working Rules (IRRR, 1976: 8). For the most part, however, as we saw in Chapter 2, those large companies and public sector employments with procedures which approach the exemption standard have few tribunal applications filed against them. The fact that their procedures do come near to fulfilling the exemption criteria means that in practice the likelihood of a dismissal being perceived as unfair is lessened. An employee who unsuccessfully challenges the dismissal through such a voluntary procedure is not likely to consider it worthwhile making an application to a tribunal, particularly as the union concerned may be unwilling to support the application for fear of undermining the procedure. Where applications are made against the large, organised companies most likely to have well-designed jointly agreed procedures, the application, as we saw in Chapter 4, is likely to fail.

The process of gaining exemption, as the Electrical Contracting JIB experience showed, can be a time-consuming one. For many the changes demanded in order to qualify may appear too high a price to pay for the limited advantages which exemption offers. It should also be noted that, at the time when the legislation was first introduced, application for exemption had to be made via the National Industrial Relations Court (NIRC), the predecessor of the EAT. The TUC unions' policy not to use institutions established by the Industrial Relations Act, including the NIRC, was then a further barrier to exemption.

Disciplinary Rules

The majority of the Donovan Commission appeared to have hoped the introduction of statutory protection would lead to discipline becoming a jointly regulated area. This requires union involvement in procedural reform and also in substantive matters. Donovan argued (1968: 121) that unofficial strikes, including those over dismissal, would continue 'until the confusion which so often surrounds the exercise by management of its "rights" has been resolved by the settlement of clear rules and procedures which are accepted as fair and reasonable by all concerned'.

Joint agreement on rules, however, has been less extensive than on procedure. The IPM survey referred to above distinguished rules from procedure when asking whether there had been negotiation with a union. Whereas 38 per cent of companies said the procedure covering manual workers had been negotiated with the union or staff association, 25 per cent said the disciplinary rules were jointly agreed: a lower proportion but one which the IPM found 'surprisingly high' (1972: 21).

Employers may wish to gain union agreement to a discipline/ dismissal procedure or to involve the union in its formulation or operation as a way of conferring acceptable legitimacy on the exercise of managerial discipline or to temper union power with union responsibility. This second consideration is revealed, for example, in the notes to the West Midlands Engineering Employers' Association model disciplinary procedure. These state that a joint appeals body might be appropriate 'where management's decisions are increasingly challenged and frequently reversed. At that point, when the union has obtained the power to influence discipline, they should accept some responsibility by means of an appeal committee' (IRRR, 1976: 5). Employers may be less willing, however, to agree disciplinary rules.

Disciplinary rules set standards of performance and behaviour. Where in practice the union, perhaps through craft control, sets such standards employers may be prepared to accept that, as Flanders suggested (1975: 172), they can only regain control by 'sharing it'. But generally the setting of such standards will be claimed as an area of managerial prerogative. For their part, unions do not seek to agree disciplinary rules in areas where they exercise control, as just discussed, and in other areas they may prefer formally to keep a free hand to challenge managerial definitions of what constitutes a disciplinary issue in any particular case.

For rules to be agreed requires that they should be clear, preferably written down. Encouragement to formalisation is also given in the legislation which requires employees to be informed of disciplinary rules which affect them (above, p. 233). There may be some reluctance, however, to formalise or rework rules in the way necessary to secure agreement to them. There is often a large gap between what works rules provide and what happens in practice. What actually happens may be the result of concessions being made to stewards by lower level management and in order to agree rules jointly management would have formally to acknowledge and legitimise informal practices and procedures. They may prefer to maintain the position that their right to discipline in accordance with the formal rules is intact and retain some freedom to attempt to withdraw concessions.

The different interests of unions and employers, therefore, may be served by not seeking to agree joint disciplinary rules or even procedures. This obviously limits the extent to which the type of voluntary reform expected by the Donovan Commission has occurred. What the existence and operation of the unfair dismissal provisions does seem to have encouraged is the adoption by management of an investigatory, quasi-judicial approach to transgressions of the standards it sets, providing for adequate review of its own actions before dismissing. The formal procedures which the legislation has stimulated embody this approach. They also display a 'corrective approach' to discipline (Anderman, 1972: 57) by providing the employee with the opportunity to show 'improvement' in cases of minor misdemeanour or incapacity and thereby possibly escaping the penalty of dismissal. The Code's advice to the effect that procedures should allow for employees to be warned and given a chance to remedy the situation before the imposition of disciplinary sanctions has been heeded universally. The 1969 Government survey found that some 48 per cent of firms claimed to have some formal or normal procedure for issuing warnings to employees being considered for dismissal (ibid.: 29). The 1980 survey found all procedures included a system of early warnings, nearly all providing for both oral and written warnings (Daniel and Millward, 1983: 165).

The legislation undoubtedly has stimulated procedural development and change. Discipline/dismissal procedures are now widespread. For the most part, however, they are management procedures without an independent element and without union agreement or involvement, other than in a representative capacity. Jointly agreed rules are even less common than jointly agreed procedures. The legislation has encouraged management to adopt an investigatory, quasi-judicial approach to indiscipline but the definitions of indiscipline remain managerially determined.

The legislation, as we noted earlier, was intended both to stimulate voluntary action in areas where unions were recognised already and to facilitate the spread of voluntary action by providing support for the establishment of collective bargaining.

Support for the Establishment of Collective Bargaining

Although by the mid-1960s public policy had been long committed to collective bargaining as the best means of settling questions arising between workers and employers, the law had been used little to encourage or aid its establishment in the face of employer reluctance or hostility. The Donovan report (1968: para. 212) argued that

> properly conducted, collective bargaining is the most effective
> means of giving workers the right to representation in decisions
> affecting their working lives, a right which is or should be the pre-
> rogative of every worker in a democratic society

and proposed various new measures which, observers argued, added up
to a right of freedom of association and a right to organise (Wedderburn, 1978: 443). Among these measures was protection from dismissal
for membership of a trade union or for participating in its activities. If
an employer could dismiss freely those who joined or attempted to
organise a union, then the establishment of the basis for collective
bargaining would be thwarted. The right to join a trade union, therefore,
was seen not merely as a question of individual civil liberty but as an
essential condition for the establishment of collective rights.

The Industrial Relations Act 1971 s.5 provided, for the first time in
Britain, the right to belong to a trade union, although it was limited
to membership of unions which registered under that Act (Weekes et
al., 1975: ch. 2 and Appendix VIII). It also provided an unqualified
right not to be a member of any trade union or other organisation of
workers. There was also enacted a right to take part in union activities
at an 'appropriate time' (outside working hours or in working hours
with the employer's consent). The dismissal of someone for exercising,
or expressing an intention to exercise, any of these rights would be
automatically unfair. The service and age qualifications which applied
to applicants for unfair dismissal did not apply to those claiming dismissal because of union membership or activity. Victimisation of workers
for trade union reasons can, of course, take forms more subtle than
sacking them and the Act also sought to cover penalising action short
of dismissal.

In repealing the Industrial Relations Act, the Trade Union and
Labour Relations Act 1974 removed the express right to join or not to
join a union but trade union membership or activities remained an invalid reason for dismissal; protection against action short of dismissal
was retained, while dismissal of someone for not joining a union would
be automatically fair where there was a closed shop and he or she did
not fall under a category exempted from membership. Where an exemption was applicable then dismissal was automatically unfair. Subsequent
legislation has provided, in effect, a general right to dissociate. The
formulation regarding closed shop dismissals remains unchanged although the range of circumstances where dismissal will be fair has been
widened considerably (see Lewis and Simpson, 1982: 234). As we discussed in the preceding chapter, the Employment Protection Act 1975

introduced a new provision, the interim relief procedure, which further recognised the special status of dismissal for union membership and activities.[3]

Statutory support for collective bargaining does not rest only on the unfair dismissal provisions. Complementary statutory provisions such as protection from victimisation short of dismissal because of union membership or activities at an appropriate time have already been mentioned. In addition, once a collective foothold has been gained through recognition various other rights are available, such as time off for union duties and activities, disclosure of information for collective bargaining purposes, and to consultation on health and safety and redundancy. Although a full assessment of legislative support for nascent collective bargaining would need to take into account the operation of these other provisions – and quite clearly they can provide useful props for newly organised workers – we are concerned here only with the unfair dismissal provisions. Refusing to employ people who are union members and dismissing any workers who take an interest in, join or attempt to recruit to a union is a thorough, if crude, way of thwarting the development of union organisation upon which the establishment of collective bargaining depends.

The law provides no redress for people refused employment because they are trade union members but it is likely that the unfair dismissal legislation has helped prevent the most blatant victimisation of unionists who are employees. Tribunals have awarded remedies to workers dismissed as soon as their union membership was discovered; in some cases where the employer made anti-union statements and where inadequate steps were taken to build up evidence of 'incompetence' or to substantiate allegations of misbehaviour to camouflage the real motive for dismissal (IDS, 1980: 3; IRLIB, 1978: 8). Where employers are more careful in dismissing trade unionists, however, workers find it difficult to get tribunals to accept that the employer's stated reason for dismissal is false or that, for example, the 'misconduct' was in fact trade union activities.

The interpretation of the provisions concerning trade union membership and activities by the courts has revealed large holes in the protection they provide for nascent collective bargaining. In the preceding chapter we discussed the *Therm A Stor* case (above, p. 212). In that case the action of a trade union official in requesting recognition from the company resulted in the dismissal of some individuals who were union members. But the Court of Appeal held that they were not protected by the relevant section of the statute since it was not their

3. EP(C)A 1978 s.77.

individual membership or activities which led to dismissal. In the *Therm A Stor* case the activity of the union official was held not to be that of the individual members. In other cases, protection has been denied because the activities of an individual union member, although of a union type, such as organising a union-vetted petition complaining about safety standards, were deemed not to be union activities.[4] Where the individual member is a shop steward the range of activities which is protected is much wider but not everything done in the name of the union will be covered; stewards have to act within the authority delegated to them and do so in a reasonable manner.

Dismissal cases where trade union reasons are alleged can be brought without the normal service period but where this happens the worker bears the burden of proving the reason for dismissal was union membership or activity. It appears that the applicant has to show at least some evidence of anti-union behaviour or attitude on the part of the employer before the burden shifts to the employer to prove that this did not motivate the dismissal, or that it was not the principal reason for it. The hardest task probably faces those union members or activists whose dismissal is defined as redundancy, particularly if part of a mass dismissal. Furthermore, in such cases, although it may be argued that selection for redundancy is because of union membership, the interim relief provisions are not available.[5]

As this discussion implies, the rate of success in applications where trade union membership or activities are the alleged reason for dismissal is very low. The Department of Employment does not publish separate statistics for this category of unfair dismissal application but information has been given in reply to Parliamentary Questions although, because of past problems with the accuracy of the data, the figures have to be treated with caution. Table 8.4 shows only 13 per cent of union membership and activities cases heard by tribunals in 1979 and 1980 were found unfair. In 1981 just over a fifth of heard cases were upheld and in 1982 the applicant's claim succeeded in 17 per cent of heard cases. This rate of success is below — in most years considerably below — the already low level achieved by unfair dismissal applicants generally, as detailed in Chapter 4.

Over the four-year period for which figures have been given there were 2,257 complaints of dismissal on grounds of union membership or activities. As Table 8.4 shows, 291 ended with an agreed settlement. This is a 13 per cent settlement rate, well under half the settlement rate achieved in unfair dismissal cases generally (see above, Chapter 6). The

---

4. For example *Chant v Aquaboats* [1978] ICR 643, EAT.
5. See *Farmeary v Veterinary Drug Co. Ltd* [1976] IRLR 322.

TABLE 8.4

OUTCOME OF UNFAIR DISMISSAL COMPLAINTS ON GROUNDS OF TRADE UNION MEMBERSHIP OR ACTIVITY

Year	Applications	Settlements	Complaints Heard	Complaints Upheld	Percentage of Heard Complaints Upheld
1979	545	50	263	33	12.6
1980	621	140	255	34	13.3
1981	271	48	82	18	21.9
1982	820	53	126	21	16.7
1979–82	2257	291	726	106	14.6

SOURCE: HC Written Reply, 26 October 1983.

NOTE: 1982 provisional figures.

106 applications which were upheld by tribunals represent 6 per cent of all membership and activities complaints in the period. No information is given on the remedies obtained by those who succeeded in obtaining an agreed settlement or a tribunal award but it is likely that, as with unfair dismissal cases generally, the usual remedy was compensation. Employers are thus still free to engage in this kind of anti-union activity but at the slight risk of having to pay a price for it.

One further limitation to the support for the establishment of collective bargaining offered by the unfair dismissal provisions is that the tribunals are not empowered to consider the fairness or otherwise of the dismissals of those sacked while taking part in industrial action other than in circumstances where the employer has discriminated between the workers taking part in such action. Where union organisation has made some progress, therefore, and the workers take industrial action to obtain recognition of the union, they will have no legal redress if the employer responds by dismissing them all. This limitation on tribunal jurisdiction has existed since the introduction of the unfair dismissal provisions. Amendments made by s.9 of the Employment Act 1982, however, allow the employer to exercise some selectivity in re-employment without the risk of unfair dismissal actions by those not re-employed. The employer escapes the possibility of unfair dismissal claims unless strikers are selectively re-employed at the same establishment within three months. Re-employment outside these constraints permits employers some scope for singling out union activists for dismissal in these circumstances (Wallington, 1983: 314).

The discussion in this section indicates that the protection of union members and activists from dismissal is weak and therefore does not provide a secure base for the development of union organisation and the establishment of collective bargaining. The right to organise, the collective social right which the Donovan Commission intended the legislation to promote, appears to rest in this respect on weak individual legal rights. Further, because the support takes the form of individual legal rights, the collective aspects may be lost sight of. This is seen in some of the judgments, discussed above, and in the development of the individual right *not* to be a trade union member, whether or not a closed shop is in force.

In terms of individual liberty or freedom of association, the right not to belong to a union (the right to dissociate) appears to balance the right to join and take part in union activities. The collective implications of each, however, are quite different. The Donovan Commission rejected the argument that the right to dissociate was comparable to the right to join a trade union, arguing (1968: para. 599) 'the former condition is designed to frustrate the development of collective bargaining, which it is public policy to promote, whereas no such objection applies to the latter'. In considering the extent to which the unfair dismissal provisions have supported the establishment of collective bargaining, therefore, we need to examine the possible counter-effect of the right not to be dismissed because of non-membership of any or a particular union.

The right of non-membership has been extended by the Employment Acts 1980 and 1982 and is now much wider than the right to non-membership on grounds of religious belief which existed from 1976 to 1980. In effect the position now resembles that under the Industrial Relations Act 1971 (Lewis and Simpson, 1982: 235). Dismissal of a non-member where there is a closed shop (union membership agreement) remains automatically fair but the range of exemptions to membership, which make any dismissal unfair, has been widened considerably.[6] Where there is a union membership agreement or arrangement dismissal of someone for non-membership will be unfair if the employee concerned objects on 'grounds of conscience or other deeply held personal conviction' to being a member of any, or a particular, trade union; if he or she was not in the union when the membership agreement came into effect and had not joined since; if he or she is being unreasonably excluded from membership of the closed shop union or if the employee's union membership would conflict with a written code of conduct applicable to his or her occupation. Further a dismissal for non-membership of a closed shop union can only be fair if there has been a ballot which obtained large majority support for continuing the union membership agreement or arrangement.[7]

In equating the right not to belong with the right to be a member, the 1982 Act made the interim relief procedure available in both instances. We noted earlier that the interim relief procedure seems to have been of only limited use to those alleging their dismissal was because of trade union membership or activities. Tribunals have not been convinced easily that there is a 'pretty good chance' of such claims succeeding at the full hearings. There are some signs, however, that applicants alleging non-union membership dismissal, particularly where a UMA applies, may find the interim relief tribunal takes a more optimistic view of the likelihood of their winning at full hearing. The first such application succeeded. The claim was brought by a worker dismissed by General Motors after he ended his membership of the Amalgamated Union of Engineering Workers (AUEW) which has a closed shop agreement with the company. The tribunal ordered continuation of the

6. EP(C)A s.58(4)–(8).
7. EP(C)A 1978 s.58A, inserted by the Employment Act 1982. The majority required is at least 80 per cent of those entitled to vote or at least 85 per cent of those actually voting.

contract of employment (*Financial Times*, 20 December 1983: 8). The applicant in the case was represented by the Freedom Association which is pursuing a number of such cases in an attempt to destroy closed shops.

The willingness of workers to assert their right to non-membership may have been increased by other changes introduced by the 1982 Act. The remedies available in union membership, activities and non-membership cases are the same as those in other dismissal cases, namely re-employment or compensation, but the increased protection of the right not to be a union member was accompanied by a great increase in the level of compensation which can be awarded where such claims succeed. Additionally, new joinder provisions enable compensation awarded in cases where dismissal for non-membership resulted from union pressure to be obtained from the trade union rather than the employer. A minimum basic award of £2,000 is introduced for unfair dismissal on trade union grounds and a special award of £10,000 or 104 weeks' pay up to a maximum of £31,850 will be made where re-employment is requested but not ordered. Where re-employment is ordered but not complied with the special award is £15,000 or 156 weeks' pay, with no upper limit. Further, the tribunals' discretion to reduce these awards is limited.

The prime aim behind these changes in compensation levels was to deter the dismissal of non-unionists in order to enforce closed shop agreements and to compensate adequately those who might be dismissed in such circumstances (DE, 1981c: 510). Compensation awards too low to deter employers from dismissing and which failed 'to provide adequate compensation to dismissed employees, particularly low paid employees, whose dismissal involves a serious loss of livelihood' were identified as problems in the context of closed shop dismissals. These problems, however, also apply to the remedies in unfair dismissal cases generally, as discussed in Chapter 5. The selective approach to remedies in the Employment Act 1982 is argued by Lewis and Simpson (1981: 238) to point

> to the conclusion that deterring employers from unfair dismissals and providing adequate compensation are in the present government's view goals to be pursued only on behalf of non unionists (or supporters of breakaway unions), especially if they can be achieved at the expense of established trade unions.

What is clear from the recent legislation is that public policy commitment to collective bargaining has weakened considerably since 1979 and the present view contrasts markedly with the statements of the Dohovan Commission (see above, p. 243). The changes to the unfair dismissal provisions to place the right to dissociate on equal footing with the right to join a union, emphasising individual liberty rather than collective rights, is only one of a number of measures aimed at removing all forms of 'compulsory unionism' (Lewis and Simpson, 1982: 227) and fostering an individual rather than collective basis for relations in industry.

Recent amendments to the unfair dismissal provisions are part of a trend encouraging individualism. It can be argued, however, that the introduction of the unfair dismissal provisions themselves, rather than just subsequent amendments to them, were likely to enhance individualism rather than underpin collective bargaining.

It is generally argued that legislation, such as that concerning dismissal, which lays down rules of employment — what Kahn-Freund termed 'regulatory legislation' — provides a safety net for those who are not covered by collective bargaining but also, by a switch of metaphor, provides a floor 'on which we can all stand ... a ground floor for an edifice of collective bargaining' (Kahn-Freund, 1977: 43). We have noted that this was, in part, the Donovan Commission's conception of the unfair dismissal provisions; they would protect the unorganised but also provide an impetus to joint regulation in this area. The question being raised here is whether the enactment of statutory rights, rather than underpinning union organisation and collective bargaining, might hinder or undermine them.

Although it has been acknowledged that, in certain circumstances, 'the existence of statutory regulation, far from promoting collective bargaining, actually proves to be a hindrance to its development or progress' (Kahn-Freund, 1977: 43), the unfair dismissal provisions and other employment protection measures generally are not seen in this way. Rather, in providing through the exemption procedure a mechanism whereby regulation through collective bargaining can supersede statutory regulation, they are seen to accord primacy to collective bargaining. They can be viewed from the hindrance perspective, however, in that, firstly, the statutory regulation takes the form of an individual legal right which makes no concession to trade unions and, secondly, what happens in the legal sphere may affect adversely what unions can achieve for their members by voluntary means.

The British legislation does not attempt to 'write in' the trade unions in respect of the individual right regarding unfair dismissal. Thus, for example, there is no duty on the employer to consult with an appropriate union prior to dismissing a worker, comparable to the consultation requirement where multiple redundancies are contemplated.[8] Nor,

8. Employment Protection Act 1975 s.99 as amended.

even in union membership and activities cases, is there any recognition of compensable injury to the union in addition to any loss on the part of the individual found to have been dismissed unfairly. The state, by enacting individual legal rights which do not depend on, or make concession to, trade union organisation presents itself as restraining the exercise of employer power. This legal protection may be seen by workers, and argued by employers and others, to lessen or obviate the need for workers to combine and seek protection through unions.

The potential for general legal employment protection to undermine the attraction of trade unionism appears to be a cause for concern among trade unions in the United States where proposals for general protection from unfair dismissal are being canvassed.[9] Access to grievance arbitration provided for in collectively bargained labour contracts, enabling review and adjudication of discharges, is thought by American unions to be a positive recruitment factor. Similar fears may have underlain the reluctance of TUC unions to see unfair dismissal legislation introduced in Britain. In 1960 the TUC questioned its affiliated unions on their attitude towards legislation against unfair dismissal. The majority of respondents, 44 out of 57 unions, said they preferred the matter to be dealt with by collective bargaining (*The Times*, 15 March 1965).

In the kind of cost-benefit analysis which the argument implies, however, there will be a range of factors other than the opportunity to challenge dismissal which affect membership decisions. Indeed, where unions are a taken-for-granted part of working life, no explicit cost-benefit calculation may be made. Further, the nature of the statutory protection in Britain is such that there are still advantages in this area accruing from effective union organisation.

Collective organisation may provide a qualitatively different kind of employment protection from that offered by individual rights. For example, as we have noted, it may affect the definition of what constitutes a disciplinary issue in the first place. Even where the legal route is used to challenge dismissal, the ability to call upon union assistance in case preparation and presentation confers a benefit on the union member (see above, Chapter 4). In some ways a certain degree of union organisation appears necessary to make individual legal rights effective. This is to some extent the case with the unfair dismissal provisions (in providing information and supervising any re-employment as well as giving advice and assistance) but is perhaps particularly the case where the individual rights are exercisable by those in employment.

Because the protection from, and redress for, unfair dismissal is weak (see Chapter 5) the force of any argument that trade union pro-

9. See, for example, *Journal of Law Reform*, 16(2) (1983).

tection is no longer necessary obviously is reduced. It might appear, therefore, to be in the unions' organisational interests, in terms of their attractiveness to non-members, that the statutory protection does display various weaknesses. But there is a dilemma for the unions here, partly because their members do sometimes use the machinery but also because what happens in the voluntary, collective bargaining sphere may be affected by what happens in the legal sphere. Bargaining over discipline/dismissal issues cannot be immune totally from the norms and values fostered by the tribunals, and workplace definitions of 'fairness' may come to be influenced by legal definitions and tribunal judgments. An awareness by the parties to negotiation that management generally have their dismissal decisions upheld by tribunals does not enhance the trade unions' bargaining power. In this rather more subtle, gradual way the existence and operation of the statutory protection may impinge on the collective bargaining process and be part of a process of juridification.

Juridification of Industrial Relations

The term juridification has been borrowed recently from the German. The concept refers to the extent and significance of legal regulation in industrial relations and has a number of elements covering both the amount, nature and scope of legal regulation and its impact. In terms of impact, juridification refers to the importation of legal norms and processes into the workplace. Clark and Wedderburn (1983: 188) suggest that the juridification of industrial relations is indicated by the extent to which

> the behaviour of line and personnel managers, shop stewards and full time officers in dealing with individual and collective employment issues [is] determined by reference to legal (or what are believed to be legal) norms and procedures, rather than to voluntarily agreed norms and procedures or to 'custom and practice'.

We noted above (p. 233), that the unfair dismissal provisions have stimulated the development, formalisation and modification of procedures for handling discipline/dismissal issues and that, in various respects, the standards laid down in the Code of Practice have been influential (above, p. 242; IPM, 1979: 51). These procedures generally incorporate notions of 'due process' or 'natural justice' and encourage quasi-judicial managerial review of decisions (p. 233). This process may be identified as an aspect of juridification in terms of the impact of legislation. Voluntarily agreed norms and procedures are not *replaced* necessarily by legal ones, but rather their form and operation may be modified and informed by an awareness of the legal provisions and their operation. Increased specialisation and importance of the personnel function which has occurred in some, but by no means all, areas (Daniel and Millward, 1983: 126) and training of union lay and full-time officials in legal matters, are possible sources of such awareness.

Detecting juridification in the sense of the impact of legal norms and concepts on the thinking and everyday activity of those involved in industrial relations is clearly far more difficult than assessing some of the direct impacts of legal regulation, discussed earlier. It is also important to note the ways in which the impact of the law can be mediated. The extent to which a party to a discipline/dismissal dispute will be willing or able to call in aid legal norms, or wish or be able to resist their importation, for instance, will vary with the political and economic context at both macro and micro level. We discussed above (p. 231) the ability of workers and their trade unions in some circumstances to resist the legalisation of discipline/dismissal disputes by refusing to accept them as issues of individual right rather than of collective interest. The impact of law depends not only on the nature of the law but the social context. This point is picked up again in the next section when we examine the impact of the unfair dismissal provisions on job security through their effect on managerial policy and practice.

One other possible impact of the legislation, however, which can be discussed under the heading of juridification is the extent to which individual rights, such as protection from unfair dismissal, have assisted the acceptability of legal regulation and the role of judicial institutions in industrial relations.

The voluntary principle in British industrial relations has never denied legislation a role but has displayed a pragmatic approach. Statutory regulation is seen as inferior to regulation by collective agreement and as best confined to areas where the latter is absent. Thus, 'protective' and 'safety net' legislation was acceptable to, and sought by, the trade unions while any legislative intervention in collectively regulated areas, or in the internal affairs of trade unions, was resisted. In practice the voluntary tradition required identification and management of a, at times difficult, line between supportive and restrictive legislation.

But if the voluntary tradition did not mean keeping the law out of industrial relations, it did embrace the desire to keep out the courts. As Flanders noted (1974: 354):

> It is when legislation has the effect, or appears to have the effect, of bringing unions and their members into the courts that it meets with almost universal disapproval and the tradition asserts

its full force. This is exactly what one would expect given the
unions' history and their accumulated lessons of experience.

The existence of the unfair dismissal provisions will have contributed
to juridification, therefore, if they have led to greater acceptance on the
part of trade unions of legal regulation in areas where it was resisted
previously, and of judicial institutions. This does appear to be the case,
with the qualification that acquiescence rather than acceptance may be
a more appropriate label.

In their successful opposition to the Industrial Relations Act 1971
the trade unions rejected the direct attempt to get them to accept
greater restriction and regulation as part of a 'balanced package' (see
above, p. 10 and Weekes et al., 1975) which included apparently
supportive legislative measures such as the unfair dismissal provisions.
But the unions' support for the retention of the unfair dismissal provisions and the restoration of full participation in the industrial tribunal
system after the repeal of that Act, opened the way for a more gradual
introduction of legal provisions which are seen by the trade unions as
harmful to their interests. This is not to say that these measures would
not have been introduced without the framework provided by the unfair dismissal provisions but that the ability of 'restrictionist' governments (Clark and Wedderburn, 1983) to build upon and modify a generally accepted framework helped make overt opposition more difficult.

The 1974–6 legislation sought to restore the closed shop (outlawed
under the Industrial Relations Act) to its pre-1971 position while
retaining unfair dismissal rights. This necessitated guidance for the
tribunals as to when dismissal of non-members of a union would be
fair: a definition of a closed shop had to be provided and those who
were to be exempted from its membership requirements had to be
identified. The provision of a legal framework within which the closed
shop has to function led to a tightening up of informally operated
closed shops with greater involvement by management in their administration and maintenance (Weekes, 1976: 217). It also gave closed
shops a high profile and provided a means – amendment to the definitions and exemptions – whereby they can be undermined. We discussed
earlier in this chapter (p. 248) the various amendments made in recent
legislation which widen and protect the right not to be a union member.
Further, although the greater part of the industrial tribunal jurisdiction
still concerns disputes between employers and employees, s.4 of the
Employment Act 1980 provides for tribunals to hear complaints against
trade unions by those claiming unreasonable exclusion or expulsion
and, as noted above (p. 249), the 1982 Act provides more opportunities
for tribunals to award compensation against trade unions rather than
employers.

This trend of course has not gone unnoticed by the trade unions. Indeed, part of the TUC campaign against the 1982 legislation was a recommendation of partial withdrawal of co-operation from the industrial tribunal system (Dickens, 1983a: 27). This was that 'no trade union member of an industrial tribunal or the Employment Appeal Tribunal should serve on cases arising from the application of a union membership agreement or arrangement' (TUC, 1982: 21). This limited proposal contrasts markedly with the strategy of non-cooperation with the Industrial Relations Act which included instructions to TUC nominees not to serve on the industrial tribunals and other institutions concerned with its implementation. This led to the resignation of some 80 per cent of union-nominated tribunal lay members (Dickens, 1983a: 29). The great increase in the number of lay members since that time will have increased the problems of getting compliance with any instruction to resign which might be issued now, but the more limited withdrawal of co-operation by the trade unions reflects also a general acceptance, and in some quarters appreciation, of the industrial tribunal system.

Just prior to the Employment Act 1982, the then President of the EAT (Browne-Wilkinson, 1982: 77) noted the success of the industrial tribunals and the EAT in 'applying law affecting industrial relations which both employer and employees voluntarily accept', a success resting in large part on the 'participation of employers and employees in the administration of industrial relations law'. This model, he suggested, 'may well point the way to the best method of bringing law into other sectors of labour relations where the law may have a role to play'. The murmurings of disquiet in the TUC about the changes affecting tribunals in the 1980 and 1982 Acts, and the fact that, in the pre-1983 election period affiliated unions' views were canvassed on a range of options concerning the tribunals including their replacement in unfair dismissal cases by arbitration bodies (IRLIB, 1983: 11–12), indicates that continued trade union involvement and acceptance of these judicial bodies is not unproblematic and may well be contingent upon the nature of the law they have to administer. But the fact that trade union acceptance and involvement *does* continue at a time when the unions see themselves attacked, inter alia, through legal regulation, does raise the question of at what stage and how easily any disengagement in the future might occur.

Employers' Policies and Security Against Job Loss

We now turn to the final area identified as likely to be affected by the unfair dismissal provisions. It was expected that employers' policies and practices would change in a way which would improve individual job security.

The impact of the statutory provisions on security against job loss cannot be gauged by considering only those cases where dismissal takes place and is challenged through the statutory machinery. Consideration must also be given to what has happened at the workplace as a result of the enactment of the right to challenge the fairness of a dismissal before an industrial tribunal. Cases come into the tribunal system only after a dismissal decision has been taken. The question we have to address here is whether such decisions are themselves less likely because of the existence of the statutory protection.

To answer this question definitively calls for detailed information on the extent of and reasons for job terminations over time, and even then there would be difficulties in isolating the impact of the legislation from other possible influences on any trend detected. As it is, the statistical information is inadequate. But writers have, with qualifications, reached conclusions on the basis of what statistics are available. By comparing their 1977 survey of manufacturing establishments employing over fifty workers with the 1969 Government survey of establishments drawn from all sectors of the economy employing at least twenty-five, Daniel and Stilgoe (1978) noted that rates of dismissal for reasons other than redundancy had fallen over the eight-year period and argue that the unfair dismissal provisions 'played a part' in this. In 1977, among establishments having five hundred or more employees, none had dismissed 3.5 per cent or more of its workers. In marked contrast the 1969 findings showed that 6 per cent of establishments in this size band had dismissed 6 per cent or more and a very few had dismissed 11 per cent or more (Daniel and Stilgoe, 1978: 62). This fall through reduced incidence of high dismissal rates was found to apply also in sectors other than manufacturing (Daniel and Millward, 1983: 171).

We cannot quantify more precisely the impact which the existence of the statutory right may have had on dismissal and job security. Instead, we indicate ways in which the legislation may be expected, on the basis of the research, to have had an impact on employer policies and practices which might affect individual job security. These are discussed under: the effect of procedural development; recruitment; definition of good employee; and classification of job loss.

Effect of Procedural Development
As documented above (p. 232), there has been a marked growth in procedures for dealing with discipline/dismissal: procedures which generally provide for a system of warnings and opportunity for higher

management to review the dismissal decisions or recommendations of lower level management. With two important provisos — one that the procedural development represents a change, rather than merely formalisation of existing practice, and two that the procedure is actually followed — this development can be expected to reduce the likelihood of dismissal by producing an improvement in an employee's conduct or performance (the corrective function of procedures) which removes management's need for dismissal and/or by removing the risk of arbitrary or ill-considered dismissal decisions. This suggests the impact on job security of procedural development would be to reduce the rate of dismissal overall.

It might be noted, however, that for any particular individual, management adherence to procedure, in some circumstances, could increase the risk of dismissal. Where management is concerned not to appear inconsistent it may not act to retain an employee, whom they would otherwise choose to make a special case, where the number of warnings warranting dismissal has been accumulated or where an offence has been committed for which summary dismissal is possible under the disciplinary rules. Some flexibility in the operation of rules and procedures in dismissal is of course permissible, not least because the tribunals look at reasonableness 'in the circumstances', but in some cases a procedure, particularly where 'three warnings and out' is operated rigidly, may act as a conveyor belt towards dismissal.

We argued earlier (p. 241) that union involvement in procedures may help legitimise management's dismissal decisions and that procedures themselves help dismissal decisions be accepted as 'fair'. Where this occurs, following a procedure may increase the likelihood of an individual dismissal in circumstances where previously the unpredictability of workforce or union reaction to the dismissal may have inhibited the employer from applying this sanction.

Overall, however, where procedures have now been introduced or improved, representing a change in practice, and are actually followed, some reduction in the number of dismissals may be expected. But this has to be seen in the context of research results which find managers in all sized establishments attributing little effect to the unfair dismissal provisions in terms of inhibiting dismissal.

Daniel and Stilgoe's findings to this effect concerned establishments with at least fifty workers. Because it was argued that firms smaller than this were suffering most from the inhibiting effects on management of the employment protection legislation, a further survey of establishments employing fewer than fifty workers was undertaken by the Department of Employment's own staff (Clifton and Tatton-Brown, 1979). Only 35 per cent of the 301 respondents said that legislation had affected them, and when asked how, 6 per cent mentioned difficulty in sacking bad workers. 'On unfair dismissal a direct question (has the law relating to unfair dismissal affected the numbers dismissed?) was answered in the affirmative by ten per cent' (ibid.: 23). When asked whether employment legislation (including such legislation as redundancy payments and the sex and race discrimination Acts as well as unfair dismissal) had made it more difficult to reduce their labour force, 27 per cent said considerably more difficult, 6 per cent slightly more difficult, and 63 per cent of respondents said it made no difference. The authors note 'what is surprising about these answers is that it is self-evident that the employment legislation – if it has any effect at all – should have made it at least *slightly* more difficult to dismiss people'.

Recruitment

The major effect attributed to the unfair dismissal provisons by respondents to the Daniel and Stilgoe survey who reported some effect was procedural reform, which was identified by 84 per cent (1978: 40). As Table 8.5 shows, the specific procedural area mentioned most often was discipline/dismissal which has been dealt with above. The second type of procedure most frequently mentioned was selection/recruitment, identified by 11 per cent. In discussing the impact of the legislation on recruitment Daniel and Stilgoe (ibid.: 50) report that the 'focus of managers' replies was upon the *quality* of recruits. They paid more attention to ensuring that new employees were competent to undertake the job and to fulfil their terms of employment before taking them on'. The small employer survey confirmed that where an impact on recruitment is reported 'the main influence appears to be on *care* in recruitment' (Clifton and Tatton-Brown, 1979: 33).

Fears (whether well-founded or not) concerning problems in dismissing workers deemed unsuitable, or the cost this would involve, act as an encouragement to some managers to review and improve their recruitment and selection procedures and practices and to effect better training and appraisal schemes. The legislation should make the method of obtaining a suitable workforce by a practice of hiring (almost) anyone and then firing those not suitable appear more costly and problematic than taking greater initial care in ensuring only suitable workers are employed or retained beyond a monitored probationary period.

Inasmuch as greater screening of job applicants helps produce a workforce satisfactory to the employer fewer dismissals might be expected. In practice, of course, the nature of the provisions allows the hire and fire method of obtaining a suitable workforce to continue without risk, if management wish, as dismissal generally can be challenged only

TABLE 8.5

NATURE OF EFFECTS ATTRIBUTED TO UNFAIR DISMISSAL LEGISLATION

	%	
Procedure	84	
(Procedures generally or unspecified)		(44)
(Disciplinary/dismissals)		(36)
(Selection/recruitment)		(11)
(Induction/training)		(1)
Supervisory/management training	10	
More tolerant/cautious	8	
Reduced management discretion	6	
Inconvenient/irritating/frustrating	3	
Extra work/costs	2	
Other answer	3	
Can't say	1	
	117	
(Base: plants where some effects reported)	(173)	

SOURCE: Table 23. Daniel and Stilgoe, 1978: 49.

if it takes place after a certain period of service which serves in effect as a probationary period. For small firms, since 1980, this period is two years (see Chapter 1).

This may be expected to reduce the likely impact on security from job loss resulting from improved selection. It is not the actual provisions which affect employer behaviour, however, but employer awareness and perception of them. If it is believed to be impossible to sack people who are unsuitable or extremely expensive to do so, then this may affect policy and practice in ways not actually necessitated by the legislative requirements or likely outcome of an unfair dismissal claim. The survey of small firms (Clifton and Tatton-Brown, 1979: 33) found 'evidence that decisions are often taken in the light of considerable ignorance of the detail of the legislation and without reference to official sources of information and advice'.

In response to the small firm lobby in particular, the Conservative government elected in 1979 introduced changes to the legislative provisions where they were thought to 'damage smaller businesses — and larger ones too — and actually prevent the creation of jobs' (DE, 1979b: 874). Although these harmful effects were argued by various bodies representing small business interests to arise from the statutory protection, the non-partisan research undertaken did not find that the unfair dismissal legislation was preventing job creation or recruitment. Where demand was increasing but recruitment was not occurring, increased labour productivity or unused capacity were given as explanations by managers questioned rather than the inhibiting effect of the unfair dismissal provisions (Daniel and Stilgoe, 1978: 68).

Inasmuch as the criticism and anxiety of small employers arose from misunderstanding or ignorance, the amendments to the legislation and regulations of themselves are unlikely to make any difference to employers' behaviour unless employers are persuaded that the position is now one where they have 'regained' the freedom to dismiss any worker who is regarded as unsatisfactory without risk of challenge or penalty. The government, through the Department of Employment, has issued a booklet providing 'a perspective on unfair dismissal claims' which contains guidance and reassurance for small firms (Henderson, 1982). The booklet gives information about the rarity of unfair dismissal claims, the lack of applicant success, and the relatively low amounts of compensation awarded to the minority who do succeed. It advises employers what measures to take to 'help make dismissal unnecessary' — such as proper selection and adequate training — and notes reassuringly that other than in special cases, such as dismissal for trade union membership or activities, 'the one or two year qualifying period gives you time in most cases to decide on a person's suitability before a claim of unfair dismissal can be made'.

The survey of small firms found that DE leaflets relating to employment legislation had been heard of by 54 per cent of firms, but only 32 per cent had got any copies and only 23 per cent had consulted them (Clifton and Tatton-Brown, 1979: 25). Assuming that the guidance booklet makes a greater impact, it would seem that while the advice given therein on recruitment and training might help reduce the likelihood of dismissal, the reassurance it contains about the odds against facing an unfair dismissal claim or suffering any penalty might remove unfounded inhibitions and produce the opposite effect.

Definition of Good Employee

In the discussion so far reference has been made to management's need and desire to obtain a suitable workforce and the ways in which the existence of the statutory provisions may influence how this is done: possibly be leading to greater emphasis on recruitment of good employees

and correction, through training and warning, of those who prove unsatisfactory rather than dismissing and replacing them. We now turn
to the question of what is a good employee.

Managerial definitions of what qualities make a good worker vary
within and between employment establishments. Even where similar
terms are used, for example, 'good attendance record', there can be
wide differences between the rates of absence considered acceptable
(Edwards and Scullion, 1982: 117; Singleton, 1975: 32). The law
allows managements wide discretion in defining these matters and does
not seek to remove management's right to rid itself of 'bad' employees.
However, the legislation in operation does not leave untouched management's freedom to define which employees are 'bad'. An obvious
example is that while unsuitable employees can be dismissed fairly,
employers are not free at law to equate 'female' or 'black' or 'trade
union member' with 'unsuitable'.

Less obviously, the interpretation of the provisions by the tribunals
and courts may have necessitated, for example, some reconsideration of
the importance attached to an employee's behaviour outside the workplace in any assessment of him or her as a good or bad worker. In setting
standards of substantive fairness the tribunals and courts may help
shape employer definitions. This effect does, however, require knowledge of tribunal decisions by the employers in question and a preparedness to take steps necessary to ensure only those dismissals are
executed which a tribunal would uphold as fair.

For this possible impact on employer definitions to lead to a reduced
likelihood of dismissal, the tribunal's definition of a 'bad' employee
(that is one who may be dismissed substantively fairly) needs also to
be more restrictive than that presently operated by employers. Therefore, as with all other possible impacts discussed here, the effect is
likely to vary between employments. But, as we argued earlier (p. 103),
the test adopted by the tribunal – that of the reasonable employer – is
not a particularly stringent one. The existence of the legislation may
call for some redefinition of the 'good' employee but this takes place
within a context which acknowledges that it is fair to dismiss workers
whose continued employment is not in the interests of the business
as defined by the reasonable employer.

Classification of Job Loss

So far in our discussion of the impact of the statutory protection on
security against job loss we have equated the reduced likelihood of dismissal with greater job security. It is now necessary to take a wider
view which encompasses other forms of job termination for it is possible that a reduction in 'dismissal' may be accompanied by an increase

in 'resignation' or 'redundancy'. The terms may have precise legal definitions but they are often used loosely, whether intentionally or not, by
those dismissing and being dismissed.

It may suit both employer and employee to have a job terminated
by reason of redundancy rather than dismissal for reasons relating to
the individual. Although redundancy is of course dismissal it does not
carry the same stigma. It is generally recognised as a neutral, no-fault
reason for termination. By the same token, certain workers, particularly
higher status staff, may prefer to 'resign' rather than be dismissed,
particularly if an ex gratia payment is made. In the period 1965 to
1971, when the Redundancy Payments Act was in force but not the
unfair dismissal provisions, employers could seek to avoid having to
make a payment by giving a reason other than redundancy for dismissal.
Since the introduction of the unfair dismissal provisions, defining the
dismissal as redundancy might be the better option for the employer,
particularly if the employee concerned does not qualify for a redundancy payment and is unlikely to succeed in a claim for unfair selection.
Even if he or she is qualified for a redundancy payment the employer
will receive a partial rebate from the state fund.

It is impossible to gauge the extent of redefinition of reason for
termination which the introduction of statutory protection against
unfair dismissal may have occasioned. The employer's freedom to
redefine the nature of the termination – perhaps with the explicit or
tacit consent of the worker – and a certain amount of ignorance about
the exact meaning of the terms, and loose usage, however, make it
difficult to assess the impact of the unfair dismissal provisions on security against job loss by considering dismissal statistics alone. A decline
in the rate of dismissal, defined in terms of dismissal for reasons relating
to the individual, cannot be taken necessarily as an indicator of increasing job security. In time of recession the amount of 'genuine' redundancy (that is in accordance with the statutory definition) is such that
employers have ample opportunity to shake out any employees whose
health, fitness, age, work or absence record make them seem less than
satisfactory employees. The need to dismiss such workers individually
does not then arise.

Even where there is no recession, changes in work organisation,
technological change or relocation all enable workers to be sacked in
circumstances which, unless unfair selection or unreasonable treatment
is alleged, generally fall outside the scope of the unfair dismissal provisions. This may not of course be the main, or even a conscious, reason
for such changes. Nevertheless such developments, including the apparently increasing practice of subcontracting, often to self-employed persons, and the putting out of work previously done by direct employees,

all have an impact on overall job security – reducing further the core of relatively protected workers and increasing the proportion of those outside the statutory protection.

Where workers are classified as self-employed rather than employees the termination of their contracts is not defined as dismissal under the legislation (see Chapter 1). This kind of contractual relationship, generally obtainable for instance by using outworkers, enables employers to escape the risk of unfair dismissal remedies. Studies into homeworking have identified a wide range of factors (summarised in Hakim and Dennis, 1982: 5) influencing employers' decisions to use homeworkers of which preferences between contractual labour and subcontracting is only one.

Research into contractual arrangements in six types of business or firm where outworking was common (Leighton, 1983: 20) tentatively concluded that the demands of employment legislation did not have a significant effect on leading employers to adopt a particular form of relationship. Interestingly, however, the research found (ibid.: 23) that in the industries studied 'employers did manage, even when using employee status for their workers, to avoid almost all employment protection burdens'. They did this through use of a series of extremely short-term contracts. Because of this, in the firms studied the employment conditions of the direct employees did not act as an incentive to use outworkers. In other cases, particularly where direct labour is organised and rights are established and protected, subcontracting may provide a way for the employer to achieve greater flexibility in use of labour (Rubery and Wilkinson, 1981).

In this section we have discussed the impact of the unfair dismissal provisions on those employer policies and practices most likely to affect individual job security. This was the last of the areas we identified where the unfair dismissal provisions were intended or expected to have an effect. In the final section of this chapter, we discuss more generally the question of the impact of the provisions on employers, seeking to differentiate groups within this category.

Impact on Employers

Earlier discussion in this book, although often indicating the limitations on the extent to which the unfair dismissal provisions have promoted job security, has none the less shown that constraints have been imposed on the exercise of the employer's right to dismiss. The perception of these constraints and their impact on policy and practice are likely to vary as between different levels and functions of management within an organisation, and between organisations. The effect of the introduction, formalisation and modification of procedures, identified above (p. 232) as an important consequence of the unfair dismissal provisions, provides a good example of this differential impact.

Most obviously, perhaps, where procedures for handling dismissal in the way encouraged by the legislation already existed and were being followed, for example in parts of the nationalised industry sector (Weekes et al., 1975: 23), the impact of the legislation will have been less than in areas where no or inadequate procedures existed and where changes were introduced. This means that different employers will have faced different requirements for expenditure of time, money and effort and, assuming that the new procedures were adhered to, there will have been a differential impact on the policy and practice of discipline/ dismissal.

Consideration of procedures indicates also the likelihood of differential impact within management in the same organisation. One of the changes identified shortly after the introduction of the unfair dismissal provisions (ibid.: 22) was in the level of management with authority to dismiss. The report of that research refers to 'responsibility for dismissal' meaning power to dismiss but it is useful to distinguish responsibility from authority. The *authority* to dismiss moved upwards in a number of organisations following the introduction of the statutory protection against unfair dismissal. In many cases, however, lower level management would have retained *responsibilities* in the discipline/ dismissal area. As Child and Partridge (1982: 47) note, they may even appear to be increased 'if as a result of increased formalisation supervisors are involved in more procedures they might perceive this as an increase in responsibility, though it would probably limit their autonomy or authority'. The responsibility of supervisory staff in the area of discipline/dismissal may continue or even increase with procedural development, for instance they often play an important role in issuing warnings. Their freedom of action in this area, however, may be limited by demands for consistency of action, adherence to rules and centralisation of control over job termination through a staged procedure.

The identification and setting of rules concerning discipline and dismissal and moving the right to dismiss up the management hierarchy, both common consequences of the introduction of the legislation, clearly affect the discretion and authority of first line supervision. Rules and procedures in fact can be seen as a means of control over lower level supervision rather than over workers; management at a higher level centralises and exercises control.

The differential impact of the consequences of the unfair dismissal provisions may occur across management functions as well as between different levels in the hierarchy. The personnel/industrial relations staff were the people who would know, or would have to find out, what the law was; how legal action against the organisation could be avoided, or won; what changes in procedures or practices would be needed and how they might be implemented. If change had to be negotiated then they would be responsible for bringing it about. If the law was becoming more important then those people who knew about it should become more important also.

There is some evidence that this is what happened with the great increase in employment protection legislation in the 1970s, of which the unfair dismissal provisions were a central element. In the manufacturing sector – particularly metals, engineering and food industries – the industrial relations function was perceived by those involved to be increasing in importance (Brown, 1981; 32). Thirty-six per cent of respondents said the position of the industrial relations function in their establishment had, in the last five years, become 'much more important', 46 per cent said it had become 'more important' and 17 per cent that it had 'stayed about the same'. The largest proportion of respondents, 57 per cent, gave the cause of perceived increased importance as the increase in legislation (ibid.: 33). Through reference to earlier studies it appeared that the number of manufacturing units employing industrial relations specialists and the number of manufacturing company boards with specialist industrial relations directors had increased (ibid.: 32).

Another study of establishments in manufacturing (Daniel and Stilgoe, 1978: 41) detected that 'as a whole, the employment legislation of recent years had increased the workload, the range of activities and the influence of the personnel function'. An increased tendency for line managers to approach the personnel function for help and advice was one indication of this development which helped contribute to the view 'that there had been some tendency for the importance of the personnel function to grow following the legislation'. Research conducted across a wider range of industries including smaller establishments (Daniel and Millward, 1983: 126), however, throws some doubt on the extent to which the trend detected in manufacturing occurred elsewhere and recent developments may lead us to question the permanence of changes which did occur (Guest, 1982).

That the legislation did produce different consequences for various types and levels of management, however, does mean that there may be no homogeneous 'employer view' of its costs and benefits, even within an organisation. The diversity is increased considerably when we consider the differential impact between organisations.

Legislation which impinges on management's right to dismiss or which reshapes that right, as the unfair dismissal provisions have done, will be experienced differently by organisations according to the saliency accorded to dismissal as a sanction in the overall system of control. The ability of employers to terminate their relationship with individual workers underlies their ability to get the capacity to work, which they purchase through the employment contract, transformed into labour done. For employers to realise the full potential of the labour they employ they have to secure the consent (which need not imply agreement), compliance and co-operation of their workforce. The way in which employers attempt to do this will vary between organisations.

It is not appropriate here to discuss in any detail the question of strategies of control of labour, on which there is a growing literature (see for example Friedman, 1977; Edwards, 1979; Burawoy, 1979; Littler, 1982). We would note, however, that because different organisations can employ different structures and methods to obtain the necessary consent, compliance and co-operation of their workforces, the importance, utility and use of dismissal as a disciplinary sanction also will vary.

Edwards (1979: 18) identified discipline as one of three elements, together with direction of work tasks and evaluation, which are co-ordinated to constitute the system of control. Edwards's work has been criticised, partly because his categories do not capture the complexities of the real world. However, brief consideration of two of the control systems he discusses — simple control and bureaucratic control — is useful for our present purpose of indicating the possibility of differential importance of dismissal. Edwards uses 'simple' control (ibid.: 19) to refer to situations where

> bosses exercised power personally, intervening in the labour process often to exhort workers, bully and threaten them, reward good performance, hire and fire on the spot, favor loyal workers, and generally act as despots, benevolent or otherwise . . . There was little structure to the way power was exercised, and workers were often treated arbitrarily.

The use of the past tense reflects Edwards's presentation of the different types of control system he identifies as associated with particular phases of capitalism but simple control is seen to survive in the entrepreneurial small business sector (ibid.: 19) and in medium-sized firms also where it is embodied in an hierarchical structure (ibid.: 31). Here

> each boss — whether a foreman, supervisor or manager — . . . would have full rights to fire and hire, intervene in production, direct workers as to what to do and what not to do, evaluate and

promote or demote, discipline workers, arrange rewards, and so on; in short, each boss would be able to act in the same arbitrary, idiosyncratic unencumbered way that entrepreneurs had acted.

In contrast to the direct, personal control of this model, bureaucratic control 'establishes the impersonal force of "company rules" or "company policy" as the basis for control'. The process of dismissal in this model becomes subject to 'the rule of (company) law' (ibid.: 143). The right to dismiss remains but 'it is reshaped by the bureaucratic form. Exceptional violations aside, workers can be dismissed only if they continue to "misbehave" after receiving written warnings specifying improper behaviour'. An important feature of bureaucratic control is that it does not rest only on sanctions but institutionalises positive incentives and rewards 'proper' behaviour. Reward and incentive structures are biased toward seniority and thus employment stability.

For companies which use carrots more than sticks in dealing with their workforces, where the right to dismiss is already exercised in the way characterised in the bureaucratic control model, there will be little difficulty in complying with the requirements and implications of the unfair dismissal provisions. The Donovan Commission concept of 'good industrial relations' and how to obtain order on the shopfloor is highly compatible with the kind of bureaucratic model just outlined. For other organisations, however, there will be a greater dissonance between the reform sought by the legislation and the particular mix of methods used in the attempt to obtain a compliant, co-operative workforce.

The Donovan Commission recommendations sought to consolidate the status of trade unionism and harness it in the joint construction of more orderly and predictable industrial relations arrangements (Hyman, 1981: 140). Management which was already in fact limited by shop floor power was encouraged to adopt procedural and other reform to regain control. But this de facto loss of power was not a problem for all employers. In some sectors worker constraints on the bald exercise of managerial prerogative were not experienced. As Edwards notes (1979: 27), in some organisations, simple control 'despite being informal, erratic and subject to favouritism and arbitrariness, provided the basis for profitable control'. It did not follow, therefore, that these sectors also would find that giving workers additional job security, relief from arbitrary supervision and the right to appeal grievances would be a better way to do business.

Particular factors can be identified which, as they interact in some organisations probably favour, at a particular point in time, bureaucratic or, drawing on a different typology (Friedman, 1977), 'responsible autonomy' strategies, but which as they apply in other organisations may produce a form of 'simple' control. Such factors include the size of the organisation, the choice of production technology and payment system, demands of the product market, employer preference or 'ideology'; the nature of the workforce (for example its substitutability); the labour market and worker resistance and organisation.

Employers are in business to make profits not to sack people. Dismissal may or may not be an important aspect of the range of policies which employers adopt at any particular time in their pursuit of profit. Where it is, the introduction of legislation affecting dismissal will be experienced as a greater intrusion than where it is not. This helps explain the locus of employer protest concerning the unfair dismissal provisions and the operation of industrial tribunals. Most protest has come from the small-firm secondary sector where not only is there likely to be a greater dissonance between the existing mode of operation and the requirements of the legislation, but where any time, effort or expense occasioned in complying with them, or penalties imposed for failing to do so, will be proportionately greater than in larger corporations operating in the primary sector.

We should note, however, that there is no exact 'read off' between the sector of the economy in which a firm operates and the kind of terms and conditions which are offered to its workers. Although the institution of bureaucratic control is associated with primary sector corporate firms with stable product markets and high levels of demand, and more direct control is associated with secondary sector firms where conditions are not conducive to employment security, the correspondence sometimes breaks down on closer examination (Lawson, 1981; Nolan, 1983: 306). Finally, the difference between organisations in saliency of dismissal in the overall package of control has been discussed, but it also may vary as between groups of workers within the same firm. Different formal and informal discipline policies can co-exist within an organisation.

The impact of the unfair dismissal provisions between different levels and functions of management were detected empirically. The differential impact between and within organisations according to the salience of dismissal just discussed is, to a large extent, a differential *potential* impact. The incentive to change policies, procedures and practice will depend in large part on the perceived advantages to be gained by so doing and the likely consequences of not doing so. We noted above that although management in large, organised firms may see advantages to be gained through procedural reform and may revise practice to improve their chances of having any dismissal challenge, particularly if union supported, upheld as fair by a tribunal, this is not necessarily the general position.

Where advantages are not perceived the likely consequences of inaction are not such as to provide a strong incentive to change: although employers are inevitably involved in some expense in defending unfair dismissal claims, the chance of a company finding itself before an industrial tribunal, although slightly greater for a small firm (see Chapter 2), is small; the employer is likely to succeed should there be a hearing and should the dismissal be found unfair a relatively small compensation payment generally is all that will be required. The circumstances and interests of smaller employers have increasingly been acknowledged in the legislative provisions anyway (see above, p. 102) weakening, for example, the initial emphasis on the need for dismissal procedures. This means that the areas where the scope for impact on policies and practtices is greatest may in fact be the areas which actually experience the least impact.

Summary

In this chapter we identified and examined five areas in particular where the unfair dismissal provisions were expected or intended to have an impact. The hope that the introduction of statutory protection and a legal route whereby dismissal could be challenged would lead to a reduction in industrial action does not appear to have been fulfilled. We identified various reasons why those able to organise a collective challenge to a dismissal continue to do so and why this was a 'rational' response where the employer's definiton of an issue as an individual matter was not shared by the workers.

It was expected that the introduction of agreed disciplinary rules and procedures, which the legislation would stimulate, would reduce the likelihood of dismissal decisions taken in accordance with them being challenged. Although adherence to a procedure may remove arbitrariness from dismissal, the nature of the procedures which have been developed reduces the extent to which decisions taken in accordance with them will be seen as fair and reasonable and, therefore, less open to challenge.

In examining procedural growth and development, we noted that the introduction and operation of the provisions had led to a great increase in the incidence of formal procedures but that for the most part they were managerial rather than joint procedures and rarely provided for appeal against management decisions to an independent body. In part, reduction in strike activity had been expected to result from 'clarification' of management's right to dismiss. Although unions have to some extent been involved in agreeing disciplinary procedures, joint agreement on rules was less extensive.

The unfair dismissal provisions had been seen as a way of giving some protection to workers outside the coverage of collective bargaining while at the same time helping bring them within that coverage by protecting freedom of association: people were not to be dismissed for joining a union or taking part in its activities. The protection of union members and activists and, therefore, the support for collective bargaining provided by the provisions, was found in practice to be very limited. Interpretation of the provisions had exposed large holes in the protection provided by the right not to be dismissed for union membership or activity. Further, the right not to be a union member, reintroduced into the provisions, although balancing the individual right of freedom of association, is counter-effective in terms of the legislation's underpinning of collective bargaining.

We discussed the extent to which the introduction of unfair dismissal provisions themselves, rather than encouraging or supporting collective bargaining, could be seen to enhance individualism. The impact of the unfair dismissal provisions on collective bargaining was dealt with also by considering the extent to which legal norms and processes are being imported into day-to-day industrial relations: an aspect of juridification. The other aspect of this phenomenon we considered was the acceptability of legal regulation and the role of judicial institutions in industrial relations. We argued that the framework provided by the unfair dismissal provisions and the general acceptability of the industrial tribunal system had made it more difficult for unions to oppose the introduction of legal provisions which they see as harmful to their interests.

In examining the indirect impact of the unfair dismissal provisions on individual job security we considered the likely effect of the procedural development we had identified; the way in which employers' recruitment policies or practices had been affected; whether the statute had influenced the definition of 'good' and 'bad' employees and the definition of job termination. The introduction and improvement of dismissal procedures, where this represented a change in actual practice, was seen overall as likely to lead to some reduction in the likelihood of dismissal. Few employers, however, actually reported that they thought the law had made it more difficult for them to dismiss workers, the main impact being perceived as procedural reform. Employers reported they were more careful over recruitment and selection but the legislation, with its service qualification, still enables the adoption of the hire and fire method of obtaining a suitable workforce. Other than in discrimination cases, the provisions are likely to have had little, if any, effect in shaping employer definitions of 'good' and 'bad' workers in a way which might improve individual job security. Their impact in shaping definitions of job termination and in influencing work organisation decisions may be greater although quantification in this area is impossible.

In noting the limitations on the impact of the provisions on individual job security through affecting employers' policies and practices, it should be borne in mind that, although increased individual job security was among the legislative intentions, the individual welfare consideration was only one element in the industrial relations reform sought, and not necessarily one to be accorded priority. As the Code of Practice associated with the Industrial Relations Act (DE, 1972: 4) made clear, management's main concern remained the operational efficiency and success of the undertaking; job security was to be pursued only in so far as it was consistent with these goals, as defined by management. Not all employers will see the operational efficiency of their enterprise as served by increasing employee job security. Even those who may have seen advantages in doing so in the 'full employment' economy of the 1960s, when workers could insist more effectively on what they considered to be their rights, may see this as less necessary in the changed economic climate of the 1980s.

The differential impact of the provisions on employers was discussed in the final section. The perception of constraints imposed by the legislation on the right to dismiss and their impact on policy and practice varies as between levels and functions of management within an organisation, and as between organisations. Increased importance of the personnel function and a shift in authority away from lower level supervision were identified as differential impacts as between management within an organisation. The different potential for impact as between organisations was argued to depend on the different saliency accorded to dismissal as a sanction in the particular mix of methods used to gain consent, compliance and co-operation from the workforce.

The Donovan Commission reform strategy was seen to be in line with the control systems of some organisations, or as applied to some groups of employees, but to be discordant with others. The differential potential impact helps explain the small-employer protest concerning the legislation and the industrial tribunals while discussion of the incentives to change suggested that the areas where the greatest potential for impact exists in fact may be those areas where the least impact has occurred.

9

An Arbitral Alternative

In 1965 the then Minister of Labour described the industrial tribunals as 'a valuable experiment in our industrial relations system'.[1] The preceding chapters have provided an assessment of that experiment. We begin this chapter by looking briefly at the success or failure of the experiment as reflected in the perceptions of those using the system.

The essence of the experiment, as we have seen, was a form of tripartite labour court. In this chapter we explore an alternative, an experiment which was not tried, namely an arbitral system for handling dismissal disputes. We argue that the combination and interplay of the distinguishing features of arbitration might have allowed an arbitration-based system, given the same statutory framework of law as the industrial tribunal system, to have escaped the tendencies towards legalism and to have fulfilled more adequately the desire for a speedy, cheap, informal and expert means of resolving dismissal disputes. We suggest also that an arbitral system might have operated more effectively than a court-based one in curbing the exercise of employer authority in the interests of employee job retention. The need to consider an alternative is prompted by the examination of the operation, outcomes and impact of the present industrial tribunal system. This places in context the satisfaction with the present system which those who use it apparently have.

Extent of Satisfaction with the Existing System

Applicants in our survey were asked 'bearing in mind your own experience, what do you think of the industrial tribunal system as a whole?' Table 9.1 shows the responses according to the outcome of the case. Seventy per cent of all applicants thought that as a whole the system was 'good' and only 16 per cent considered it 'bad'. The outcome of

1. 711 HC Deb, 26 April 1965, 46.

TABLE 9.1

APPLICANTS' OPINIONS OF THE TRIBUNAL SYSTEM

	All	Heard		Not Heard	
		Applicant Won	Applicant Lost	Settlement	No Settlement
	%	%	%	%	%
Very good	38	56	18	52	22
Fairly good	32	33	31	32	26
Total good	70	89	49	84	58
Neither good nor bad	12	3	15	10	22
Rather bad	8	4	17	4	5
Very bad	8	3	16	2	12
Total bad	16	7	33	6	17
	N = 1063	N = 145	N = 284	N = 447	N = 187

SOURCE: IRRU survey of applicants.

the individual case did appear to influence the judgment made but almost half of those applicants who lost their claims at tribunal none the less considered the system at least 'fairly good'.

Employers' opinions of the industrial tribunal system as a whole, bearing in mind the case they had been involved in, were less favourable than those of applicants. As Table 9.2 shows, 40 per cent of all employers thought the system 'good', a similar proportion, 39 per cent, thought it 'bad' and 17 per cent considered it neither good nor bad. The outcome of the case in which the respondent had been involved once again appeared to have some influence on the assessment. Employers who lost at the tribunal hearing were the group most likely to have an unfavourable view of the system although 30 per cent of this group was still prepared to describe the system as at least 'fairly good'.

It is important, however, to place the opinions of those using the system in context. As we saw in Chapter 2, applicants to industrial tribunals generally have no alternative means of seeking redress of their grievances. They therefore are not evaluating the tribunal system by comparing it with an alternative form of dispute resolution but with the absence of any means of complaining about their dismissal. The most frequent response to an open-ended question asking applicants to explain their opinion of the tribunal system reflects this fact: 37 per cent of those 750 applicants thinking the system good gave reasons coded as 'it gives the working person a chance/provides an opportunity which did not exist otherwise'. Next came a response made by 29 per cent of those thinking the system good, which was that, it was 'a good idea/worked well/seemed to be impartial'.

Those employers holding a favourable view of the system generally explained this by reference to what the system represented, namely a means of providing protection for employees or an impartial method of dispute settlement. Thirteen per cent of those employers in the survey giving an opinion of the system, and 23 per cent of those who said the system was good, stated that the system provided necessary protection for employees. This was the most frequent favourable response. Next came the view that it provided an impartial method of resolving dismissal disputes, a reason given by 10 per cent of all employers expressing an opinion and 22 per cent of those saying the system was good.

The main explanation for the opinions given by employers holding unfavourable views of the industrial tribunal system was that it was biased against employers. A quarter of all employers and 41 per cent of those who thought the system was bad said this. It is likely that this evaluation of the industrial tribunal system is influenced by the employers' view of the legislation it operates. The unfair dismissal provisions, in giving workers rights against their employers, is thus, in a

TABLE 9.2

EMPLOYERS' OPINIONS OF THE TRIBUNAL SYSTEM

| | All | Heard | | Not Heard | |
| | | Employer Won | Employer Lost | Settlement | No Settlement |
	%	%	%	%	%
Very good	11	17	7	7	10
Fairly good	29	35	23	24	37
Total good	40	52	30	31	47
Neither good nor bad	17	14	10	21	19
Rather bad	19	14	27	20	19
Very bad	20	17	33	21	10
Total bad	39	31	60	41	29
No opinion	4	2	—	5	5
	N = 1080	N = 309	N = 134	N = 449	N = 189

SOURCE: IRRU survey of employers.

sense, to the disadvantage of or 'biased against' employers. Other explanations, however, referred to the operation of the system itself: almost a quarter of the 414 employers who thought the system was bad thought it was too easy to apply and 27 per cent thought it involved excessive time and cost. As we noted (p. 104) such employer criticism has led to changes such as the introduction of pre-hearing assessment.

Whilst the opinions of those experiencing the system are important, we would argue that it is necessary to evaluate the industrial tribunal system by wider criteria and this we have done. In looking at the industrial tribunals in their operation of the unfair dismissal jurisdiction we examined whether certain expectations and intentions had been met. Some expectations, discussed in Chapters 6 and 7, concerned the industrial tribunal system itself, in particular that it would provide 'a procedure which is easily accessible, informal, speedy and inexpensive and which gives (the parties) the best possible opportunity of arriving at an amicable settlement of their differences' (Donovan, 1968: para. 572). Others, discussed in Chapter 8, concerned the statutory right, for example that it would improve individual job security, reduce industrial action and underpin the growth of collective bargaining.

In discussing the efficiency of industrial tribunals in Chapter 7, we noted that the quasi-court nature of the tribunals and the particular legal context within which they operate constrain the *extent* to which they display the operational advantages over the ordinary courts identified in the Franks Report. We saw, for example, that legal representation is seen as beneficial and increasingly is being used. This is in part a reflection of the nature of the industrial tribunal system but also feeds back into the system, emphasising its court-like features. Use of legal representation was found to be associated with less expedition, reduced accessibility, greater expense and more technicality.

The examination of various aspects of the industrial tribunal system in earlier chapters identified ways in which constraints imposed by the quasi-court nature and legal context of the tribunal system affect its ability to provide an ideal adjudication mechanism in dismissal disputes. Such constraints show themselves for instance in the fact that tribunals, despite the presence of lay members, have not succeeded in eschewing legalism and in distancing themselves from the mainstream of English legal method (see above, Chapter 3, and Munday, 1981: 150). The ability of tribunals to pay attention to considerations wider than black letter law is limited by appeal being from expert bodies to ordinary courts. This, we saw, limits the potential influence of lay members on the bodies where they sit and means they have no input at all where the final decision is made. As Aaron notes (1980 383), in support of his preference for expert lay involvement in final decision-making in employment disputes, professional judges

> seeking to resolve all disputes in accordance with abstract or 'pure' legal principles are likely to render judgments in labour disputes which, though irreproachable in a legal sense, may not necessarily bring about a particularly wise or fair result.

As we discussed in Chapter 7 in relation to union membership and activity dismissals, the approach of the professional judge shows itself in an emphasis on individual, legalistic considerations rather than a concern for the collective, industrial relations aspects of a case. This is part of the explanation for the apparent failure of the industrial tribunal system to emerge as an acceptable alternative to collective action in certain cases, as discussed in Chapter 8. We saw that for some dismissal disputes — those which at least some participants define as collective, industrial relations disputes rather than individual, legal disputes — another form of independent adjudication, arbitration, is preferred by the parties to that of the industrial tribunal.

Some of those who have identified problems with the operation and outcomes of the industrial tribunal system in its operation of the unfair dismissal jurisdiction have suggested that an arbitration-based system might provide a preferable alternative but the case has not been argued in any detail (IRLIB, 1983: 12; Lewis, 1982: 87). As we have noted at points in our examination, different interests will perceive or emphasise different problems with the industrial tribunal system and obviously this will influence views as to what may constitute a 'preferable' alternative. The rarity of re-employment awards by tribunals, for example, is not perceived as a problem by employers although it is not in keeping with the legislative intention as to remedies for unfair dismissal and is regretted by employee representatives (Chapter 5). Similarly, the relative ease of application, part of the intended accessibility of the system, has been criticised by employers but not by employees (for example, see National Chamber of Trade, 1977: 12, and p. 103 above). The criticism that tribunals show a tendency to legalism, however, is one apparently shared by all, with the possible exception of some lawyers. The point here is not that lawyers will not criticise legalism but that they may not share lay perceptions that it exists. Although legalism is concerned primarily with the way in which the industrial tribunal system operates and generally refers to the aspects which make tribunals appear more like courts, as we discussed earlier it also affects other aspects of the system, including its outcomes.

Existing Arbitration Examined

The reference point here is arbitration as experienced in Britain. While it may be useful to consider, for example, the American grievance arbitration system which operates in the unionised sector (see Elkouri and Elkouri, 1973), the different industrial relations and wider contexts warn against simply searching for ready-made foreign packages to import. Also, common labelling may conceal different goods. Thus, an 'arbitration system' may be judicial and court-like, as in Australia for example, where the criticism of legalism is often made of the arbitration system (Cupper, 1976: 387; Donn, 1976: 327). Our examination, therefore, centres on contemporary state-provided arbitration in Britain, identifying how its decision-making differs from that in the industrial tribunal system and exploring whether it offers a preferable alternative to that system.

Types of Arbitration Arrangements

Each year a small number of dismissal disputes are handled by arbitration set up through ACAS under its general statutory duty, conferred by s.3 of the Employment Protection Act 1975, to provide such services as conciliation and arbitration where there is a 'trade dispute'. The legal definition of a trade dispute includes a dispute between employer and workers over termination of employment of one or more workers.[2] When approached to provide arbitration under its general duty ACAS will see first if the dispute can be resolved through conciliation; if not arbitration will be arranged. ACAS arranged arbitration in 51 disputes over discipline and dismissal in 1983 having attempted conciliation in 178. These 51 cases accounted for a quarter of the mediation/arbitration case load that year (ACAS, 1984: 74).

Such arbitration is 'voluntary' in that it is provided at the request of the parties who may be using it on an ad hoc basis or because it is provided for as an automatic or optional stage in their grievance or disputes procedure. Arbitration also may be set up privately at the expense of the parties without using ACAS. As noted in the previous chapter, procedural provision for third-party intervention in dismissal disputes is still found only infrequently, mainly in large unionised establishments. In the 1980 workplace survey most establishments had a procedure for discipline/dismissal disputes; 29 per cent contained provision for reference to ACAS. Use of outsiders specified in the procedure was rare: only 17 per cent of the minority who had used an outsider to help settle the most recent dispute in the twelve months preceding the

2. Trade Union and Labour Relations Act 1974 s.29, amended.

survey had used ACAS (Daniel and Millward, 1983: 168, 169). An earlier survey of manufacturing industry found that it was very unusual for an establishment without formal provision for third-party intervention to make use of it and only 7 per cent of establishments in that survey which had no such provision said they had used it on an ad hoc basis to settle a discipline or dismissal dispute in the two years preceding the survey (Brown, 1981: 48).

A dispute can be referred to any of three types of arbitration: the single arbitrator, a board of arbitration or the Central Arbitration Committee (CAC). The Central Arbitration Committee is a permanent body, the successor to the Industrial Court set up in 1919, more appropriately renamed the Industrial Arbitration Board in 1971 (Dickens, 1979: 290). Cases are normally heard by a committee of three consisting of the CAC chairperson, or one of the thirteen deputy chairpersons, together with two members drawn from two panels, which together (as at December 1983) consist of some thirty-eight people who have experience as representatives respectively of employers and employees (CAC, 1984: 1–6). A board of arbitration may be appointed by ACAS to deal with a particular dispute. It is similar to the CAC in that an independent chairperson will sit with an equal number of members, normally one each side, but, unlike the CAC, the members are appointed by ACAS to represent the respective general interests of the parties to the dispute.

These larger scale arbitrations generally are not used for dismissal disputes and are less common for other types of dispute also. The CAC has only a small voluntary arbitration case load in addition to its statutory duties, although it is trying to attract more cases (Dickens, 1983b: 263). In 1983 it received ten references for voluntary arbitration. Boards of arbitration are generally used only for 'more important issues' (ACAS, 1981: 3) such as a national industry-wide pay dispute or where a dispute is unusually complex and it is felt that side members would be of assistance to the chair. There were twenty-five references to boards of arbitration in 1983 (ACAS, 1984: 74).

The most common type of arbitration, and that used most often to resolve dismissal disputes, is the single arbitrator. This provides the model for an arbitration-based alternative to industrial tribunals. ACAS maintains a list of arbitrators who can be called upon on a fee-paid basis to help resolve disputes. Those on the list who are used fairly regularly are predominantly middle-ranking and senior academics, particularly from the subject areas of economics, industrial relations and law (Jones et al., 1983: 14). A number of them will have had some industrial experience (Towers and Wright, 1983: 84). There are also retired civil servants and some retired employers and union officials on the list. The aim is to appoint people with knowledge and experience of industrial relations who are seen to be impartial. Hence, those actively involved in a trade union or employer capacity are unlikely to be appointed (Lockyer, 1979: 59).

Single arbitration is a relatively quick and inexpensive process. The fees and expenses of the arbitrator are borne by public funds. This kind of arbitration is not highly paid as it is regarded as a public service. The fee in 1984 was £88 per day. Hearings are normally arranged between two or three weeks after the application but can be set up more quickly if required. The award is sent to the parties generally a week or so after the hearing. Hearings are held often at the place of employment but can be held at ACAS regional offices or elsewhere. The hearings are not subject to any set procedure; this is a matter for the arbitrator. The hearings generally are conducted informally and in private. There is no oath taking and the parties remain seated in the same places. The parties make written submissions to the arbitrator prior to the hearing and are asked to exchange these with each other. At the hearing they make oral presentations. The arbitrator questions both sides and they may ask questions of each other, but through the arbitrator rather than by cross-examination. The arbitrator may decide to visit the workplace if this would help his or her understanding of the case. Advisors and witnesses may be brought to the hearing; any witnesses being questioned by the arbitrator. The parties normally are represented by those people who would have attempted to settle the case through negotiation at any earlier stage, for example the personnel manager and union full-time official. In dismissal arbitrations the cases normally are presented by full-time officials of the unions with shop stewards present (Concannon, 1980: 16). Legal representation is extremely rare and notice is required if it is intended that a legal representative be used so the other party may consider whether to employ one also (Lockyer, 1979: 66).

Arbitration awards are the property of the parties and are not published. Awards in voluntary arbitrations are not legally enforceable but the parties undertake to be bound by them. Where the parties in dispute are reluctant to agree beforehand to accept an arbitrator's award, they may agree to mediation instead. Mediators, appointed in the same way as arbitrators, produce recommendations rather than awards which may be accepted by the parties or which may provide the basis for a negotiated settlement. Mediation is often more of a fact-finding exercise which, writ large, may be undertaken by a Committee of Inquiry which ACAS is also empowered to set up to help resolve a dispute. This type of dispute resolution machinery is used far less frequently than arbitration, however, and is not usually resorted to in dismissal disputes.

This brief sketch of arbitration arrangements indicates clear points of difference from the industrial tribunal system. First, the personnel is different: the involvement of lawyers in the arbitral system is minimal, most notably they are not automatically the decision-makers. Second, there is no published record of decisions and so there can be no build up of 'case law' or reliance on precedent in decision-making; each dispute has to be decided on a case by case basis. Third, the procedure adopted is that of inquiry rather than the adversarial one which forms the basis of tribunal hearings. Finally, it appears to operate with greater speed and informality.

Arbitral Decision-Making

The differences discussed so far relate to personnel, form and procedure. We would seek to distinguish arbitration from the judicial decision-making of the industrial tribunal also in terms of its objectives and the nature of the process. Attempts at producing typologies of dispute settlement machinery are complicated by the fact that labels such as 'arbitration' often are attached to quite different processes in different national or other contexts (for a comparative exercise see Aaron, 1969) and because apparently distinguishable processes in any particular context blur at the edges. Some broad distinctions, however, can be drawn.

Schmidt (1969: 47) distinguished adjudication (the judicial method) from administration, under which he placed British voluntary arbitration. The latter, he argued, unlike adjudication 'does not make vested rights a matter of principal concern but aims at the adjustment of the relations of the parties with a view to the future'. Another way of expressing this distinction is that an arbitrator seeks to resolve the dispute, whereas a judge seeks to determine and apply the law. The different approaches to determining an issue which this distinction implies were seen to arise at times as between lay members and legal members of the industrial tribunals but in a context where, because the requirement is to produce a decision which is legally right (and will be held to be so on appeal) lay members had to subordinate their 'arbitral instincts' or feelings of what constituted industrial, common sense to their judicial duty (see above, p. 67).

We argued in the preceding chapter that while the industrial tribunal is concerned to discover who is legally right and focuses on the reasonableness of employer action in the circumstances of the individual dismissal, in voluntary arbitration the problem is seen as one of industrial relations, not law, and the search is for a workable and acceptable solution which takes account of the wider context. In his study of dismissal arbitrations arranged by ACAS between 1972 and 1977, Concannon (1980: 21) observed that

> as arbitrators are not constrained by any external criteria of relevance and as they necessarily have a sensitivity to industrial relations understanding to be on the arbitral panel, an arbitration case is relatively 'rich' in the breadth and depth of the contextual information available to it. It is, in that way, a method of adjudication without legal constraints, able to lift the veil of formality to see the reality of the power relations and collective bargaining dynamics.

The lack of 'external criteria' does not mean that the arbitrator may not be faced with a job of interpretation and application of rules, that is, be required to exercise a kind of judicial function. Such rules however are likely to be those provided by the parties themselves, for example in collective agreements or procedures.

The arbitral process appears more appropriate than the judicial process for certain kinds of dismissal disputes. Our discussion of tribunal decisions in trade union membership cases (p. 244), for example, indicates one area where 'industrial relations sensitivity' and an ability to take account of the wider context might produce decisions more in accord with the aim of preventing victimisation of trade unionists. In such cases the individual dismissal unmistakably raises questions of concern to the group – in this case trade union members. Hepple (1983b: 84) has suggested that as arbitration is better suited to considering the interests of groups, it might be more appropriate than judicial determination in dealing with other 'individual' disputes at present handled by industrial tribunals, such as those concerned with race and sex discrimination, which may overlap with the unfair dismissal jurisdiction. In such cases individual rights are given to members of groups who are collectively deprived.

A distinction between collective interests and individual rights often lies behind the allocation of certain disputes to arbitral or judicial bodies. It is a distinction, however, which in practice is not viable (see, for example, Wedderburn, 1969). The dismissal arbitrations studied by Concannon concerned individual dismissals treated as collective disputes and thus concerned the interests of groups of workpeople as well as the rights of individuals. They arose in organised workplaces and the 'union had exercised its organisation and power to remove the dismissal decision from being merely a matter of individual rights to one of collective interest'. In such a context the arbitrator, even when interpreting given rules and procedures, can be expected to bring to bear 'a sense of what is practical and politically necessary in the situation, bearing in mind the power realities of the parties' and the desirability of 'enabling the collective relation itself to be maintained' (1980: 16–18).

This discussion would suggest that for those one in three unfair dismissal claims which are brought by union members, an arbitration hearing might offer various advantages in terms of producing an acceptable solution in a quick, inexpensive and non-legalistic way. If an arbitration-based system were preferred generally to the industrial tribunal system, however, one would have to face the fact that most dismissal disputes currently handled by the industrial tribunals cannot be 'collectivised' as the applicants are not members of trade unions. In Britain, unlike in America, there is no duty on a recognised union to represent any non-members in the bargaining unit. Anyway, the lack of union membership among applicants reflects the non-union employment from which many applications arise (see Chapter 2). We need to consider therefore whether, as British legislators have assumed, arbitration is suitable only for disputes where trade unions are involved, where inequality in bargaining power is less stark than as between an individual employee and employer.

At present dismissal arbitrations take place in the absence of any external guidelines or criteria for decision-making. The parties themselves determine the terms of reference for the arbitrator. They are usually fairly broad, for example 'to determine whether the Company was justified in dismissing X . . . and to award accordingly' (Concannon, 1980: 18). It has been suggested (Hyman, 1977: 110) that as 'there exists no "neutral" body of industrial jurisprudence to guide the arbitrator . . . he can never deviate too far from his estimate of the likely outcome if the disputants had fought the matter out for themselves'. Although this power-reflecting view of arbitration is not universally accepted (for instance Guillebaud, 1970: 40), it does raise the question of how a system at present geared to dealing with collective disputes (in which even if the union does not 'own' the grievance, it plays the major part in processing it) would function if faced with individualised disputes.

The implication of the 'lion gets the lion's share' argument outlined above is that a weaker party (in a non-union dismissal case, the applicant) will lose. The argument, however, rests on there being no external guidelines which the arbitrator could use to give the weaker party more than it might otherwise obtain and this is not necessarily the case. Even in such interest arbitrations as those concerned with pay bargaining, where the only explicit reference point is the parties' own terms of reference, arbitrators may do more than arrange surrender terms (Dickens, 1979: 305). They may bring to bear considerations such as the going rate in industry generally or the trend in settlements elsewhere in addition to their own conception of equity and fairness. Unlike conciliation where, as we discussed in Chapter 6, the dispute is adjusted according to the parties' views and strengths, in arbitration the dispute is adjusted according to the outsider's views. But, more importantly, an arbitration-based system for resolving unfair dismissal cases arising from the existence of a statutory right would have a framework provided by the statute which enacts the right not to be unfairly dismissed, which could be supplemented by guidance from a code of practice.

It is useful to distinguish dispute resolution which takes place within the parties' terms of reference from that which occurs within a framework of rules which, in a sense, takes the place of the parties' terms of reference. Rideout (1982: 51) has suggested the terms 'equitable' and 'regulated' to distinguish these two kinds of arbitration. If the adjudication of unfair dismissal disputes were given to an arbitration-based system rather than the industrial tribunal system it would be a system of regulated arbitration. Although on a continuum of dispute settlement mechanisms, regulated arbitration is nearer judicial decision-making than is equitable arbitration, it retains the distinguishing features of arbitration.

The Basis of an Arbitral System

Regulated Arbitration

Single arbitration, described above, provides the basic model for an arbitral alternative to the industrial tribunal system but the work of the CAC, in connection with Schedule 11 of the Employment Protection Act 1975 and the Fair Wages Resolution (both now repealed), provides an example of how regulated arbitration can operate. In simplified terms, both Schedule 11 and the Fair Wages Resolution allowed claims to the CAC against employers offering less than 'fair' or agreed terms and conditions of employment. It is not possible or necessary to review here in any detail the CAC's operation of these provisions, it has been done elsewhere (Jones, 1980; Wood, 1978; Lockyer, 1979: ch. 8; CAC, 1977–82), but some features should be indicated, Reference to arbitration under these statutory provisions could be made unilaterally by a trade union, unlike voluntary arbitration where both parties to the dispute need to agree. If not settled by ACAS conciliation which was offered, the claims had to be determined in the light of criteria set out in the various enactments whihc had to be operationalised; for example 'the general level' of pay, 'trade or industry', 'comparable employment', 'a substantial proportion', 'the district' 'less favourable'. The awards were legally enforceable.

The arbitrator in regulated arbitration, like the judge, has to interpret a statute and has scope to exercise discretion. The interpretation of statutes, and the perception of facts, is influenced by social knowledge and experience. What distinguishes the exercise of discretion by the British arbitrator from that of the judge or legal chairperson of a tribunal is, to a large extent, a result of differences in these factors and the perceived objective of their activity. Rideout, himself a deputy chairperson of the CAC, noted (1982: 52) that since the CAC members 'were mostly composed of experienced arbitrators and practitioners of industrial relations it would be surprising if they did not primarily react as problem solvers rather than as appliers of rules'. The latitude allowed by the rules was used by the arbitrator to attempt to solve the problem underlying the claim. Rideout notes that this was not necessarily done consciously: 'non-lawyers with great experience of industrial relations would often adopt what to them was the obvious common sense application of a rule without noticing that lawyers would not hesitate to come to a different conclusion'. Whereas in the industrial tribunals the non-lawyers have to defer to lawyers where the answer they reach is not legally correct, Rideout suggests that in a case where the CAC happens to be chaired by a lawyer who knows there is a better legal answer than that reached by the non-lawyers, he or she would be wrong to impose the legally correct decision since the chairperson is primarily an arbitrator (ibid.: 57).

Unlike under voluntary arbitration, the decisions reached by the CAC under its statutory functions are published and there is an indication of the considerations which led to the particular award. There was a conscious attempt by the CAC, however, to avoid building up a system of binding precedent and so there was no attempt to offer a detailed 'judgment-like' explanation of every detail of the award. The Chairman of the CAC (Wood, 1979: 11) noted that: 'No decision making body wants to produce a succession of awards that lack pattern or coherence. Yet the use of precedents, as seen in the courts and to a lesser extent tribunals, imposes a stifling rigidity'. The CAC took the view (1978: 23) 'that its composition is clear indication that [the statute's] words are to be applied in a commonsense way with industrial and industrial relations practice in mind'. Thus, for example, the term 'district' was interpreted in different contexts as the travel to work district, the recruitment area and the area of inter-transfer of labour. Its geographical extent varied from 'Greater Manchester' in award 160 to 'Great Britain' in award 219 (Lockyer, 1979: 101).

Although the CAC interpreted the provisions in a flexible manner, taking into account the underlying problems of industrial relations involved in each case, it had to operate within the statutory framework. There is no appeal on law or fact from decisions of the CAC but the Committee is subject to the supervisory jurisdiction of the ordinary courts through the prerogative orders such as certiorari. In the case of *R v CAC ex parte Deltaflow* ([1977] IRLR 486), the Divisional Court acted to constrain the CAC in its interpretation of the rules by applying a stricter construction than that which the Committee had used as it did again in *R v CAC ex parte Hy-Mac* ([1979] IRLR 461). In other cases, however, the courts recognised the non-court nature of the CAC and endorsed the view that an arbitral body should be allowed 'common sense' interpretations of statute and that it was not for the court 'to say that one dictionary definition is preferable to another' (Wein J in *R v CAC ex parte TI Tube Division Services Ltd* [1978] IRLR 183). The relationship between the arbitration body and the courts is an important point to which we return later in this chapter.

Potential Problems Discussed

Among the advantages claimed for an arbitral system is that there is a finality in its decision-making and it is free from rigidities imposed by an appeal system. But some would see disadvantages in the lack of appeal provision in the handling of unfair dismissal disputes. A major perceived disadvantage is lack of uniformity. A past president of the EAT (Browne-Wilkinson, 1982: 72) has argued:

> although each case must, in the end, depend on its own facts, it is not right that the principles by which the 'fairness' of conduct is judged should differ according to the region in which the case is heard.

An aspect of the undesirability of this anticipated lack of uniformity, it is argued, is the engendering of uncertainty. It is argued that a uniform view needs to be imposed as 'individuals need to know their rights and duties before taking any particular step so that they can know the consequences of their actions'. With the kind of regulated arbitration which we have been discussing, however, a Code of Practice would provide guidance additional to that in the statute and thus there would be some degree of certainty in that individuals would know what factors the arbitrator would take into account and what the determinants of fairness would be. It is interesting to note that the past EAT President's argument for a body of precedent for tribunals to be provided by an appeal court rests to some extent on the absence at present of a sufficiently up to date and detailed Code of Practice (see for example *Grundy (Teddington) Ltd v Plummer and Salt* [1983] IRLR 98). It should be noted, however, that one reason why the current Code is regarded by some as out of date is that the standards of procedural fairness it suggests have been weakened rather than followed by the courts and tribunals (see above, p. 102). One way in which a Code of Practice might be kept up to date in the context of an arbitral system would be for ACAS to provide regular supplements, perhaps annually, drawing on arbitrators' reports to distill guidelines on good employer practice and fairness in discipline and dismissal.

Under voluntary arbitration the parties can exercise a degree of choice over the identity of the arbitrator. If a further degree of consistency were sought, therefore, the same arbitrator could be selected for all dismissal disputes arising in a particular company, or a small group of arbitrators could handle all cases arising in a particular industry. Any advantages this offers by way of consistency, however, would have to be set against possible disadvantages which might arise where an arbitrator's future use would depend upon his or her continued acceptability to the parties. This may be a reason for denying the parties choice in the selection of an arbitrator, particularly in disputes involving non-union employees.

The lack of uniformity in decisions which it is thought would arise from a system which operated without a body of precedent is sometimes seen as inimical to justice which demands that people be treated equally; that in similar circumstances similar outcomes are obtained (Munday, 1981: 151). But this requirement of universal consistency rests on a particular concept of justice. It is not the one which is applied in the system of voluntarily agreed dispute procedures which the unfair dismissal legislation sought to encourage. Here only local, internal consistency is sought. Any decision-making system which has some flexibility, some room for discretion – as indeed is intended for the industrial tribunals – contains within it the possibility of inconsistency. This apparent inconsistency is necessary, however, if justice is to be done in any particular case as between the parties in that case. Although the outcome of two apparently similar cases may differ, justice is served by individuals being dealt with equally in terms of the way in which those cases are heard, the rules which are operated and the way in which the decision is reached. That is to say, equality and consistency in arbitration are to be sought more in the treatment of cases than in their final outcomes.

Underlying this of course is the point we emphasised earlier which is that arbitration locates dispute settlement in its wider industrial relations context, a context which can be expected to vary as between individual cases. Interestingly, as the ordinary courts have wrestled with industrial relations disputes there has been some judicial acknowledgment of this last point. Lord Wilberforce, in reaching a different decision on union liability in *General Aviation Services (UK) Ltd v TGWU* ([1976] IRLR 224) to that reached in an earlier, similar case noted:

> industrial relations and industrial disputes are, as both this case and *Heatons* show, so complex, so opaque, that it may be the exception when the ultimate result reached with difficulty in one case, can be applied to another (quoted in Ewing, 1982c: 223).

The industrial tribunal system, under the weight of law built up by precedent, appears to have failed to strike the necessary balance for unfair dismissal disputes between certainty and flexibility (Browne-Wilkinson, 1982: 72). The Court of Appeal's attempt to curb the EAT in its operation of its appellate jurisdiction (above, p. 211) and even the new EAT President's encouragement to tribunals not to place too much emphasis on the guideline authority of case law, but to base their decisions on the language of statute (*Anandarajah v Lord Chancellor's Department* [1984] IRLR 131) will not be sufficient to overcome the range of problems grouped under the label 'legalism' which we indicated earlier. An arbitration-based system may provide a better approach.

At present the annual single arbitration case load of ACAS is fewer than two hundred (ACAS, 1984: 74) while the unfair dismissal case load of the tribunals runs to several thousands (above, p. 6). The question therefore arises whether there would be a sufficient supply of arbitrators to meet the unfair dismissal case load arising from the statutory right without jeopardising the expertise and speed which are attractive features of the single arbitrator system. ACAS normally does not advertise for arbitrators, who are usually recommended by existing arbitrators, but recently it did advertise for experts to be called upon in disputes over equal pay for equal value (Lowry, 1983: 29). Despite the specialised nature of the expertise required several hundred applications were received for the dozen or so places on the list. Advertising for arbitrators to hear dismissal cases would probably produce an even greater response. Those presently sitting in industrial tribunals may of course be suitable for the arbitrators' list. Freed from the constraints within which they have to operate at present, a number of the two thousand lay members, and possibly some of the legal members, might fulfil the requirements necessary for arbitration work: these are industrial relations experience, expertise and understanding coupled with perceived impartiality and acceptability.

Some problems which we discussed in relation to the industrial tribunal system, however, remain to be addressed in an arbitration-based system, notably the difficulties faced by unrepresented parties, particularly employees. As our examination of these difficulties in Chapter 4 indicated, unrepresented applicants to industrial tribunals are generally ignorant of provisions, such as the ability to request better details of the other side's case, which may help them prepare their cases, and feel themselves disadvantaged at hearings. The arbitration system as it operates at present places reliance on the written submissions which the parties provide to the arbitrator and to each other prior to the hearing. Those workers who cannot call upon a union for assistance might find the preparation of such a submission almost as difficult as preparing a case for an industrial tribunal. It ought to be possible, however, to build upon the inquisitorial approach of arbitration to overcome this potential difficulty. The inquisitorial approach, unlike the adversarial, places responsiblity for elucidating facts and information, requesting documents and calling witnesses on the adjudicator and not the parties to the disputes. Holding arbitration hearings at the place of employment should facilitate this fact-finding approach since information should be readily available.

An arbitration system where the hearing is based on the inquisitorial, rather than adversarial model; where non-lawyer decision-makers are not bound by case law precedent and where a flexible 'common sense' approach is taken in interpreting the legal framework is a system in which legal representation would appear far less useful or necessary than it does in the present industrial tribunal system. As a safeguard against 'creeping legalism' external legal representation could be banned but some legal representation might still occur, through use of in-house legal specialists. Even if legal representation were to be allowed, however, it is likely that, just as the court-like nature of the industrial tribunal system has encouraged legal representation, the quite different nature of an arbitral system would make such representation appear inappropriate.

The complexity of the law facing industrial tribunals owes much to the multiplicity of decisions handed down by the appellate courts which would be absent in an arbitral system which did not allow appeal on law or fact. But there would be, of course, interpretative difficulties with any statute, however clearly worded. We have seen above (p. 285) that the CAC in its statutory arbitration function had to grapple with a range of terms enacted in statute. It did so in a flexible, common sense manner with an awareness of the context in which the interpretation would be given effect and of the underlying purpose of the legislation. It did not follow the courts' judicial approach to statutory interpretation which confines itself to linguistic analysis of statute.

Where an arbitration system involves the courts it rapidly loses its advantages. This is demonstrated by the experience of the Workmen's (Compensation for Accidents) Act 1897. Disputes concerning liability for accidents or the amount of compensation could be referred to arbitration. But there was also reference to the county courts and this is where most claims were decided, to the detriment of the operation of the scheme as intended (Wilson and Levy, 1941: 258 Beveridge, 1942: 36).

The discussion has indicated that an arbitration system independent of the courts could avoid the shortcomings now associated with the industrial tribunal system, in particular the slide to legalism. A major factor, however, is whether the courts would restrain themselves from interfering with the decisions of arbitrators in ways which would undermine the advantages of an arbitral system. As we noted above (p. 286), while there is no right of appeal from decisions in regulated arbitration, the courts could and did intervene if decisions of the CAC were challenged on certain grounds. Operating within a statutory framework, a system of regulated arbitration for handling dismissal disputes inevitably would entail the possibility of legal restraint by the courts.

The courts would have to develop a willingness to recognise wider policy considerations or to practice a degree of self-abnegation to ensure an arbitral system did not 'degenerate'. The example of the courts' intervention concerning ACAS's operation of the recognition procedure contained in the Employment Protection Act 1975 unfortunately is not particularly encouraging. A small number of applications were made to the High Court for declarations that ACAS was in breach of its statutory duty in its handling of recognition cases. The resultant decisions gave 'the Act an interpretation which . . . made it more difficult for the Service to operate its procedures' (ACAS, 1979: 27), undermining the discretion which ACAS believed parliament had intended it to have. In his analysis of the judicial opinions in these cases, Simpson (1979: 78) detected two main types of approach by the courts which he labels 'individualist' and 'legalistic'. Neither involved a sympathetic judicial attitude to the functioning of ACAS in its attempt to promote the improvement of industrial relations.

The way in which statutory provisions are worded can make legal control more or less possible or likely. The case of *R v CAC ex parte Hy-Mac* ([1979] IRLR 461) provides an illustration of the Divisional Court intervening to restrict the CAC's interpretation of its duties under the Equal Pay Act, an interpretation guided by the spirit and intention of the legislation rather than its actual wording. The better the spirit and intention of legislation is encapsulated in its wording, of course, the more likely it can be pursued. The happier experience of ACAS's counterpart in Northern Ireland, the Labour Relations Agency, in operating a slightly different recognition procedure illustrates this

(IRRR, 1979: 11). But any statutory provisions will allow some scope for judicial amplification (Simpson, 1979: 83) and therefore this has to be seen as a possible limitation on an arbitral system's ability to operate in the long term without interference. This may mean that the degree to which it overcomes the shortcomings of the industrial tribunal system will be constrained.

The extent to which the courts seek to interfere with arbitrators' decisions depends not only on their own attitudes but also on the extent to which employers and workers are prepared to accept the arbitration decisions as fair and final rather than seek to have them put aside. The success of existing arbitration in settling dismissal disputes to some degree must depend on the fact that the parties do agree voluntarily to be bound by its outcomes. There is a propensity to accept the imposition of an outcome by a third party which may be expected to be lacking among some employers whose dismissal decisions may be challenged using statutory access to arbitration. In this connection, however, given the predominance of small employers in unfair dismissal cases, it is perhaps worth noting that it is not only large employers who at present turn to voluntary conciliation and arbitration for dismissal dispute settlement (Jones et al., 1983: 9; Concannon, 1980: 22).

The kind of arbitral system we have outlined should avoid the employee being in the relatively disadvantaged position at hearing, vis-à-vis the employer, which he or she occupies in the industrial tribunal system (see Chapter 4). This would affect any conciliation stage which might be built into an arbitration-based system.

Conciliation in Arbitral System

In Chapter 6 we argued that the form and outcome of individual conciliation in unfair dismissal disputes is influenced very much by the industrial tribunal system in which it is located. Conciliation as part of an arbitration-based system, therefore, could be expected to operate rather differently, reflecting the industrial relations problem-solving approach discussed above. It might be seen as time and cost saving for the arbitrator to perform also the function of conciliator, handing down a decision only if the parties failed to develop one themselves. This kind of approach, known in the United States as med./arb. an abbreviation of mediation/arbitration, is not much used in this country. ACAS maintains a strict distinction between conciliation and arbitration, the former being provided by its own staff, the latter by appointed outsiders. In practice, however, the line between conciliation and arbitration may blur. Arbitrators may attempt quasi-conciliation in the process of deciding an issue, particularly where there is an emphasis on involving the parties in the construction of the outcome of the dispute

(Wood, 1979: 11). Various problems with a dual role arbitrator may be identified, however, for instance confidence in the adjudicator's impartiality may be jeopardised by involvement in a conciliation process. Further, the parties may be reluctant to confide certain information, or to show a preparedness to compromise, to a conciliator who may shortly become an arbitrator in the dispute. For such reasons it seems likely that if conciliation were thought desirable it would need to be provided as a separate stage. Time saving could be effected by adopting the practice of the arbitrator undertaking preliminary fact-finding, if necessary, in the presence of an ACAS conciliator, something the CAC has done successfully (CAC, 1983: 20). If during the fact-finding a conciliated outcome appeared possible the ACAS conciliator could try to facilitate it.

Our examination of the conciliation stage in the industrial tribunal system showed how, in performing their conciliation role, ACAS officers inevitably marshal and channel pressures in the industrial tribunal system which tend to encourage settlement or abandonment of the claim. Such pressures include the time and expense of going to a tribunal hearing and, for the applicant, the odds against winning the case at hearing. Inasmuch as an arbitration-based system would be cheaper, speedier, and less formal than the industrial tribunal system at least some of these pressures would not exist. In the context of an arbitral system, a more 'reconciliating' form of conciliation rather than one concerned to arrange the terms of severance might be expected. This indicates that the outcomes of an arbitral system probably would differ from those produced by the industrial tribunal system.

Outcomes of Arbitration

There is no doubt that the TUC, and others, who have suggested replacing the industrial tribunal system by an arbitral one do so in part because they think it would increase workers' chances of winning claims and retaining employment. Certainly the experience of voluntary arbitration in dismissal disputes encourages such a view. In Concannon's study of 24 dismissal dispute arbitrations in 1977 (1980: 18), 16 dismissals were found to be unjustified and in 14 cases re-employment was awarded. This two-thirds success rate for workers and the high level of re-employment contrasts markedly with outcomes of industrial tribunals where under a third of the claims heard succeed and re-employment is extremely rare (see Chapter 5). Voluntary arbitration references do not normally allow for compensation as a remedy. This, and the greater likelihood of re-employment being sought and obtained in larger, unionised employment, which we noted earlier (p. 116), obviously is part of the explanation for this difference in remedies. But the type of remedies obtained in arbitration is also in part a reflection of the nature and aims of this form of adjudication.

It is often thought that arbitration is a process of 'splitting the difference', handing down compromise awards (for some discussion of this see Sullivan, 1980: 197). This is an over-simplistic view but it does touch upon the problem-solving emphasis of arbitration, mentioned above. A 'compromise' award is likely to be one which, at least, allows both parties to feel that they did not lose their case completely and which, therefore, may be more acceptable and workable as a solution to the dispute.

On the face of it a dispute over dismissal requires an award which supports one side or the other: is the dismissal justified or not? We have shown, however, that the industrial tribunals themselves produce decisions which are more complex than this, for example finding the dismissal unfair but then reducing the compensation award because of contribution to dismissal by the applicant (above, p. 132). We have suggested (p. 134) that, if the tribunals were to make greater use of the re-employment award, a greater range of flexibility in outcomes could be achieved. This greater flexibility in outcomes is a feature of the voluntary arbitration of dismissal disputes. Generally where re-employment is awarded by the arbitrator it is 'on terms'. These may, for example, involve a disciplinary suspension or downgrading, a loss of pay or other benefits, or the recording of a warning on the worker's record (Concannon, 1980: 18; above, p. 229). Reinstatement may be conditional upon some undertaking by the employee, or proof of fitness, or be on probation (Elkouri and Elkouri, 1973: 648–50).

The arbitrator, as an industrial relations expert and problem-solver, may also make suggestions about, for example, the need for training, or procedural changes aimed at improving the industrial relations situation which produced the dismissal dispute. Thus, while the industrial tribunal system focuses on the problem of the individual dismissal, the arbitrator may see the problem as bad working practices or procedural disorder or whatever, of which the individual dismissal dispute is a symptom. In this way, even in non-unionised companies, an individual dismissal can raise questions of concern to the employer and employees more generally. Arbitration, rather than judicial determination, is better able to deal with them.

In Chapter 5 a two-pronged explanation was forwarded for the low applicant success rate at industrial tribunals: applicants' relative disadvantage and the nature of the legal tests. We suggested above that an arbitral system could overcome some of the problems at present experienced in case preparation and presentation by industrial tribunal applicants. The question which now needs to be considered is whether decisions reached in an arbitral system would be less supportive of managerial prerogative than those of the industrial tribunal system have been. That is to say, is the inference to be drawn from the outcomes of voluntary arbitration that an arbitral system for dismissal disputes would go further than the tribunal system in curbing managements' right to dismiss, or, rather, that the context in which voluntary dismissal arbitration occurs at present is one in which outcomes favourable to the applicant are more likely?

Obviously the legal framework within which an arbitral system might operate would be a crucial factor. It is possible that a framework for a system of regulated arbitration could underpin what employers regard as their prerogatives in this area, and by providing extremely limited scope for discretion by the arbitrator, simply provide a cheaper, speedier, and less formal mechanism for legitimising managerial authority and sanctioning most dismissal decisions. The legal framework in statute and code which was given to the industrial tribunal system, however, is not of this kind and does provide the necessary scope for discretion. To address this question, therefore, we need to consider, if the framework provided by statute and Code of Practice (but not case law) were the same, whether an arbitral system would operate more effectively than a court-based one in terms of curbing the exercise of employer authority in the area of discipline and dismissal in the interests of employee job security.

In Chapter 4 we observed that the courts' apparent willingness to protect the individual employee in holding on to his or her job only in so far as it does not undermine the employer's interest in running the business to make a profit, mirrored the ideological perspective of the statute. In Chapter 8 we raised doubts concerning the priority which the objective of job security was afforded in the range of legislative intentions and noted that the original Code of Practice had made it clear that job security was to be pursued only in so far as it was consistent with the operational efficiency and success of the undertaking. But, while the courts may mirror the ideological perspective of the statute, we have shown in earlier chapters that the mirror is a magnifying one. The courts have not gone as far in curbing managerial prerogative in this area as the statute could allow.

The legal framework, both of necessity and by design, left scope for discretion in working out the concept of fairness. The way in which the courts used the discretion left to them in interpreting and applying the law — for instance in developing the 'range of reasonable responses' test, discussed in Chapter 4, and in dealing with re-employment, discussed in Chapter 5 — is an important explanation for the fact that the law of unfair dismissal has been

> sterilised to such an extent that it is reasonable to conclude that, far from controlling managerial discretion and therefore protecting the interest of employees in job security, the law generally endorses and legitimates a strong conception of managerial authority (Collins, 1982: 177).

It is because arbitration differs from the industrial tribunal system in its procedure, in the flexibility and objective of its decision-making and in its personnel, that it is reasonable to suppose that the exercise of discretion would differ also.

The areas of difference we identified are interrelated. For instance those trained in the law, such as tribunal chairpersons, are likely to see certain types of procedures, for example the examination/cross examination technique, as the best way of arriving at the 'truth'; those unused to such techniques are unlikely to adopt them. The objective of arbitration compared to that of judicial adjudication also reflects and reinforces differences in personnel. The 'wider-view' compromise-seeking, problem-solving approach of the arbitrator, described earlier, is not generally that of the trained lawyer. The trained lawyer will be influenced in his or her approach by the traditional ideologies of the common law which emphasise the individual rights basis of conflict. As Kahn-Freund observed 'the common law knows nothing of a balance of collective forces. It is . . . inspired by the belief in the equality (real or fictitious) of individuals' (1977: 1). The lawyer will also be trained to approach a dispute by looking for some authority which decides the problem in hand. 'In many lawyers the constant search for guidance in the past leads to the view that whatever is, is right, or at least is normally right. The lawyers' outlook is profoundly conservative. He becomes the defender of the status quo. To him justice lies in the application of the law' (Pain, 1981: 138). There is obviously a problem in expecting a conservative judiciary, steeped in common law, to operate radical legislation such as that, like the unfair dismissal provisions, which seeks to curb managerial prerogatives (see, also, Hepple, 1983a: 415; Lustgarten, 1980: 226).

We have discussed the ideology of the judiciary so far in terms of their professional training; others would place stress on their social background (Griffith, 1977; Wedderburn, 1971: 25–6). Boothman and Denham (1981: 13) argue that decisions in union membership dismissal cases consistently favour managerial ideology because 'when faced with the most controversial cases of the employment relationship . . . judges are frequently extended not only to the limits of the law but also to the limits of their own social perceptions'. The different social knowledge and experience of arbitration when compared with judges, which we mentioned earlier, can be expected to feed through into decision-making. But, we would argue, it is the *interplay* of the various differences discussed, the different way in which the decision-making process is structured and approached in arbitration which suggests that, given similar legislative scope for discretion, an arbitral system would have been less likely to develop a concept of fairness as supportive of managerial authority as that developed by the industrial tribunal system. The right not to be unfairly dismissed constituted a challenge to employer prerogative. Arbitrators would have displayed greater willingness to impose their own 'intuitive' view of what is fair and to question managerial rules, assessing their necessity and appropriateness in the circumstances rather than concentrating, as do the industrial tribunals, on whether they have been conformed with.

Ultimately, however, as we noted at the start of this section, the legal framework will act as a constraint. If it were intended, therefore, to achieve a marked shift in favour of employees in the balance between employee protection and employer freedom of action, substantive legislative changes would be required. These might include a move away from considering whether the employer acted reasonably at the time of dismissal, as judged by employer standards, towards considering whether the employee has suffered any injustice, as viewed at the time of the hearing.

Time for Change?

We have discussed whether an arbitral system *would have* operationalised the unfair dismissal provisions in the same way as the industrial tribunal system and decided it probably would have avoided legalism and gone further in challenging managerial prerogative. There may be a difference, however, between what an arbitration-based system might have achieved had it been given the unfair dismissal jurisdiction in 1972, the time the tribunals began operating it, and what such a system might be able to achieve were it decided to transfer the unfair dismissal jurisdiction to it *now*. It is, we suggest, perhaps unlikely that arbitrators, or the parties to disputes, would be able now to distance themselves totally from the norms and values concerning fairness in dismissal which the industrial tribunal system has fostered. It is also likely that such safeguards against legalism as no right of appeal and discouraging legal representation at hearing would be argued to be a denial of justice, a deterioration from the industrial tribunal system, particularly by those in the legal profession (for example, Best, 1978: 19).

If it were thought desirable to change gradually from the industrial tribunal system to an arbitral system for unfair dismissal disputes then a start could be made by giving unionised workers the option of unilateral binding arbitration rather than application to an industrial tribunal. The industrial tribunal system would remain for non-union applicants but more could be done to recognise and meet the needs of such people, for example by making skilled lay and legal advice and representation or 'rights enforcement' help more easily available (see above, p. 49 and p. 191).

An arbitral system is more likely than the industrial tribunal system to appear attractive to those organised workers who are able to pursue collective action to seek redress for their grievances and, as we discussed in Chapter 8, have continued to do so despite the existence of the industrial tribunal system. Unionised workers, rather than trade unions, should be given the right of application because if the system is to be widened to non-union workers it would be incongruous to allow unions rather than their members to 'own' the grievances. While this may cause some problems for unions, these problems already exist with an application to the industrial tribunals and part of the wider context which the arbitrator may be expected to take into account would be in the fact that the individual failed to gain the support of the union in challenging the employer's dismissal decision.

Extending arbitration into non-union areas would obviously be something of a leap in the dark and it is possible that for non-union employees in small firms, who are the majority of those seeking to challenge their dismissal through law at present, the gains from an arbitral system ultimately might be more procedural than substantive, although, as we have argued, the two are linked. None the less, for the reasons we have outlined, it appears reasonable to suppose that a generally applicable arbitral system, operating within a framework of law which allowed the kind of discretion which the tribunal system has had in determining the fairness of a dismissal, would produce outcomes better than are being obtained from the industrial tribunal system for at least some of those who challenge employer dismissal decisions.

Any radical restructuring of the system for resolving dismissal disputes, such as that being discussed here, however, obviously would provide an opportunity for changes in the statutory framework to be made which might aid the achievement of the various objectives identified earlier concerned with the efficiency of the system and its outcomes. Thus, for example, employers could be required, when giving notice of dismissal, to inform workers in writing of their right to have the dispute arbitrated and how to request this. Such a requirement could be balanced by a reduction in the time allowed to workers to appeal against their dismissal. For example a worker could be required to indicate within two weeks of notice whether the dismissal decision was to be challenged. This kind of change would increase the accessibility of the system, by countering ignorance, and its speed. It would mean also that employers would face a much reduced period of uncertainty over whether their decision was likely to be subject to challenge by a dismissed worker and also alleviate the problem of trying to reconstruct distant events in order to prepare a defence to an unfair dismissal claim.

Such a requirement would mean that conciliation, and possibly arbitration of the case, would be more likely to occur during the notice period, a development which we argued earlier would tend to place more emphasis, where dismissal is unjustified, on whether the employment relationship should continue and on what terms rather than determining the price of dismissal as now. This changed emphasis, we suggest, would be more likely to produce the continued employment of workers whose dismissal is not justified, something which the legislation has sought but so far has been unable to effect through the industrial tribunal system (Chapter 5). Rather than leaving it to chance whether or not the dispute is adjudicated before the expiration of notice, the legislation could be changed so that, where a challenge to a dismissal decision is made, the employment contract continues in existence until the matter is resolved (Dickens et al., 1981: 174–5). This would give the employee a continuing right to wages despite any employer reluctance actually to provide work. A change of this kind appears less onerous on the employer when viewed in the context of a system of adjudication which disposes of cases within three weeks rather than taking about ten to reach the first instance decision.

But, in discussing these possible changes, it is important not to lose sight of the limitations of the law. Whether the unfair dismissal law is operated by an arbitral or judicial system, we are concerned with the *extent* to which the employers' right to discipline labour by dismissal is restrained. The legislation on unfair dismissal was described earlier (p. 295) as radical in that it seeks to curb the exercise of employer power. However 'radical' legislation may be in this respect, it is concerned only to *regulate* the power of the employer; it does not seek fundamentally to alter it (Kahn-Freund, 1977: 6; Picciotto, 1979: 171–7).

Summary

A senior judge has expressed the view that 'there is nothing an arbitrator can do that a specialised labour court cannot do better' (Donaldson,

1975: 68). In this chapter we have presented the contrary view, arguing that an arbitral system could have provided a way of overcoming some of the perceived failings of the industrial tribunal system.

The distinguishing features and possible advantages of an arbitral system were examined by exploring the British experience of single arbitration, used voluntarily by the parties to settle dismissal disputes, and the work of the CAC in 'regulated arbitration' that is, unilateral binding arbitration within a framework of law. Differences between arbitration and industrial tribunal decision-making in terms of procedure, objectives, personnel and outcomes were explored. We argued that the inquisitorial, rather than adversarial, basis of arbitration; the problem-solving approach, which locates the dismissal dispute in its wider context rather than seeking to discover who is 'right'; and the use as key decision-makers of those knowledgeable and experienced in industrial relations rather than those qualified in law, all combined to make an arbitral system preferable for dealing with unfair dismissal disputes. This was thought to be particularly the case where the interests of groups, in addition to the rights of individuals, clearly were involved.

Our examination of the differences in the two types of system suggested that with the same legislation an arbitral system was likely to have produced outcomes more favourable to applicants. That is to say, we argued that an aribitral system would have gone further than has the judicial one in curbing the exercise of managerial prerogative in the interests of individual job retention as well as avoiding the tendency to legalism.

For this reason, and because attention could be paid to the collective dimensions of individual disputes, an arbitral system would probably be more attractive than the industrial tribunals have been as an option for those capable of challenging managerial decisions through collective action. In this way an arbitral system might provide a more effective way of achieving some of the intentions of the unfair dismissal legislation. We raised some caveats, however, concerning possible change to an arbitral system noting that what an arbitration-based system might have achieved had it been given the unfair dismissal jurisdiction in 1972 may not necessarily be obtainable as easily now.

In considering the likelihood of change, it should be recalled also that, as we noted earlier, the unfair dismissal legislation was introduced in the context of a particular set of circumstances prevailing in the late 1960s. A particular complex of problems was identified which concerned a loss of managerial control; lack of 'order' on the shop floor and workers' insistence through collective action on what they saw as their rights, including that of job security. It was thought these problems could be addressed by, among other things, granting certain statutory rights and providing peaceful channels for dispute resolution. Some legal restriction on employer freedom of action was seen as necessary and desirable in order to achieve ends generally subsumed under the label of 'good industrial relations'. In the changed circumstances of the 1980s, policy makers may see less need to act in this area to provide a mechanism potentially capable of fulfilling the intentions of the original legislation.[4]

4. Indicative of this is the present government's decision not to ratify ILO Convention 158 or accept Recommendation 166, which set new standards concerning Termination of Employment at the Initiative of the Employer, because of the 'unacceptable' extra burden they would place on employers (DE, *International Labour Conference*, Cmnd 9078 (London: HMSO, November 1983),4).

Appendix I

Survey Details

Interviews with Applicants and Respondents

This part of the research was undertaken with the assistance of Social and Community Planning Research.

Sample Design and Selection

The sample was designed with the aim of achieving a thousand interviews with applicants and a thousand with respondents, with as many as possible of these being matched pairs — that is the applicant and respondent in the same tribunal case. The sample of cases was drawn from the publicly available register of applications held at the Central Office of the Industrial Tribunals in London and Glasgow. In the interests of efficiency, an element of clustering was introduced into the design, in preference to selecting a national random sample of all unfair dismissal cases. It was then necessary to group cases into practicable workloads for individual interviewers. The first stage was the decision to limit selection to cases dealt with by four tribunal regional offices:

> Scotland (Glasgow office)
>
> Leeds
>
> East Anglia and
>
> London South

Scotland was chosen because some of the tribunal procedures differ from those operating in England; Leeds and London South were included to obtain both northern and southern representation of large metropolitan areas. However, both these regions cover a considerable area and, therefore, variety of area types: for example London South cases extend down to the Kent coast as well as stretching into Essex and Hertfordshire. East Anglia was included as a more rural area in which agricultural workers' cases might be represented.

At the initial sample selection stage it was decided to aim for an equal, rather than a proportional representation of each region. The number of cases initially selected had to be very much larger than the number of case interviews it was hoped to achieve (250 per region) to allow for:

1. Discarding cases under jurisdictions other than unfair dismissal;
2. Discarding cases in which the address of one, or both, sides were 'inaccessible' in terms of interviewer workloads e.g. the only case from a particular town or village);
3. Discarding cases in which the address of either applicant or respondent was outside *any* of the regions in which we were interviewing (e.g. a case handled by the head office of an organisation located in a different region from the establishment where the applicant worked. Many of these cases did not have to be discarded since head office was within the same region or in London, where we were interviewing anyway);
4. Discarding selections in which more than one case occurred in the sample for the same employer address, in order to avoid interviewing the same organisation about more than one case;
5. Non-response at the interview stage.

The initial selection was carried out from the registers of applications dated 1 October 1976 to 30 September 1977. Although fieldwork was scheduled to start early in 1978, later cases could not safely be included because our sample could only cover completed cases (cases are registered by the date that the application is made, not by date of completion). We had undertaken not to approach any parties in cases not finally determined.

The central register for England and Wales lists all applications in date order, and it is only subsequently that they are allocated for hearing at a regional centre. A count was made of all cases allocated to the chosen regions and a sampling interval worked out to yield around 450 cases per region. The intervals were:

> every 5th case from London South
>
> every 5th case from Leeds
>
> every 7th case from East Anglia.

(This interval did not produce the required number for East Anglia so a small subsidiary sample was selected by the same method.)

The public register in England and Wales provided inadequate details of many respondent employers and, at the time of the research, did not identify cases by jurisdiction. As we could not have access to case files to overcome this problem, Department of Employment staff kindly supplied the missing information. A similar procedure was followed for Scotland but not so many stages were required since the central public register there included the jurisdiction and respondent information. Cases heard in Aberdeen or with addresses in Dundee, Inverness and north of there were excluded. The case information was then sent to Social and Community Planning Research (SCPR) for the remaining phases of grouping into interviewer workloads, and discarding non-accessible and multiple case selections. With the latter, the case retained was that with the most recent date of application.

A total of 1,339 cases were issued to interviewers, 75 per cent of the total received by SCPR. The number of cases received for each region varied considerably and it was not possible completely to restore the balance at the discarding stage, because of the difficulty of organising economical workloads for interviewers.

	Cases received	Cases issued		
	No.	No.	% of Received	(% of Total)
Scotland	565	397	70	(30)
Leeds	446	342	77	(25)
East Anglia	404	305	75	(23)
London South	367	295	80	(22)
	1782	1339	75	100

Questionnaire Design
A postal questionnaire survey of applicants and respondents in one tribunal region (Dickens, 1978–9) provided a basis for the design of questionnaires for the interview survey. Four different questionnaires were designed, with assistance from SCPR, for sub-groups within the sample:

1. Applicants in cases that went through to a decision by the tribunal – i.e. 'heard' cases.

2. Applicants in cases that were withdrawn or settled prior to a tribunal hearing, i.e. 'withdrawn cases.

matched to either

3. Respondents (employers) in 'heard' cases.
4. Respondents in 'withdrawn' cases.

Many questions were identical in all four questionnaires so that exactly comparable results could be obtained for both applicants and respondents. Other questions, of necessity, were different for these two groups. Similarly with heard and withdrawn cases, questioning was identical in following the development of the case from the time of application through to the outcome of, or attempts at, conciliation. Heard cases interviews then continued with detailed questioning about the hearing itself while the withdrawn cases interview dealt with reasons for withdrawal and the kind of settlement, if any, that was reached.

In the majority of cases, therefore, questionnaires 1 and 3 or 2 and 4 were linked (at the data processing stage) to form a single record for an individual case. The questionnaires were piloted in the field prior to the main fieldwork. A small sample of cases was selected with addresses in the Croydon area. Two very experienced SCPR interviewers carried out a total of nineteen interviews, nine with applicants and ten with respondents (employers), between 30 November and 11 December 1977. The questionnaire was shortened and other revisions made as a result of the pilot experience.

Interviewing

The bulk of the interviewing was carried out from 25 January 1978 to mid-April, with final interviews completed by 10 May. Members of the research team took part in the briefings held for the interviewers in the selected area. In the case of applicants, interviewers called at the given address personally and either took the interview then or arranged a suitable appointment. At least four attempts at contact were made before an address was abandoned as unproductive.

The approach to respondents (employers) was initially by letter, mailed four to five days prior to the interviewer's intention to make the first personal contact. This gave time for the letter to be channelled to the correct individual or department since the registers gave named individuals in only a small proportion of cases. The interviewer then telephoned or called personally at the address to arrange an appointment for the interview.

Response

Interviews were achieved with 979 applicants and 1,013 respondents, 73 per cent and 76 per cent respectively of all issued addresses. However, many of the unproductive addresses were 'out of scope', that is, no interview was possible because the premises were empty or because firms or individuals had moved and could not be followed up etc. The response from 'in scope' addresses was high though there was considerable variation between regions with London South losing most through both out of scope addresses and non-response. SCPR informed us that this is a pattern common to most surveys over the past few years.

	Out of Scope	Achieved		
	% of Total Issued	*No.*	*% of in Scope*	*(% of Total)*
APPLICANTS				
Scotland	10	330	93	(34)
Leeds	14	243	83	(25)
East Anglia	13	236	89	(24)
London South	27	170	79	(17)
Total	16	979[a]	87	(100)
RESPONDENTS				
Scotland	12	313	89	(31)
Leeds	9	255	83	(25)
East Anglia	10	240	87	(24)
London South	9	206	77	(20)
Total	10	1013[a]	84	(100)

NOTE

a. Unweighted analysis bases for applicants and respondents were 971 and 999 respectively. The discrepancy is due to some questionnaires being rejected at the data processing stage (e.g. interview incomplete; wrong jurisdiction; case waiting appeal, etc.) and minor clerical errors in booking-in questionnaires as they were returned from the field.

The figures above show response separately for applicants and respondents. Of the achieved interviews 61 per cent were matched, that is, both the applicant and the respondent in the same case were interviewed.

Interviewed	No.	%
Applicant and respondent	745	61
Applicant only	226	18
Respondent only	254	21
Total cases (unweighted)	1225	100

The remainder were cases in which an interview with only one side was achieved. In the table on p. 307, the survey figures are compared to Department of Employment figures for *all* unfair dismissal cases registered (and completed) from October 1976 to December 1977. The two sets of figures are fairly similar although the time periods covered are not identical: survey cases were drawn from October 1976 to September 1977 registrations.

Data Processing
We played a major role in developing coding frames for the open-ended questions, the editing and coding being undertaken by SCPR staff. The code lists for the open-ended questions were prepared using listings of all verbatim responses to 100 questionnaires (50 applicants and 50 respondents).

In the selected sample a number of instances were found where the same employer was the respondent in more than one case. As only one case could be included for interview, weighting was needed to restore the correct representation of multi-case organisations. The weight applied was simply the number of cases drawn in the initial sample for one establishment, up to a maximum weight of five. There were very few instances of more than five cases down to one establishment and the most common weight applied was two.

Weight applied	1	2	3	4	5	Total
No. of cases	1145	56	17	1	6	1225
Weighted sample	1145	112	51	4	30	1342

In accordance with our specification SCPR provided tabulations (covering some 1,400 pages) which we analysed.

| | Survey Results from: | | Department of Employment analysis, all cases:[1] | | |
Outcome	Applicants	Respondents	Total	Oct.–Dec. 76	1977
	%	%	%	%	%
HEARD CASES					
Applicant won	14	12	12	14	11
Applicant lost	27	29	26	27	25
Total	40	41	37	42	36
WITHDRAWN CASES					
With a settlement	42	42	41	41	41
Without a settlement	18	17	21	18	22
Don't know[a]			1		
Total[b]	60	59	63	61[c]	64
(base for percentages)	(1,063)	(1,080)	(44,046)	(8,657)	(35,389)

SOURCES: (1) *Employment Gazette* (October 1977 and May 1978).

NOTES:
a. These were cases not conciliated by ACAS which we could not allocate between 'settlement' and 'no settlement'.
b. Percentages do not always add exactly to totals due to rounding up or down of decimal points.
c. The 1976 figures include a small amount of duplication because a minority of cases were awarded more than one remedy and the duplication could not be taken out for the summary.

Postal Surveys of Tribunal Members

Separate questionnaires were designed for those who chair tribunals, full-time and part-time, and for lay members nominated by the TUC and by employers' organisations.

Chairpersons.

At the time of the survey in 1978 there were 77 full-time chairpersons, excluding the two Presidents, in Scotland, England and Wales. Thirty-eight (a one in two sample) of these were selected from lists provided by the Central Offices of Industrial Tribunals to receive a postal quest-ionnaire, ensuring a reasonable spread across regions.

A one in three sample was selected from the 145 part-time chair-persons. Four of the selected sample resigned making a total sample of 44. The questionnaires were sent out via the regional offices to which the chairpersons were attached, with a covering letter from the Presi-dent of Industrial Tribunals explaining the non-official nature of our research and emphasising that co-operation was completely voluntary.

A 50 per cent response was obtained from full-time chairpersons and a 43 per cent response from part-timers which are acceptable response rates for a postal questionnaire survey.

Lay Members

A 15 per cent sample was selected from the 1,139 trade-union-nominated lay members and a similar sample from the 1,310 employer-nominated lay members listed by the Department of Employment for us. There is an imbalance between men and women among lay members and to ensure representation of women among our final sample we selected the 15 per cent samples separately for men and women within each of the panels. The final trade union sample was 171, the employer sample 196. The questionnaires and, in some cases, reminder letters, were sent to the lay members via the regional tribunal offices to which they were attached. Completed questionnaires were received from 60 per cent of the trade-union-nominated lay members and 55 per cent of the employer-nominated lay members.

Appendix II

Extracts from Employment Protection (Consolidation) Act 1978 as Amended

This appendix reproduces some of the major sections concerning unfair dismissal from the EP(C)A 1978, as amended by the Employment Acts 1980 and 1982.

Right of employee not to be unfairly dismissed

54.–(1) In every employment to which this section applies every employee shall have the right not to be unfairly dismissed by his employer.

(2) This section applies to every employment except in so far as its application is excluded by or under any provision of this Part or by section 141 to 149.

Meaning of 'dismissal'

55.–(1) In this Part, except as respects a case to which section 56 applies, 'dismissal', and 'dismiss' shall be construed in accordance with the following provisions of this section.

(2) Subject to subsection (3), an employee shall be treated as dismissed by his employer if, but only if,–

- (*a*) the contract under which he is employed by the employer is terminated by the employer, whether it is so terminated by notice or without notice, or
- (*b*) where under that contract he is employed for a fixed term, that term expires without being renewed under the same contract, or
- (*c*) the employee terminates that contract, with or without notice, in circumstances such that he is entitled to terminate it without notice by reason of the employer's conduct.

*   *   *

General provisions relating to fairness of dismissal

57.–(1) In determining for the purposes of this Part whether the dismissal of an employee was fair or unfair, it shall be for the employer to show–

(*a*) what was the reason (or, if there was more than one, the principal reason) for the dismissal, and

(*b*) that it was a reason falling within subsection (2) or some other substantial reason of a kind such as to justify the dismissal of an employee holding the position which that employee held.

(2) In subsection (1)(*b*) the reference to a reason falling within this subsection is a reference to a reason which–

(*a*) related to the capability or qualifications of the employee for performing work of the kind which he was employed by the employer to do, or

(*b*) related to the conduct of the employee, or

(*c*) was that the employee was redundant, or

(*d*) was that the employee could not continue to work in the position which he held without contravention (either on his part or on that of his employer) of a duty or restriction imposed by or under an enactment.

(3) Where the employer has fulfilled the requirements of subsection (1), then, subject to sections 58 to 62, the determination of the question whether the dismissal was fair or unfair, having regard to the reason shown by the employer, shall depend on whether in the circumstances (including the size and administrative resources of the employer's undertaking) the employer acted reasonably or unreasonably in treating it as a sufficient reason for dismissing the employee; and that question shall be determined in accordance with equity and the substantial merits of the case.

(4) In this section, in relation to an employee,–

(*a*) 'capability' means capability assessed by reference to skill, aptitude, health or any other physical or mental quality;

(*b*) 'qualifications' means any degree, diploma or other academic, technical or professional qualification relevant to the position which the employee held.

Dismissal relating to trade union membership

58.–(1) Subject to subsection (3), the dismissal of an employee by an employer shall be regarded for the purposes of this Part as having been unfair if the reason for it (or, if more than one, the principal reason) was that the employee–

(*a*) was, or proposed to become, a member of an independent trade union, or (*b*) had taken part, or proposed to take part, in the activities of an independent trade union at an appropriate time, or

(*c*) was not a member of any trade union or of a particular trade union, or of one of a number of particular trade unions, or had refused or proposed to refuse to become or remain a member.

(2) In subsection (1) 'an appropriate time', in relation to an employee taking part in the activities of a trade union, means a time which either—

(*a*) is outside his working hours, or

(*b*) is a time within his working hours at which, in accordance with arrangements agreed with or consent given by his employer, it is permissible for him to take part in those activities;

and in this subsection 'working hours', in relation to employee, means any time when, in accordance with his contract of employment, he is required to be at work.

(3) Subject to the following provisions of this section, the dismissal of an employee by an employer shall be regarded for the purposes of this Part as having been fair if—

(*a*) it is the practice, in accordance with a union membership agreement, for employees of the employer who are of the same class as the dismissed employee to belong to a specified independent trade union, or to one of a number of specified independent trade unions; and

(*b*) the reason (or, if more than one, the principal reason) for the dismissal was that the employee was not, or had refused or proposed to refuse to become or remain, a member of a union in accordance with the agreement; and

(*c*) the union membership agreement had been approved in relation to employees of that class in accordance with section 58A through a ballot held within the period of five years ending with the time of dismissal.

(4) Subsection (3) shall not apply if the employee genuinely objects on grounds of conscience or other deeply-held personal conviction to being a member of any trade union whatsoever or of a particular trade union.

(5) Subsection (3) shall not apply if the employee—

(*a*) has been among those employees of the employer who belong to the class to which the union membership agreement relates since before the agreement had the effect of requiring them to be or become members of a trade union, and

(*b*) has not at any time while the agreement had that effect been a member of a trade union in accordance with the agreement.

(6) Subsection (3) shall not apply if—

   (*a*) the union membership agreement took effect after 14th August 1980 in relation to the employees of the employer who are of the same class as the dismissed employee, and

   (*b*) the employee was entitled to vote in the ballot through which the agreement was approved in accordance with section 58A or, if there have been two or more such ballots, in the first of them, and

   (*c*) the employee has not at any time since the day on which that ballot was held been a member of a trade union in accordance with the agreement.

(7) Subsection (3) shall not apply if the dismissal was from employment in respect of which, at the time of dismissal, either—

   (*a*) there was in force a declaration made on a complaint presented by the employee under section 4 of the Employment Act 1980 (unreasonable exclusion or expulsion from trade union), or

   (*b*) proceedings on such a complaint were pending before an industrial tribunal,

unless the employee has at any time during the period beginning with the date of the complaint under section 4 and ending with the effective date of termination been, or failed through his own fault to become, a member of a trade union in accordance with the union membership agreement.

(8) In any case where neither subsection (4) nor subsection (7) has the effect of displacing subsection (3) and the employee—

   (*a*) holds qualifications which are relevant to the employment in question,

   (*b*) is subject to a written code which governs the conduct of those persons who hold those qualifications, and

   (*c*) has—

      (i) been expelled from a trade union for refusing to take part in a strike or other industrial action, or

      (ii) refused to become or remain a member of a trade union,

subsection (3) shall not apply if the reason (or, if more than one, the principal reason for his refusal was, in a case falling within paragraph (*c*)(i), that his taking the action in question would be in breach of the code or, in a case falling within paragraph (*c*)(ii), that if he became, or as the case may be remained, a member he would be required to take part in a strike, or other industrial action, which would be in breach of that code.

*   *   *

Dismissal on ground of redundancy

59. Where the reason or principal reason for the dismissal of an employee was that he was redundant, but it is shown that the circumstances constituting the redundancy applied equally to one or more other employees in the same undertaking who held positions similar to that held by him and who have not been dismissed by the employer, and either—

(a) that the reason (or, if more than one, the principal reason) for which he was selected for dismissal was one of those specified in section 58(1); or

(b) that he was selected for dismissal in contravention of a customary arrangement or agreed procedure relating to redundancy and there were no special reasons justifying a departure from that arrangement or procedure in his case,

then, for the purposes of this Part, the dismissal shall be regarded as unfair.

Dismissal on ground of pregnancy

60.—(1) An employee shall be treated for the purposes of this Part as unfairly dismissed if the reason or principal reason for her dismissal is that she is pregnant or is any other reason connected with her pregnancy, except one of the following reasons—

(a) that at the effective date of termination she is or will have become, because of her pregnancy, incapable of adequately doing the work which she is employed to do;

(b) that, because of her pregnancy, she cannot or will not be able to continue after that date to do that work without contravention (either by her or her employer) of a duty or restriction imposed by or under any enactment.

(2) An employee shall be treated for the purposes of this Part as unfairly dismissed if her employer dismisses her for a reason mentioned in subsection (1)(a) or (b), but neither he nor any successor of his, where there is a suitable available vacancy, makes her an offer before or on the effective date of termination to engage her under a new contract of employment complying with subsection (3).

*   *   *

Dismissal in connection with a lock-out, strike or other industrial action

62.—(1) The provisions of this section shall have effect in relation to an employee (the 'complainant') who claims that he has been unfairly dismissed by his employer where at the date of dismissal—

(*a*) the employer was conducting or instituting a lock-out, or

(*b*) the complainant was taking part in a strike or other industrial action.

(2) In such a case an industrial tribunal shall not determine whether the dismissal was fair or unfair unless it is shown—

(*a*) that one or more relevant employees of the same employer have not been dismissed, or

(*b*) that any such employee has, before the expiry of the period of three months beginning with that employee's date of dismissal, has been offered re-engagement and that the complainant has not been offered re-engagement.

(3) Where it is shown that the condition referred to in paragraph (*b*) of subsection (2) is fulfilled, the provisions of sections 57 to 60 shall have effect as if in those sections for any reference to the reason or principal reason for which the complainant was dismissed there were substituted a reference to the reason or principal reason for which he has not been offered re-engagement.

(4) In this section—

(*a*) 'date of dismissal' means—

(i) where the employee's contract of employment was terminated by notice, the date on which the employer's notice was given, and

(ii) in any other case, the effective date of termination;

(*b*) 'relevant employees' means—

(i) in relation to a lock-out, employees who were directly interested in the dispute in contemplation or furtherance of which the lock-out occurred, and

(ii) in relation to a strike or other industrial action, those employees at the establishment who were taking part in the action at the complainant's date of dismissal; 'establishment', in sub-paragraph (ii), meaning that establishment of the employer at or from which the complainant works; and

(*c*) any reference to an offer of re-engagement is a reference to an offer (made either by the original employer or by a successor of that employer or an associated employer) to re-engage an employee, either in the job which he held immediatly before the date of dismissal or in a different job which would be reasonably suitable in his case.

Pressure on employer to dismiss unfairly

63. In determining, for the purposes of this Part any question as to the reason, or principal reason, for which an employee was dismissed or any question whether the reason or principal reason for which an employee was dismissed was a reason fulfilling the requirements of section 57(1) (*b*) or whether the employer acted reasonably in treating it as a sufficient reason for dismissing him,—

(*a*) no account shall be taken of any pressure which, by calling, organising, procuring or financing a strike or other industrial action, or threatening to do so, was exercised on the employer to dismiss the employee, and

(*b*) any such question shall be determined as if no such pressure had been exercised.

Qualifying period and upper age limit

64.—(1) Subject to subsection (3), section 54 does not apply to the dismissal of an employee from any employment if the employee—

(*a*) was not continuously employed for a period of not less than one year ending with the effective date of termination, or

(*b*) on or before the effective date of termination attained the age which, in the undertaking in which he was employed, was the normal retiring age for an employee holding the position which he held, or, if a man, attained the age of sixty-five, or, if a woman, attained the age of sixty.

(3) Subsection (1) shall not apply to the dismissal of an employee if it is shown that the reason (or, if more than one, the principal reason) for the dismissal was one of those specified in section 58(1).

Extended qualifying period where no more than twenty employees

64A.—(1) Subject to subsection (2), section 54 does not apply to the dismissal of an employee from any employment if—

(*a*) the period (ending with the effective date of termination) during which the employee was continuously employed did not exceed two years; and

(*b*) at no time during that period did the number of employees employed by the employer for the time being of the dismissed employee, added to the number employed by an associated employer, exceed twenty;

(2) Subsection (1) shall not apply to the dismissal of an employee by reason of any such requirement or recommendation as is referred to in section 19(1), or if it is shown that the reason (or, if more than one, the principal reason) for the dismissal was one of those specified in section 58(1).

Exclusion in respect of dismissal procedures agreement

65.—(1) An application may be made jointly to the Secretary of State by all the parties to a dismissal procedures agreement to make an order designating that agreement for the purposes of this section.

(2) On any such application the Secretary of State may make such an order if he is satisfied—

(*a*) that every trade union which is a party to the dismissal procedures agreement is an independent trade union;

(*b*) that the agreement provides for procedures to be followed in cases where an employee claims that he has been, or is in the course of being, unfairly dismissed:

(*c*) that those procedures are available without discrimination to all employees falling within any description to which the agreement applies;

(*d*) that the remedies provided by the agreement in respect of unfair dismissal are on the whole as beneficial as (but not necessarily identical with) those provided in respect of unfair dismissal by this Part;

(*e*) that the procedures provided by the agreement include a right to arbitration or adjudication by an independent referee, or by a tribunal or other independent body, in cases where (by reason of an equality of votes or for any other reason) a decision cannot otherwise be reached; and

(*f*) that the provisions of the agreement are such that it can be determined with reasonable certainty whether a particular employee is one to whom the agreement applies or not.

(3) Where a dismissal procedures agreement is designated by an order under this section which is for the time being in force, the provisions of that agreement relating to dismissal shall have effect in substitution for any rights under section 54; and accordingly that section shall not apply to the dismissal of an employee from any employment if it is employment to which, and he is an employee to whom, those provisions of the agreement apply.

(4) Subsection (3) shall not apply to the right not to be unfairly dismissed for any reason mentioned in subsection (1) or (2) of section 60.

Remedies for unfair dismissal

68.—(1) Where on a complaint under section 67 an industrial tribunal finds that the grounds of the complaint are well-founded, it shall explain to the complainant what orders for reinstatement or re-engagement may be made under section 69 and in what circumstances they may be made and shall ask him whether he wishes the tribunal to make such an order, and if he does express such a wish the tribunal may make an order under section 69.

(2) If on a complaint under section 67 the tribunal finds that the grounds of the complaint are well-founded and no order is made under section 69, the tribunal shall make an award of compensation for unfair dismissal, calculated in accordance with sections 72 to 76 to be paid by the employer to the employee.

Order for reinstatement or re-engagement

69.—(1) An order under this section may be an order for reinstatement (in accordance with subsections (2) and (3)) or an order for re-engagement (in accordance with subsection (4)), as the industrial tribunal may decide, and in the latter case may be on such terms as the tribunal may decide.

(2) An order for reinstatement is an order that the employer shall treat the complainant in all respects as if he had not been dismissed, and on making such an order the tribunal shall specify—

(*a*) any amount payable by the employer in respect of any benefit which the compainant might reasonably be expected to have had but for the dismissal, including arrears of pay, for the period between the date of termination of employment and the date of reinstatement;

(*b*) any rights and privileges, including seniority and pension rights, which must be restored to the employee; and

(*c*) the date by which the order must be complied with.

(3) Without prejudice to the generality of subsection (2), if the complainant would have benefited from an improvement in his terms and conditions of employment had he not been dismissed, an order for reinstatement shall require him to be treated as if he had benefited from that improvement from the date on which he would have done so but for being dismissed.

(4) An order for re-engagement is an order that the complainant be engaged by the employer, or by a successor of the employer or by an associated employer, in employment comparable to that from which he was dismissed or other suitable employment, and on making such an order the tribunal shall specify the terms on which re-engagement is to take place including—

(*a*) the identity of the employer;

(*b*) the nature of the employment;

(*c*) the remuneration for the employment;

(*d*) any amount payable by the employer in respect of any benefit which the complainant might reasonably be expected to have had but for the dismissal, including arrears of pay, for the period between the date of termination of employment and the date of re-engagement;

(*e*) any rights and privileges, including seniority and pension rights, which must be restored to the employee; and

(*f*) the date by which the order must be complied with.

(5) In exercising its discretion under this section the tribunal shall first consider whether to make an order for reinstatement and in so doing shall take into account the following considerations, that is to say—

(*a*) whether the complainant wished to be reinstated;

(*b*) whether it is practicable for the employer to comply with an order for reinstatement;

(*c*) where the complainant caused or contributed to some extent to the dismissal, whether it would be just to order his reinstatement.

(6) If the tribunal decides not to make an order for reinstatement it shall then consider whether to make an order for re-engagement and if so on what terms; and in so doing the tribunal shall take into account the following considerations, that is to say—

(*a*) any wish expressed by the complainant as to the nature of the order to be made;

(*b*) whether it is practicable for the employer or, as the case may be, a successor or associated employer to comply with an order for re-engagement;

(*c*) where the complainant caused or contributed to some extent to the dismissal, whether it would be just to order his re-engagement and if so on what terms;

and except in a case where the tribunal takes into account contributory fault under paragraph (*c*) it shall, if it orders re-engagement, do so on terms which are, so far as is reasonably practicable, as favourable as an order for reinstatement.

Enforcement of s.69 order and compensation

71.—(1) If an order under section 69 is made and the complainant is reinstated or, as the case may be, re-engaged but the terms of the order are not fully complied with, then, subject to section 75, an industrial tribunal shall make an award of compensation, to be paid by the employer to the employee, of such amount as the tribunal thinks fit having regard to the loss sustained by the complainant in consequence of the failure to comply fully with the terms of the order.

(2) Subject to subsection (1), if an order under section 69 is made but the complainant is not reinstated or, as the case may be, re-engaged in accordance with the order—

(*a*) the tribunal shall make an award of compensation for unfair dismissal, calculated in accordance with sections 72 to 76 to be paid by the employer to the employee; and

(*b*) except in a case in which the dismissal is to be regarded as unfair by virtue of section 58 or 59(*a*) or in which the employer satisfies the tribunal that it was not practicable to comply with the order, the tribunal shall make an additional award of compensation to be paid by the employer to the employee of an amount—

(i) where the dismissal is of a description referred to in subsection (3), not less than twenty-six nor more than fifty-two weeks' pay, or

(ii) in any other case, not less than thirteen nor more than twenty-six weeks' pay.

(3) The descriptions of dismissal in respect of which an employer may incur a higher additional award in accordance with subsection (2)(*b*) (i) are the following, that is to say,—

(*a*) [*Repealed by the Employment Act 1982, Sched. 4,*]

(*b*) a dismissal which is an act of discrimination within the meaning of the Sex Discrimination Act 1975 which is unlawful by virtue of that Act;

(*c*) a dismissal which is an act of discrimination within the meaning of the Race Relations Act 1976 which is unlawful by virtue of that Act.

(4) Where in any case an employer has engaged a permanent replacement for a dismissed employee the tribunal shall not take that fact into account in determining, for the purposes of subsection (2)(*b*) whether it was practicable to comply with the order for reinstatement or re-engagement unless the employer shows that it was not practicable for him to arrange for the dismissed employee's work to be done without engaging a permanent replacement.

(5) Where in any case an industrial tribunal makes an award of compensation for unfair dismissal, calculated in accordance with sections 72 to 76 and the tribunal finds that the complainant has unreasonably prevented an order under section 69 from being complied with, it shall, without prejudice to the generality of section 74(4), take that conduct into account as a failure on the part of the complainant to mitigate his loss.

Compensation for unfair dismissal

72. Where a tribunal makes an award of compensation for unfair dismissal under section 68(2) or 71(2) the award shall consist of—

(*a*) a basic award (calculated in accordance with section 73), and (*b*) a compensatory award (calculated in accordance with section 74), and

(*c*) where the dismissal is to be regarded as unfair by virtue of section 58 or 59(*a*), a special award (calculated in accordance with section 75A);

but paragraph (*c*) shall not apply unless the complainant requested the tribunal to make an order under section 69, and shall not in any event apply in a case within section 73(2).

Calculation of basic award

73.–(1) The amount of the basic award shall be the amount calculated in accordance with subsections (3) to (6) subject to—

(*a*) subsection (2) of this section (which provides for an award of two weeks' pay in certain redundancy cases);

(*b*) [*Repealed by the Employment Act 1982, Sched. 4*]

(*ba*) subsection (7A) (which provides for the amount of the award to be reduced where the employee has unreasonably refused an offer of reinstatement);

(*bb*) subsection (7B) (which provides for the amount of the award to be reduced because of the employee's conduct);

(*d*) subsection (9) (which provides for the amount of the award to be reduced where the employee received a payment in respect of redundancy); and

(*e*) section 76 (which prohibits compensation being awarded under this Part and under the Sex Discrimination Act 1975 or the Race Relations Act 1976 in respect of the same matter).

(2) The amount of the basic award shall be two weeks' pay where the tribunal finds that the reason or principal reason for the dismissal of the employee was that he was redundant and the employee—

(*a*) by virtue of section 82(5) or (6) is not, or if he were otherwise entitled would not be, entitled to a redundancy payment; or

(*b*)| by virtue of the operation of section 84(1) is not treated as dismissed for the purposes of Part VI.

(3) The amount of the basic award shall be calculated by reference to the period, ending with the effective date of termination, during which the employee has been continuously employed, by starting at the end of that period and reckoning backwards the numbers of years of employment falling within that period, and allowing—

(*a*) one and a half weeks' pay for each such year of employment in which the employee was not below the age of forty-one;

(*b*) one week's pay for each year of employment not falling within paragraph (*a*) in which the employee was not below the age of twenty-two; and

(*c*) half a week's pay for each such year of employment not falling within either of paragraphs (*a*) and (*b*).

(4) Where, in reckoning the number of years of employment in accordance with subsection (3), twenty years of employment have been reckoned no account shall be taken of any year of employment earlier than those twenty years.

(4A) Where the dismissal is to be regarded as unfair by virtue of section 58 or 59(*a*), the amount of the basic award (before any reduction under the following provisions of this section) shall not be less than £2,000.

*   *   *

Calculation of compensatory award

74.—(1) Subject to sections 75 and 76, the amount of the compensatory award shall be such amount as the tribunal considers just and equitable in all the circumstances having regard to the loss sustained by the complainant in consequence of the dismissal in so far as that loss is attributable to action taken by the employer.

(2) The said loss shall be taken to include—

(*a*) any expenses reasonably incurred by the complainant in consequence of the dismissal, and

(*b*) subject to subsection (3), loss of any benefit which he might reasonably be expected to have had but for the dismissal.

(3) The said loss, in respect of any loss of any entitlement or potential entitlement to, or expectation of, a payment on account of dismissal by reason of redundancy, whether in pursuance of Part VI or otherwise, shall include only the loss referable to the amount, if any, by which the amount of that payment would have exceeded the amount of a basic award (apart from any reduction under section 73 (7A) to (9)) in respect of the same dismissal.

(4) In ascertaining the said loss the tribunal shall apply the same rule concerning the duty of a person to mitigate his loss as applies to damages recoverable under the common law of England and Wales or of Scotland, as the case may be.

(5) In determining, for the purposes of subsection (1), how far any loss sustained by the complainant was attributable to action taken by the employer no account shall be taken of any pressure which, by calling, organising, procuring or financing a strike or other industrial action, or threatening to do so, was exercised on the employer to dismiss the employee, and that question shall be determined as if no such pressure had been exercised.

(6) Where the tribunal finds that the dismissal was to any extent caused or contributed to by any action of the complainant it shall reduce the amount of the compensatory award by such proportion as it considers just and equitable having regard to that finding.

(7) If the amount of any payment made by the employer to the employee on the ground that the dismissal was by reason of redundancy, whether in pursuance of Part VI or otherwise, exceeds the amount of the basic award which would be payable but for section 73(9) that excess shall go to reduce the amount of the compensatory award.

Calculation of special award

75A.—(1) Subject to the following provisions of this section, the amount of the special award shall be—

(*a*) one week's pay multiplied by 104, or

(*b*) £10,000,

whichever is the greater, but shall not exceed £20,000.

(2) If the award of compensation is made under section 71(2)(*a*) then, unless the employer satisfies the tribunal that it was not practicable to comply with the preceding order under section 69, the amount of the special award shall be increased to—

(*a*) one week's pay multiplied by 156, or

(*b*) £15,000,

whichever is the greater, but subject to the following provisions of this section.

(3) In a case where the amount of the basic award is reduced under section 73(5), the amount of the special award shall be reduced by the same fraction.

(4) Where the tribunal considers that any conduct of the complainant before the dismissal (or, where the dismissal was with notice, before the notice was given) was such that it would be just and equitable to reduce or further reduce the amount of the special award to any extent, the tribunal shall reduce or further reduce that amount accordingly.

(5) Where the tribunal finds that the complainant has unreasonably—

(*a*) prevented an order under section 69 from being complied with; or

(*b*) refused an offer by the employer (made otherwise than in compliance with such an order) which if accepted would have the effect of reinstating the complainant in his employment in all respects as if he had not been dismissed;

the tribunal shall reduce or further reduce the amount of the special award to such extent as it considers just and equitable having regard to that finding.

(6) Where the employer has engaged a permanent replacement for the complainant, the tribunal shall not take that fact into account in determining, for the purposes of subsection (2), whether it was practicable to comply with an order under section 69 unless the employer shows that it was not practicable for him to arrange for the complainant's work to be done without engaging a permanent replacement.

(7) The Secretary of State may by order increase any of the sums of £10,000, £20,000 and £15,000 specified in subsections (1) and (2), or any of those sums as from time to time increased under this subsection, but no such order shall be made unless a draft of the order has been laid before Parliament and approved by a resolution of each House of Parliament.

Awards against third parties

76A.—(1) If in proceedings before an industrial tribunal on a complaint against an employer under section 67 either the employer or the complainant claims—

(*a*) that the employer was induced to dismiss the complainant by pressure which a trade union or other person exercised on the employer by calling, organising, procuring or financing a strike or other industrial action, or by threatening to do so, and

(*b*) that the pressure was exercised because the complainant was not a member of any trade union or of a particular trade union or of one of a number of particular trade unions,

the employer or the complainant may request the tribunal to direct that the person who he claims exercised the pressure be joined, or in Scotland sisted, as a party to the proceedings.

(2) A request under subsection (1) shall be granted if it is made before the hearing of the complaint begins, but may be refused if it is made after that time; and no such request may be made after the tribunal has made an award under section 68(2) or an order under section 69.

(3) Where a person has been joined, or in Scotland sisted, as a party to proceedings before an industrial tribunal by virtue of subsection (1) and the tribunal—

(*a*) makes an award of compensation under section 68(2) or 71 (2)(*a*) or (*b*), but

(*b*) finds that the claim mentioned in subsection (1) is well founded,

the award may be made against the person instead of against the employer, or partly against that person and partly against the employer, as the tribunal may consider just and equitable in the circumstances.

Interim relief pending determination of complaint of unfair dismissal

77.–(1) An employee who presents a complaint to an industrial tribunal under section 67 alleging that the dismissal is to be regarded as unfair by virtue of section 58 may apply to the tribunal for an order under the following provisions of this section.

(2) An industrial tribunal shall not entertain an application under this section unless—

(*a*) it is presented to the tribunal before the end of the period of seven days immediately following the effective date of termination (whether before, on or after that date); and

(*b*) in a case in which the employee relies on section 58(1)(*a*) or (*b*) before the end of that period there is also so presented a certificate in writing signed by an authorised official of the independent trade union of which the employee was or had proposed to become a member stating that on the date of the dismissal the employee was or had proposed to become a member of the union and that there appear to be reasonable grounds for supposing that the reason for his dismissal (or, if more than one, the principal reason) was one alleged in the complaint.

(3) An industrial tribunal shall determine an application under this section as soon as practicable after receiving the application and (where appropriate) the relevant certificate,

*   *   *

(5) If on hearing an application under this section it appears to an industrial tribunal that it is likely that on determining the complaint to which the application relates the tribunal will find that the complainant is by virtue of section 58 to be regarded as having been unfairly dismissed the tribunal shall announce its findings and explain to both parties (if present) what powers the tribunal may exercise on an application under this section and in what circumstances it may exercise them, and shall ask the employer (if present) whether he is willing, pending the determination or settlement of the complaint—

(*a*)| to reinstate the employee, that is to say, to treat the employee in all respects as if he had not been dismissed; or

(*b*) if not, to re-engage him in another job on terms and conditions not less favourable than those which would have been applicable to him if he had not been dismissed.

*   *   *

(7) If the employer states that he is willing to reinstate the employee, the tribunal shall make an order to that effect.

(8) If the employer states that he is willing to re-engage the employee in another job and specifies the terms and conditions on which he is willing to do so, the tribunal shall ask the employee whether he is willing to accept the job on those terms and conditions, and—

(a) if the employee is willing to accept the job on those terms and conditions, the tribunal shall make an order to that effect; and

(b) if the employee is unwilling to accept the job on those terms and conditions, then, if the tribunal is of the opinion that the refusal is reasonable, the tribunal shall make an order for the continuation of his contract of employment, but otherwise the tribunal shall make no order under this section.

(9) If, on the hearing of an application under this section, the employer fails to attend before the tribunal or he states that he is unwilling either to reinstate the employee or re-engage him as mentioned in subsection (5), the tribunal shall make an order for the continuation of the employee's contract of employment.

* * *

Functions of conciliation officers on complaint under s.67

134.—(1) Where a complaint has been presented to an industrial tribunal under section 67 by a person (in this section referred to as the complainant) and a copy of it has been sent to a conciliation officer, it shall be the duty of the conciliation officer—

(a) if he is requested to do so by the complainant and by the employer against whom it was presented, or

(b) if, in the absence of any such request, the conciliation officer considers that he could act under this section with a reasonable prospect of success,

to endeavour to promote a settlement of the complaint without its being determined by an industrial tribunal.

(2) For the purpose of promoting such a settlement, in a case where the complainant has ceased to be employed by the employer against whom the complaint was made,—

(a) the conciliation officer shall in particular seek to promote the reinstatement or re-engagement of the complainant by the employer, or by a successor of the employer or by an associated employer, on terms appearing to the conciliation officer to be equitable; but

(b) where the complainant does not wish to be reinstated or re-engaged, or where reinstatement or re-engagement is not practicable, and the parties desire the conciliation officer to act under this section, he shall seek to promote agreement between them as to a sum by way of compensation to be paid by the employer to the complainant.

(3) Where—

> (*a*) a person claims that action has been taken in respect of which a complaint could be presented by him under section 67, and
>
> (*b*) before any complaint relating to that action has been so presented, a request is made to a conciliation officer (whether by that person or by the employer) to make his services available to them,

the conciliation officer shall act in accordance with subsections (1) and (2) above as if a complaint had been presented.

(4) In proceeding under subsections (1) to (3), a conciliation officer shall where appropriate have regard to the desirability of encouraging the use of other procedures available for the settlement of grievances.

(5) Anything communicated to a conciliation officer in connection with the performance of his functions under this section shall not be admissible in evidence in any proceedings before an industrial tribunal, except with the consent of the person who communicated it to that officer.

Restrictions on contracting out

140.—(1) Except as provided by the following provisions of this section, any provision in an agreement (whether a contract of employment or not) shall be void in so far as it purports—

> (*a*) to exclude or limit the operation of any provision of this Act; or
>
> (*b*) to preclude any person from presenting a complaint to, or bringing any proceedings under this Act before, an industrial tribunal.

(2) Subsection (1) shall not apply—

*   *   *

> (*d*) to any agreement to refrain from presenting a complaint under section 67, where in compliance with a request under section 134(3) a conciliation officer has taken action in accordance with that subsection;
>
> (*e*) to any agreement to refrain from proceeding with a complaint presented under section 67 where a conciliation officer has taken action in accordance with section 134(1) and (2);

*   *   *

Appendix III

Industrial Tribunals (Rules of Procedure) Regulations 1980

This appendix reproduces the regulations governing industrial tribunals in England and Wales (SI 1980 No. 884). Similar regulations govern tribunals in Scotland (SI 1980 No. 885). Rules relating to the procedure for hearing equal pay for equal value claims, inserted into the Regulations in 1983, are not included.

Originating application

1.–(1) Proceedings for the determination of any matter by a tribunal shall be instituted by the applicant (or, where applicable, by a court) presenting to the Secretary of the Tribunals an originating application which shall be in writing and shall set out:–

    (*a*) the name and address of the applicant; and

    (*b*) the names and addresses of the person or persons against whom relief is sought or (where applicable) of the parties to the proceedings before the court; and

    (*c*) the grounds, with particulars thereof, on which relief is sought, or in proceedings under section 51 of the 1966 Act the question for determination and (except where the question is referred by a court) the grounds on which relief is sought.

(2) Where the Secretary of the Tribunals is of the opinion that the originating application does not seek or on the facts stated therein cannot entitle the applicant to a relief which a tribunal has power to give, he may give notice to that effect to the applicant stating the reasons for his opinion and informing him that the application will not be registered unless he states in writing that he wishes to proceed with it.

(3) An application as respects which a notice has been given in pursuance of the preceding paragraph shall not be treated as having been received for the purposes of Rule 2 unless the applicant intimates in writing to the Secretary of the Tribunals that he wishes to proceed with

it; and upon receipt of such an intimation the Secretary of the Tribunals shall proceed in accordance with that Rule.

Action upon receipt of originating application

2. Upon receiving an originating application the Secretary of the Tribunals shall enter particulars of it in the Register and shall forthwith send a copy of it to the respondent and inform the parties in writing of the case number of the originating application entered in the Register (which shall thereafter constitute the title of the proceedings) and of the address to which notices and other communications to the Secretary of the Tribunals shall be sent. Every copy of the originating application sent by the Secretary of the Tribunals under this paragraph shall be accompanied by a written notice which shall include information, as appropriate to the case, about the means and time for entering an appearance, the consequences of failure to do so, and the right to receive a copy of the decision. The Secretary of the Tribunals shall also notify the parties that in all cases under the provisions of any enactment providing for conciliation the services of a conciliation officer are available to them.

Appearance by respondent

3.—(1) A respondent shall within 14 days of receiving the copy originating application enter an appearance to the proceedings by presenting to the Secretary of the Tribunals a written notice of appearance setting out his full name and address and stating whether or not he intends to resist the application and, if so, setting out sufficient particulars to show on what grounds. Upon receipt of a notice of appearance the Secretary of the Tribunals shall forthwith send a copy of it to any other party.

(2) A respondent who has not entered an appearance shall not be entitled to take any part in the proceedings except—

   (i)   to apply under Rule 13(1) for an extension of the time appointed by this Rule for entering an appearance;

   (ii)   to make an application under Rule 4(1)(i);

   (iii) to make an application under Rule 10(2) in respect of Rule 10(1)(*b*);

   (iv) to be called as a witness by another person;

   (v)   to be sent a copy of a decision or specification of reasons or corrected decision or specification in pursuance of Rule 9(3), 9(7) or 10(5).

(3) A notice of appearance which is presented to the Secretary of the Tribunals after the time appointed by this Rule for entering appearances shall be deemed to include an application under Rule 13(1) (by

the respondent who has presented the notice of appearance) for an
extension of the time so appointed. Without prejudice to Rule 13(4), if
the tribunal grants the application (which it may do notwithstanding
that the grounds of the application are not stated) the Secretary of the
Tribunals shall forthwith send a copy of the notice of appearance to
any other party. The tribunal shall not refuse an extension of time
under this Rule unless it has sent notice to the person wishing to enter
an appearance giving him an opportunity to show cause why the extension should be granted.

*Power to require further particulars and attendance of witnesses and to
grant discovery*

   4.–(1) A tribunal may—
   (*a*) subject to Rule 3(2), on the application of a party to the
          proceedings made either by notice to the Secretary of the
          Tribunals or at the hearing of the originating application, or
   (*b*) in relation to sub-paragraph (i) of this paragraph, if it thinks
          fit of its own motion—
       (i)   require a party to furnish in writing to the person
             specified by the tribunal further particulars of the
             grounds on which he or it relies and of any facts and
             contentions relevant thereto;
      (ii)   grant to the person making the application such
             discovery or inspection (including the taking of
             copies) of documents as might be granted by a county
             court; and
     (iii)   require the attendance of any person (including a
             party to the proceedings) as a witness or require the
             production of any document relating to the matter
             to be determined, wherever such witness may be
             within Great Britain;
and may appoint the time at or within which or the place at which any
act required in pursuance of this Rule is to be done.
   (2) A party on whom a requirement has been made under paragraph (1)(i) or (1)(ii) of this Rule on an *ex parte* application, or (in
relation to a requirement under paragraph 1(i)) on the tribunal's own
motion, and a person on whom a requirement has been made under
paragraph (1)(iii) may apply to the tribunal by notice to the Secretary
of the Tribunals before the appointed time at or within which the
requirement is to be complied with to vary or set aside the requirement. Notice of an application under this paragraph to vary or set aside
a requirement shall be given to the parties (other than the party making

the application) and, where appropriate, in proceedings which may involve payments out of the Redundancy Fund or Maternity Pay Fund, the Secretary of State if not a party.

(3) Every document containing a requirement under paragraph (1)(ii) or (1)(iii) of this Rule shall contain a reference to the fact that under paragraph 1(7) of Schedule 9 to the 1978 Act, any person who without reasonable excuse fails to comply with any such requirement shall be liable on summary conviction to a fine not exceeding £100.

(4) If the requirement under paragraph (1)(i) or (1)(ii) of this Rule is not complied with, a tribunal, before or at the hearing, may dismiss the originating application, or, as the case may be, strike out the whole or part of the notice of appearance, and, where appropriate, direct that a respondent shall be debarred from defending altogether: Provided that a tribunal shall not so dismiss or strike out or give such a direction unless it has sent notice to the party who has not complied with the requirement giving him an opportunity to show cause why such should not be done.

Time and place of hearing and appointment of assessor

5.—(1) The President or a Regional Chairman shall fix the date, time and place of the hearing of the originating application and the Secretary of the Tribunals shall (subject to Rule 3(2)) not less than 14 days (or such shorter time as may be agreed by him with the parties) before the date so fixed send to each party a notice of hearing which shall include information and guidance as to attendance at the hearing, witnesses and the bringing of documents (if any), representation by another person and written representations.

(2) In any proceedings under the 1966 Act in which the President or a Regional Chairman so directs, the Secretary of the Tribunals shall also take such of the following steps as may be so directed, namely—

    (*a*) publish in one or more newspapers circulating in the locality in which the port in question is situated notice of the hearing;

    (*b*) send notice of the hearing to such persons as may be directed;

    (*c*) post notices of the hearing in a conspicuous place or conspicuous places in or near the port in question;

but the requirement as to the period of notice contained in paragraph (1) of this Rule shall not apply to any such notices.

(3) Where in the case of any proceedings it is provided for one or more assessors to be appointed, the President or a Regional Chairman may, if he thinks fit, appoint a person or persons having special knowledge or experience in relation to the subject matter of the originating application to sit with the tribunal as assessor or assessors.

Pre-hearing assessment

6.–(1) A tribunal may at any time before the hearing (either, subject to Rule 3(2), on the application of a party to the proceedings made by notice to the Secretary of the Tribunals or of its own motion) consider, by way of a pre-hearing assessment, the contents of the originating application and entry of appearance, any representations in writing which have been submitted and any oral argument advanced by or on behalf of a party.

(2) If upon a pre-hearing assessment, the tribunal considers that the originating application is unlikely to succeed or that the contentions or any particular contention of a party appear to have no reasonable prospect of success, it may indicate that in its opinion, if the originating application shall not be withdrawn or the contentions or contention of the party shall be persisted in up to or at the hearing, the party in question may have an order for costs made against him at the hearing under the provisions of Rule 11. A pre-hearing assessment shall not take place unless the tribunal has sent notice to the parties to the proceedings giving them (and, where appropriate, in proceedings which may involve payments out of the Redundancy Fund or Maternity Pay Fund, the Secretary of State, if not a party) an opportunity to submit representations in writing and to advance oral argument at the pre-hearing assessment if they so wish.

(3) Any indication of opinion made in accordance with paragraph (2) of this Rule shall be recorded in a document signed by the chairman a copy of which shall be sent to the parties to the proceedings and a copy of which shall be available to the tribunal at the hearing.

(4) Where a tribunal has indicated its opinion in accordance with paragraph (2) of this Rule no member thereof shall be a member of the tribunal at the hearing.

The hearing

7.–(1) Any hearing of or in connection with an originating application shall take place in public unless in the opinion of the tribunal a private hearing is appropriate for the purpose of hearing evidence which relates to matters of such a nature that it would be against the interests of national security to allow the evidence to be given in public or hearing evidence from any person which in the opinion of the tribunal is likely to consist of—

(a) information which he could not disclose without contravening a prohibition imposed by or under any enactment; or

(b) any information which has been communicated to him in confidence, or which he has otherwise obtained in consequence of the confidence reposed in him by another person; or

(c) information the disclosure of which would cause substantial injury to any undertaking of his or any undertaking in which he works for reasons other than its effect on negotiations with respect to any of the matters mentioned in section 29(1) of the Trade Union and Labour Relations Act 1974.

(2) A member of the Council on Tribunals shall be entitled to attend any hearing taking place in private in his capacity as such member.

(3) Subject to Rule 3(2), if a party shall desire to submit representations in writing for consideration by a tribunal at the hearing of the originating application that party shall present such representations to the Secretary of the Tribunals not less than 7 days before the hearing and shall at the same time send a copy to the other party or parties.

(4) Where a party has failed to attend or be represented at the hearing (whether or not he has sent any representations in writing) the contents of his originating application or, as the case may be, of his entry of appearance may be treated by a tribunal as representations in writing.

(5) The Secretary of State if he so elects shall be entitled to apply under Rules 4(1), 13(1) and (2), 15 and 16(1) and to appear as if he were a party and be heard at any hearing of or in connection with an originating application in proceedings in which he is not a party which may involve payments out of the Redundancy Fund or Maternity Pay Fund.

(6) Subject to Rule 3(2), at any hearing of or in connection with an originating application a party and any person entitled to appear may appear before the tribunal and may be heard in person or be represented by counsel or by a solicitor or by a representative of a trade union or an employers' association or by any other person whom he desires to represent him.

Procedure of hearing

8.—(1) The tribunal shall conduct the hearing in such manner as it considers most suitable to the clarification of the issues before it and generally to the just handling of the proceedings, it shall so far as appears to it appropriate seek to avoid formality in its proceedings and it shall not be bound by any enactment or rule of law relating to the admissibility of evidence in proceedings before the courts of law.

(2) Subject to paragraphs (1)(2A) (2B) (2C) and (2D) of this Rule, at the hearing of the originating application a party (unless disentitled by virtue of Rule 3(2)), the Secretary of State, (if, not being a party, he elects to appear as provided in Rule 7(5)) and any other person entitled to appear shall be entitled to give evidence, to call witnesses, to question any witnesses and to address the tribunal.

(3) If a party shall fail to appear or to be represented at the time and place fixed for the hearing, the tribunal may, if that party is an applicant dismiss, or, in any case, dispose of the application in the absence of that party or may adjourn the hearing to a later date: Provided that before deciding to dismiss or disposing of any application in the absence of a party the tribunal shall consider any representations submitted by that party in pursuance of Rule 7(3).

(4) A tribunal may require any witness to give evidence on oath or affirmation and for that purpose there may be administered an oath or affirmation in due form.

Decision of tribunal

9.—(1) A decision of a tribunal may be taken by a majority thereof and, if the tribunal shall be constituted of two members only, the chairman shall have a second or casting vote.

(2) The decision of a tribunal shall be recorded in a document signed by the chairman which shall contain the reasons for the decision.

(3) The clerk to the tribunal shall transmit the document signed by the chairman to the Secretary of the Tribunals who shall as soon as may be enter it in the Register and shall send a copy of the entry to each of the parties and to the persons entitled to appear who did so appear and, where the originating application was sent to a tribunal by a court, to that court.

(4) The specification of the reasons for the decision shall be omitted from the Register in any case in which evidence has been heard in private and the tribunal so directs and in that event a specification of the reasons shall be sent to the parties and to any superior court in any proceedings relating to such decision together with a copy of the entry.

(5) The Register shall be kept at the Office of the Tribunals and shall be open to the inspection of any person without charge at all reasonable hours.

(6) Clerical mistakes in documents recording the tribunal's decisions, or errors arising in them from an accidental slip or omission, may at any time be corrected by the chairman by certificate under his hand.

(7) The clerk to the tribunal shall send a copy of any document so corrected and the certificate of the chairman to the Secretary of the Tribunals who shall as soon as may be make such correction as may be necessary in the Register and shall send a copy of the corrected entry or of the corrected specification of the reasons, as the case may be, to each of the parties and to the persons entitled to appear who did so appear and, where the originating application was sent to the tribunal by a court, to that court.

(8) If any decision is—
(*a*) corrected under paragraph (6) of this Rule,
(*b*) reviewed, revoked or varied under Rule 10, or
(*c*) altered in any way by order of a superior court,
the Secretary of the Tribunals shall alter the entry in the Register to conform with any such certificate or order and shall send a copy of the new entry to each of the parties and to the persons entitled to appear who did so appear and where the originating application was sent to the tribunal by a court, to that court.

Review of tribunal's decisions

10.—(1) A tribunal shall have power to review and to revoke or vary by certificate under the chairman's hand any decision on the grounds that—
(*a*) the decision was wrongly made as a result of an error on the part of the tribunal staff; or
(*b*) a party did not receive notice of the proceedings leading to the decision; or
(*c*) the decision was made in the absence of a party or person entitled to be heard; or
(*d*) new evidence has become available since the making of the decision provided that its existence could not have been reasonably known of or foreseen; or
(*e*) the interests of justice require such a review.

(2) An application for the purposes of paragraph (1) of this Rule may be made at the hearing. If the application is not made at the hearing, such application shall be made by the Secretary of the Tribunals at any time from the date of the hearing until 14 days after the date on which the decision was sent to the parties and must be in writing stating the grounds in full.

(3) An application for the purposes of paragraph (1) of this Rule may be refused by the President or by the chairman of the tribunal which decided the case or by a Regional Chairman if in his opinion it has no reasonable prospect of success.

(4) If such an application is not refused under paragraph (3) of this Rule it shall be heard by the tribunal which decided the case or—
(*a*) where it is not practicable for it to be heard by that tribunal, or
(*b*) where the decision was made by a chairman acting alone under Rule 12(4),
by a tribunal appointed either by the President or a Regional Chairman, and if it is granted the tribunal shall either vary the decision or revoke the decision and order a rehearing.

(5) The clerk to the tribunal shall send to the Secretary of the Tribunals the certificate of the chairman as to any revocation or variation of the tribunal's decision under this Rule. The Secretary of the Tribunals shall as soon as may be make such correction as may be necessary in the Register and shall send a copy of the entry to each of the parties and to the persons entitled to appear who did so appear and where the originating application was sent to a tribunal by a court, to that court.

Costs

11.—(1) Subject to paragraphs (2), (3) and (4) of this Rule, a tribunal shall not normally make an award in respect of the costs or expenses incurred by a party to the proceedings but where in its opinion a party (and if he is a respondent whether or not he has entered an appearance) has in bringing or conducting the proceedings acted frivolously, vexatiously or otherwise unreasonably the tribunal may make—

(*a*) an order that that party shall pay to another party (or to the Secretary of State, if, not being a party, he has acted as provided in Rule 7(5)) either a specified sum in respect of the costs or expenses incurred by that other party (or, as the case may be, by the Secretary of State) or the whole or part of those costs or expenses as taxed (if not otherwise agreed);

(*b*) an order that that party shall pay to the Secretary of State the whole, or any part, of any allowances (other than allowances paid to members of tribunals or assessors) paid by the Secretary of State under paragraph 10 of Schedule 9 to the 1978 Act to any person for the purposes of, or in connection with, his attendance at the tribunal.

(2) Where the tribunal has on the application of a party to the proceedings postponed the day or time fixed for or adjourned the hearing, the tribunal may make orders against or, as the case may require, in favour of that party as at paragraph (1)(*a*) and (*b*) of this Rule as respects any costs or expenses incurred or any allowances paid by that party as a result of the postponement or adjournment.

(3) Where, on a complaint of unfair dismissal in respect of which—

(i) the applicant has expressed a wish to be reinstated or re-engaged which has been communicated to the respondent at least 7 days before the hearing of the complaint, or

(ii) the proceedings arise out of the respondent's failure to permit the applicant to return to work after an absence due to pregnancy or confinement,

any postponement or adjournment of the hearing has been caused by the respondent's failure, without a special reason, to adduce reasonable evidence as to the availability of the job from which the applicant was dismissed, or, as the case may be, which she held before her absence, or of comparable or suitable employment, the tribunal shall make orders against that respondent as at paragraph (1)(*a*) and (*b*) of this Rule as respects any costs or expenses incurred or any allowances paid as a result of the postponement or adjournment.

(4) In any proceedings under the 1966 Act a tribunal may make—

(*a*) an order that a party, or any other person entitled to appear who did so appear, shall pay to another party or such person either a specified sum in respect of the costs or expenses incurred by that other party or person or the whole or part of those costs or expenses as taxed (if not otherwise agreed);

(*b*) an order that a party, or any other person entitled to appear who did so appear, shall pay to the Secretary of State a specified sum in respect of the whole, or any part, of any allowances (other than allowances paid to members of tribunals) paid by the Secretary of State under paragraph 10 of Schedule 9 to the 1978 Act to any person for the purpose of, or in connection with, his attendance at the tribunal.

(5) Any costs required by an order under this Rule to be taxed may be taxed in the county court according to such of the scales prescribed by the county court rules for proceedings in the county court as shall be directed by the order.

Miscellaneous powers of tribunal

12.—(1) Subject to the provisions of these Rules, a tribunal may regulate its own procedure.

(2) A tribunal may, if it thinks fit,—

(*a*) extend the time appointed by or under these Rules for doing any act notwithstanding that the time appointed may have expired;

(*b*) postpone the day or time fixed for, or adjourn, any hearing (particularly as respects cases under the provisions of any enactment providing for conciliation for the purpose of giving an opportunity for the complaint to be settled by way of conciliation and withdrawn);

(*c*) if the applicant shall at any time give notice of the withdrawal of his originating application, dismiss the proceedings;

(*d*) except in proceedings under the 1966 Act, if both or all the parties (and the Secretary of State, if not being a party, he has acted as provided in Rule 7(5)) agree in writing upon the terms of a decision to be made by the tribunal, decide accordingly;

(*e*) at any stage of the proceedings order to be struck out or amended any originating application or notice of appearance or anything in such application or notice of appearance on the grounds that it is scandalous, frivolous or vexatious;

(*f*) on the application of the respondent, or of its own motion, order to be struck out any originating application for want of prosecution: Provided that before making any order under (*e*) or (*f*) above the tribunal shall send notice to the party against whom it is proposed that any such order should be made giving him an opportunity to show cause why such an order should not be made.

(3) Subject to Rule 4(2), a tribunal may, if it thinks fit, before granting an application under Rule 4 or Rule 13 require the party (or, as the case may be, the Secretary of State) making the application to give notice of it to the other party or parties. The notice shall give particulars of the application and indicate the address to which and the time within which any objection to the application shall be made being an address and time specified for the purposes of the application by the tribunal.

(4) Any act other than the holding of a pre-hearing assessment under Rule 6, the hearing of an originating application, or the making of an order under Rule 10(1), required or authorised by these Rules to be done by a tribunal may be done by, or on the direction of, the President or the chairman of the tribunal, or any chairman being a member of the panel of chairmen.

(5) Rule 11 shall apply to an order dismissing proceedings under paragraph (2)(*c*) of this Rule.

(6) Any functions of the Secretary of the Tribunals other than that mentioned in Rule 1(2) may be performed by an Assistant Secretary of the Tribunals.

Extension of time and directions

13.–(1) An application to a tribunal for an extension of the time appointed by these Rules for doing any act may be made by a party either before or after the expiration of any time so appointed.

(2) Subject to Rule 3(2), a party may at any time apply to a tribunal for directions on any matter arising in connection with the proceedings.

(3) An application under the foregoing provisions of this Rule shall be made by presenting to the Secretary of the Tribunals a notice of

application, which shall state the title of the proceedings and shall set out the grounds of the application.

(4) The Secretary of the Tribunals shall give notice to both or all the parties (subject to Rule 3(2)) of any extension of time granted under Rule 12(2)(*a*) or any directions given in pursuance of this Rule.

Joinder and representative respondents

14.–(1) A tribunal may at any time either upon the application of any person or, where appropriate of its own motion, direct any person against whom any relief is sought to be joined as a party to the proceedings, and give such consequential directions as it considers necessary.

(2) A tribunal may likewise, either upon such application or of its own motion, order that any respondent named in the originating application or subsequently added, who shall appear to the tribunal not to have been, or to have ceased to be, directly interested in the subject of the originating application, be dismissed from the proceedings.

(3) Where there are numerous persons having the same interest in an originating application, one or more of them may be cited as the person or persons against whom relief is sought, or may be authorised by the tribunal, before or at the hearing, to defend on behalf of all the persons so interested.

Consolidation of proceedings

15. Where there are pending before the industrial tribunals two or more originating applications, then, if at any time upon the application of a party or of its own motion it appears to a tribunal that—

(*a*) some common question of law or fact arises in both or all the originating applications, or

(*b*) the relief claimed therein is in respect of or arises out of the same set of facts, or

(*c*) for some other reason it is desirable to make an order under this Rule,

the tribunal may order that some (as specified in the order) or all of the originating applications shall be considered together, and may give such consequential directions as may be necessary: Provided that the tribunal shall not make an order under this Rule without sending notice to all parties concerned giving them an opportunity to show cause why such an order should not be made.

Transfer of proceedings

16.–(1) Where there is pending before the industrial tribunals an originating application in respect of which it appears to the President or a Regional Chairman that the proceedings could be determined by an industrial tribunal (Scotland) established in pursuance of the Industrial Tribunals (Scotland) Regulations 1965 and that the originating application would more conveniently be determined by such a tribunal, the President or a Regional Chairman may, at any time upon the application of a party or of his own motion, with the consent of the President of the Industrial Tribunals (Scotland), direct that the said proceedings be transferred to the Office of the Industrial Tribunals (Scotland): Provided that no such direction shall be made unless notice has been sent to all parties concerned giving them an opportunity to show cause why such a direction should not be made.

(2) Where proceedings have been transferred to the Office of the Industrial Tribunals (England and Wales) under Rule 16(1) of the Industrial Tribunals (Rules of Procedure) (Scotland) Regulations 1980 they shall be treated as if in all respects they had been commenced by an originating application pursuant to Rule 1.

Notices, etc.

17.—(1) Any notice given under these Rules shall be in writing.

(2) All notices and documents required by these Rules to be presented to the Secretary of the Tribunals may be presented at the Office of the Tribunals or such other office as may be notified by the Secretary of the Tribunals to the parties.

(3) All notices and documents required or authorised by these Rules to be sent or given to any person hereinafter mentioned may be sent by post (subject to paragraph (5) of this Rule) or delivered to or at—

(*a*) in the case of a notice or document directed to the Secretary of State in proceedings to which he is not a party, the offices of the Department of Employment at Caxton House, Tothill Street, London SW1H 9NA or such other office as may notified by the Secretary of State;

(*b*) in the case of a notice or document directed to the Board, the principal office of the Board;

(*c*) in the case of a notice or document directed to a court, the office of the clerk of the court;

(*d*) in the case of a notice or document directed to a party:—

   (i)   his address for service specified in the originating application or in a notice of appearance or in a notice under paragraph (4) of this Rule; or

   (ii) if no address for service has been so specified, his last known address or place of business in the United Kingdom or, if the party is a corporation, the corporation's registered or principal office in the United Kingdom or, in any case, at such address or place outside the United Kingdom as the President or a Regional Chairman may allow;

(*e*) in the case of a notice or document directed to any person (other than a person specified in the foregoing provisions of this paragraph), his address or place of business in the United Kingdom, or if such person is a corporation, the corporation's registered or principal office in the United Kingdom;

and if sent or given to the authorised representative of a party shall be deemed to have been sent or given to that party.

(4) A party may at any time by notice to the Secretary of the Tribunals and to the other party or parties (and, where appropriate, to the appropriate conciliation officer) change his address for service under these Rules.

(5) The recorded delivery service shall be used instead of the ordinary post:—

(*a*) when a second set of documents or notices is to be sent to a respondent who has not entered an appearance under Rule 3(1);

(*b*) for service of an order made under Rule 4(1)(iii) requiring the attendance of a witness or the production of a document.

(6) Where for any sufficient reason service of any document or notice cannot be effected in the manner prescribed under this Rule, the President or a Regional Chairman may make an order for substituted service in such manner as he may deem fit and such service shall have the same effect as service in the manner prescribed under this Rule.

(7) In proceedings brought under the provisions of any enactment providing for conciliation the Secretary of the Tribunals shall send copies of all documents and notices to a conciliation officer who in the opinion of the Secretary is an appropriate officer to receive them.

(8) In proceedings which may involve payments out of the Redundancy Fund or Maternity Pay Fund, the Secretary of the Tribunals shall, where appropriate, send copies of all documents and notices to the Secretary of State notwithstanding the fact that he may not be a party to such proceedings.

(9) In proceedings under the Equal Pay Act, the Sex Discrimination Act 1975 or the Race Relations Act 1976 the Secretary of the Tribunals shall send to the Equal Opportunities Commission or, as the case may be, the Commission for Racial Equality copies of all documents sent to the parties under Rule 9(3), (7) and (8) and Rule 10(5).

List of Cases Cited

List of Statutes

Bibliography

Aaron, Benjamin (ed.). 1969. *Dispute Settlement Procedures in Five Western European Countries.* Los Angeles: University of California Press.
———. 1980. 'The Administration of Justice in Labor Law: Arbitration and the Role of the Courts, an International Survey'. *In Memoriam Sir Otto Kahn-Freund.* Munich: C.H. Beck'sche Verlagsbuchhandlung.
Abel-Smith, B., and R. Stevens. 1968. *In Search of Justice.* London: Allen Lane.
Advisory, Conciliation and Arbitration Service (ACAS). 1977. 'Disciplinary Practice and Procedures in Employment'. *Code of Practice 1.* London: HMSO.
———. 1977. *Annual Report 1976.* London: HMSO.
———. 1979. *Annual Report 1978.* London: HMSO.
———. 1981. *Voluntary Arbitration in Trade Disputes.* London: HMSO.
———. 1982. *Conciliation by ACAS in Complaints by Individuals to Industrial Tribunals.* London: HMSO.
———. 1983a. *Annual Report 1982.* London: HMSO.
———. 1983b. 'Report and Award of a Panel of Arbitration Appointed to Resolve a Dispute between the Ford Motor Company Ltd and the Transport and General Workers' Union'. May 1983. (Unpublished.)
———. 1984. *Annual Report 1983.* London: HMSO.
Anderman, S.D. 1972. *Voluntary Dismissals Procedure and the Industrial Relations Act.* London: PEP.
———. 1978. *The Law of Unfair Dismissal.* London: Butterworths.
———. 1979. 'Legal Restrictions on Trade Unions'. *The Imposition of Law.* Ed. S.B. Burman and B.E. Harrell-Bond. London: Academic Press.
Angel, John. 1980. *How to Prepare Yourself for an Industrial Tribunal.* London: IPM.
Atkinson, J. Maxwell. 1982. 'Understanding Formality: The Categorisa-

tion and Production of "Formal" Interaction'. *British Journal of Sociology*, 33 (1), 86–117.

Bain, G.S., and R. Price. 1980. *Profiles of Union Growth. A Comparative Statistical Portrait of Eight Countries.* Oxford: Blackwell.

Barnes, Denis, and Eileen Reid. 1980. *Governments and Trade Unions. The British Experience 1964–79.* London: Heinemann Educational Books.

Bell, Kathleen. 1969. *Tribunals in the Social Services.* London: Routledge and Kegan Paul.

———. 1982. 'Social Security Tribunals – A General Perspective'. *Northern Ireland Legal Quarterly*, 33 (2), 132–47.

Benson. 1979. Royal Commission on Legal Services. *Final Report.* Cmnd 7648. London: HMSO.

Best, G. 1978. 'Tribunals – Justice for All?'. *Industrial Society* (March/April), 18–21.

Beveridge, William. 1942. *Social Insurance and Allied Services. Report.* London: HMSO.

Boothman, Fred, and David Denham. 1981. 'Industrial Tribunals: Is there an Ideological Background?'. *Industrial Relations Journal*, 12 (May/June), 6–14.

Bourn, C. 1979. 'Statutory Exemptions for Collective Agreements'. *Industrial Law Journal*, 8 (2), 85–99.

Bowers, John. 1984. 'Alternative Remedies for Dismissal'. *Industrial Relations Legal Information Bulletin*, no. 260 (July), 2–8.

———, and A. Clarke. 1981. 'Unfair Dismissal and Managerial Prerogative: A Study of "Other Substantial Reason" '. *Industrial Law Journal*, 10 (1), 34–44.

Brown, William (ed.). 1981. *The Changing Contours of British Industrial Relations: A Survey of Manufacturing Industry.* Oxford: Blackwell.

Browne-Wilkinson, The Hon Mr Justice. 1982. 'The Role of the Employment Appeal Tribunal in the 1980s'. *Industrial Law Journal*, 11 (2), 69–77.

Burawoy, Michael. 1979. *Manufacturing Consent.* Chicago: University of Chicago Press.

Cairns, B. 1980. 'Twelve Months of Tribunal Exemption'. *Electrical Contractor* (November), 23, 28.

Cavenagh, W.E., and D. Newton. 1971. 'Administrative Tribunals: How People Become Members'. *Public Administration*, 49 (Summer), 197–218.

Central Arbitration Committee (CAC). 1976. *First Annual Report.* London: HMSO.

———. 1978–84. *Annual Reports, 1977–83.* London: HMSO.

Central Office of Industrial Tribunals (COIT). 1981a. 'Industrial

Tribunals in England and Wales. Fact Sheet'. (March). London. (Mimeographed.)

COIT. 1981b. *Industrial Tribunals Procedure*. London: HMSO.

——. 1984. 'Industrial Tribunals in England. Fact Sheet'. (February). London. (Mimeographed.)

Child, J., and B. Partridge. 1982. *Lost Managers. Supervisors in Industry and Society*. Cambridge: Cambridge University Press.

Clark, G. de N. 1970. *Remedies for Unjust Dismissal*. London: PEP.

Clark, Jon, and Lord Wedderburn. 1983. 'Modern Labour Law: Problems, Functions and Policies'. *Labour Law and Industrial Relations: Building on Kahn-Freund*. Ed. Lord Wedderburn, Roy Lewis and Jon Clark. Oxford: Clarendon Press.

Clifton, B., and C. Tatton-Brown. 1979. *Impact of Employment Legislation on Small Firms*. Research Paper no. 7. London: Department of Employment.

Collins, Hugh. 1982. 'Capitalist Discipline and Corporatist Law – Part II'. *Industrial Law Journal*, 11 (3), 170–77.

Concannon, Harcourt. 1980. 'Handling Dismissal Disputes by Arbitration'. *Industrial Relations Journal*, 11 (May/June), 13–23.

Conroy, Diarmaid. 1971a. 'Do Applicants Need Advice or Representation?'. *The Future of Administrative Tribunals*. Edited transcript of proceedings of a conference held at Institute of Judicial Administration, University of Birmingham, April 1971. Birmingham: Institute of Judicial Administration.

——. 1971b. 'Tribunals and the Courts: An Interview with the President of the Industrial Tribunals'. *New Law Journal*, 19 November, 1069–71.

Conservative Party. 1968. *Fair Deal at Work*. London: Conservative Political Centre.

Cupper, Les. 1976. 'Legalism in the Australian Conciliation and Arbitration Commission: The Gradual Transition'. *Journal of Industrial Relations*, 18 (December), 337–64.

Danet, Brenda, and Bryna Bogoch. 1980. 'Fixed Fight or Free for All? An Empirical Study of Combativeness in the Adversary System of Justice'. *British Journal of Law and Society*, 7 (Summer), 36–60.

Daniel, W.W., and Neil Millward. 1983. *Workplace Industrial Relations in Britain*. The DE/PSI/SSRC Survey. London: Heinemann Educational Books.

——, and Elizabeth Stilgoe. 1978. *The Impact of Employment Protection Laws*. London: PSI.

Davies, P.L. 1979. 'Arbitration and the Role of the Courts in the United Kingdom'. *Comparative Labor Law*, 3 (1), 31–51.

——, and Mark Freedland. 1979. *Labour Law Text and Materials*.

London: Weidenfeld and Nicolson.

Department of Employment (DE). 1970. *Industrial Relations Bill: Consultative Document.* London: HMSO.

———. 1972. *Industrial Relations Code of Practice.* London: HMSO.

———. 1974a. *Employment Protection Bill: Consultative Document.* London: HMSO.

———. 1974b. 'Unfair Dismissal Applications in 1972 and 1973'. *Employment Gazette*, 82 (June), 503–4.

———. 1975. 'Unfair Dismissal Applications in 1974'. *Employment Gazette*, 83 (June), 529–34.

———. 1976. 'Unfair Dismissal Cases in 1975'. *Employment Gazette*, 84 (April), 354–5.

———. 1977a. 'Unfair Dismissal Cases in 1976'. *Employment Gazette*, 85 (October), 1079–80.

———. 1977b. 'Unfair Dismissal Cases in 1976. Characteristics of the Parties'. *Employment Gazette*, 85 (November), 1214–17.

———. 1978. 'Unfair Dismissal Cases in 1977'. *Employment Gazette*, 86 (May), 555–6.

———. 1979a. 'Unfair Dismissal Cases in 1978'. *Employment Gazette*, 87 (September), 866–7.

———. 1979b. 'Employment Protection Legislation. Working Paper on Proposed Amendments'. *Employment Gazette*, 87 (September), 874–7.

———. 1981a. 'Unfair Dismissal Cases in 1979'. *Employment Gazette*, 89 (February), 82.

———. 1981b. 'Unfair Dismissal Cases in 1980'. *Employment Gazette*, 89 (December), 539.

———. 1981c. 'Proposals for Industrial Relations Legislation'. *Employment Gazette*, 89 (December), 510–14.

———. 1982a. 'Unfair Dismissal Cases in 1981'. *Employment Gazette*, 90 (December), 520

———. 1982b. 'Labour Market Data'. *Employment Gazette*, 90 (October), S1-S64.

———. 1982c. 'Stoppages Caused by Industrial Disputes in 1981'. *Employment Gazette*, 90 (July), 289–94.

———. 1983a. 'Unfair Dismissal Cases in 1982'. *Employment Gazette*, 91(October), 449.

———. 1983b. 'Stoppages Caused by Industrial Disputes in 1982'. *Employment Gazette*, 91 (July), 297–304.

———. 1983c 'Labour Market Data'. *Employment Gazette*, 91 (September), S1-S64.

———. 1983d. 'Industrial Disputes'. *Employment Gazette*, 91 (April), S42.

Department of Employment (DE). 1984a. 'Questions in Parliament'. *Employment Gazette*, 92 (March), 127.

———. 1984b. 'Retail Prices Index'. *Employment Gazette*, 92 (February), S58.

Department of Employment and Productivity. 1969. *In Place of Strife: A Policy for Industrial Relations*. Cmnd 3888. London: HMSO.

Dickens, Linda. 1978. 'ACAS and the Union Recognition Procedure'. *Industrial Law Journal*, 7 (3), 160–77.

———. 1978–9. 'Unfair Dismissal Applications and the Industrial Tribunal System'. *Industrial Relations Journal*, 9 (4), 4–18.

———. 1979. 'Conciliation, Mediation and Arbitration in British Industrial Relations'. *Industrial Relations: A Social Psychological Approach*. Ed. G. Stephenson and C. Brotherton. Chichester: John Wiley.

———. 1983a. 'Tribunals in the Firing Line'. *Employee Relations*, 5 (1), 27–31.

———. 1983b. 'Whither Third Party Intervention in the 1980s?' *Industrial Law Journal*, 12 (4), 261–4.

———, Moira Hart, Michael Jones, and Brian Weekes. 1979. 'A Response to the Government Working Papers on Amendments to Employment Protection Legislation'. Discussion Paper. Coventry: SSRC Industrial Relations Research Unit, University of Warwick. (Mimeographed.)

———, Moira Hart, Michael Jones, and Brian Weekes. 1981. 'Re-employment of Unfairly Dismissed Workers: The Lost Remedy'. *Industrial Law Journal*, 10 (3), 160–75.

Donaldson, John. 1975. 'The Role of Labour Courts'. *Industrial Law Journal*, 4 (2), 63–8.

———. 1984. Transcript of speech given at Engineering Employers' Federation Dinner, 14 February. (Unpublished.)

Donn, Clifford B. 1976. 'Australian Compulsory Arbitration – Some Proposed Modifications'. *Journal of Industrial Relations*, 18 (December), 326–36.

Donovan. 1968. Royal Commission on Trade Unions and Employers' Associations. *Report*. Cmnd 3623. London: HMSO.

Edwards, P.K. 1982. 'Britain's Changing Strike Problem?'. *Industrial Relations Journal*, 13(2), 5–20.

———, and Hugh Scullion. 1982. *The Social Organisation of Industrial Conflict*. Oxford: Blackwell.

Edwards, Richard. 1979. *Contested Terrain*. London: Heinemann.

Elcock, H.J. 1969. *Administrative Justice*. London: Longmans.

Elias, P. 1981. 'Fairness in Unfair Dismissal: Trends and Tensions'. *Industrial Law Journal*, 10 (December), 201–17.

Elkouri, F., and E.A. Elkouri. 1973. *How Arbitration Works*. 3rd edn. Washington, DC: Bureau of National Affairs.

Equal Opportunities Commission (EOC). 1978. *Women in the Legal Services.* Manchester: EOC.

Evans, S., L.C. Hargreaves, and J.F.B. Goodman. 1984. 'The Operation of Recent Employment Legislation: Interview Programme with Full-time Representatives of Twenty Trade Unions'. (January). Manchester: UMIST. (Unpublished.)

Ewing, K. D. 1982a. 'Homeworking: A Framework for Reform'. *Industrial Law Journal*, 11 (2), 94–110.

——. 1982b. 'Trade Union Political Fund Complaints'. *British Journal of Industrial Relations*, 20 (July), 218–30.

——. 1982c. 'Industrial Action: Another Step in the "Right" Direction'. *Industrial Law Journal*, 11 (4), 209–26.

Farmer, J. A. 1974. *Tribunals and Government.* London: Weidenfeld and Nicolson.

Flanders, Allan. 1974. 'The Tradition of Voluntarism'. *British Journal of Industrial Relations*, 12 (3), 352–70.

——. 1975. *Management and Unions.* London: Faber and Faber.

Franks. 1957. Committee on Administrative Tribunals and Enquiries. *Report.* Cmnd 218. London: HMSO.

Freedland, M.R. 1976. *The Contract of Employment.* Oxford: Clarendon Press.

Friedman, A.L. 1977. *Industry and Labour.* London: Macmillan.

Frost, Anne, and Coral Howard. 1977. *Representation and Administrative Tribunals.* London: Routledge and Kegan Paul.

Fryer, R.H. 1973. 'Redundancy, Values and Public Policy'. *Industrial Relations Journal*, 4 (2), 2–19.

Fulbrook, J., R. Brooke, and P. Archer. 1973. 'Tribunals: A Social Court?'. *Fabian Tract* 427 (December).

Goodrich, C.L. 1975. *The Frontier of Control.* London: Pluto Press.

Gregory, J. 1982. 'Equal Pay and Sex Discrimination: Why Women Are Giving up the Fight'. *Feminist Review*, 10, 75–89.

Griffith, John. 1977. *The Politics of the Judiciary.* London: Fontana.

Grunfeld, C. 1980. *The Law of Redundancy.* London: Sweet & Maxwell.

Guest, D. 1982. 'Has the Recession Really Hit Personnel Management?'. *Personnel Management* (October), 36–9.

Guillebaud, C.W. 1970. *The Role of the Arbitrator in Industrial Wage Disputes.* Welwyn: Nisbet.

Hakim, Catherine, and Roger Dennis. 1982. *Homeworking in Wages Council Industries.* Research Paper 37. London: Department of Employment.

Hawes, W.R., and G. Smith. 1981. *Patterns of Representation of the Parties in Unfair Dismissal Cases: A Review of the Evidence.* Research Paper 22. London: Department of Employment.

Henderson, Joan. 1982. *The Law on Unfair Dismissal. Guidance for Small Firms.* London: HMSO.

Hendy, John. 1983. 'The Farce of Industrial Tribunals'. *Haldane Society Employment Law Bulletin* (Summer).

Hepple, B.A. 1982. 'The Transfer of Undertakings (Protection of Employment) Regulations'. *Industrial Law Journal*, 11 (1), 29–40.

———. 1983a. 'Individual Labour Law'. *Industrial Relations in Britain.* Ed. G.S. Bain. Oxford: Blackwell.

———. 1983b. 'Judging Equal Rights'. *Current Legal Problems*, 36, 71–90.

———, and P. O'Higgins. 1981. *Employment Law.* 4th edn. London: Sweet & Maxwell.

Hughes. 1980. Royal Commission on Legal Services in Scotland. *Vol. One Report.* Cmnd 7846. London: HMSO.

Hyman, R. 1977. *Strikes.* 2nd edn. London: Fontana-Collins.

———. 1981. 'Green Means Danger? Trade Union Immunities and the Tory Attack'. *Politics and Power*, 4, 129–45.

Incomes Data Services (IDS). 1980. *Employing Union Members.* Handbook Series no. 18. Old Woking, Surrey: Incomes Data Services.

Inns of Court Conservative and Unionist Society. 1958. *A Giant's Strength.* London: Inns of Court Conservative and Unionist Society and Christopher Johnson Publishers.

Institute for Employment Research (IER). 1983. *Review of the Economy and Employment.* Coventry: Institute for Employment Research, University of Warwick.

Institute of Personnel Management (IPM). 1979. *Disciplinary Procedures and Practice.* Information Report 28. London: IPM.

IRLIB. 1978. 'Dismissal for Trade Union Membership or Activity'. *Industrial Relations Legal Information Bulletin*, no. 111, 26 April.

———. 1983. 'TUC Paper on Unfair Dismissal'. *Industrial Relations Legal Information Bulletin*, no. 231 (April).

IRLR. 1983. 'Highlights'. *Industrial Relations Law Reports*, 12 (February).

IRRR. 1976. 'Union Involvement in Discipline'. *Industrial Relations Review and Report*, no. 131 (July), 2–8.

———. 1979. 'The Labour Relations Agency: Northern Ireland's Answer to ACAS'. *Industrial Relations Review and Report*, no. 214, 10–16.

Jenkins, Peter. 1970. *The Battle of Downing Street.* London: Charles Knight.

Jones, Michael. 1980. 'CAC and Schedule 11: The Experience of Two Years'. *Industrial Law Journal*, 9 (1), 28–44.

———, Linda Dickens, Brian Weekes, and Moira Hart. 1983. 'Resolving Industrial Disputes: The Role of ACAS Conciliation'. *Industrial Rela-*

tions Journal, 14 (2), 6–17.

Jukes, M. 1978. 'Reply: Tribunals – Justice for All?'. *Industrial Society*, 60 (September/October), 5–6.

Kahn-Freund, O. 1931. 'The Social Ideal of the Reich Labour Court – A Critical Examination of the Reich Labour Court'. Otto Kahn-Freund *Labour Law and Politics in the Weimar Republic*. Ed. R. Lewis and J. Clark. 1981. Oxford: Blackwell.

——. 1977. *Labour and the Law*. 2nd edn: London: Stevens.

——. 1978. 'Uses and Misuses of Comparative Law'. *Selected Writings*. London: Stevens.

Komarovsky, M. 1967. 'The Quality of Domestic Life'. *The Woman Question*. Ed. M. Evans. 1982. Oxford: Fontana.

Lawson, Tony. 1981. 'Paternalism and Labour Market Segmentation Theory'. *The Dynamics of Labour Market Segmentation*. Ed. F. Wilkinson. London: Academic Press.

Leighton, Patricia E. 1983. *Contractual Arrangements in Selected Industries*. Research Paper no. 39. London: Department of Employment.

——. 1984. 'Employment Status and the "Casual" Worker'. *Industrial Law Journal*, 13 (March), 62–6.

Lewis, Paul. 1981. 'An Analysis of Why Legislation has Failed to Provide Employment Protection for Unfairly Dismissed Employees'. *British Journal of Industrial Relations*, 19 (3), 316–26.

——. 1982. 'Industrial Tribunals: Time to Re-consider?'. *Industrial Society*, 64 (March), 36–7.

——. 1983. 'A Note on Applicants' Choice of Remedies in Unfair Dismissal Cases'. *British Journal of Industrial Relations*, 21 (2), 232–3.

Lewis, Roy, and Bob Simpson. 1981. *Striking a Balance? Employment Law after the 1980 Act*. Oxford: Martin Robertson.

——, and Bob Simpson. 1982. 'Disorganising Industrial Relations: An Analysis of Sections 2–8 and 10–14 of the Employment Act 1982'. *Industrial Law Journal*, 11 (4), 227–44.

Littler, Craig R. 1982. *The Development of the Labour Process in Capitalist Societies*. London: Heinemann.

Lockyer, John. 1979. *Industrial Arbitration in Great Britain – Everyman's Guide*. London: IPM.

Lord Chancellor's Department (LCD). 1983. 'Interest on County Court Judgments and Orders: Consultation Paper', 24 August.

Lowry, P. 1983. 'Equal Pay for Work of Equal Value: How the New Regulations will Work'. *Personnel Management* (September), 28–30.

Lustgarten, Laurence. 1980. *Legal Control of Racial Discrimination*. London: Macmillan.

McCarthy, W.E.J. 1967. *The Role of Shop Stewards in British Industrial Relations.* Royal Commission on Trade Unions and Employers' Associations, Research Paper 1. London: HMSO.

McIlroy, J. 1980. 'Conciliation'. *Industrial Law Journal*, 9 (3), 179–83.

——. 1983. *Industrial Tribunals: How to Take a Case and Win it.* London: Pluto Press.

McPherson, W.H., and F. Meyers. 1966. *The French Labour Courts: Judgment by Peers.* Urbana: University of Illinois.

Martin, R., and R. Fryer. 1973. *Redundancy and Paternalist Capitalism.* London: Allen and Unwin.

Massey, Doreen, and Richard Meegan. 1982. *The Anatomy of Job Loss.* London: Methuen.

Mellish, M., and N. Collis-Squires. 1976. 'Legal and Social Norms in Discipline and Dismissal'. *Industrial Law Journal*, 5 (September), 164–77.

Meyers, F. 1964. *Ownership of Jobs.* Los Angeles: University of California Press.

Ministry of Labour. 1967. *Dismissal Procedures.* London: HMSO.

Munday, Roderick. 1981. 'Tribunal Lore: Legalism and the Industrial Tribunals'. *Industrial Law Journal*, 10 (3), 146–59.

Napier, B. 1979. 'The French Labour Courts – An Institution in Transsition'. *Modern Law Review*, 42 (May), 270.

National Association of Citizens Advice Bureaux (NACAB). 1978. 'Assistance to Tribunal Applicants'. (February). London: NACAB. (Internal Document.)

National Chamber of Trade. 1977. *Unfair Dismissal and the Smaller Business.* Report of Working Party to the Board of Management. London: National Chamber of Trade.

National Economic Development Council (NEDC). 1963. *Conditions Favourable to Faster Growth.* London: HMSO.

Nolan, Peter. 1983. 'The Firm and Labour Market Behaviour'. *Industrial Relations in Britain.* Ed. G.S. Bain. Oxford: Blackwell.

Pain, The Hon Mr Justice Peter. 1981. 'Contract and Contact: The Trade Unionist and the Lawyer'. *Industrial Law Journal*, 10 (3), 137–45.

Phillips, The Hon Mr Justice. 1978. 'Some Notes on the Employment Appeal Tribunal'. *Industrial Law Journal*, 7 (3), 137–42.

Picciotto, S. 1979. 'The Theory of the State, Class Struggle and the Role of Law'. *Capitalism and the Role of Law from Deviancy Theory to Marxism.* Ed. B. Fine, R. Kinsey, J. Lea, S. Picciotto and J. Young. London: Hutchinson.

Pitt, G. 1980. 'Individual Rights under the New Legislation'. *Industrial Law Journal*, 9 (4), 233–42.

Price, R., and G.S. Bain. 1983. 'Union Growth in Britain: Retrospect and Prospect'. *British Journal of Industrial Relations*, 21 (1), 46–68.

Rideout, R. 1968. 'The Industrial Tribunals'. *Current Legal Problems*, 21, 178–94.

———. 1982. 'Arbitration and the Public Interest – Regulation Arbitration'. *Labour Law and the Community: Perspectives for the 1980s*. Ed. Lord Wedderburn and W.T. Murphy. London: Institute of Advanced Legal Studies.

Robertson, J.A.S., and J.M. Briggs; 1979. 'Part-time Working in Great Britain'. *Employment Gazette*, 87 (7), 671–7.

Rubery, Jill, and Frank Wilkinson. 1981. 'Outwork and Segmented Labour Markets'. *The Dynamics of Labour Market Segmentation*. Ed. Frank Wilkinson. London: Academic Press.

Schmidt, Folke. 1969. 'Conciliation, Adjudication and Administration: Three Methods of Decision-Making in Labor Disputes'. *Dispute Settlement Procedures in Five Western European Countries*. Ed. B. Aaron. Los Angeles: University of California Press.

Schofield, P. 1983. 'The British Labour Pump Principle'. *Industrial Law Journal*, 12 (September), 171–5.

Scottish Central Office of Industrial Tribunals (SCOIT). 1984. 'Industrial Tribunals in Scotland. Fact Sheet'. (April). Glasgow. (Mimeographed.)

Simpson, R.C. 1979. 'Judicial Control of ACAS'. *Industrial Law Journal*, 8 (2), 69–84.

Singleton, N. 1975. *Industrial Relations Procedures*. Department of Employment Manpower Report no. 14. London: HMSO.

Smailes, G. 1971. 'The Industrial Tribunals – How Well Will They Cope?'. *The Future of Administrative Tribunals*. Edited transcript of proceedings of a conference held at Institute of Judicial Administration, University of Birmingham, April 1971. Birmingham: Institute of Judicial Administration.

Smith, C.T.B. et al. 1978. *Strikes in Britain*. Department of Employment Manpower Papers 15. London: HMSO.

Sullivan, Terry. 1980. 'The Process of Industrial Arbitration'. *Journal of Management Studies*, 17 (2), 185–204.

Terry, Michael. 1983. 'Shop Steward Development and Managerial Strategies'. *Industrial Relations in Britain*. Ed. G.S. Bain. Oxford: Blackwell.

Thompson, A.W.J., and S.R. Engleman. 1975. *The Industrial Relations Act*. London: Martin Robertson.

Towers, Brian, and Mike Wright. 1983. 'The Disclosure of Financial Information in Pay References at Arbitration: Survey, Discussion and Conclusions'. *Industrial Relations Journal*, 14 (4), 83–91.

Trades Union Congress (TUC). 1982. *Industrial Relations Legislation: Report by the TUC General Council*. London: TUC.

Upex, R. 1982. 'Conciliation Agreements'. *Industrial Law Journal*, 11 (2), 124–6.

Wallington, P. 1983. 'The Employment Act 1982: Section 9 – A Recipe for Victimisation?'. *Modern Law Review*, 46 (3), 310–17.

Wedderburn, K.W. (Lord). 1965. 'Labour Courts?'. *New Society*, 9 December.

———. 1969. 'Conflicts of "Rights" and Conflicts of "Interests" in Labor Disputes'. *Dispute Settlement Procedures in Five Western European Countries*. Ed. B. Aaron. Los Angeles: University of California Press.

———. 1971. *The Worker and the Law*. 2nd edn. Harmondsworth: Penguin.

———. 1976. 'The Employment Protection Act 1975 – Collective Aspects'. *Modern Law Review*, 39 (2), 169–83.

———. 1978. 'The New Structure of Labour Law in Britain'. *Israel Law Review*, 13 (4), 435–58.

———. 1980. 'Industrial Relations and the Courts'. *Industrial Law Journal*, 9 (June), 65–94.

———. 1983. 'Otto Kahn-Freund and British Labour Law'. *Labour Law and Industrial Relations: Building on Kahn-Freund*. Ed. Lord Wedderburn, R. Lewis and J. Clark. Oxford: Clarendon Press.

———, and P.L. Davies 1969. *Employment Grievances and Disputes Procedures in Britain*. Berkeley and Los Angeles: University of California Press.

Weekes, B.C.M. 1976. 'Law and the Practice of the Closed Shop'. *Industrial Law Journal*, 5 (December), 211–22.

———, M. Mellish, L. Dickens, and J. Lloyd. 1975. *Industrial Relations and the Limits of Law*. Oxford: Blackwell.

Whitesides, K., and G. Hawker. 1975. *Industrial Tribunals*. London: Sweet & Maxwell.

Williams, K. 1975. 'Job Security and Unfair Dismissal'. *Modern Law Review*, 38 (May), 292–310

———, and D. Lewis. 1981. *The Aftermath of Tribunal Reinstatement and Re-engagement*. Research Paper no. 23. London: Department of Employment.

Wilson, A.W., and H. Levy. 1941. *Workmen's Compensation*, 2. London: Oxford University Press.

Wood, John C. 1979. 'The Central Arbitration Committee – A Consideration of its Role and Approach'. *Employment Gazette*, 87 (1), 9–17.

Wood, Penny. 1978. 'The Central Arbitration Committee's Approach to Schedule 11 of the Employment Protection Act 1975 and the Fair Wages Resolution 1946'. *Industrial Law Journal*, 7 (2), 65–83.

Wraith, R.E., and P.G. Hutchesson. 1973. *Administrative Tribunals.* London: Allen and Unwin.

Zander, M. 1980. *The State of Knowledge about the English Legal Profession.* Chichester: Barry Rose.

Index

Dismissed

Warwick Studies in Industrial Relations

General Editors: G.S. Bain, W.A. Brown and H.A. Clegg

Also available in this series